WILD
Wyoming

Help Us Keep This Guide Up to Date

Every effort has been made by the author and editors to make this guide as accurate and useful as possible. However, many things can change after a guide is published—trails are rerouted, regulations change, techniques evolve, facilities come under new management, etc.

We would love to hear from you concerning your experiences with this guide and how you feel it could be improved and kept up to date. While we may not be able to respond to all comments and suggestions, we'll take them to heart and we'll also make certain to share them with the author. Please send your comments and suggestions to the following address:

The Globe Pequot Press
Reader Response/Editorial Department
P.O. Box 480
Guilford, CT 06437

Or you may e-mail us at:

editorial@globe-pequot.com

Thanks for your input, and happy travels!

WILD
Wyoming

A Guide to 63 Roadless Recreation Areas

By

Erik Molvar

FALCON®

Guilford, Connecticut
An imprint of The Globe Pequot Press

A **FALCON**GUIDE ®

Front cover photo: Cheyenne Rouse Photography
All interior photographs and back cover photo are by Erik Molvar.

Library of Congress Cataloging-in-Publication Data
Molvar, Erik.
  Wild Wyoming : a guide to 63 roadless recreation areas / by Erik Molvar.--1st ed.
    p. cm.
  Includes index.
  ISBN 1-56044-780-X
    1. Recreation areas--Wyoming--Guidebooks. 2. Wilderness areas--Wyoming--Guidebooks. 3. Wyoming--Guidebooks. I. Title.

GV54.W8 M65 2001
917.8704'34--dc21   2001031548

Manufactured in the United States of America
First Edition/First Printing

Leave it as it is. You cannot improve on it; not a bit.
The ages have been at work on it, and man can only mar it.

—Theodore Roosevelt

ACKNOWLEDGMENTS

This book was not the work of one person, but was built upon the combined works of thousands of lands managers, historians, and scientists over the course of decades. It is a synthesis of the life's work of many of Wyoming's most dedicated scientists, conservationists, and seekers of knowledge. Too many people have made contributions to this book to be named here, but the efforts of all are profoundly appreciated. In particular, I would like to thank Linda Merigliano, Benton Smith, Adrian Villaruz, Susan Marsh, Megan Bogle, Mike Bree, Craig Cope, Joe Harper, Dale Gomez, and Cindy Stein of the Forest Service for contributing their time and knowledge to this book. Tom Shirn, Bob Lanka, and Ben Jarrett of the Wyoming Game and Fish Department and Helen Larsen of Grand Teton National Park were also wellsprings of information. Thanks to Kirk Koepsel and Rob Schmitzer for introducing me to the wild side of the Thunder Basin. Ray Hanson, Neil Schicke, David Baker, and Andy Tenney of the BLM shared their copious knowledge of Wyoming's lesser-known wildlands. David Love of Wyoming Geological Survey and Liz Howell of the Sierra Club made significant contributions, each in their own way. Thanks to the staff of the University of Wyoming Library and the Montana State University map collection, where much of the background research was performed. And thanks to Margo of Margo's Pottery in Buffalo, where the ball first got rolling in its own weird and wobbling way.

CONTENTS

LEGEND

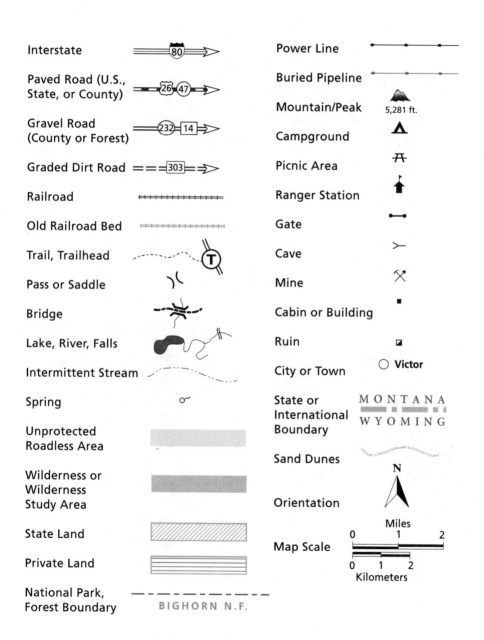

Interstate	
Paved Road (U.S., State, or County)	
Gravel Road (County or Forest)	
Graded Dirt Road	
Railroad	
Old Railroad Bed	
Trail, Trailhead	
Pass or Saddle	
Bridge	
Lake, River, Falls	
Intermittent Stream	
Spring	
Unprotected Roadless Area	
Wilderness or Wilderness Study Area	
State Land	
Private Land	
National Park, Forest Boundary	BIGHORN N.F.

Power Line	
Buried Pipeline	
Mountain/Peak	5,281 ft.
Campground	
Picnic Area	
Ranger Station	
Gate	
Cave	
Mine	
Cabin or Building	
Ruin	
City or Town	Victor
State or International Boundary	MONTANA / WYOMING
Sand Dunes	
Orientation	N
Map Scale	Miles 0 1 2 / 0 1 2 Kilometers

STATEWIDE OVERVIEW MAP

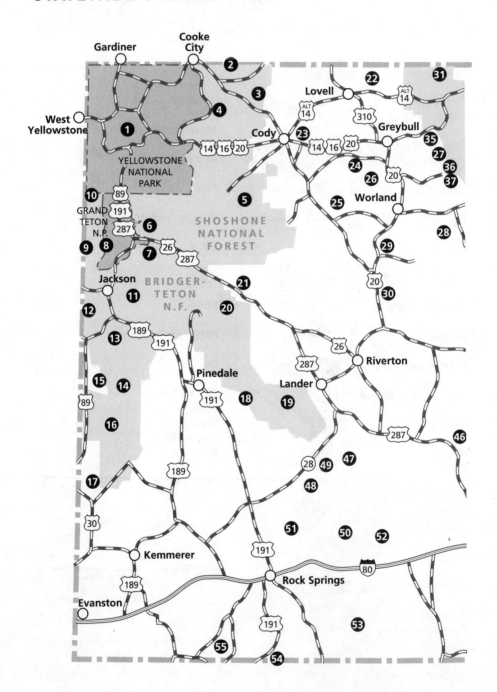

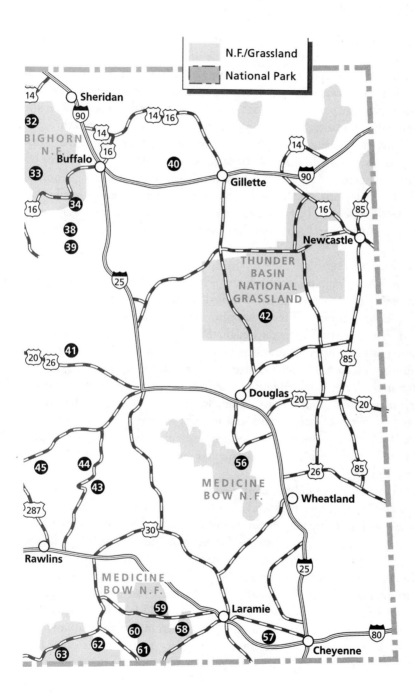

N.F./Grassland

National Park

INTRODUCTION

Wyoming is a raw land of craggy mountains, empty deserts, and limitless plains. The last bastion of the Old West, the lifestyle here is a throwback to a simpler time when people lived closer to the land. But even in this least populated state in the lower 48, wild and pristine landscapes are scarce. The state boasts two national parks and fifteen designated wilderness areas, all in the high mountains. But there are millions of acres of wildlands scattered throughout the state, from the climax forests to the shrub deserts, from the Great Plains to the Great Divide Basin. Most of these are managed primarily for industrial use—logging, mining, oil and gas drilling, and cattle grazing. Some of these areas are currently under consideration for wilderness status, while others have been overlooked by federal agencies. These pristine areas are all suited to wilderness pursuits and represent the last, best remnants of wild Wyoming.

WHAT IS WILDERNESS?

Wilderness has a very specific legal definition under federal law. With the Wilderness Act of 1964, Congress identified wilderness as a place "where the Earth and its community of life are untrammeled by man, where man is a visitor who does not remain." Federally designated wilderness is designed to provide outstanding opportunities for primitive and unconfined recreation. Wilderness areas must be at least 5,000 acres in size or, if less, they must be manageable in a pristine state. A potential wilderness may include primitive roads and other signs of human activity, but it must "generally appear to have been affected primarily by the forces of nature, with the imprint of man's work substantially unnoticeable." Motor vehicles, bicycles, and even chainsaws are typically prohibited in wilderness areas in order to preserve the opportunity for solitude in a primeval setting.

Wilderness status can only be conferred by an act of Congress. The process begins when Congress directs federal agencies to inventory the public lands to determine which ones are eligible for wilderness status. During this inventory, the agency draws up an Environmental Impact Statement (EIS), which is supposed to be drawn up by experts and scientists (too often this is not the case). The EIS contains a description of the eligible areas and presents several alternatives for managing them. This analysis is by no means all encompassing, and many lands eligible for wilderness status may be excluded. The draft EIS is then submitted for public comment, and any citizen may register approval or concern by letter or in public hearings. The agency then issues a Final EIS, complete with the "preferred alternative" that it seeks for the management of each area.

Once the Final EIS is submitted, the wilderness process goes into limbo until Congress decides to act on it. The drafting of a state wilderness bill is traditionally left up to the Congressional delegation from that state. Meanwhile, eligible roadless areas become Wilderness Study Areas (WSAs). These lands are managed as if they already had wilderness status so that their pristine character can be retained until Congress decides whether to confer wilderness status or remove the area from wilderness consideration. Representatives may choose to enact the preferred alternatives of the agency, or may call for more wilderness—or less, as they see fit. The current Wyoming Congressional delegation has proven itself to be pro-industry and anti-environment, and may have been waiting to gain political control of both the U.S. Congress and the Presidency before it submits a bill.

THE TEN MOST ENDANGERED WILD AREAS

Wild Area	Nature of the Threat
Adobetown	Oil and gas development
Yellowstone National Park	Bison slaughter, endangered wolf and grizzly populations, overpopulation, thermal resource development
Mount Leidy Highlands	Timber harvesting, oil and gas development, grazing
Killpecker Dunes	Oil and gas development, coal-bed methane development
The Pinnacles	Oil and gas development
Mount Laramie	ORV use, radio transmitter development
Red Lake Dunes	Oil and gas development
McCullough Peaks	Oil and gas development, ORV use
Bobcat Draw	Oil and gas development
Vedauwoo	ORV use, heavy recreational pressure

WILDERNESS AND MULTIPLE USE

Some opponents of wilderness complain that wilderness status "locks away" lands, preventing public use. In fact, federal agencies are required by law to manage the public lands for multiple use (although every acre does not necessarily have to be managed for every use). The multiple uses recognized in federal law are timber, mining, grazing, watershed, recreation, and wildlife. How does multiple use square with wilderness designation?

Wilderness designation is generally seen to improve the land's value for recreation. Because motorized vehicles are prohibited, horsemen and hikers gain a greater sense of quiet and solitude. It is well known that most game animals flee from motorized traffic. Off-road vehicles can push the game animals into the deepest recesses of the backcountry, where they are inaccessible to most hunters. By restricting motorized traffic, land managers can effectively move the game closer to the public. It is certain that motorized recreation deserves a place on public lands. If all the areas in this book were instantly given wilderness status, motorized travel would still be allowed on 95 percent of Bureau of Land Management (BLM) lands and over half of national forest lands.

It is an absolute certainty that wilderness designation is beneficial to wildlife and watershed values. Fewer roads and industrial developments mean less erosion, which translates into higher water quality and less siltation downstream. Wilderness status is a boon to wildlife species that shun human presence, and wilderness areas typically become reservoirs for game species from which the animals can re-populate neighboring lands that have been over-hunted or developed.

Many kinds of industrial uses are compatible with wilderness designation. Livestock grazing has continued in all areas that have so far been granted wilderness status, and cattle and sheep can still be found in most of Wyoming's wilderness areas. Indeed, wilderness status can improve the range for livestock by excluding motorized vehicles that spook livestock and cause them to lose weight. Oil and gas exploration can continue beneath a wilderness under a "no surface occupancy" stipulation. Oil companies have the technology to drill diagonally to reach subsurface oil and gas reservoirs beyond political boundaries. The only industrial uses prohibited by wilderness status are strip mining and logging.

Federal law requires agencies to consider public input whenever land management decisions are made. As citizens, we all have the responsibility to make our voices heard and see to it that industrial development is limited to activities that do not conflict with the public interest.

PUBLIC ACCESS AND WYOMING STATE LAW

Wyoming legal code differs from most western states when it comes to access to public lands. Landowners have the right under Wyoming law to close any roadway that crosses private property unless it has a formal public easement. Public easements apply only to county roads, state and federal highways, and other roads for which a public easement has been purchased or condemned. Just because a road runs onto public lands and has a federal road number does not mean that it has a public easement. Landowners can deny access on such roads regardless of whether they were "usual and accustomed" public thoroughfares in the past. Any person who crosses private land on a non-public roadway may be prosecuted for trespassing.

To make matters more complicated, landowners are not required to place "no trespassing" signs at their legal boundaries. In fact, most boundaries between private and public lands are not marked in any way. Under Wyoming law, it is the traveler's responsibility to know the land ownership, and ignorance of the land ownership will not protect you from prosecution. State-owned lands are unconditionally open to the public. They are typically leased to ranchers for grazing, and in a few cases the ranchers have illegally posted "no trespassing" signs on state lands. If you come across such illegal postings, notify the Wyoming Game and Fish Department.

In Wyoming, a landowner cannot be denied access to his or her land just because the intervening holdings of another private owner prevent access from the public roadway. Therefore, under Wyoming state law, as a landowner any member of the public ought to be able to demand access to any parcel of federal land. In fact, however, this is not the current legal interpretation of the law, and the conflict between trespass law and public landowner rights has yet to be resolved in the courts. This is a lawsuit waiting for a plaintiff, and anyone who has the time and money to take on this legal battle would do the public a great favor by helping to resolve the issue.

A number of large parcels of BLM land are entirely surrounded by private lands and the public has no legal access to them. The ranchers who lease the grazing rights to these lands sometimes consider them to be private holdings and often band together to fight public access. In fact, some landowners charge the public admission fees to use private roads on the way to public lands. It is unethical for private individuals to decide who can and who cannot access public lands, and it is outrageous that private citizens are charging tolls for public land access.

The Bureau of Land Management and other federal agencies are on record as striving to "increase legal access into large blocked-up areas of public land that have high values for public recreation and use." In practice, federal agencies move slowly and cautiously to acquire access corridors. It would be perfectly reasonable for federal agencies to create public easements along existing roads to landlocked public parcels, but federal agencies typically lack the willpower for condemnation proceedings.

Perhaps a better solution would be to ban motorized traffic on all roads leading to federal lands that have no legal public access. The public has absolutely no interest in the maintenance of roads that it cannot access, and one can hardly justify allowing a few private landowners special access that is denied to the rest of the public. Indeed, closures to motorized use would yield public benefits by improving wildlife habitats, decreasing erosion, and increasing the acreage of roadless areas. Under threat of road closure, landowners who hold grazing leases on public lands might be more inclined to grant access to public lands, so that they themselves could use the roads to move livestock and maintain range improvements.

TRAVELERS ADVISORIES

- **Severe storms** can strike without warning in the Wyoming high country even on cloudless days. Cold temperatures can occur even during the height of summer, and nighttime temperatures routinely dip into the 40s and even 30s on clear nights. Thunderstorms may suddenly change cloudless days into drenching misery, so carry appropriate rain gear at all times. Ponchos are generally sufficient for day hikes, but backpackers should carry full rain suits. Snowfall is always a distinct possibility in the high country, and backpackers should carry clothing and gear with this in mind. If you are traveling in an area that is prone to severe storms, plan your trip to avoid open country and high ridgetops during the afternoon, when most thunderstorms strike.

- **Flash floods** are common in areas with clay soils and little plant cover. When traveling in desert badlands and High Plains locales, never pitch your tent in a dry wash or draw; instead, choose high ground that will remain above the floodwaters. Do not be fooled by the banks of arroyos or other dry watercourses; flash floods typically rise above the banks and spread across the entire bottomlands of dry watercourses. In the Great Divide Basin, be wary of camping in low basins where vegetation is completely absent and a crust of salt or cracked mud is present. Such areas may be dry lakebeds that fill with water during rainstorms.

- **Drinking water** from the pristine streams and lakes of the Wyoming mountains is quite refreshing, but all such sources may contain a microorganism called *Giardia lamblia*. Giardia is readily spread to surface water supplies through the feces of mammals (especially beaver) and infected humans, causing severe diarrhea and dehydration when ingested by humans. Water can be rendered safe for drinking by boiling it for at least 5 minutes or by passing it through a filter system with a mesh no larger than 2 microns. Iodine tablets and other purification additives are not considered

100 percent effective against giardia. No natural water source is safe, and a single sip of untreated water can transmit the illness. Symptoms (gas, cramps, nausea, and diarrhea) usually appear within three weeks and demand medical attention.

- **Bad water** can be found in areas with saline soils and alkaline deposits, particularly in the Red Desert and High Plains areas. Alkaline water cannot be rendered safe to drink by any amount of filtering because it contains dissolved salts. Drinking from alkaline water sources can result in dehydration and stomach disorders. If you will be traveling in an area with bad water, bring along at least one gallon of fresh water per person per day of your trip.

- **Altitude Sickness.** Many of Wyoming's wildlands are at or above 10,000 feet. If you live at low elevations, you should plan to spend a day or two in leisurely activities at the high altitude before exerting yourself. Visitors who fail to acclimate themselves to the thin air may develop a medical condition known as *altitude sickness*, in which the victim becomes dizzy and nauseous and may also experience headaches or a lack of appetite. If one of your party suffers from this condition, get them to a low elevation *immediately* and rehydrate them with plenty of water or juice (not alcohol, which will make their condition worse). Bottled oxygen helps, but it is rarely available when you need it. Altitude sickness is debilitating and potentially fatal in extreme cases, particularly if the victim suffers from other health problems.

- **Grizzly bears** are at the top of the food chain in the mountains of western Wyoming. In most cases, grizzlies will flee from human contact, but may react aggressively when they are surprised or feel threatened. When traveling in bear country, make noise in areas where heavy brush or timber blocks visibility. In an encounter, back away slowly, talking in a loud but calm voice and wave your arms slowly so that the bear can identify you as human. Under no circumstances should you run from a grizzly, because fleeing will trigger the bear's predatory instinct.

   Bears can be particularly troublesome in their quest for human food. A bear that manages to get food even once from humans is likely to become a repeat offender and pose a threat to future visitors. When camping in bear country, it is advisable (and often required) to secure food in a bear-proof manner at all times. In camp, hang all food at least 10 feet above the ground and 5 feet away from the tree trunk. Black bears are able climbers and will raid food containers that are hung too close to the trunk. Cosmetics and food-scented items should also be kept well out of a bear's reach.

- **Mountain lions** are scattered sparsely throughout Wyoming, although their numbers may be on the increase. Because of their reclusive habits, hikers rarely see them. However, they can present a real threat if encountered at close range. The current wisdom is that hikers encountering a cougar should behave aggressively in order to scare it off. Remain standing and never turn your back on a cougar or attempt to run away. Such behavior may incite an attack. Report all sightings at the nearest ranger station.

- **Rattlesnakes** are common in the sage steppes and low deserts of Wyoming below 8,000 feet. The species that is present here is the northern prairie rattler; they're smaller than diamondbacks and have less-potent venom. Their bites are painful but rarely life threatening; seek medical attention if you are bitten.

  Northern prairie rattlesnakes are nocturnal during the summer months but they may be encountered on rock ledges during the morning and evening hours. During spring and autumn, rattlesnakes migrate to caves where they hibernate by the dozens. They are often seen in broad daylight during these migrations, and may be more aggressive at this time. These snakes are usually quite reclusive and will most often flee if given the chance. To avoid being bitten, pay close attention to the trail ahead when you are in rocky country, and never put your hands in places that you can't see. Avoid disturbing downed logs and don't overturn large boulders. If you encounter a rattlesnake, hold still for a few minutes and allow the snake to retreat to a place of safety.

  Other animals are more of a nuisance than a danger. Deer may hang around campsites and try to steal sweat-soaked clothing and saddle tack. At higher elevations, rodents dwelling in rockslides may chew their way into a pack in search of food or salt.

FOLLOWING FAINT TRAILS

Some of the trails that appear on maps are quite faint and difficult to follow. Visitors should have a few elementary trail-finding skills in their bag of tricks, in case a trail peters out or a snowfall covers the pathway. A topographic map and compass—and the ability to use them—are essential insurance against disaster when a trail takes a wrong turn or disappears completely.

Maintained trails are marked in a variety of ways. Signs bearing the name of the trail are present at some trail junctions. They're usually fashioned of plain wood, with the script carved into them. They sometimes blend in well with the surrounding forest and may go unnoticed at junctions where a major trail meets a lightly traveled one. These signs may contain mileage information, but it's often inaccurate.

Along the trail, several kinds of markers indicate the location of maintained trails. In forested areas, old blazes cut into the bark of trees may mark the path. In spots where a trail crosses a gravel streambed or rock outcrop, piles of rocks called *cairns* may mark the route. Cairns are also used in windswept alpine areas. They are typically constructed of three or more stones stacked one on top of the other in a formation that almost never occurs naturally. In open meadows, guideposts mark the route where a trail is overgrown by the grasses. They can take the form of large cairns with fenceposts sticking up, or they may be plastic composite strips with "Trail" decals on them.

In the case of a long-abandoned trail, markings of any kind may be impossible to find. On such a trail, the techniques used to build the trail may serve as clues to its location. Well-constructed trails have rather wide, flat beds. Let your feet seek level spots when traveling across a hillside, and you will almost always find yourself on the trail. Old sawed logs from previous trail maintenance can be used to navigate in spots where the trail bed is obscured; if you find a sawed log, then you must be on a trail that was maintained at some point. Switchbacks are also sure signs of an official trail; wild animals travel in straight lines and rarely zigzag across hillsides.

Trail specifications often call for the clearing of all trees and branches for several feet on each side of a trail. In a forest, this results in a distinct "hall of trees" effect, where a corridor of cleared vegetation extends continuously through the woods. Trees grow randomly in a natural situation, so a long, thin clearing bordered by tree trunks usually indicates an old trail bed. On more open ground, look for trees that have lost all of their lower branches on only one side. Such trees often indicate a spot where the old trail once passed close to a lone tree.

When attempting to find a trail that has disappeared, ask yourself where the most logical place would be to build a trail, given its source and destination. Trail builders tend to seek level ground where it is available, and they often follow the natural contours of stream courses and ridgelines. Bear in mind that most trails avoid up-and-down motion in favor of long, sustained grades culminating in major passes or hilltops. Old trail beds can sometimes be spotted from a distance as they cut across hillsides at a constant angle.

FORDING STREAMS AND RIVERS

Bridges are the exception rather than the rule in mountainous areas managed for wilderness, and many trails or cross-country routes cross substantial streams without the benefit of a bridge. Streams are typically highest in early summer, when snowmelt swells the watercourses with silty discharge. Water levels also rise following rainstorms. Stream crossings should always be approached with caution; even a shallow stream can harbor slippery stones that can cause a sprained ankle or worse. However, wilderness travelers can almost always make safe crossings by exercising good judgment and employing a few simple techniques.

When you get to the water's edge, the first thing you'll probably think is, "This is going to be really cold!" It will be even colder if you try to cross barefooted. Since most folks don't like to hike around in wet boots all day, we recommend bringing a pair of lightweight canvas sneakers or river sandals specifically for the purpose of fording streams. Wearing something on your feet will prevent heat from being conducted from your feet to the stream cobbles and will give you superior traction for a safer crossing. Walking staffs add additional stability when wading streams. Some manufacturers make special staffs for wading with metal tips, and some even telescope down to manageable proportions. If you use one of these, remember not to lean too hard on it; your legs should always bear most of the burden.

Before entering the stream, unclip your hip belt and other restrictive straps; this can save you from drowning if you fall in. Water up to knee-depth can usually be forded without much difficulty; mid-thigh is the outer-limit safe depth for crossing unless the water is barely moving. Once you get in up to your crotch, your body starts giving the current a broad profile to push against, and you can bet that it won't be long before you are swimming.

When wading, discipline yourself to take tiny steps. The water will be cold, and your first impulse will be to rush across and get warm again, but this kind of carelessness frequently results in a dunking. While inching your way across, your feet should seek the lowest possible footing, so that it is impossible to slip downward any farther. Use boulders sticking out of the streambed as braces for your feet. These boulders will have tiny underwater eddies on their upstream and downstream sides, and thus the force of the current against you will be reduced by a fraction. When emerging from the water, towel off as quickly as possible with an absorbent piece of clothing. If you let the water evaporate from your body, it will take with it additional heat that you could have used to warm up.

Some streams will be narrow, with boulders sticking up from the water beckoning you to hopscotch across without getting your feet wet. Be careful, because you are in prime ankle-spraining country. Rocks that are damp at all may have a film of slippery algae on them, and even dry rocks might be unstable and roll out from underfoot. To avoid calamity, step only on boulders that are completely dry, and do not jump onto an untested boulder, since it may give way. The best policy is to keep one foot on the rocks at all times, so that you have firm footing to fall back on in case a foothold proves to be unstable.

SHARING THE TRAIL

A wide variety of different user groups seek out the Wyoming backcountry as a setting for outdoor recreation. The state's wild areas are a magnet for hunters, anglers, and solitude seekers of all descriptions. In the interest of a safe and pleasant outdoor experience for all, follow established regulations and exercise consideration and good manners when meeting other parties on the trail. Respect for others is the cornerstone of the traditional western ethic, a code that remains in force throughout Wyoming. A few common-sense guidelines will help you avoid bad experiences when encountering other backcountry visitors.

Motorized vehicles are allowed on many of Wyoming's roadless areas. Knowing the current regulations is the responsibility of the visitor: All-terrain vehicles (ATVs) may be allowed off-trail on some National Forest lands and only on established trails in other areas. Some trails are closed to all motorized recreation. On BLM land, ATVs are never allowed off established roads and trails and they may be excluded from some trails entirely. Wilderness and wilderness study areas are closed to motorized vehicles. Non-motorized users should expect to encounter ATVs in areas where they are allowed. Many ATV users are courteous and thoughtful visitors who try to minimize their impacts just as other backcountry users do.

When several parties meet on the trail, the following order of priority is observed: Hikers should yield to livestock parties; move well off the trail and talking softly to the animals so they don't spook. Mountain bikers and motorized users should yield to both horse and foot parties. When two horse parties meet, generally it is the smaller party that should pull to the side. Motorized travelers should yield the right-of-way to all other visitors.

DRIVING WYOMING BACK ROADS

Driving in Wyoming's remote corners requires special skills. Although county roads are typically well marked at intersections, secondary roads and jeep trails often have no markings, and you will have to navigate by map and compass. Public access is not allowed across private lands except on county, state, and federal roadways, and on secondary roads with public easements. The DeLorme Wyoming Atlas shows back roads and land ownership, as do National Forest maps and the BLM 1:100,000 scale topo maps. When driving, be sure to bring one of these maps along to help you find your way.

While most county roads and forest trunk roads are passable to passenger cars, secondary roads require high clearance and may also require four-wheel drive. These roads are most often marked on maps by dashed lines, and on Forest Service maps by vertical road markers. They are often no more than two-track vehicle ways worn into the landscape; they are typified by large boulders, deep ruts, springs, and even stream fords. It is best to inquire about current road conditions, because most secondary roads receive little if any maintenance and are susceptible to washouts.

Fifty million years ago, volcanoes spewed forth a thick layer of bentonite ash that was deposited in many of Wyoming's western basins. Bentonite has the unique property of being capable of holding water in quantities 15 times its own volume. As a result, surface soils often liquefy into a sucking, slippery mud whenever a wetting rain falls. This applies equally to jeep trails and well-graded county roads that are made from the local soils. Four-wheel drive is of no assistance on these soils and chains only increase the diameter of the mud layer that will quickly coat your tires. If you are traveling on gravel roads and expect rain, get out quickly or prepare to stay put until the roads dry out.

ZERO IMPACT

One of the aims of this book is to encourage people to strike out into the wildest corners of Wyoming. But many of these same areas already receive moderate to heavy use, and they're showing signs of wear. Erosion is a problem where an army of boots and hooves has short-cut switchbacks. Litter seems to beget more litter, especially near trailheads and at backcountry campsites. Unofficial trails have proliferated across some high alpine meadows, marring the otherwise pristine environment. Fortunately, all of these problems are avoidable—as are most impacts caused by backcountry visitors—if a few simple guidelines are heeded. Remember: the goal is to *leave no trace* of your passing.

ADVANCE PLANNING TO MINIMIZE IMPACT

Much of the wear and tear that occurs in the Wyoming backcountry could be reduced by careful planning before the trip. Visitors should contact local authorities (see Appendices) to find out about areas that are particularly sensitive to disturbance or receive heavy use. Since the goal of most wilderness travelers is to visit pristine and untrammeled areas, the avoidance of the most popular sites can only enhance your wilderness experience.

We encourage travelers to plan their routes using established trails whenever possible, since these travel corridors are least susceptible to damage. Alpine habitats and high deserts are particularly fragile, and travelers who cross them are encouraged to use designated trails. Backcountry visitors can also travel more lightly by moving about in small groups. Small groups stress the landscape to a much smaller degree, especially around campsites, and they also lend themselves to greater flexibility in route choice and on-the-spot problem solving. Groups of two to six are optimal, while groups larger then ten hikers have a much greater potential for environmental damage and should be split up into smaller components.

The proper equipment can also help visitors reduce their visual presence and trampling effects in the wilderness. Dark-hued or muted clothing, tents, and packs help make you less conspicuous to other travelers. One bright-yellow or orange shirt can be carried to attract attention in an emergency. Hiking shoes with a shallow tread design are gentler on plants and soils and also won't clog with mud. Backpackers can also carry a pair of smooth-soled camp shoes—sport sandals, boat shoes, or moccasins. These feel terrific after a day on the trail and they greatly reduce wear and tear on plants and soils around camp.

ON THE TRAIL

Plan your trip on established trails. Cutting switchbacks or crossing previously untracked ground leaves behind footprints and trampled plants—signs that may invite the next person to follow in your footsteps. Eventually, enough footsteps lead to damaged plants and soils, erosion, and unwanted "social" trails.

If you must travel off trail, look for trample-resistant surfaces: rock, gravel, snow (if it's not too steep), or a streambed below the high water mark. Parties traveling cross-country should spread out in a line abreast rather than traveling single file. This reduces the potential for creating new and unwanted trails and erosion in pristine areas. Leave your route unmarked—no blazes, cairns, flagging, or arrows scratched in the dirt.

As you hike along, always be conscious to reduce short- and long-term disturbances to the environment. Making loud noises can be helpful in avoiding encounters with bears and mountain lions where visibility is limited, but it disturbs the less dangerous wildlife as well as other travelers. If you do spot wildlife along the trail, take care to stay outside the animal's comfort zone. If an animal changes its behavior as a result of your presence, you are too close. You may also chance upon sites of historical or archaeological significance as you travel in the Wyoming backcountry. These sites are an irreplaceable treasure of national importance and are protected by federal law. Enjoy them as they are and leave them unchanged.

SELECTING A CAMPSITE

National parks have well-marked backcountry campsites. On Forest Service and BLM lands, established campsites will not be marked. If there is no established site, you will need to choose an impact-resistant spot to set up camp. Shorelines of lakes and stream banks are particularly sensitive to disturbance. Keep all campsites at least 200 feet from the nearest lake or stream. Alpine meadows (particularly wet meadows) are very fragile and should also be avoided by campers. Camp well away from travel corridors—this will increase your own seclusion and help other parties enjoy their wilderness experience. The larger wilderness areas have special limits on the location of campsites.

When leaving a campsite, be sure that it is returned to its natural state. Make an extra check around the area to be sure that you don't leave any belongings or litter. Leaves, duff, and twigs should be scattered about to camouflage your tent site and all high foot-traffic areas.

CAMPFIRES

In many established wilderness areas, campfires are prohibited or restricted to certain areas. Even where campfires are allowed, consider doing without one. A lightweight stove is a far superior alternative for cooking, and a flashlight or candle lantern is a better light source.

If you build a fire, do so only where downed dead wood is abundant. Use sticks small enough to be broken by hand, and gather only as much as you need. Keep the fire small and brief. All fire rings must be dismantled and the fire site completely restored to a natural appearance before you leave the site. The backcountry of the Wyoming is a pristine environment; if you find a fire ring left by less considerate visitors, dismantle it and camouflage the site. A fire should never be left unattended, and once it's out make sure the ashes are cold. Pack out any unburned trash left over after the fire is doused.

ARCHAEOLOGICAL RELICS AND FOSSILS

In years past, searching for dinosaur bones or arrowheads was a common pastime of Wyoming visitors. Thousands of archaeological sites and prehistoric digs were raided to stock private collections or sell to wealthy collectors. As a result, a priceless part of our prehistory was lost forever. In 1906 Congress passed the Antiquities Protection Act forbidding the collection or disturbance of any human artifact (both historical and prehistoric) or vertebrate fossils of any kind. Even such prosaic finds as arrowheads and teepee rings must not be disturbed; violators face federal prosecution. It is legal to collect fossils of plants and invertebrates such as clams, crinoids, and snails, but any fossil that has a backbone must be left as you found it. That way, an archaeologist or paleontologist can interpret the find in its proper context of surrounding soils or rock strata, and reliable dates can be assigned to the find. Feel free to enjoy fossils or any other evidence of past human activity, but leave them undisturbed for future visitors.

HOW TO USE THIS BOOK

This book was designed to present broad and general information about each major roadless area in Wyoming. It contains information about the landscape, ecology, geology, and history of each area, as well as its outlook for the future.

This information may help you decide which wild area you wish to visit, or it may perhaps encourage you to voice your opinion on the management of that area. Each description is accompanied by one or more suggested trips, which give a representative sample of the country. All of these trips have been organized into a quick-reference table in Appendix A.

Each of the 63 wildlands described in this book consists of contiguous lands that are either roadless or essentially pristine in character, and each meets all the criteria for wilderness designation. Each of these areas is dominated by federal lands, but may also include small state and private parcels that are roadless and natural. In some cases, lands from several different agencies have been combined into a single wild area to give an accurate impression of the true extent of the roadless area. Only 15 of the 63 eligible wildlands presented here have been granted wilderness status by Congress; the remaining ones face the threat of future development.

INFORMATION BLOCKS

1) *Location*—the direction and distance by road from the largest or nearest town. This is intended to give a general idea of the wildland's location.

2) *Size*—measured as the total contiguous roadless area or complex in acres, regardless of land ownership, based on the best available information. Size matters, since areas must be at least 5,000 acres or be manageable as a separate unit to achieve wilderness status.

3) *Administration*—lists the agencies responsible for managing the wild areas listed in this book. See the Appendices for addresses of these agencies.

4) *Management status*—reveals the area's designation by acreage as wilderness, wilderness study area, national park, national recreation area, or unprotected roadless area. Readers are encouraged to obtain more detailed information from the managing agency and then work with the agency, conservation groups, and Congress toward improved management and protection of our public wildlands.

5) *Ecosystem*—based on the Bailey-Kuchler system used by federal agencies for ecosystem management. More detailed information on plant communities present in the wildlands are found in the text of the description.

6) *Elevation range*—the minimum and maximum elevations above sea level to give an idea of vertical relief.

7) *System trails*—an enumeration of the miles of officially recognized trails within the area, which may or may not be actively maintained.

8) *Maximum core to perimeter distance*—the greatest distance in air miles that a visitor can get from the nearest road. This figure gives a rough index to the remoteness and solitude one can achieve within a given area. In cases where several roadless units are described in one complex, the figure applies to the unit with the largest core to perimeter distance.

9) *Activities*—those non-motorized pursuits for which the area is best suited, both from a legal standpoint and based on the topography and vegetation. Hunting and fishing are subject to State of Wyoming regulations and, in some cases, special federal limitations.

10) *Best season*—the time of year that is most conducive to outdoor pursuits in a given area. Consideration is given to snowpack conditions, runoff and flooding, average temperature, and insect outbreaks.

11) *Maps*—a list of the applicable agency travel maps, surface management maps, or topographic maps, all of which are generally small scale and give a general impression of the area. In general, more detailed topographic quadrangles are needed for backcountry trips.

12) *Overview*—the heart of the area's description. It gives a detailed account of the landscapes, special features, flora and fauna, geology, history, and management status of the area. It is intended to give you a mental image of the landscape as an ecological unit.

13) *Recreational uses*—expands on suitable activities and seasons, with special attention to the unique recreational attributes of the area. This section often includes information on use patterns in order to help you avoid heavily used areas and find solitude.

14) *Access*—general descriptions of the best legal access to each area, including prevailing driving conditions and vehicle requirements.

15) *Trip ideas*—one or more suggested backcountry trips that highlight the unique features of the area. These suggestions cover a variety of travel modes and seasons, and range from well-maintained trails to map-and-compass wilderness routes. Detailed driving directions to the trailhead are included, as well as necessary topographical maps, distance information, and difficulty ratings. In general, *easy* trips are suitable for travelers of all ages and abilities while *moderate* trips will challenge beginners but will be easy for experienced backcountry travelers. *Moderately strenuous* trips will exhaust beginners and challenge experts, while *strenuous* trips will test the limits of even the most Herculean traveler.

1

Greater Yellowstone Ecosystem

T he Yellowstone plateaus form the centerpiece of one of the largest essentially wild areas remaining in the United States. Unbroken stands of coniferous forest stretch for hundreds of square miles, interspersed with broad meadows that are the feeding grounds for vast herds of elk and bison. Grizzly bears roam at will here, and wolves have been successfully returned to their natural role in the ecosystem. In all, the Greater Yellowstone area has most of the components of a fully functioning ecosystem.

Yellowstone and Grand Teton National Parks form the core of the ecosystem and its flanking wilderness areas—the Absaroka-Beartooth, North Absaroka, Washakie, Teton, Lee Metcalf, Winegar Hole, and Jedediah Smith. In addition, there are a number of unprotected roadless areas that complement the protected areas, highlighted by the Madison and Gallatin Ranges, Henrys Fork Mountains, Line Creek area, and Mount Leidy Highlands. Logging roads could penetrate these areas at any time, destroying their value to large mammal populations for which the region has become known.

But the Greater Yellowstone Ecosystem is still struggling with a number of challenges. First and foremost is the problem of winter range for the wildlife species that inhabit Yellowstone National Park. When the park was created in 1872, Congress drew the boundaries to include the geological wonders for which the park has become world famous. At the time, bison, elk, and grizzly bears were so plentiful everywhere that they did not warrant special consideration as park inhabitants. As a result, Yellowstone National Park includes only summer ranges above 8,000 feet in elevation. The neighboring lowlands that were the traditional winter range of elk and bison were soon fenced off by ranchers and put into cattle production. As the twentieth century progressed, conflicts between ranching interests and wintering elk and bison escalated steadily.

At the end of the nineteenth century, the U.S. Army was the caretaker of the new national park. In pursuing an active policy of predator extermination, it drove wolves to extinction, and mountain lion and bear populations were greatly reduced. In the absence of predators, elk populations exploded; by the 1960s the elk were so overpopulated that they were beginning to destroy their own range. The Yellowstone Fires of 1988 created new range to relieve some of the pressure, and the reintroduction of wolves may help control the elk populations. When the burned areas grow into pole-sized pines, however, the elk herd may be in trouble again.

At the turn of the twentieth century, trumpeter swans were driven to the brink of extinction by market hunters harvesting their feathers and skins to adorn fashionable ladies' hats. The swans' numbers have been slow to recover, most significantly because of lead shot used by duck hunters along swan migration routes. Swans are bottom feeders, and pick up lead shot with their diet of algae and invertebrates. They then develop lead poisoning, which leads to low egg production, failed nests, and even death.

The Greater Yellowstone Ecosystem's health is critical to the regional economy of southwest Montana, eastern Idaho, and northwest Wyoming. Tourism is the single largest industry in these areas. In summer, tourists flock to Yellowstone to see exotic creatures like bison and bears roaming free in their natural habitats. In the fall, outfitters and guides take thousands of clients into the wilderness areas that surround the park to hunt for trophy elk and bighorn sheep. During the winter, hundreds of thousands of skiers and a lesser number of snowmobilers visit the area, and they consider wildlife sightings to be an important part of their vacations. The collapse of the Greater Yellowstone Ecosystem would lead to an economic collapse in these already cash-poor states.

Yet, for all of these economic facts of life, federal, state, local, and private interest in the Greater Yellowstone Ecosystem have shown much less cooperation that should be expected when common interests are at stake. Each local interest has been reluctant to compromise on conservation issues that face the region. This has slowed the full recovery of the Greater Yellowstone Ecosystem. Rancor and lawsuits are the rule here, dialogue the exception. The Greater Yellowstone Coalition has succeeded in bringing together many of the local ranchers, merchants, outdoorsmen, and preservationists. It is unfortunate that this spirit of cooperation has not had greater influence on federal and state policies in the region.

But with all of its problems, the Greater Yellowstone area remains one of the great treasure chests of wilderness in our nation. High plateaus, jagged mountain ranges, and forested foothills offer an infinite array of wild country recreation. Visitors who seek solitude or spectacular landforms, short hikes or hundred-mile trails, completely untouched watersheds or boardwalk-bordered geysers, can find them in the Greater Yellowstone Ecosystem.

Yellowstone National Park

Location: Occupies the northwest corner of the state, 50 miles west of Cody and 55 miles north of Jackson.
Size: 2.2 million acres.
Administration: National Park Service.
Management status: 2,016,200 acres of roadless backcountry under consideration for wilderness status.
Ecosystems: Douglas fir forest, lodgepole pine, sagebrush steppe, western spruce-fir forest, abundant wetlands.
Elevation range: 6,400 feet to 11,139 feet.
System trails: 1,210 miles.
Maximum core to perimeter distance: 8.1 miles.
Activities: Hiking, backpacking, horseback riding, wildlife viewing, fishing, canoeing.
Best season: Mid-June–September.
Maps: Yellowstone (USGS 1:125,000), *Earthwalk Yellowstone*, *Trails Illustrated Yellowstone*, *Yellowstone North and South* (American Adventures).

TRAVELERS ADVISORY:
SUDDEN STORMS, GRIZZLY COUNTRY

Yellowstone National Park occupies a region of high, forested plateaus guarded to the north and east by craggy mountains. The park is larger than the state of Rhode Island, and its forested plateaus are dotted with vast lakes, broad meadows, and thermal basins where geysers and hot springs boil up from the depths of the Earth. Its wildlife diversity is world famous, and resident animals are much more tolerant of humans than hunted populations. Although the road system teems with tourists, its vast network of trails receives light use, making solitude easy to find in the backcountry.

World's First National Park

Yellowstone National Park was established by Congress in 1872 to preserve the region's geological wonders for public enjoyment. The earliest tourists traveled in by buckboard over rough roads and camped in the high country. The first of Yellowstone's grand hotels was built in 1883 at Mammoth Hot Springs. Its architecture reflected a mixture of rustic frontier flavor with opulent comfort. It

YELLOWSTONE NATIONAL PARK

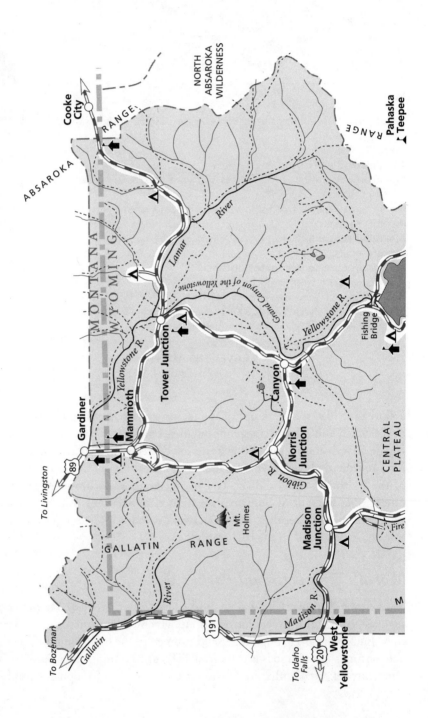

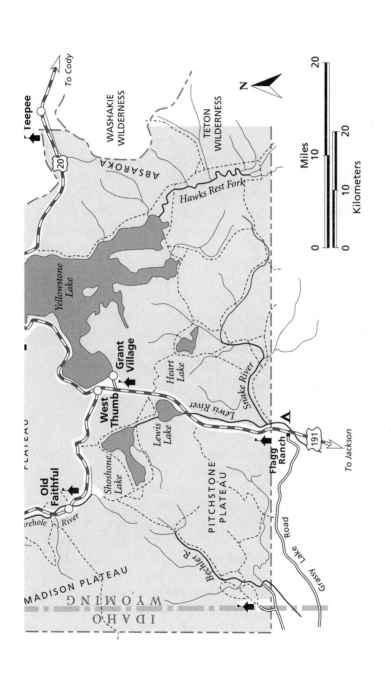

was built to appeal to the wealthy East Coast tourists who took extensive excursions by rail throughout the American West.

The U.S. Army took over Yellowstone's administration between 1886 and 1918, instituting a program of predator eradication during which mountain lions, wolves, and coyotes were driven extinct in the park. By the early 1900s, the National Park Service was actively marketing Yellowstone as a vacation destination. Private entrepreneurs moved into the park, setting up camps of wall tents and clusters of cabins and mercantile stores to accommodate the growing influx of visitors. Wagon roads were built to link the most outstanding of Yellowstone's natural wonders.

Following World War II, an increase in the middle class coupled with improved highway systems and a proliferation of automobiles led to a radical increase in visitation. This was the high-water mark of park development, which included immense visitor centers, sprawling campgrounds, and vast marinas. With the lodges came massive outdoor garbage dumps, which soon became a favorite feeding site for grizzly bears. The lodges built bleachers at the dumps so their guests could be entertained by the massive grizzlies sifting through the garbage.

During the late 1960s, the National Park Service's role began to change. Spurred on by a new generation of preservationists, many of the cabins, outbuildings, and marinas were dismantled. The National Park Service no longer advertised Yellowstone's wonders, and the marketing role fell to the local and regional chambers of commerce. Realizing that garbage-fed bears were a danger to park visitors, the Park Service closed down the garbage dumps in 1972 and replaced them with incinerators.

A Land of Geological Wonders

The story of Yellowstone is a tale of volcanism. The plateau forming the park's core was built up by a succession of eruptions that sent fiery clouds of ash billowing into the sky and incandescent flows of magma and mud across the landscape. The two largest eruptions occurred 1.3 million years ago, laying down beds of basalt, rhyolite, and welded tuff to form the major outcrops of surface rock that dominate the high plateaus. Some of the ash falls buried living trees, which became fossilized in the petrified forest of Specimen Ridge. A minor eruption followed some 150,000 years ago, issuing from a ring of vents that later collapsed to form the West Thumb Caldera. The most recent eruptions occurred only 70,000 years ago, a mere eye blink in geologic time. Over the eons, the eruptions have formed a series of overlapping *calderas*. A caldera is formed by a ring of volcanic vents that collapses to form a circular depression.

The eruptions, geysers, and hot springs derive from a tongue of magma that lies 100–200 miles beneath the surface of Yellowstone, known as the Yellow-

The Grand Canyon of Yellowstone.

stone Hotspot. As the North American plate has moved westward across this plume of magma, the magma plume has produced outbreaks of volcanic activity on a cycle of 630,000 years. The first series of eruptions occurred in the Columbia Basin, filling it with volcanic material. The next occurred near the present site of Boise, Idaho, while the third created the Craters of the Moon lava fields in the eastern Snake River Basin, also in Idaho. The modern activity of geysers, steam vents, and hot springs in Yellowstone may represent the last gasps of an episode of volcanism that began here 52 million years ago.

Between 75 and 12 million years ago, a period known as the Pleistocene Epoch, a cooling climate brought on several episodes of glaciation in Yellowstone country. During much of this time, the entire Yellowstone Plateau was buried beneath a massive icecap. The ice lapped up against the Absaroka Range, mingling with montane glaciers that poured down from the high peaks. To the west and south, valley glaciers flowed along the Madison valley, the Bechler valley, and into Jackson Hole, flowing out into the surrounding lowlands.

Geologists believe that the pool of magma that underlies the Park is partially solidified, but evidence of new volcanic activity is still cropping up. Near Mammoth, a 1995 study showed that Opal Hot Springs is slowly moving away from its former position. During the same year, a steam vent along Astringent Creek expanded into a series of mud cauldrons and boiling springs, and a new mud volcano sprang up. All told, Yellowstone currently boasts over 200 active geysers and more than 10,000 other thermal features.

Yellowstone's hot springs are inhabited by ancient bacteria that have changed little in the last 3.5 billion years. Scientists believe that these bacteria represent the most primitive forms of life on the planet, forms from which all other plants, animals, and protozoans have evolved. The primitive bacteria give the hot springs their brilliant colors, and some are photosynthetic and can manufacture their own energy from sunlight. Currently, the Park Service allows companies to "mine" the bacteria for research and genetics work in the private sector. The primitive bacteria of Yellowstone's hot springs have already yielded a key enzyme for replicating DNA. There have been suggestions that the National Park Service should share in the royalties from these discoveries, but so far biotechnology companies can sample the Yellowstone bacteria at no charge.

An American Serengeti

Visitors who travel through Yellowstone National Park will find the largest assemblage of wild herbivores in the contiguous United States. Over 50,000 elk summer within the borders of the park, grazing in the lush, subalpine meadows of the high plateau. This is the largest concentration of elk in the world. Almost 6,000 moose haunt Yellowstone's waterways, feeding on aquatic vegetation and browsing on streamside shrubs. The mountainous arc of high country across the northern and eastern edges of Yellowstone supports a population of almost 4,000 bighorn sheep. American bison roam freely across the sagebrush prairies of the Madison, Hayden, and Lamar valleys.

The Yellowstone Plateau is dotted with large lakes, broad rivers fed by hot springs, and extensive marshes, which results in a burgeoning population of wetland species. River otters and mink hunt for fish along lakes and rivers, and beaver thrive on the smaller streams and in the back sloughs of the major rivers. Pelicans nest on the islands of Yellowstone Lake, and ospreys and bald eagles raise their young along most of the major waterways of the park. The trumpeter swan is known to nest in some of the smaller lakes and ponds. Small numbers of the endangered whooping crane have been known to summer in Yellowstone National Park, but currently the only nesting populations are in Alberta and the Northwest Territories. Sandhill cranes are common residents of Yellowstone's marshes.

The grizzly bear is the unofficial emblem of Yellowstone National Park, although bears are not sighted as often as they once were. With the closure of park dumps and the elimination of feeding by tourists, these magnificent creatures have reverted to a wild state. A grizzly bear's home range can cover over 100 square miles, which accounts for the relative rarity of bear sightings. The bear population has been growing over the last decade, but population estimates vary widely between 250 and 600 animals for the Greater Yellowstone Ecosystem. The Yellowstone grizzly is listed as "threatened" under the Endangered Species Act and is still vulnerable to population decline because of low birth rates, the high potential for inbreeding, and the relatively low numbers of breeding females.

The last timber wolves in Yellowstone were driven extinct during the 1930s, but were reintroduced in 1995. Since that time, wolves have reclaimed their natural place in the Yellowstone ecosystem, with a population now in excess of 100 animals. Wolves are an endangered species in Wyoming, but the transplanted animals were given the status of an "experimental, nonessential population." This exempted them from the Endangered Species Act so wolves that killed livestock could be shot. Ranchers have filed lawsuits to remove the wolves, but their efforts are likely to fail: Wild wolves were spotted in the park before the transplants, and these wolves would receive full protection under the Endangered Species Act. It would be impossible to ascertain whether any wolf without a radio collar was an "experimental and nonessential" wolf or an endangered native one that may not legally be disturbed. Visitors occasionally spot wolves in the Lamar Valley and infrequently throughout the rest of the park. Wolves present no danger to humans.

The vast lodgepole forests of the Yellowstone Plateau are the result of forest fires that raged over the high country in the early 1700s. In 1988, the cycle repeated itself during an unusual drought. More than 249 individual fires caused by both lightning strikes and humans swept through old stands of lodgepole pine that had lots of downed wood to burn. Many of the natural fires were allowed to burn, but low humidity and high wind soon blew the blazes into vast infernos. By the time the Park Service decided to suppress the fires, it was too late. The federal government spent over $120 million to fight the blazes in Yellowstone, but the fires never came under control until the first snows of September put them out. In the end, almost 800,000 acres had burned.

Critics bemoaned the "loss" of the landscapes of their childhoods, but in fact the fires of 1988 have benefited Yellowstone's ecosystem. By clearing away stands of lodgepole that contained little forage for wildlife, the fire made way for new meadows and brushfields where forage plants grow vigorously in direct sunlight. The many snags created by the blaze are a bonanza for woodpeckers, cavity-nesting songbirds, and ants, which have emerged as a new staple in the diets of grizzly bears. The fire burned in patches, creating a mosaic of regenerating stands that will serve as natural firebreaks during future blazes. The real culprit in the 1988 fires was a century of fire suppression: In a natural state, small to medium-sized fires would have burned through the forest periodically, creating a patchy mosaic of young, fire-resistant stands within the highly combustible mature forest. Because wildfires were systematically extinguished during 100 years of "Smokey the Bear" firefighting, Yellowstone's lodgepole stands aged into a uniform cover of 200-year-old forest, which is vulnerable to catastrophic fire.

Lodgepole pine is a "fire-adapted" species, which means it requires forest fires to complete its life cycle. Lodgepole pine seedlings grow only in direct sunlight; in the absence of fire, stands of lodgepole will inevitably be replaced by shade-tolerant Douglas fir and spruce. But lodgepole pine has evolved a special adaptation to fire: serotinous cones, sealed in sap that opens only in the high temperatures of a forest fire. After a blaze sweeps through a stand of lodgepole, cones open on the dead trees, and seeds are scattered across the nutrient-rich ashes. In this way, the lodgepole pine renews its hold on the landscape and dominates areas like Yellowstone that have dry climates and frequent lightning storms.

Embattled Yellowstone Ecosystem

With the tourists has come an unwelcome influx of non-native species. Some of the most devastating pests include white pine blister rust, two species of knapweed, hounds-tongue, musk thistle, and Dalmatian toadflax, all of which strangle the native vegetation. Lake trout were illegally introduced into Yellowstone Lake in the recent past, threatening the indigenous population of cutthroat trout that has provided anglers with a world-class fishery for decades. To compound the problem, whirling disease has recently appeared in Yellowstone Lake. It can be deadly to the cutthroat, but lake trout are unaffected by this European parasite. The New Zealand mud snail has invaded the Firehole and Madison Rivers, threatening populations of aquatic insects that are the principal food supply of trout.

It has long been recognized by geologists that the volcanic plateau of Yellowstone is underlain by oil-bearing strata. Oil seeps in the Grand Canyon of the Yellowstone point to the possibility of significant pools of oil beneath the eastern half of the park. Although it would be absurd to turn the world's first national park into a drilling field for private profit, one only needs to consider the oil industry's continuing pursuit of drilling permits for the Arctic National Wildlife Refuge to recognize that nothing is sacred.

Plans to tap the subterranean steam of the Island Park Caldera for geothermal power threatens to disrupt the activity of Old Faithful and the other geysers of Yellowstone. Although the project's proponents assure the public there is no threat to the Yellowstone geysers, there's little scientific data to support their claims. There are known records of active geyser fields in Iceland and New Zealand becoming extinct as a result of nearby geothermal projects. The Old Faithful Protection Act, which would limit geothermal development, has been repeatedly defeated in the U.S. Congress.

Not all of the park's ecological policies have yielded sound results. Following an outcry by animal rights activists, the Park Service in 1968 abandoned its policy of culling overpopulated elk. The new policy has favored natural self-regulation of elk numbers through cyclic population booms and die-offs. The end result was an explosion of elk during the 1980s, followed by widespread starvation. In their desperate attempt to find food, the elk wreaked havoc on plant communities in winter range areas. The extensive fires of 1988 resulted in an increase in forage for elk, but eventually many of the burned areas will mature into pole-stage stands of lodgepole pine, which offer little forage. When this occurs, biologists expect the newly inflated elk population to undergo a population crash worse than any in history.

In an effort to starve out the hostile Plains tribes, President Grant ordered a systematic program of bison eradication in the 1870s. By 1902 Yellowstone's bison population was limited to 23 animals in the Pelican Valley. This ancestral herd was augmented by plains bison and was managed like domestic livestock until the late 1930s, when the herd was allowed to roam free. It reached a peak population of about 3,500 animals in 1996. During the following winter, the State of Montana slaughtered bison that left the park during the winter, with the intention of preventing the transmission of brucellosis from bison to domestic cattle.

Brucellosis is a disease that causes spontaneous abortion in domestic cattle; it is also carried by elk. If cattle in Montana were to be diagnosed with brucellosis, Montana ranchers would be unable to export their beeves beyond the state line. It is not currently known whether brucellosis can be transmitted from bison to cattle. Despite the public outcry that came about in response to the bison slaughter, state and federal agencies continue to favor spending millions of taxpayer dollars each year to slaughter the bison, rather than taking the common-sense approach of removing 20,000 head of cattle from traditional bison winter ranges. The federal acquisition of ranch lands near Gardiner, Montana, is a step in the right direction, but the new interagency management plan for bison will continue to allow bison slaughters to occur.

RECREATIONAL USES: Yellowstone National Park receives over 3 million visitors every year, and almost all of them come between the first of June and the last days of August. The road system bears the brunt of the onslaught, with 95 percent of recreational use occurring at developed sites like rest areas, nature trails, visitor centers, lodges, and roadside campgrounds. Most of the Yellowstone backcountry, vast and varied, receives few visitors at all. Solitude can be found easily in the more remote quadrants of the park. Some of the streams and even rivers in Yellowstone's backcountry have no bridges, and many fords will be impassable during the spring runoff. Some of the less popular trails may be difficult to follow, but most are marked with orange markers or cairns.

Backpackers and horsemen must obtain a backcountry permit (free of charge at ranger stations and visitor centers) before sallying forth into the wilds. Optional advance reservations can be made by mail for a fee and permits can be picked as early as two days before you set out. Trails may be closed for protracted periods of time due to the presence of grizzly bears, especially during early summer. Backcountry camping is permitted at established campsites, each of which is secluded away from neighboring sites so that visitors get a feeling of solitude. Most campsites are provided with a cache pole to help you hang your food in a bear-proof manner. You must stick rigidly to the itinerary on your permit, and camping at sites other than those specified on the permit for that date is strictly prohibited.

Geyser basins are typified by thin and fragile pans of minerals that overlie subterranean channels of boiling water. In the backcountry, there are no fences to keep visitors from venturing onto dangerous surfaces around thermal features. Use common sense and avoid walking on the excreted minerals that surround geysers and hot springs. It is illegal to bathe in hot springs in Yellowstone (which at any rate average over 200°F), but visitors may bathe in cold-water rivers and streams that have hot spring waters flowing into them.

Although Yellowstone has never been popular with the horse crowd, its backcountry trails do offer fine opportunities for riding. Horses are excluded from trails during the early part of the season (generally before July 1), when muddy conditions lead to trail damage. About 30 percent of backcountry camps are open to stock; check at a ranger station for details. Guided trail rides are available at Mammoth Hot Springs, Canyon Village, and Roosevelt Lodge, and through local outfitters.

Fishermen will find outstanding opportunities in Yellowstone National Park. The Firehole and Madison rivers are nationally known meccas for fly fishing, and many of the lesser-known streams also provide outstanding angling. Anglers must obtain a Yellowstone fishing permit; the Wyoming fishing license is not valid here. This permit was once free of charge, because these fisheries belong equally to all Americans. In recent years, a fee has been imposed on all anglers over the age of 16 to make up for shortfalls in federal funding.

Three species of cutthroat trout are native to Yellowstone National Park: the fine-spotted Snake River cutthroat, the west-slope or greenback cutthroat, and the famed Yellowstone cutthroat with its bright colors and large spots. Brook, brown, and rainbow trout have been planted in some of the park's waterways and they have established self-sustaining populations. The grayling is also native to some of the rivers and streams of Yellowstone National Park. This distant relative of the trout has an enormous, lobe-shaped dorsal fin and iridescent scales. Grayling are commonly caught on flies, as are mountain whitefish, a scaly stream-dweller with a mouth that opens downward.

The population of Yellowstone cutthroats that inhabit Yellowstone Lake and breed in the waters under Fishing Bridge is thought to be declining, spurred by the illegal introduction of lake trout. Lakers prey on young cutthroats and are known to drive native populations to the brink of extinction. Since lake trout tend to stabilize at low population densities, fishing opportunities typically disappear following their introduction.

Boating and rafting in Yellowstone are allowed only on Yellowstone Lake, Lewis Lake, Shoshone Lake, and the Lewis River channel between Lewis and Shoshone Lakes. Lewis Lake and most of Yellowstone Lake are open to motorboats, with the exception of some of the southern bays. Boat-accessible backcountry campsites can be found along Shoshone and Yellowstone Lakes; backcountry permits are required. Prevailing southwesterly winds make for hazardous paddling on all of these lakes during the afternoon, and Yellowstone Lake can have ocean-like swells. All boats (even anglers' float tubes) must be outfitted with a boating permit, which can be obtained for a fee at any ranger station.

Climbing opportunities in Yellowstone are poor, due to the crumbly nature of the volcanic bedrock. Climbing is allowed at your own risk except in the Grand Canyon of the Yellowstone, where it is prohibited. Bicycling is allowed only on park roads, where touring is of moderate popularity. Mountain bikes are permitted on a limited number of trails. Most park roads are narrow and winding with no shoulders, and drivers often pay more attention to the sights than to the road. Cyclists should wear bright clothing and full protective gear.

In winter, Yellowstone National Park offers a number of wilderness opportunities. Be aware that snowmobiles are allowed on all park roads, and plan your trip accordingly to avoid the noise and pollution generated by these machines. With the overwhelming support of the public, a ban on snowmobiles was slated to be phased in over a four-year period starting in 2001. This ban may be reversed, however, by presidential direction. The easiest access for cross-country skiing and snowshoeing is from Mammoth Hot Springs and from the Gallatin Valley on the Montana side of the park. The mountains of the northern and eastern parts of the park are prone to avalanches, and visitors who venture here should carry avalanche transponders and shovels, and they should educate themselves about avalanche potential and self-rescue. Thermal areas are known for treacherous ice and snow, and a number of careless winter visitors have died over the years. Remember that all overnight stays require a backcountry permit.

ACCESS: Yellowstone is accessed through five main gateways. The west entrance is at the edge of the town of West Yellowstone, which can be reached from Bozeman, Montana, by driving U.S. Highway 191 down the Gallatin Canyon, and from southern Idaho via US 20 through Targhee Pass. The north entrance lies at the edge of the town of Gardiner, Montana, which is served by US 89. Cooke City, Montana is the northeast gateway to the park, and it can be reached from the Montana side via the scenic Beartooth Highway (US 212), or from Cody, Wyoming via the Chief Joseph Scenic Byway (Wyoming 296). The east entrance of the park can be reached by driving up the canyon of the Shoshone River from Cody on US 20. Finally, the south entrance to Yellowstone can be reached by driving north through Grand Teton National Park on US 191.

Some roads open as early as mid-April, while all of the roads in Yellowstone are generally open by Memorial Day. In recent years, many of the park roads have been under construction. The park roads close as snow covers them, typically in late fall. US 191 between West Yellowstone and the north boundary of the park is open year round, as is US 89 to Mammoth and Gardner. A rather steep entrance fee ($20 per vehicle as of this writing) is charged at all entrances.

Once in the park, you will be able to access most trailheads via a paved network of two intersecting ring roads. These narrow parkways have lower speed limits than are found outside the park, and tourists often drive slowly or stop in the roadway, further impeding progress. Paved pullouts are available throughout the park; slower drivers should use them to allow other cars to pass, and tourists are advised (in the name of courtesy and basic self-preservation) *never* to stop in the middle of a roadway. To make matters worse, the road system in the park has been under reconstruction for the last several years, and judging from the glacial speed of construction, this roadwork will continue for years to come. Sections of road may be closed for much of the day during construction periods. Ask about current delays and closures at the entrance station. An average trip across the park from one side to the other takes a minimum of 2 hours.

The wilderness areas that surround Yellowstone National Park on almost all sides have trail systems that interconnect with park trails. If your journey will take you into the national park from one of these wildernesses, you must obtain a backcountry permit with campsite reservations from the park.

Day Trip on Foot or Horseback

Turbid Lake

Distance: 3.3 miles one way.
Difficulty: Moderate.
Starting and maximum elevation: 7,760 feet, 7,920 feet.
Topo map: Lake Butte.
Getting there: The hike to Turbid Lake begins and ends at the Pelican Valley Trailhead, which is reached by driving 3 miles east from Fishing Bridge, then following a narrow dirt road northeast from Indian Pond to the trailhead.

This route follows the rolling meadows of Pelican Creek and offers some distant views of the Absarokas. This is the home of the Pelican Valley bison herd, and grizzly bears are also abundant here. The final leg of the journey is an off-trail route requiring some map and compass use. The old trail that once ran from Turbid Lake back to the trailhead has been erased.

Verdant meadows along Pebble Creek, in the Absarokas.

The trek begins on an old road that runs eastward through open meadows, revealing jagged peaks to the east. Before long, a well-beaten footpath veers left. Follow this path through grassy swales and stands of lodgepole pine. Upon reaching the broad valley of Pelican Creek, fine views of the Absarokas stretch to the east. The trail now enters an important summer range for elk and bison. Ducks nest beside the looping curves and oxbow sloughs of the creek.

The trail runs east along the edge of the valley to a point where a large meadow extends southward from creek. A signpost marks the spot where our route departs from the established trail. The cone-shaped hill to the south is Lake Butte; use it as a guidepost as you cross the trackless meadows. Near the head of the grassland, watch for an open gap in burned-over timber. This gap leads to Turbid Lake. Turbid Lake is home to moose and Canada geese, and hot springs bubble up along its western shore. Return via the same route.

Backpack

Bliss Pass

Distance: 20.6 miles overall.
Difficulty: Strenuous.
Starting and maximum elevation: 6,240 feet, 9,360 feet.
Topo maps: Abiathar Peak, Mount Hornaday, Cutoff Mountain, Roundhead Butte.
Getting there: The Bliss Pass trek begins at the Slough Creek Campground, at the end of a wide gravel road that runs north from US 212 about 5 miles east of Tower Junction. The hike ends at the Pebble Creek Campground, 3 miles east of Soda Butte on the same highway.

This backpack penetrates the Absaroka Range in the northeastern corner of the park. Moderate out-and-back day trips along Slough Creek and Pebble Creek are possible on either end of the route. The intervening trail over Bliss Pass is fairly steep and primitive, and negotiates some burned-over country en route to the high pass. Anglers will enjoy fine spring-creek fishing on Slough Creek (watch out for the ever-present grizzlies).

The trek begins with a hearty climb around a rocky hillock. After you pass through a saddle, the terrain is dominated by aspen parklands lit by wildflowers. The trail tops out after 0.8 mile, then descends to the Slough Creek Cabin. Broad and fertile meadows stretch across the valley floor, and the silvery ribbon of Slough Creek meanders lazily through the bottomlands. The trail follows the edge of the vast and boggy meadows, then climbs into rolling country to the south of the creek. It returns to the bottoms near Plateau Creek, staying in the lowlands for the remaining distance to the Bliss Pass junction, just beyond Elk Tongue Creek.

An eastward view from Bliss Pass.

Turn east on the Bliss Pass Trail, a footpath not maintained for horse use. It climbs aggressively through the timber, spruce at first and then lodgepole pine and Douglas fir as the path reaches higher, drier slopes. After a hearty climb, south-facing meadows offer a broad vista that stretches all the way to the Tetons.

The path now climbs in ever-steeper spurts, entering country that burned during the 1988 fires. It finally levels off in the headwaters of Elk Tongue Creek. Burned snags and low ridges block the distant views, but a low saddle near two small ponds yields mountain vistas to the north. A final steep pitch leads to Bliss Pass, a barren saddle guarded by hulking summits. From the east side of the pass, you can look eastward toward the heart of the Beartooth Mountains, while the emerald meadows of Pebble Creek stretch out below.

The trail now zigzags down a burned slope beneath the cliffs of Cutoff Peak. During the descent, watch for views of slender waterfalls on its south face. The many majestic summits of Baronette Peak reveal themselves to the southwest. Upon reaching the meadows of the valley floor, make a knee-deep ford of Pebble Creek to join the Pebble Creek Trail. Turn right and follow the trail down the valley, through the grassy glades and spruce forests of the bottoms. There are two more fords early on, each mid-thigh in depth.

After a while, the path moves inland, gradually climbing onto eastern slopes as the valley drops away. At the toe of the ridge are open meadows, where you can enjoy superb views of Mount Norris and The Thunderer. A steady descent then leads to the Pebble Creek Trailhead on US 212.

Backpack

Bechler Canyon

Distance: 12.0 miles one way.
Difficulty: Moderate.
Starting and maximum elevation: 6,400 feet, 7,360 feet.
Topo maps: Cave Falls, Bechler Falls, Trischman Knob.
Getting there: To reach the Bechler River Trailhead, you must begin in Idaho and drive east from Ashton on Idaho 47. After 5 miles, the highway bends north; follow it 1.2 miles, then turn right on the unmarked Cave Falls Road. It runs east for 5.5 miles to enter the Targhee National Forest, then continues about 10 miles to the Wyoming border. Just beyond the border, take the first left, which leads 1 mile to the trailhead at the Bechler Ranger Station.

This trail follows the Bechler River into a remote corner of the Pitchstone Plateau, visiting vast prairies, waterfalls, and thermal features along the way. From the Bechler Ranger Station, follow the Bechler Meadows Trail across a nondescript flatland of lodgepole forests and woodland swamps. After 2 miles, it breaks out into Bechler Meadows, a broad grassland interlaced with sluggish streams and stagnant sloughs. Near the far edge of the clearing, you can look back for views of the northern Tetons.

A footbridge leads across the Bechler River; turn left and follow the Bechler River Trail toward the mouth of a low and narrow canyon in the volcanic rock. Ouzel Falls can be seen to the west as the path enters the canyon. Soon, talus slopes guard the bottomland forest of spruce. The trail follows the crystalline waters of the Bechler River up to Colonnade Falls, where the water plummets over two drop-offs for a combined height of 100 feet. The trail climbs steadily past equally stunning Iris Falls, then continues upriver past a series of foaming rapids.

The valley levels off somewhat as the trail makes two knee-deep fords of the river, then continues through the woods to the head of the valley. It passes a series of hot springs opposite a ranger cabin, then climbs to reach Ragged Falls, which marks the head of the canyon.

Absaroka-Beartooth Wilderness

2

Location: 10 miles east of Cooke City, Montana.
Size: 44,800 acres within Wyoming.
Administration: Shoshone National Forest (Clarks Fork District).
Management status: 943,610 acres in Absaroka-Beartooth Wilderness (23,283 acres in Wyoming); Beartooth High Lakes WSA (21,517 acres).
Ecosystems: Douglas fir forest, lodgepole pine, western spruce-fir forest, and vast stretches of alpine tundra.
Elevation range: 6,890 feet to 11,450 feet.
System trails: 37 miles.
Maximum core to perimeter distance: 4.0 miles.
Activities: Hiking, horseback riding, fishing, cross-country skiing, nature study, upland bird hunting.
Best season: July–August.
Maps: Shoshone National Forest North Half; Absaroka-Beartooth Wilderness Map; Cody 1:100,000.

TRAVELERS ADVISORY:
SUDDEN STORMS, GRIZZLY COUNTRY, ALTITUDE SICKNESS

The Absaroka-Beartooth Wilderness stretches north over the Montana border to encompass the high granite domes of the Beartooth range as well as the northern end of the volcanic Absaroka Range. The Wyoming section of the wilderness consists mostly of low granite benches covered in a forest of lodgepole pines, pocked with a few woodland lakes. Across the border are craggy peaks and high, rolling plateaus robed in tundra. To the east of the wilderness is the Beartooth High Lakes Wilderness Study Area, where sparkling alpine tarns are set amid a timberline mixture of fir groves and open meadows. This popular area is easily accessible from the Beartooth Scenic Highway and has a network of well-worn trails.

The Beartooth Mountains are part of an uplift that occurred 30 million years ago, while volcanoes were spewing out the magma and ash that was to build the neighboring Absaroka Range. The granite pluton that forms the core of the Beartooth Mountains is over 3.7 billion years old, representing some of the oldest rock known to man. Atop it is a series of marine shales and sandstones that were laid down as the first fishes evolved in ancient seas. Remnants

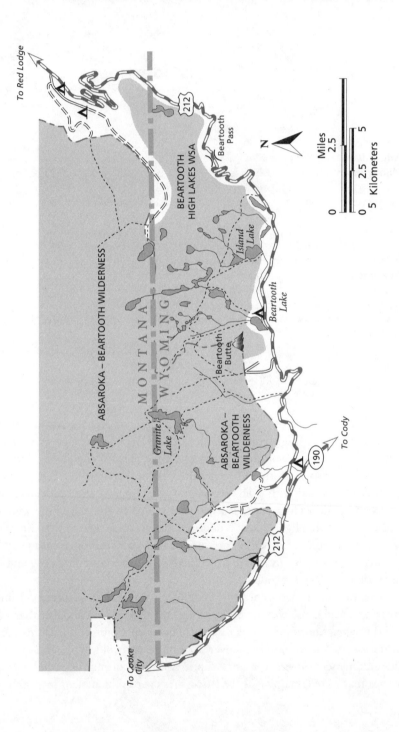

of these sedimentary rocks form some of the high peaks of the Beartooths. On the Wyoming side, Beartooth Butte and the rounded plateaus that flank Colter Pass are composed of old seafloor sediments.

Paleolithic peoples made summer forays into the timberline meadows to hunt and gather edible plants as early as 9,000 years ago. They left behind few traces of their passage, but archaeologists have been able to locate a number of primitive campsites.

The Beartooth Mountains offer an important summer range for wildlife. Parts of the Yellowstone elk population summer here. Grizzly bears range throughout the Beartooth Mountains. Bighorn sheep are widely scattered throughout the wilderness, and mountain goats may be spotted in the headwaters of Hellroaring Creek and the Buffalo Fork. Moose can be found in all major drainages and are common in the forested lowlands on the Wyoming side of the border. Peregrine falcons nest among the high peaks. Golden eagles and prairie falcons also build their nests here, feeding their young with the plentiful marmots, pikas, and ground squirrels found at the timberline.

RECREATIONAL USES: The Beartooth High Lakes are a very popular day-hike destination for tourists following the Beartooth Scenic Highway. Most of the use occurs near the roads and campgrounds, and the crowds dissipate once you get a few miles from the trailhead. Island Lake receives the heaviest summer use; it is a major starting point for both horse and foot parties bound for the high peaks of the Beartooths, which lie just across the Montana border. Granite Lake is a popular destination for backpackers, and should be avoided by solitude seekers. Perhaps as important as its backcountry, the roadless character of the Beartooth High Lakes provides a breathtaking scenic backdrop for auto tourists on the Beartooth Scenic Highway.

The off-trail areas are the exclusive domain of hikers, since the glacier-scoured bedrock that crops up at frequent intervals is dangerous for horses. Thin soils and a short growing season make the timberline areas especially vulnerable to impacts by recreational users. Beware of mosquitoes, which are abundant during the first half of summer. ATVs are strictly prohibited in both the Absaroka-Beartooth Wilderness and the Beartooth High Lakes WSA.

Some of the streams have native cutthroats, and many of the lakes have been planted with brook, rainbow, and cutthroat trout. Almost all the lakes are fishable, but the streams tend to have poor fishing due to their cold temperatures and lack of nutrients. Granite Lake (at 210 acres) is the largest of the 32 Wyoming lakes that have fish. Brook trout are the most common species. Beartooth and Island Lakes have loading ramps for motorboats.

After Labor Day, the crowds that throng the Beartooth Scenic Highway disappear. Early autumn is an excellent time to visit the Beartooth Plateau, al-

A storm rolls in over Beartooth Butte and the High Lakes proposed wilderness.

though winter storms are an ever-present possibility. Most of the game animals leave the high country at this time, migrating eastward to lower elevations. Hunters may find a few blue grouse, but little else of interest.

In the winter, the Pilot Creek Trailhead on US 212 becomes a hub of recreational activity. Snowmobilers park here and drive their machines up the unplowed highway grade, then roam free throughout the Beartooth High Lakes Wilderness Study Area. Cross-country skiing and snowshoeing are also popular in this high country; plan an extra day to make the long climb up the grade before making sallies into the backcountry. The Forest Service maintains a warming hut at Island Lake for public use. Be aware that winter weather at this altitude is highly capricious, with gale-force winds and sub-zero temperatures a common occurrence. The skiing can be good as late as early June in this area, and the highway is plowed for the Memorial Day weekend, offering easier access to the high plateaus.

ACCESS: The Beartooth Scenic Highway (US 212) makes the big climb from Cooke City to the top of the Beartooth Plateau before making a winding descent to Red Lodge, Montana. Along the way, it offers access to the Wyoming part of the Absaroka-Beartooth Wilderness as well as the Beartooth High Lakes Wilderness Study Area. The highway is typically open from Memorial Day through mid-October. The principal access points to the Absaroka-Beartooth Wilderness are the Lost Lake and Granite Lake Trailheads. Farther east, US 212 runs past Beartooth Lake and Island Lake, which are the jumping-off points for trails that run through the Beartooth High Lakes WSA and continue into the Absaroka-Beartooth Wilderness.

Day Hike

Lost Lake

Distance: 2.4 miles one way.
Difficulty: Moderate.
Starting and maximum elevation: 7,760 feet, 8,220 feet.
Topo map: Muddy Creek.
Getting there: Drive northeast up U.S. Highway 212 for a short distance from its junction with Wyoming 296, then turn left (northwest) on Forest Road 130. Follow this road to reach a hilltop junction; passenger cars should park here. High-clearance vehicles can turn left, following the rutted and often muddy jeep road that descends westward. Turn right at mile 2.7, following signs for Lost Lake, and park at the road's end at the wilderness boundary.

This short trail penetrates the forested foreland that stretches along the south edge of the Absaroka-Beartooth Wilderness. Attractions include waterfalls and woodland lakes, but there are limited views of the high mountains. Initially, the Lost Lakes Trail climbs up a timbered slope and then levels off to cross sagebrush meadows. It soon descends into the lush, bottomland forest along Gilbert Creek. After a rock-hop of this stream, the trail splits. Bear right as the Lost Lakes Trail climbs heartily across sagebrush slopes, then contours across timbered hillsides to cross Gilbert Creek at the foot of a broad and delicate waterfall.

The path now continues eastward, crossing rocky slopes robed in lodgepole pine and passing through shady spruce bottoms. Ultimately, it follows a small brook upward between steep knobs of granite to reach Lost Lake. This broad tarn occupies a rocky pocket surrounded by steep hills. Its deep waters are stained brown by the tannic acids that leach from decaying pine needles in the surrounding forest.

Waterfall on Crazy Creek.

Day Hike

Beartooth Butte Loop

Distance: 6.5 to 8.5 miles total.
Difficulty: Moderate.
Starting and maximum elevation: 9,570 feet, 10,000 feet.
Topo maps: Muddy Creek, Beartooth Butte.
Getting there: To reach the Granite Lake Trailhead, continue up US Highway 212 almost to the top of the grade, then turn left on the marked road to the Clay Butte Fire Lookout. Follow this high-standard gravel road to find the trailhead below the road on its west side just before it makes the big switchback to reach the lookout at the summit if the butte. The hike ends at the Beartooth Lake Campground, a little farther up US 212.

This route makes a circuit around Beartooth Butte, traveling through the Beartooth High Lakes WSA. Along the way are panoramic views of the Beartooth Mountains, flower-filled alpine meadows, and sparkling lakes set amid shallow granite basins sculpted by ice sheets. The route is poorly marked and faint in places, and requires some route-finding skill. Set up a two-car shuttle to get from the Beartooth Lake Campground back to the Granite Lake Trailhead near Clay Butte (hitchhiking is difficult here).

From the Granite Lake Trailhead, the path descends across meadowy slopes that offer an unbroken vista of the Absaroka Range. Before long, it levels off through stands of subalpine fir. Turn right at the junction to reach the Clay Butte Trail, which climbs lazily across alpine grasslands. Beartooth Butte's limestone walls rise above, and the high peaks of the Beartooth Mountains stretch across the northern horizon.

As the trail enters a maze of granite hillocks, watch carefully for a spur trail that heads upward to the right (east). Follow this trail past Native Lake, then cross the divide at the base of Beartooth Butte. The path now swings south, crossing the flower-spangled meadows below the cliffs. The High Lakes Trail junction is 0.7 mile beyond the divide. If time is limited, continue straight ahead for the direct descent to Beartooth Lake. Otherwise, turn left onto the High Lakes Trail and enjoy the best scenery of the trek.

The High Lakes Trail follows cairns northward to cross a gap in the granite hills. The path emerges above a string of nameless lakes, and a striking panorama of the Beartooth Mountains unfolds ahead. The path now swings east, following a chain of alpine tarns bordered by tundra and exposed granite. As whitebark pines and firs become prevalent, the path works its way past snow-melt ponds and through a series of granite gaps.

A pair of hearty descents soon leads down to the head of Beauty Lake. After crossing two broad but shallow streams, turn right onto the Beauty Lake Trail. It runs past two large lakes set amid the timberline forest, and it reveals excellent views of Beartooth Butte along the way. The trail then descends through the timber and makes a final stream ford to reach its end at the Beartooth Lake Campground.

Line Creek   3

Location: 5 miles west of Clark and 20 miles east of Cooke City, Montana.
Size: 98,560 acres (65,280 in Wyoming).
Administration: Shoshone National Forest (Clarks Fork District); Custer National Forest (Beartooth District).
Management status: Unprotected Wyoming lands (65,280 acres).
Ecosystems: Douglas fir forest, lodgepole pine, western spruce-fir forest, sagebrush steppe.
Elevation range: 5,575 feet to 10,990 feet.
System trails: 59 miles.
Maximum core to perimeter distance: 4.2 miles.
Activities: Mountain biking, hiking, horseback riding, fishing, big game hunting, backcountry skiing.
Best season: July–August.
Maps: Red Lodge and Cody 1:100,000; Shoshone National Forest North Half map.

TRAVELERS ADVISORY:
SUDDEN STORMS, GRIZZLY COUNTRY, ALTITUDE SICKNESS

Just across the highway from the Beartooth High Lakes WSA is a much larger stretch of roadless country that has received little public attention. Its terrain varies from the high, rolling tundra of the Beartooth Plateau down through subalpine parklands of upper Littlerock Creek and the Douglas fir forests of the foothills. Known as the Line Creek roadless area, it offers outstanding recreational opportunities.

On the highest ground near Beartooth Pass, the tundra plateaus are strewn with boulders left behind by long-extinct ice sheets. "Patterned ground" occurs atop these high, windswept balds that form the summit of the Beartooth Plateau. This unusual phenomenon occurs as a result of permafrost—ground that never melts, even during the height of summer. Beneath the tundra, wedges of ice form in a polygonal pattern, and as they grow, they thrust the soil above them upward. The result is a series of polygonal depressions separated by tundra-clad ridgelets.

Between 8,000 and 10,000 feet, the landscape is loosely forested in spruce, subalpine fir, and whitebark pine growing from thin soils interspersed with exposed bedrock. Along the eastern edge of the roadless area, the plateau drops off into steep mountainsides dissected by granite canyons with exposed strata

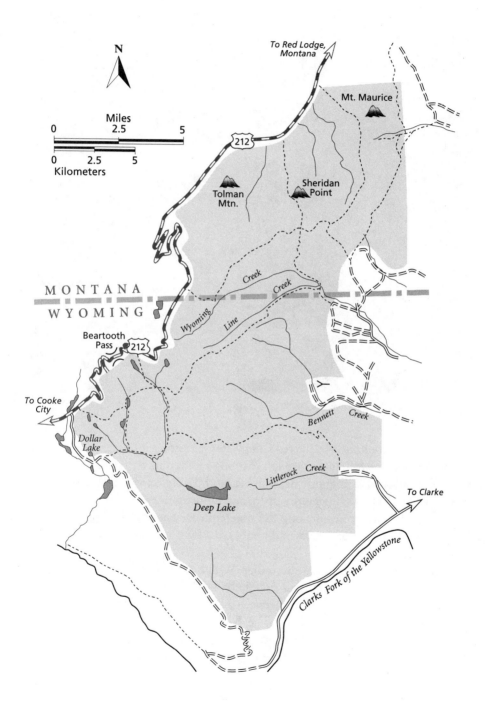

Alpine meadows near Gardner Lake.

of Madison limestone and the red Chugwater sandstone at their mouths. Here, fast-flowing streams churn through foaming rapids and waterfalls en route to the flatlands of the Bighorn Basin. This foothills region is characterized by a mixed woodland of Douglas fir, aspen, and limber pine, with cottonwoods and other hardwoods growing along the watercourses. South-facing slopes in this area are robed in an arid grassland punctuated by sagebrush, yucca, and prickly pear cactus.

One of the last battles of the Indian Wars occurred in 1878 at the foot of these highlands near the current site of Clark, Wyoming. Known as the Battle of Bennett Butte, it was fought between a troop of infantry with Crow scouts and a band of Bannock Indians. The Bannocks had left their reservation in eastern Idaho after a failure of the camas crop (a wild root that was a staple of the Bannock tribe) as a result of depredations by pigs owned by white settlers.

Starving and hopeless, the Bannocks made their way along their traditional trail over the Yellowstone Plateau. They were taken by surprise at the mouth of Little Sand Coulee, and half of their men, women, and children were killed or captured in the ensuing battle. The survivors fled north to the Crow Reservation in Montana and merged into that tribe's population.

Although fur trappers probably plied the Beartooth Plateau during the early 1800s, the first record of white exploration comes from 1882. In that year, General Phil Sheridan led a small military party from Cooke City up over the Beartooth Plateau to Billings. In later years, the windswept tundra of the Beartooth Plateau became summer pasture for large herds of domestic sheep. Sheep are no longer grazed here, with the exception of a small band that grazes the eastern slopes above Littlerock Creek. Camp Sawtooth was established in the heart of the roadless area in 1922. This cluster of cabins was run as a dude ranch for many years. Its rotting structures were dismantled in the 1970s.

RECREATIONAL USE: The Beartooth Loop National Scenic Trail receives comparatively heavy use from hikers, but most visitors never venture beyond Losekamp and Stockade Lakes. The high alpine tundra affords easy traveling for cross-country hikers, but it is a poor place to camp due to the gale force winds that are common here. The remainder of the area is well-suited to horses, but horse parties are seldom numerous. The trail from the Dollar Lake Trailhead to Camp Sawtooth is open to motorized vehicles; other parts of the area are closed to motor vehicles during summer.

In autumn, elk congregate along the eastern side of the roadless area, luring big game hunters from around the region. Hunting season sees the highest use of the roadless area. Poor access to the east means that the foothills receive mainly local use. The lakes and streams in this area are populated by brook trout and provide fair to good fishing for pan-sized specimens.

ACCESS: The best access to the Line Creek WSA is via US 212, the Beartooth Scenic Highway, which runs across the high country along its western boundary and offers several trailheads. The Morrison jeep trail (FR 120) runs from the highway down to the mouth of Clarks Fork Canyon, where roads lead to the settlement of Clark. This road is extremely rough and prone to mud, with steep, tight switchbacks. It should only be attempted (with great trepidation) with jeeps and similar vehicles.

The eastern side of the roadless area, with its unmarked roads and rampant subdivisions, has very poor public access. Access to Bennett Creek is blocked by "no trespassing" signs. You can reach the mouth of Little Rock Creek by driving the old highway to the Clarks Fork Canyon to County 8RA (the next road after 8SA), which is unmarked.

Looking south toward Table Mountain and Sawtooth Peak.

Day Hike or Backpack

Beartooth Loop National Recreation Trail

Distance: 12.3 miles overall.
Difficulty: Moderate.
Starting and maximum elevation: 9,792 feet, 10,050 feet.
Topo map: Deep Lake.
Getting there: Drive east on U.S. Highway 212 from its junction with Wyoming 296. The Beartooth Loop trail can be accessed at marked trailheads 1 mile beyond the Top of the World Store or above Gardner Lake at the top of the grade.

This loop trail can be accessed from several points and is moderately popular with tourists traveling on the Beartooth Scenic Highway. It crosses rolling country near the timberline and features alpine meadows, sparkling lakes, and a few mountain vistas along the way. The trail is faint in places, and hikers should be prepared to follow cairns and consult their topo maps frequently.

From the marked trailhead on US 212, follow a spur trail east through timberline meadows and groves of whitebark pine. It soon passes Hauser Lake, then wanders among granite hillocks and alpine wetlands. The Absaroka Mountains appear in the south periodically, and Table Mountain rises close at hand to the southeast. As low but craggy summits close in on the north, the path descends to Losekamp Lake, where it joins the loop trail.

Turn left (north) as the route rounds the head of the lake and then climbs lazily into the tundra-clad pass behind Tibbs Butte. Here, a carpet of alpine wildflowers stretches in all directions and majestic peaks rise to the north. As the path descends into the valley of Littlerock Creek, a spur trail runs north across the level meadows to reach Gardner Lake, set in an alpine basin at the foot of the peaks.

The loop trail descends southwest across the paths that lead down from Tibbs Butte Pass. Upon reaching the valley floor, the path follows Littlerock Creek through broad and marshy meadows. The Highline Trail splits away to the left as Sawtooth Butte appears ahead. The loop trail soon crosses Littlerock Creek and swings west into the valley of Stockade Lake.

A gentle climb through the trees leads up this wooded vale; stay right as the trail to Sawtooth Camp splits away. The scenery improves as the path passes Stockade Lake, then traces the pretty cascades that lead from its head to the alpine Basin of Losekamp Lake. Acquire the original entry trail on the southwest shore of this lake to return to your vehicle.

North Absaroka Wilderness   4

Location: 20 miles northwest of Cody and 5 miles south of Cooke City, Montana.
Size: 486,388 acres.
Administration: Clarks Fork Ranger District, Shoshone National Forest.
Management status: North Absaroka Wilderness (350,488 acres); adjacent roadless lands (135,900 acres).
Ecosystem: Douglas fir forest, lodgepole pine, western spruce-fir forest.
Elevation range: 5,575 feet to 12,200 feet.
System trails: 217 miles.
Maximum core to perimeter distance: 11.8 miles.
Activities: Horseback riding, hiking, backpacking, fishing, big game hunting.
Best season: Mid-June–mid-September.
Maps: Shoshone National Forest North Half Map, Cody 1:100,000.

TRAVELERS ADVISORY:
GRIZZLY COUNTRY, FORDS

The North Absaroka Wilderness was originally part of the Yellowstone Timberland Reserve, set aside in 1891 as the predecessor to the National Forest system. The Absarokas are the remnants of a vast volcanic plateau which has been dissected by rivers and streams and carved into sharp horns and razorback ridges by long-extinct glaciers. Big reefs and mesas of volcanic rock are found along the southern edge of the wilderness. The name *Absaroka* means "people of the large-beaked bird," referring to the Crow tribe.

Volcanic activity in the Absarokas began 53 million years ago during the uplifts that created the Rocky Mountains and lasted until 38 million years ago. During this time, the land that now forms the Absarokas was part of the broad, shallow basin some 7,000 square miles in extent that is known as the Absaroka Basin. During the period of volcanic cataclysm, huge stratovolcanoes rose from the floor of the depression. These classic, cone-shaped volcanoes were built up from ash and mudflows expelled during the eruptions. At their peak they rose over 10,000 feet above sea level, but the forces of erosion soon leveled them. Some of these extinct volcanoes can be found in the Sunlight Basin. Other lava flows were extruded from small vents in the earth's surface; many of these vents were buried beneath later flows of volcanic rock.

4   NORTH ABSAROKA WILDERNESS

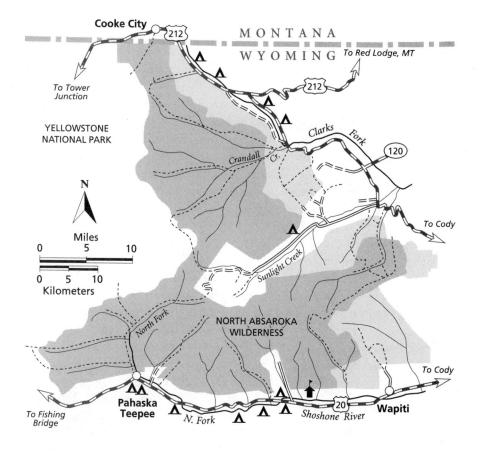

About 4 million years ago, the entire region was part of a broad uplift, and the volcanic rocks that were to become the Absarokas formed a high and unbroken plateau. Erosion immediately began its work on the newly formed uplands. Then, during the Pleistocene ice ages between 50,000 and 12,000 years ago, the Absaroka highlands were subjected to several episodes of glaciation. Once-shallow depressions were deepened by glacial ice which ultimately formed great valley glaciers that gouged canyons 3,000 feet deep and whittled the high summits into sharp horns and sawtooth ridges. During this time, a massive trunk glacier flowed down the valley of the Clarks Fork, damming the valley of Sunlight Creek to form Glacial Lake Sunlight. Permafrost formed within the soils above the glaciers, and relict patches of this permafrost can be found today on top of Carter Mountain. Here, the trained eye can find patterned ground, *solifluction deposits* that resulted from the downhill creep of frozen soil, relict *pingos* (or ice-cored mounds), and *felsenmeers*, or level plains of ice-shattered rock.

Along the southern edges of the wilderness are outcrops of volcanic conglomerate known as *breccia*. The larger cobbles in this pastiche of sediments are resistant to erosion, and over time pillars and fins form beneath them as the surrounding rock erodes away along vertical fractures. Also in this area, volcanic gravels contain petrified stumps of trees that were killed by mudflows. Thick layers of basalt resulting from ancient lava flows form the eastern ramparts of the Absarokas. The tall cliffs of the Absaroka Mountain front are the result of a north-south thrust-fault known as the Heart Mountain Fault. During the Laramide uplift, the Absaroka volcanics and the older limestone that underlies them were thrust eastward, overtopping newly deposited ash beds. As a result, you can now find 300 million-year-old limestones atop beds of ash that formed only 52 million years ago.

Sunlight Peak boasts its own glacier, a small remnant of the great valley glaciers that coursed through the range during the Pleistocene Epoch. There are also several active rock glaciers in the upper basin of Sunlight Creek. These ice-cored slopes of broken rock creep gradually downhill, and their surface is marked by a curvaceous, billowy pattern that betrays the movement of the ice underneath. Elsewhere in the range, U-shaped valleys, horn peaks, and knife-edge ridges display the sculpting power of long-extinct rivers of ice.

During the Clover Mist Fire of 1988, intense fires spread through the northern half of the wilderness. The sterile stands of mature lodgepole were converted into ash and minerals, and a riot of shrubs and wildflowers sprang up in the open sunlight. This created ideal feeding habitat for elk and other game animals, which have become abundant. The grizzly bear has also benefited from the blaze, thriving on plentiful spring greenery and a new abundance of ants. Fire is no stranger to the North Absarokas. In 1955, some 6,600 acres of timber burned during a fire along Sunlight Creek. With the new "let burn" policy that applies to wilderness areas, the North Absarokas are steadily returning to their natural and beneficial cycle of small-scale wildfires.

Because it shares a border with Yellowstone National Park, the North Absaroka Wilderness is a critical corridor for wildlife migrations. The Sunlight Basin is a winter range for elk, mule deer, and bighorn sheep. Two herds of bighorn sheep use this wilderness, each fluctuating around 500 animals. One herd centers its activity in the peaks above the Clarks Fork, while the other ranges south of Sunlight Creek, with Trout Peak as it focal point. The North Absarokas have also been the site of recent efforts to reestablish breeding populations of peregrine falcons.

Indigenous peoples were making summer forays into the Absarokas for thousands of years before the arrival of the first white explorer. North of Blackwater Creek, archaeologists discovered a tunnel—known as Mummy Cave—which was used continuously as a shelter by prehistoric hunter-gatherers for over 9,000 years, beginning around 7,280 B.C. The Sheepeater Indians were year-round residents of the Sunlight Basin when the first European explorers arrived.

Sunlight Creek was also part a traditional Indian trail used by the Bannock Indians. The trail ran from the Snake River Plain up over Targhee Pass, then crossed the Yellowstone plateau and forded the Madison and Yellowstone rivers before descending into the Sunlight Basin. The trail then followed Sunlight Creek down to the Clarks Fork and thence out into the Bighorn Basin, where the Bannocks hunted for bison during the summer months. Parts of this route were used by Chief Joseph and his tribe of Nez Perce as they made their ill-fated run for Canada in 1877.

The first white visitors to the region were fur trappers working on behalf of large trading companies based in St. Louis and Canada. John Colter is believed to have made a solo trip into the Sunlight Basin during the winter of 1806–07. The trappers moved through the area but few stayed to settle, and the Absarokas remained in pristine condition until late in the 1800s.

As the twentieth century approached, several mining towns sprang up along Galena Creek in the Sunlight Basin. Goods were brought in to the miners by buckboard, a long and costly journey from the nearest supply point. The towns disappeared almost as soon as they arose, and now only a few foundations with interpretive signs mark the sites of the mining boom. There has been little mining activity here since the turn of the 20th century. There are several inactive mining claims in the Sunlight Creek drainage, inholdings within the wilderness that remain in private hands. Geological surveys have noted significant deposits of porphyry in this area, an ore mineral that contains both copper and molybdenum.

Oil companies have long looked to the North Absarokas as a possible site for development. The sedimentary strata that lie beneath the Absaroka volcanics are known to contain significant quantities of oil. Mineral springs and oil seeps along Sweetwater Creek show quantities of crude oil seeping to the surface through fissures in the bedrock, associated with intrusive dikes of younger volcanic rock. At one time, oil companies advocated the removal of wilderness designation from the North Absarokas so they could pursue full-scale development here, but long-range thinking prevailed and the wilderness survived.

RECREATIONAL USE: During the summer months, much of the North Absaroka backcountry is free from human incursions. The Pahaska-Sunlight

Trail receives heavy use from backpackers and horse parties, and guest ranches send horse tours up several of the valleys that drain into the North Fork of the Shoshone. But to the north of Sunlight Creek, only a few hardy souls venture into the primeval wilds, where the Clover Mist Fire has created trail-finding challenges and numerous deadfalls. This area is a good place to seek a genuinely primitive wilderness experience and put your wilderness skills to the test.

If you venture into the Clover Mist burn, be especially wary of dead snags, which can fall without warning and cause serious injury. Expect steep climbs, difficult route finding, and few trail signs in this area. Streams are typically impassable before the end of June, and thunderstorms may bring high water throughout the season. Day trips are few in the North Absarokas; most trails are better suited to extended backpacks and horse trips.

Most of the visitors who penetrate far into the North Absaroka backcountry do so on horseback. Heaviest use occurs during the autumn hunting season, when an influx of hunters arrives to pursue the elk that migrate down from the high plateaus of Yellowstone National Park. Guides and outfitters often set up extensive camps in the backcountry. Hunters traditionally concentrate on the valleys of Dead Indian, Sunlight, North Crandall, and Pilot Creeks. By rifle season, a large percentage of the elk have reached private lands owned by the Twodot Ranch, but hunters bag a healthy number of stragglers each year. Horsemen should be aware that forage is limited in the backcountry; very few camping spots offer any grazing. As a result, the few meadows that offer forage tend to be overused, so minimum impact techniques are a must for all.

There are few lakes in the North Absarokas, but stream fishing can be productive. Rainbow, brook, and cutthroat trout are the most prevalent species, and you might find brown trout in some of the larger streams. Volcanic soils in this area erode easily, so the waters muddy easily and the fishing deteriorates with every passing rainstorm.

ACCESS: The Chief Joseph Scenic Byway (Wyoming 296) links Cooke City, Montana with Cody, Wyoming. It offers access to a number of trailheads along the eastern flank of the North Absaroka Wilderness, including the popular Crandall Creek Trailhead. From this highway, the gravel road to Sunlight Basin makes a westward foray, penetrating deep into the heart of the mountains and offering rapid access to the heart of the wilderness. Private ranch lands surround the southeastern lobe of the North Absaroka Wilderness, and public access to many wilderness trails in this area is disputed. Farther west, however, U.S. Highway 20 follows the Shoshone Canyon and visits several trailheads on Forest Service land.

Day Hike

Pilot Creek

Distance: 7.0 miles one way.
Difficulty: Moderate (first falls); strenuous (second falls).
Starting and maximum elevation: 6,990 feet, 9,140 feet.
Topo maps: Jim Smith Peak, Pilot Peak.
Getting there: Drive east from Cooke City, Montana, on U.S. Highway 212 to reach the large Pilot Creek Trailhead some 1.5 miles east of Fox Creek Campground. When approaching from the east, the trailhead is 2.3 miles west of Crazy Creek Campground.

This obscure trail follows the valley to the south of Pilot Peak and crosses country that burned during the Clover Mist Fire. Downed snags are common obstacles, making horse travel difficult. The high ridges at the head of the drainage offer good views of the surrounding peaks.

The south face of Pilot Peak.

Grinnell Meadows.

The hike begins by climbing along the sinuous ridge that separates Pilot Creek from the Clarks Fork of the Yellowstone. After a gentle climb, it crosses through post-fire salvage clearcuts before entering the wilderness. The sharp pinnacle of Pilot Peak rises ahead, and to the north is a panorama of the Beartooth Mountains.

An old roadbed soon carries the trail higher into Douglas fir savannas. The road ends as the trail descends into the Pilot Creek valley, where scorched snags are underlain by a lush growth of wildflowers. A striking peak rises at the head of the valley, and the south face of Pilot Peak emerges as the path reaches the valley floor.

A rock-hop of a nameless tributary leads into the wilderness. A few stands of spruce have survived along upper Pilot Creek, and before long the trail reaches a lush meadow. Deadfalls become more numerous as the trail climbs modestly through burned-over spruce bogs.

Upon reaching the base of the divide, the trail reveals a striking waterfall. This is a good turn-around point. More ambitious hikers can continue on the increasingly primitive trail as it climbs steeply up the valley's headwall. It ultimately turns south and traverses the slopes to enter a hanging basin. The trail ends near the timberline, beside a steep watercourse with sheet-like waterfalls.

Day Trip on Foot or Horseback

Grinnell Creek

Distance: 5.0 miles one way
Difficulty: Moderate.
Starting and maximum elevation: 6,675 feet, 8,075 feet.
Topo maps: Pahaska Teepee, Sunlight Peak.
Getting there: Drive U.S. Highway 20 east from Pahaska Teepee. The Grinnell Creek Trailhead is at the end of an unmarked dirt road on the north side of this highway, just east of the Shoshone Lodge.

This trail follows a pretty, unburned valley into the mountains near Pahaska Teepee. Grinnell Creek is known for its fine fishing for cutthroat trout, so anglers should bring fishing gear.

The journey begins with a steady climb on the mountainside to the east of Grinnell Creek. It makes its way through a lush coniferous forest, with periodic gaps in the canopy to provide views of the cliffs and peaks that flank the valley. After passing a confluence where the West Fork pours in, the cliffs of Sleeping Giant Mountain rise skyward above the trail. Before long, avalanche slopes offer clear views of the surrounding grandeur. The gabled cliffs of Hurricane Mesa now stretch in an unbroken wall across the far side of the valley.

After 4 miles, the stream gradient eases, and grassy meadows offer pleasant rest spots. The path approaches Grinnell Creek several times as it continues up the valley, passing through verdant meadows and young stands of conifers. Just beyond the 5-mile mark, the trail appears to descend to a ford of Grinnell Creek. Stay on the east bank, following a rough path to an eastern tributary. Here, the trek ends amid sedge meadows that allow glorious views of the peaks at the head of the valley.

Washakie Wilderness   5

Location: 30 miles southwest of Cody, 25 miles west of Meteetsee, and 15 miles north of Dubois.
Size: 1,019,544 acres.
Administration: Shoshone National Forest (Wapiti, Greybull, and Wind River ranger districts); BLM (Lander District).
Management status: Washakie Wilderness (704,274 acres); Owl Creek BLM Wilderness Study Area (710 acres); adjacent roadless lands (314,560 acres).
Ecosystems: Rocky Mountain Douglas fir forest, lodgepole pine, sagebrush steppe, western spruce-fir forest, with extensive grasslands on south-facing slopes and at the timberline.
Elevation range: 6,600 feet to 13,153 feet.
System trails: 473 miles, most of which receive low maintenance.
Maximum core to perimeter distance: 10.7 miles.
Activities: Horseback riding, hiking, backpacking, hunting, fishing.
Best season: July–September.
Maps: Shoshone National Forest North Half Map; The Ramshorn and Carter Mountain 1:100,000.

TRAVELERS ADVISORY:
GRIZZLY COUNTRY, SUDDEN STORMS, FORDS

In 1891, Congress established the Yellowstone Timberland Reserve, encompassing all of the present Washakie Wilderness as well as forestlands to the north. A portion of the original reserve was set aside in 1932 as the South Absaroka Wilderness. The South Absaroka Wilderness and Stratified Primitive Area were redesignated as the Washakie Wilderness in 1972. It was named in honor of Chief Washakie, a prominent leader from the Shoshone tribe.

The southern end of the Absaroka Range is typified by rolling, tundra-clad plateaus separated by deep, glacier-carved valleys. A handful of towering summits rise above the high plateaus. The highest point in the range is Francs Peak, which rises 13,153 feet above sea level. In the drainage headwaters, streams are defined by narrow valleys and bedrock canyons, with wet meadows commonplace along the flats. Farther downstream, the major waterways flow along braided courses through wide plains of alluvial outwash.

The drainages and the steep slopes that guard them are timbered loosely in spruce, lodgepole and limber pine, and aspen. Grassy swards are common on the south-facing slopes. Only about 35 percent of the wilderness is forested,

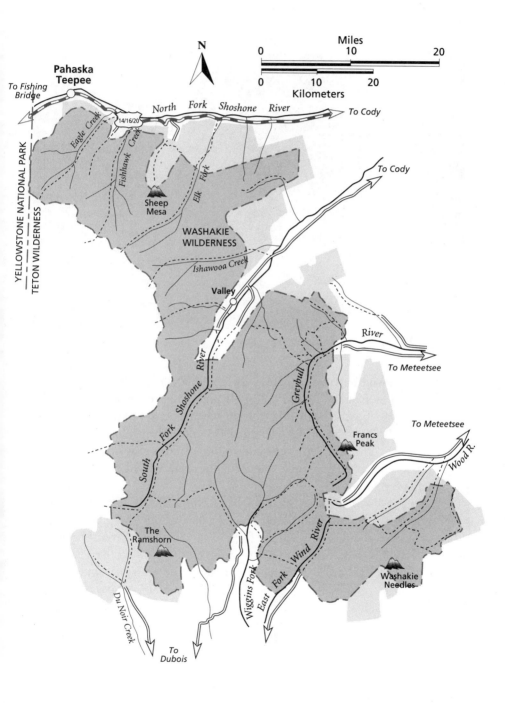

Miles

Kilometers

Looking west across Anderson Creek to the heart of the Absarokas.

and extensive wildfires are rare here. Between 6,500 and 9,000 feet, the forest is dominated by Douglas fir and lodgepole pine. Engelmann spruce and sub-alpine fir make up the timberline forest, which occurs between 8,000 and 10,000 feet. Almost half of the wilderness lies above the timberline elevation of 10,000 feet. The rounded ridges and rolling plateaus that occupy the core of the range are robed in fragile alpine tundra characterized by shallow soils and fragile vegetation.

Wildlife is abundant here, including over 8,000 elk, twice as many mule deer, hundreds of moose, and more than 1,000 bighorn sheep. The Wapiti Ridge sheep herd ranges between the forks of the Shoshone River. The slightly smaller Younts Peak sheep herd occupies the southern end of the wilderness. Pronghorn antelope are occasionally spotted in the grassy uplands of the Washakie Wilderness, wandering into the high mountain steppes during the height of the summer. The ridgetops along the Anderson-Stuart Creek divide are a major winter range for the Yellowstone elk. In the northwestern corner of the wilderness, the valleys of Canfield and Fishhawk Creeks are critical grizzly bear habitat. Other endangered species are also present here, including the bald eagle, peregrine falcon, and gray wolf.

The geological story of the Washakie Wilderness began about 55 million years ago. During this time, tectonic movement associated with the uplift of the Rocky Mountains caused the uplift of a new range of granite. Known as the Washakie Range, it stretched from Yellowstone Lake far out into the Wind River Basin, to a point northeast of modern Dubois. As it rose, existing streams and rivers that straddled the uplift began to cut downward through the granite, and ultimately excavated a series of deep transverse canyons.

This uplift also marked the beginning of a protracted period of volcanic activity in the region. Beginning 52 million years ago, huge cones rose along the lowlands, spewing forth lava and incandescent ash that covered the region and buried the Washakie Range beneath 2,500 feet of volcanic debris. Fossil forests of petrified wood occur where ancient stratovolcanoes buried the primordial landscape in mudflows and ash deposits. The volcanic flows completely buried the existing Washakie Range, which is made up of older granite. These weak beds of ash, lava, and conglomerates were later intruded by dikes of magma, which solidified underground into much harder and more resistant volcanic plugs.

The sedimentary strata that were buried beneath the Absaroka volcanics crop up along the South Fork of the Shoshone River and along the eastern and southern edges of the mountains. Tectonic movement is also evident here. Sheep Mountain is a block of Madison limestone that is 300 million years old. Due to thrust faulting that pushed the Absarokas eastward over younger strata, these limestones now lie atop the ash beds of the Willwood formation, which is only 55 million years old.

During the Pleistocene Epoch, valley glaciers filled all of the major drainages in the southern Absarokas. Small remnant glaciers can still be found in the valleys of Fishhawk, Du Noir, and Barron creeks. Since that time, erosion has carved pinnacles, natural bridges, fluted cliffs, vertical faces, and sawtooth peaks into the loose volcanic rock.

The southern reaches of the Absaroka Range were once a principal hunting ground of the Sheepeater tribe. These Native Americans were of Shoshonean descent, but they never acquired the horse and thus hunted on foot within the protection of the mountains. They constructed V-shaped drivelines using piles of stones to capture herds of bighorn sheep. The drivelines funneled the sheep uphill to a chokepoint, where a ramp led into a corral of logs and boulders. Once penned, the sheep could easily be dispatched with spears and arrows. Several of these drivelines have been found in the southern end of the Washakie Wilderness. In addition, a number of Precolumbian camp sites have been found in alpine areas.

In historical times, visitors to the southern Absarokas have been relatively few. In 1835, a party of trappers led by Osborn Russell forced their way up Du

Noir Creek and over the Absaroka divide in the midst of a blinding winter snowstorm. Later, ranchers discovered the vast alpine grasslands of the range and began driving herds of sheep up to the high country during summer. Broad tracts of the alpine grasslands within the wilderness are still leased to ranchers for summer grazing of domestic sheep and goats. Cattle and horse grazing within the wilderness occurs along the Greybull River. Check with rangers to ascertain the location and timing of livestock grazing if you wish to avoid it.

Petroleum geologists project that there is moderate to high potential for the presence of oil and gas in the sedimentary layers that lie buried beneath the Absaroka volcanics. Geologic formations such as the Cody Arch near the north end of the wilderness and the Dubois Arch along its southern flank have the highest potential for petroleum production. Oil and gas leasing was once proposed for the Washakie Wilderness, but because of the steep and highly erosive nature of the Absaroka Mountains, oil companies would have to engage in prohibitively expensive mitigation in order to drill even in the neighboring non-wilderness areas.

A number of small roadless tracts surround the Washakie Wilderness, and were identified during the RARE II process in the 1970s. The Wiggins Fork of the Wind River has been proposed as a National Wild and Scenic River. The Owl Creek WSA consists of three small tracts of BLM land in the steep country along the South Fork of Owl Creek, near the Washakie Needles. It is accessible only through the Washakie Wilderness. It has been recommended for wilderness status.

The Du Noir Special Management Area is one of the largest candidates for expansion of the Washakie Wilderness. It includes the Du Noir Glacier, which occupies the east face of Coffin Butte. The big walls of the mesas that guard Du Noir Creek are made up of welded tuff and volcanic mudflows. The area was extensively logged to supply railroad ties between 1920 and 1940, but it has since returned to a pristine state. There has been documented wolf activity along Du Noir Creek, including known incidents of wolf depredations on livestock. The Phosphoria formation underlies the eastern third of this roadless area. This formation has produced oil in paying quantities elsewhere in Wyoming, but oil potential in the Du Noir area is rated as negligible.

RECREATIONAL USES: The Washakie Wilderness has a system of long trails that extends deep into the mountains. Some trails cross over passes to enter Yellowstone National Park or the Teton Wilderness, allowing extended trips of several weeks or more. Bear in mind that a backcountry permit is required for overnight stays in the national park. Campers must pitch their tents at least 50 feet away from lakeshores, streams, and trails.

Although the long distances and abundant graze make the area ideal for horse excursions, only about 14 percent of visitors rely on horses for transportation. Eagle Creek Meadows and Five Pockets receive the heaviest horse use during the summer months, while Elk Fork Meadows and Bliss Creek Meadows become hubs of equestrian activity during the autumn hunting seasons. The Greybull-Venus area also receives comparatively heavy use by horsemen. The heaviest use of the Washakie Wilderness occurs in autumn, during the hunting season. Many Yellowstone elk migrate through the mountains at this time, en route to winter range to the east and south. There are few lakes in the Washakie Wilderness, but fishing is good in the rivers and larger creeks.

ACCESS: The Washakie Wilderness is bounded to the north by U.S. Highway 20, which follows the Shoshone River and offers good access to national forest trailheads. From the western edge of Cody, Wyoming 291 runs southwest past Buffalo Bill Reservoir and up the South Fork of the Shoshone, providing access to the Ishawooa area, which is the principal gateway to the northeastern quadrant of the wilderness.

Wyoming 120 runs along the base of the Absarokas; from it gravel roads run westward to the edge of the Washakie Wilderness. Private holdings along the foothills and unsigned roads make trailhead access a challenge in this area. The Greybull River (via the Jack Creek Trailhead) and Wood River are the principal entry points. Direct access to the southeastern corner of the range, including the Washakie Needles, is blocked by private lands to the east and the Wind River Indian Reservation to the south. There is, however, public access to the southwestern corner of the wilderness via the Horse Creek and Du Noir Creek roads near the town of Dubois.

Day Hike or Backpack

Sheep Mesa

Distance: 5.3 to 6.3 miles one way.
Difficulty: Strenuous.
Starting and maximum elevation: 6,600 feet, 11,000 feet.
Topo map: Chimney Peak.
Getting there: To reach the Blackwater Creek Trailhead, drive to the Firefighter Memorial on U.S. Highway 20, about halfway between Pahaska Teepee and Wapiti. Just east of the large, brick memorial, turn south at the sign for the Blackwater Ranch and follow the narrow dirt road across the Shoshone River. Passenger cars will find a parking area on the far side of the bridge, but high-clearance vehicles can drive 2 miles farther to the end of this rocky, rutted, and sometimes steep roadway.

This hike follows the Natural Bridge Trail up Blackwater Creek to its subalpine basin, then makes a steep, off-trail scramble to the top of Sheep Mesa. Natural

Sheep Mesa.

arches have formed in the volcanic breccia that guards the mesa rims. Schedule your hike to avoid the mesa tops during afternoon, when lightning is a major hazard.

The hike begins with a ford of Blackwater Creek, then runs upstream through a Douglas fir forest. After 1.1 miles, an old signpost marks the junction of two trails. Bear right as the route climbs beside the West Fork Blackwater Creek. After a steady slog, the forest takes on a subalpine character, and gaps in the canopy reveal the cliffs of Sheep Mesa. The trail ultimately fords the West Fork and soon zigzags up into a timberline woodland. It then resumes its southwesterly course to recross the West Fork just below an outfitter's camp at mile 5.3. Watch for the Blackwater Natural Bridge, a free-standing keyhole arch in the high cliffs to the east.

The trail ends at the camp; follow the finger ridge upward to emerge into a vast alpine meadow, then contour northeast across the slopes. As you hike, identify the grassy couloir to the north of Blackwater Natural Bridge. This gully offers a steep scramble up through the pinnacles and cliffs of breccia. At the top of the climb, the rounded surface of Sheep Mesa offers limitless vistas of the high Absarokas. If the weather isn't threatening, you can easily run the ridgetops around the head of the valley.

Backpack or Horse Loop

Warhouse Loop

Distance: 17.3 miles overall.
Difficulty: Moderately strenuous.
Starting and maximum elevation: 7,600 feet, 10,360 feet.
Topo maps: Phelps Mountain, Irish Rock, Aldrich Basin, North Fork Pickett Creek.
Getting there: To reach the Jack Creek Trailhead, take Wyoming 120 to Meteetsee, then drive west on Wyoming 290, following signs for Sunshine Recreation Area. Continue to the end of the pavement, go straight ahead at the junction with the Sunshine Reservoir road and turn left just before reaching the first bridge over the Greybull River. Follow the signs for the Jack Creek Trailhead through a maze of roads that run past hayfields, pastures, and oil wells. The road ends up at a trailhead and campground at the spot where the Greybull River flows out of a narrow canyon in the mountains.

This journey follows trails and primitive tracks on a loop route into the high grasslands to the north of the Greybull River. Substantial portions of the route are above the timberline, where trails are very faint and marked only infrequently with cairns; they're difficult to follow in places. Major fords of Jack Creek, Pine Creek, and the Greybull River make the route impassable during spring runoff. A number of old cabins can be found along the way; camping at the cabins is not allowed.

The trail begins with a ford of Jack Creek, and the trail splits on the far side. Horsemen should use the Greybull River Trail, which makes additional fords, while hikers will follow the High Water Trail. This good trail climbs high onto the slopes above the Greybull River for aerial views of its canyon. Open meadows and scattered limber pines ultimately give way to stands of Douglas fir, and soon the path makes its way to the valley floor. Turn right as the Greybull River Trail joins in, and after fording the river, follow the Anderson Creek Trail upriver.

The trail soon reaches the canyon of Anderson Creek, where the foaming rapids churn through a shady spruce forest. The path soon climbs high onto arid slopes studded with pinnacles of volcanic rock. After crossing Vick Creek, the path turns northwest to follow this tiny tributary. The climb leads to a miniature canyon replete with waterfalls, and after passing through it climbs to a junction. Bear right as the route continues up Vick Creek through rolling sagebrush meadows and spruce groves to reach an old cabin.

Pinnacles above Warhouse Creek.

Turn north at the cabin as the faint trail leads up a steep and grassy draw, then climb to the ridgetop for panoramic views. Dropping into the grassy valley of Warhouse Creek, a stunning landscape of jagged peaks unfolds at the head of the valley. The trail makes a long descent to the valley floor, where good camping spots can be found. After crossing Warhouse Creek, turn left and follow the stream up to another log cabin.

From here, the path doglegs sharply eastward, climbs through several gaps and then ascends a tributary valley. At its head is a cockscomb of rock; in the upper basin, seek out a faint path that runs southwest as it climbs a grassy ridge. Splendid views unfold as the path crests the divide, then cuts across the headwalls of the Betty Creek and West Fork Betty Creek valleys. Upon reaching a third drainage, the path descends to the watercourse and follows it to a cabin.

The path then runs southeast, glides up to the next ridgetop, and then begins the foot-pounding descent to Pine Creek. After fording this brawling stream, the trail descends through open country. A second ford leads the trail around the mountainside and into the Greybull River Canyon. After a long traverse and a brief descent, a ford of the swift-running river leads back to the Jack Creek Trailhead.

Teton Wilderness   6

Location: 35 miles northeast of Jackson.
Size: 638,105 acres.
Administration: Bridger-Teton National Forest (Jackson District).
Management status: Teton Wilderness (585,468 acres), adjacent roadless lands (52,637 acres).
Ecosystem: Douglas fir forest, lodgepole pine, western spruce-fir forest.
Elevation range: 7,500 feet to 12,165 feet.
System trails: 450 miles.
Maximum core to perimeter distance: 26.2 miles.
Activities: Horseback riding, hiking, backpacking, hunting, fishing, spelunking, cross-country skiing, dogsledding.
Best season: Mid-June–mid-September.
Maps: Bridger-Teton National Forest Buffalo and Jackson Ranger Districts map.

TRAVELERS ADVISORY:
GRIZZLY COUNTRY, FAINT TRAILS, FORDS

The Teton Wilderness stretches to the south of Yellowstone National Park and ranges from rolling, timbered hills in the west to craggy volcanic peaks of the Absaroka Range in the east. Its name derives not from the Teton Mountains but from the former Teton National Forest. Glacier-carved valleys lead into the heart of the peaks, and a handful of passes lead onward into the neighboring Washakie Wilderness. Backed by support of such wilderness lights as Olaus Murie and Bob Marshall, the Teton Wilderness was set aside as a primitive area in 1934, and it attained wilderness status with the passage of the Wilderness Act 30 years later.

The lowlands along the western end of the wilderness are made up of topography left behind after the area was repeatedly overrun by glacial ice during the Pleistocene Epoch. The lowlands are typically lush and brushy, and are considered to be prime grizzly habitat. The Teton Wilderness is part of a grizzly bear recovery area, and the bears are doing quite well here. The Heart Lake wolf pack also uses the northwestern corner of the wilderness in the autumn months as the elk migrate out of Yellowstone toward the game refuge in Jackson.

Lodgepole pine is the dominant forest type throughout the wilderness, mediated by frequent wildfires. About 200,000 acres of the northern Teton

6   THE TETON WILDERNESS

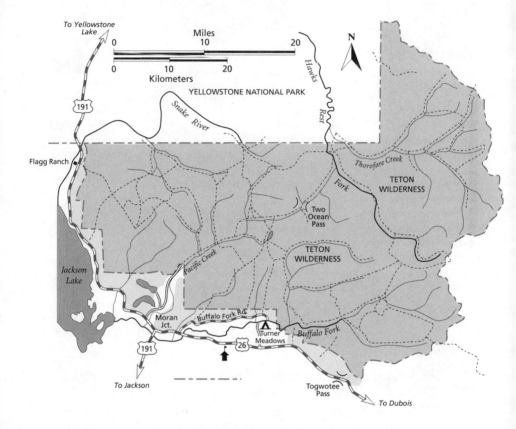

Wilderness burned during the Huckleberry Fire of 1988, and fireweed blooms among the charred snags during late summer. The pine forest is associated with meadows of elk sedge, pinegrass, and Wheeler's bluegrass, which are important forage for elk and deer. Elk summer feeding concentrates on the south-facing slopes where limber pines grow in grassy, arid savannas. Some of the rare inhabitants include lynx, wolverines, peregrine falcons, and trumpeter swans.

During the summer of 1987, a tornado ripped through the Lava Creek and Box Creek drainages of the Teton Wilderness, then continued over Enos Lake and Two Ocean Plateau before crossing the Hawks Rest Fork in Yellowstone National Park. The tornado caused a timber blowdown covering 14,000 acres, and it was the highest elevation tornado ever recorded.

The high Absarokas north of Togwotee Pass.

Both the Snake and the Yellowstone Rivers have their beginnings in the Teton Wilderness. At Two Ocean Pass, a single stream trickles down from the hills to enter a swampy depression. From this one swamp, Pacific Creek drains southwest into the Pacific watershed, while the Hawks Rest Fork of the Yellowstone drains northward, ultimately carrying its water to the Gulf of Mexico. This unique joining of drainages has historically allowed fish species to swim across the Continental Divide and colonize waters on the other side.

Togwotee Pass was a traditional travel corridor for bands of Shoshones and Bannocks during their seasonal migrations. *Togwotee* (pronounced TOAG-uh-tee) means "lance thrower" in the Shoshone language. Later, the pass became a well-known travel route for the mountain men who trapped for beaver and marten in the distant valleys and converged in the low basins of the region for their annual fur rendezvous.

RECREATIONAL USES: Hiking opportunities are fairly extensive in the Teton Wilderness, although many system trails have been abandoned. Long distances make this area favorable for long horse trips, and the trail network extends into Yellowstone National Park and the Washakie Wilderness for trips of any length. Hikers should be prepared to share the trail with horsemen, who make up the majority of visitors. Holmes Cave offers spelunking possibilities for the hard-core—there are steep drop-offs within that require rope and harness. It is reached by the good trail described below.

In recent years, Congress has failed to provide adequate funding for trail maintenance within the Teton Wilderness. A skeleton trail crew covers the hundreds of miles of trail found here. Many of the trails in the western lowlands are marshy and overgrown, and as a result you should expect route-finding challenges. Much of the trail maintenance within the wilderness is performed on a volunteer basis by the outfitters and guides who operate in the area. As a result, trails may be maintained as far as hunting camps that do not appear on maps, then disappear entirely beyond them.

About 60 percent of visitor use comes during the summer. There is heavy horse traffic up Pacific Creek to the Hawks Rest Fork via Two Ocean Pass. Gravel Creek and the lakes region of the Buffalo Fork also receive fairly heavy use. Some of the big lodges run horse concessions in the vicinity of Lake Emma Matilda and Turpin Meadows. The wilderness has a group size "limit" of 20 people and 35 pack and saddle stock. As a result of this virtually unregulated bonanza for outfitters, you are likely to encounter small regiments of cavalry and muddy conditions on the more popular trails. Do not vent your spleen at the outfitters, who are only doing their jobs. Instead, object to the Forest Service administrators who set these "limits."

Hunting big game accounts for 40 percent of the annual visitation to the Teton Wilderness. Elk and moose are the most sought-after species, and much of the hunting pressure is focused in the Thoroughfare area. Hunting within the Teton Wilderness has caused conflicts with bear recovery because grizzly bears have come to associate rifle shots with an easy meal. For this reason, hunters may have difficulty in getting their game out of the mountains without a confrontation.

In winter, the Togwotee Lodge becomes a hub of both snowmobile and cross-country skiing activity. The Teton Wilderness is entirely closed to snowmobiles; the low-lying western half provides the best opportunities for backcountry skiing. There are very few visitors at this time of year, and solitude is easy to find. The mountainous eastern half of the wilderness is prone to avalanches; visitors who venture into this region should carry avalanche beacons, shovels, and probes, and be prepared for self-rescue.

ACCESS: The Teton Wilderness shares its north boundary with Yellowstone National Park, and backpackers who carry a permit from Yellowstone can enter the Teton Wilderness via the Snake River, South Boundary, or Thoroughfare Trails. US 191 runs to the west of the wilderness, accessing the Sheffield Creek, Arizona Creek, and Bailey Creek Trails.

US 26 delineates the south boundary of the wilderness near Togwotee Pass. Just east of Moran Junction, the paved Buffalo Valley road follows the Buffalo Fork, leading past several obscure trailheads to end at Turpin Meadows, which is the major gateway into the Teton Wilderness. To the east of Togwotee Pass, a spur road to Brooks Lake offers good access to the high mountain reaches of the wilderness.

Day Trip on Foot or Horseback

Holmes Cave

Distance: 5.0 miles one way.
Difficulty: Moderately strenuous.
Starting and maximum elevation: 8,840 feet, 10,080 feet.
Topo map: Angle Mountain, Togwotee Pass.
Getting there: Drive east from Moran Junction on US 26. The trail to Holmes Cave leaves from a dirt road on the north side of the highway, 3 miles east of its Flagstaff Road junction.

This trail climbs over a high divide near Togwotee Pass, then descends through grassy basins to reach Holmes Cave, where a small stream disappears into a hole in the ground. Sweeping views and excellent chances to spot elk and other wildlife abound along the way.

To begin, hike up the road to the cow camp. Follow the trail along a fence-line as it passes through meadows overgrown with wildflowers. After topping the first rise, the fences disappear and the path follows a verdant vale toward the base of the Breccia Cliffs. Near the cliffs, the path swings north into a grassy draw, climbing heartily to reach the top of the divide.

The trail enters the Teton Wilderness as long vistas of reefs, flatirons, and razorback ridges stretch to the horizon. The route now follows cairns to the northeast down into a pristine basin guarded by the serrated walls of the Breccia Cliffs. After crossing the basin, the trail climbs again, passing several peaceful tarns set among the wooded hills. It then drops into a grassy bowl where a mountain brook gathers into a substantial flow before plummeting down a hole beneath a limestone outcrop. This sink is Holmes Cave, and it marks the end of the trail. This trail requires technical climbing gear for climbing over subterranean waterfalls and should not be attempted by casual explorers.

One-Day or Overnight Ski Trip

Pacific Creek

Distance: 10.3 to 13.2 miles one way.
Difficulty: Moderate.
Starting and maximum elevation: 6,800 feet, 7,330 feet.
Topo map: Gravel Mountain, Whetstone Mountain, Davis Hill.
Getting there: Drive north from Moran Junction for one mile and turn right onto Pacific Creek Road. Turn left at the major intersection (winter visitors will park at this intersection) as the gravel Pacific Creek Road runs north for the remaining 6 miles to the trailhead just past a camping area.

This level ski leads up to the open meadows of lower Pacific Creek. It begins by following the unplowed Pacific Creek Road north from the "private residences" sign. The road leads through open meadows and past stands of mature cottonwood en route to the trailhead. The forests on either side of the valley floor are dominated by spruce and lodgepole, with an occasional stand of ivory-barked aspen. Once you reach the trailhead, a wide path leads up Pacific Creek, staying on the timbered benches to the north of the stream. The hills crowd in around the stream, and there are a few sharp inclines mixed in with the largely level traveling. Pocket meadows allow frequent views of the watercourse.

Upon reaching Whetstone Creek, the valley widens. Extensive flats stretch eastward to yield views of the Absarokas, and thickets of willow grow along Pacific Creek. A westward glance now yields views of the Tetons. Gravel Creek makes a good turn-around point for a day trip, but overnighters may want to continue along the north edge of the increasingly brushy flats, then ski up the timbered shelves to camp in the protected glade where the Pacific Creek trail turns northward into the hills.

Mount Leidy Highlands 7

Location: 25 miles northeast of Jackson.
Size: 158,500 acres.
Administration: Bridger-Teton National Forest (Jackson District).
Management status: Unprotected roadless lands.
Ecosystem: Douglas fir forest, western spruce-fir forest, lodgepole pine, and sagebrush steppe, with locally dominant aspen communities.
Elevation range: 7,050 feet to 10,340 feet.
System trails: 126 miles.
Maximum core to perimeter distance: 4.2 miles.
Activities: Horseback riding, hiking, mountain biking, hunting, fishing, cross-country skiing.
Best season: Mid-June–mid-September.
Maps: Bridger-Teton National Forest Teton Division map, Jackson Lake 1:100,000.

TRAVELERS ADVISORY:
FAINT TRAILS, GRIZZLY COUNTRY

The Mount Leidy Highlands is a collection of rolling and forested hills sandwiched between the Teton Wilderness and the Gros Ventre Range. Along the crest of the uplands, lush meadows abloom with wild geraniums are scattered amid groves of conical spruce trees. The soils that underlie this area are high in selenium, which may account for the low birth rate among the elk that calve here. The sedimentary strata that underlie the hills tilt upward to the south, exposing palisades of tan and gray cliffs that rise above sagebrush slopes. The striking Red Hills escarpment is also exposed in this area.

The high point of the uplands is Mount Leidy, an eroded summit composed of cobbles and sediments similar to those found on the valley floor of Jackson Hole. Depending on where you are, you can view the Tetons, the Gros Ventre Range, or the southern tail of the Absarokas from the crest of the range. Some 140,000 years ago, the most extensive glaciation of the Yellowstone Plateau occurred, and ice reached almost to the 9,000-foot level in Jackson Hole and all but overran the Mount Leidy Highlands. During a later glacial episode, a valley glacier filled Jackson Hole, dammed the Gros Ventre River and created a glacial lake that reached up into the Mount Leidy highlands.

The Mount Leidy Highlands contain an important slice of wildlife habitat. It is a grizzly bear recovery area that harbors a small population of resident bears.

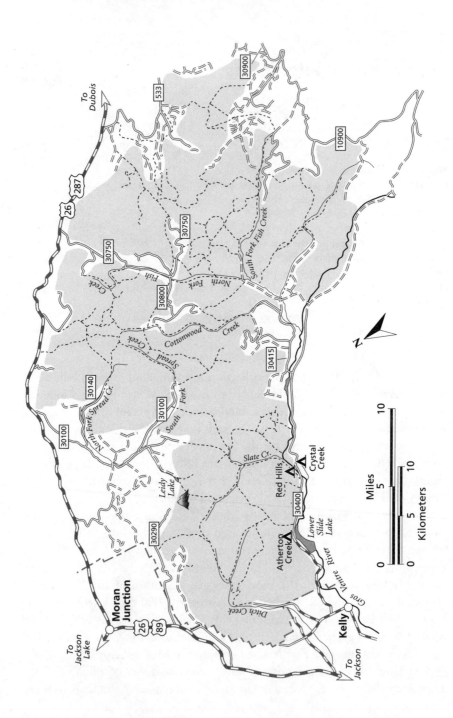

These hills are also a critical corridor for bear migration linking Yellowstone with the Gros Ventre and Wind River ranges. Beaver are abundant in the Slate Creek watershed and in the upper forks of Spread Creek. Trumpeter swans nest in Upper Slide Lake. The Forest Service has been successfully assisting these endangered birds by building artificial islands in the lake to provide predator-free nesting habitat. Peregrine falcons and bald eagles are known to nest among the higher peaks. Sandhill cranes forage along the edges of mountain wetlands and isolated ponds, and may also be spotted on open, grassy slopes.

Before the coming of white explorers, the Gros Ventre River was an important travel corridor for bands of Indians bound for Union Pass and the Wind River Basin. Archaeologists have identified several campsites at the mouths of Cottonwood and Dry Cottonwood Creeks along the margins of the Mount Leidy uplands where bands of people paused to capitalize on an abundance of trout. A summer trail also ran from the Gros Ventre River up through the meadows of the North Fork of Fish Creek and then on to Togwotee Pass.

The Mount Leidy highlands is among the most embattled roadless areas in the state of Wyoming. Grazing allotments and timber sales are currently in conflict with the habitat needs of grizzly bears, which shun human activity and require large tracts of roadless country. The upper reaches of the Cottonwood Creek watershed have been nominated for oil and gas development. A dry oil well was once drilled in the upper reaches of the Ditch Creek valley, and this drainage also saw a good deal of clearcutting in the past.

RECREATIONAL USES: The Mount Leidy Highlands is a good place to test your wilderness skills. Trails are poorly marked in this area, and junctions typically lack signs. Many of the trails that are obvious on the ground are not listed in the official inventory, and thus do not appear on maps. These factors make route-finding a serious challenge in the Mount Leidy area, and each hike will seem like a fresh exploration. Mosquitoes are abundant during the first half of summer, so bring plenty of repellent. Mountain biking is popular in the northeast quadrant of the roadless area, following a network of closed logging roads near Pilot Knob.

The Togwotee Lodge to the north is a hub of winter activities. Snowmobilers based at the lodge roam freely throughout the north and east quadrants of the roadless area. The rolling country of the highlands is practically avalanche-free, making it ideal for cross-country ski trips. The southern reaches of the area, bordering the Gros Ventre valley, are a critical winter range for wildlife, and are closed to all human intrusion during wintertime.

ACCESS: U.S. Highway 20 runs to the north of the Mount Leidy Highlands, and from it the Flagstaff Road—a good gravel trunk road—penetrates the foothills and connects to secondary roads along the north edge of the roadless area. East of Togwotee Pass, Forest Road 537 provides access to the northeastern corner of the wildland. Many of the roads in this area have been gated, necessitating long road walks to reach the roadless area.

The western edge of the roadless area is served by the old Ditch Creek Road, which runs into the foothills from the Teton Science School. The Gros Ventre Road follows the Gros Ventre River along the south side of the highlands and provides paved access as far as Lower Slide Lake. It turns to gravel at this point but remains accessible to all vehicles as far as Dry Cottonwood Creek. A fairly easy ford of the Gros Ventre River is required to reach Slate Creek, the gateway to the southern heart of the roadless area. The Fish Creek watershed is more remote and difficult to access; the mouth of its valley is blocked by private ranches and washouts, while the roads that access its upper reaches are open only to loggers. Many of the roads in the Gros Ventre River valley turn into an impassable morass when it rains.

Day Trip on Foot or Horseback

Spread Creek Loop

Distance: 16.2 miles overall.
Difficulty: Easy.
Starting and maximum elevation: 8,560 feet, 9,180 feet.
Topo maps: Angle Mountain, Tripod Peak.
Getting there: Drive east from Togwotee Lodge or west from Togwotee Pass on US 26 to reach the eastern end of the Flagstaff Road (FR 30100). Follow it for 6.5 miles, then bear left onto the North Fork Spread Creek Road (FR 30120). This road is good for the first 1.8 miles, but after you bear right at the split, you must ford the North Fork to drive the remaining 2.4 miles to the road's end.

This route visits the rolling hills and meadowy drainages at the northern edge of the Mount Leidy Highlands. Faint and unmarked trails and junctions make for challenging route finding. To begin the trip, follow the closed road along North Spread Creek through open meadows that border the willow-choked stream course. As the road ends, a good trail runs northeast across a grassy basin, then ascends through pocket meadows to reach a divide. It now descends into the headwaters of Cottonwood Creek, follows the stream as it gathers strength, and turns south into a broad valley.

Upon reaching an old road, follow it west across a bridge to a hitching post. Follow the trail that starts just south of the post. It ascends into timbered hills, passing old clearcuts en route to the top of the divide. Here, it follows a timbered ridgetop to a broad meadow. The trail now descends along the stream that drains this meadow, tracking its steep descent to South Spread Creek. Upon

View across the Red Hills toward the Teton Range.

reaching the grassy creek bottom, turn right (east) and follow the trail that runs the length of the valley. There is a low divide at its head, whereupon the trail descends into the headwaters of Cottonwood Creek and joins the North Spread trail. Turn left to retrace your steps over the divide and back to the trailhead.

Day Hike

Red Hills

Distance: 1.5 miles one-way.
Difficulty: Moderately strenuous.
Starting and maximum elevation: 7,100 feet, 8,200 feet.
Topo map: Grizzly Lake.
Getting there: Drive north from Jackson to Gros Ventre Junction, then turn right (east) on the Gros Ventre River Road. The road turns north at the settlement of Kelly; turn east at the next intersection to follow the paved road into the valley of the Gros Ventre River. The rough pavement ends at Lower Slide Lake. Keep going, and pull to the north side of the road at the unmarked trail some 100 yards east of the Red Hills Ranch entrance. (If you reach Red Hills Campground, you've gone too far.)

This trail climbs into the colorful hills that guard the southern flank of the Mount Leidy Highlands. It initially wanders north across a grassy flat to reach

Trumpeter swans nest along the Gros Ventre River just south of the Mount Leidy Highlands.

the mouth of a small canyon. It follows the canyon floor upward at a steady pace as aspens and conifers encroach from the east. Eroded outcrops and washouts of Chugwater sandstone glow crimson, forming an otherworldly landscape of spires and pillars. After a steep climb leads up a grassy rise, veer left on a trail that splits away just below the head of the draw. This well-beaten trail wanders west through ancient groves of Douglas fir to emerge at a grassy overlook with fine views of the Tetons.

Day Trip on Foot, Horseback, or Mountain Bike

Ditch Creek—Horsetail

Distance: 12.2 miles total.
Difficulty: Moderate.
Starting and maximum elevation: 7,360 feet, 8,625 feet.
Topo map: Mount Leidy, Shadow Mountain.
Getting there: The hike begins at the end of the Ditch Creek Road. To reach it, follow the paved road north from Kelly for 3 miles to turn right at signs for the Teton Science School. Drive through its campus and follow the dirt road up the valley of Ditch Creek. Passenger cars are advised to stop after a mile or so, but high-clearance vehicles can make it to the road closure gate 3 miles beyond the school. The hike ends at the Horsetail Creek Trailhead, which is reached by following the Gros Ventre River Road past Lower Slide Lake. The trail emerges from the first major valley east of Atherton Campground.

This route follows a closed road into the highlands, then visits lush meadows and spruce forests before descending to the head of Slide Lake. Motorized vehicles are allowed here, so be prepared to meet them along the way. Unmarked trails and junctions make this route a challenge to follow.

The trek begins with a gradual climb along an old logging road that follows Ditch Creek. Signs of human activity fade with increasing altitude, and by the time the road ends at the last of the regenerating clearcuts, a pretty mixture of subalpine meadows and spruce groves covers the rolling high country. The path wanders among the meadows, then seeks out a high divide for views of the Gros Ventre Range. Bear left at an unmarked junction as the route wanders again through the spruce-lined meadows of upper Ditch Creek.

The trail ultimately reaches a grassy pass that bears the ruins of an old cabin. The trail to the Carmichael Fork climbs into the trees, while our route continues through the pass and turns southeast across aspen-clad slopes. It ultimately descends to cross the head of Horsetail Creek before climbing high along the rim of the drainage for views of the Teton Range. A long descent beside the creek then leads down to open country to meet the Gros Ventre Road 2 miles east of Atherton Campground.

Grand Teton National Park   8

Location: 10 miles northwest of Jackson.
Size: 115,807 acres.
Administration: Grand Teton National Park.
Management status: Roadless national park backcountry recommended for wilderness status.
Ecosystem: Douglas fir forest, lodgepole pine, western spruce-fir forest, sagebrush steppe.
Elevation range: 6,600 feet to 13,770 feet.
System trails: 137 miles.
Maximum core to perimeter distance: 7.7 miles.
Activities: Hiking, backpacking, horseback riding, fishing, mountaineering, bird watching, field geology, canoeing.
Best season: July–early September.
Maps: USGS Grand Teton National Park (1:62,500); *Earthwalk Grand Teton*; *Trails Illustrated Grand Teton*.

TRAVELERS ADVISORY:
GRIZZLY COUNTRY, SUDDEN STORMS

The spectacular and jagged spires of the Teton Range soar 7,000 feet above the flat lowlands of Jackson Hole, forming one of the most-photographed landscapes in North America. The mountains were a prominent landmark to the fur trappers, to whom the range was known as the Trois Tetons. This translates from French as "Three Breasts." According to historical authority Orrin Bonney, the application of Trois Tetons to the jagged peaks that guard Jackson Hole is an error perpetrated by Peter Skene Ogden in 1825: The original Trois Tetons more likely referred to the rounded profiles of Big Southern Butte and Twin Buttes, which rise from the Snake River Plain near Rexburg, Idaho.

The original uplift of the Teton Range occurred between 60 and 70 million years ago. Called the Targhee Uplift, it also included the Gros Ventre Range. Erosion soon set in, and the sedimentary strata were removed from the ancient gneiss and granite that would eventually become the Tetons. During the Laramide Orogeny that spawned the Rocky Mountains, the land that would become the Tetons was actually sinking. It was at the end of the Laramide episode that the great volcanic flows of Yellowstone began, and a great flood of

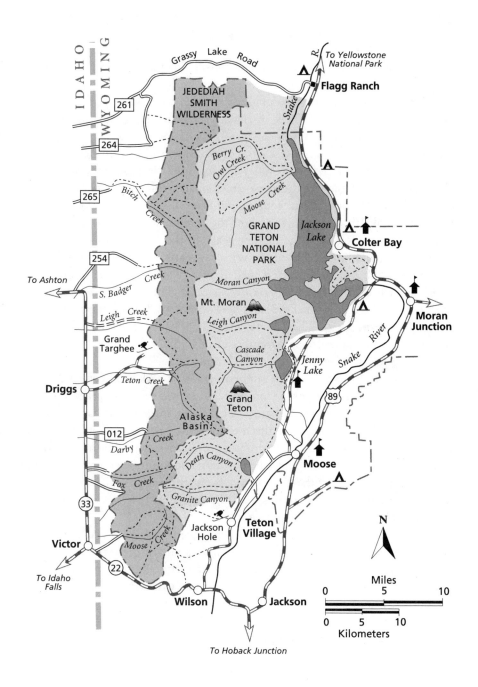

rhyolite poured southward from Yellowstone, split at the Tetons, and flowed down both sides of the range.

Much later, a north-south normal fault developed along the eastern foot of the mountains. During a long series of small, upward shifts over the last 9 million years, the rocks were pushed upward a vertical distance of over 6,000 feet to form a high plateau. Small streams formed along the secondary faults that ran westward from the foot of this new massif. The mountains are still rising, making the Tetons the youngest range in the Rocky Mountains. During this same period, the basin of Jackson Hole was sinking, and its bedrock would ultimately drop some 24,000 feet. It filled with sediments as it subsided, and during much of this time it was occupied by a freshwater lake.

The Pleistocene ice ages saw a series of glacial episodes in this region. During the height of glaciation, a valley glacier 3,000 feet thick flowed down through Jackson Hole. At the same time, smaller montane glaciers coursed down from the Teton Plateau, gouging out deep, U-shaped canyons along the secondary faults that ran westward into the core of the range. At their upper ends, these glaciers carved the highest peaks of the Tetons into sharp, horn-shaped spires and knife-edge ridges. With the warming climate that followed the ice ages, most of these glaciers melted away. They left behind mounds of debris at their endpoints called *terminal moraines*. These piles of rock became the natural dams that formed the lakes now known as Phelps, Taggart, Bradley, String, Jenny, and Leigh. The Yellowstone icefield left behind the moraine that dammed Jackson Lake. Today, a number of small montane glaciers can be seen on the slopes of the Grand Teton and Mount Moran.

At the core of the range is Precambrian gneiss, a rock that formed 2.5 billion years ago when seafloor sand and volcanic ash were metamorphosed under heat and pressure into a much harder rock. Later, magma that had forced its way into cracks and fissures in the metamorphic rock formed dikes of pale granite and dark diabase. The Precambrian core is overtopped by layers of sedimentary rock of marine origin in the northern and southern ends of the range, but the highest peaks of the Tetons have been stripped bare of their overburden. These highest peaks are made of the pale, intrusive granite, which is harder than gneiss and resists erosion.

Indians carved bowls from the talc deposits that are found in the northwestern corner of the range. Prehistoric hunters ranged high into the mountains, and the earliest explorers found circular rock shelters atop some of the highest summits. When the first white explorers arrived here, the Shoshone, Bannock, Crow, Blackfoot, and Gros Ventre summered in Jackson Hole.

Surrounded by forested ranges brimming with beaver and other furbearers, Jackson Hole became a traditional meeting point for fur trappers and mountain men. In 1829, Captain William Sublette named the broad depression at the foot of the Tetons "Jackson Hole" in honor of David Jackson, a prominent trapper of that time. The fur industry died out after the beaver prices imploded, and a few gold prospectors sifted through these mountains. They found little ore in this young range; a silver-lead deposit was mined briefly in upper Death Canyon in 1907 and 1908, then abandoned.

The soils of Jackson Hole are primarily glacial outwash, embedded with cobbles that allow rainfall to percolate deep into the earth. Some of the flats have become covered in a blanket of wind-blown glacial silt, called *loess*. The lack of available groundwater favors the establishment of a sagebrush steppe community. On the higher slopes, thin and fragile soils support a growth of lodgepole pine and huckleberry, with subalpine fir and Engelmann spruce in the cooler and wetter locales. Dense swards of wildflowers can be found on moist slopes above the timberline, while rocky areas host an alpine desert populated by cushion-forming plants.

Grizzly bears are abundant in the forested drainages at the north end of the Teton Range, and sightings are on the increase in the more southerly areas as well. The endangered peregrine falcon is known to nest within the Teton Range and is sometimes sighted by visitors to the high alpine country. The same beaver that drew the mountain men to this region in the 1820s are still here in abundance, damming small waterways to create ponds and canals. An estimated 5,000 head of elk use Grand Teton National Park as a summer range. Moose inhabit all of the major canyons among the peaks, foraging in the riparian vegetation beside the streams.

The Teton Range once sustained a substantial population of bighorn sheep. The sheep declined during the turn of the century, when an influx of domestic sheep to the pastures on the western slope of the range brought exotic diseases that decimated the native bighorns. A small population of these magnificent animals can still be found in the northern end of the range.

Bald eagles are common visitors in the lowlands, and whooping cranes are occasionally spotted here. Trumpeter swans nest in ponds within the park, and other waterfowl species, such as mallard, Canada goose, and cinnamon teal, can also be found here. Bison and pronghorn antelope are found on the sagebrush flats of Jackson Hole. The sage grouse also thrives here, feeding on the buds of sagebrush.

RECREATIONAL USES: Grand Teton National Park receives around 4.2 million visitors annually, but fewer than 1 percent of them venture into the backcountry. Nonetheless, because of the limited trail system, short distances, and topography that tends to concentrate hikers into only a few areas, crowds are commonplace on the Teton trails. The Jackson Hole ski area operates its aerial tram to the top of Rendezvous Peak throughout the summer for hikers who want to visit the high country without paying for it in sweat and effort.

The north face of the Grand Teton.

Cascade and Paintbrush Canyons receive very heavy use by hikers, while the sedimentary peaks at the southern end of the park receive fewer visitors. The remote and timbered valleys at the north end of Jackson Lake receive the fewest visitors, and also have the highest density of grizzly bears.

Some of the canyons on the western shore of Jackson Lake are managed as trail-free zones. Some improvements may have been made in these canyons in order to prevent erosion, but as a whole they should be viewed as bushwhacking hikes. Inquire at the Jenny Lake Ranger Station for current hiking conditions in these areas.

Backpackers must obtain a permit from any ranger station before setting out. Backcountry camping is limited to specific sites or zones, and you must camp in the area on your permit each night. Food storage must be bear-proof. Backcountry reservations for the summer can be made by mail between January 1 and May 15 for a fee of $15 per reservation.

The vertical granite of the Teton Range has become a magnet for mountaineers and rock climbers from around the world. Most of the climbing found here is traditional mountaineering, featuring a mixture of rock faces and snow and ice climbing to reach the summit. Opportunities for technical rock climbing are more limited, as they are hampered by long approaches to relatively short pitches of rock. Technical difficulty is typically lower than in the neighboring Wind River Range. "Sport climbing" power tools are not permitted in the park.

The Grand Teton has become overcrowded with climbers in recent years, particularly on the popular Exum route. The Lower Saddle between the Grand and Middle Tetons has seen particularly heavy impacts, and its fragile alpine community needs restoration. More remote summits like Mount Moran and Mount Owen are equally challenging without the crowds and heavily impacted routes. The Jenny Lake Ranger Station is the center for climbing information.

Jackson Lake, Jenny Lake, and Phelps Lake are open to some motorboats, which diminishes the wilderness experience that one can have along these waterways. On Jackson Lake, most of the motorboats (and, perversely, jet skis) stay close to the developed areas along the eastern shore, and thus canoeists and sea kayakers can find more seclusion along the mountainous western shore of the lake. Afternoon winds can be gusty on Jackson Lake, so canoeists should

Looking down Moran Canyon at Mount Moran.

plan to do their traveling before noon. Lakeshore campsites have bear boxes for safe food storage. String Lake and Leigh Lake are open only to hand-propelled boats and offer a more pristine experience for canoeists and sea kayakers. All watercraft users must pay a user fee and obtain a permit that must be attached to the hull of their craft.

Fishing in the Teton backcountry is rather limited due to the small and swift streams that are found in the mountains and the relative shortage of alpine lakes. The fishing in the large lakes at the foot of the range is rated as fair. A Wyoming fishing license is required for all fishing in the park, including for minors and catch-and-release.

ACCESS: Paved roads offer easy access to the southern reaches of the Teton Range. The Teton Park Road parallels US 191 along the base of the range, visiting Jenny Lake as well as the southern shore of Jackson Lake. Farther south, a winding, paved byway runs from the park headquarters at Moose past Teton Village to meet US 22 at Wilson, just west of Jackson. The Granite Canyon trail leaves directly from this road, while the Death Canyon Trailhead lies at the end of a pot-holed spur road just south of Moose. The aerial tram at Teton Village is operated during the summer to carry hikers to the top of the range at the south end of the national park.

The only trailhead at the north end of the range can be reached by driving north on US 191 almost to the boundary of Yellowstone National Park, then driving west on the gravel thoroughfare known as the Grassy Lake Road. After crossing the Snake River, drive downstream to meet the trailhead just as the road leaves the river for its westward journey. If you have a canoe or even a raft, you can avoid a lot of extra hiking by paddling across the head of Jackson Lake from the Lizard Creek picnic area to reach the trails that climb Berry, Owl, and Moose Creeks. By boat is also the easiest way to access the untracked valleys that drain into Moran Bay and Leigh Lake.

Day Hike or Backpack

Mount Hunt Divide

Distance: 7.5 miles one way.
Difficulty: Moderately strenuous.
Starting and maximum elevation: 6,790 feet, 9,710 feet.
Best season: Late July–mid-September.
Topo map: Grand Teton.
Getting there: Drive U.S. Highway 191 north from Jackson to Moose Junction, then turn left to reach the park headquarters. Turn left on the Moose-Wilson Road, which runs south opposite the visitor center. Follow it for 3 miles, then turn right on the Death Canyon road, a badly pot-holed dirt track that runs the remaining 1.5 miles to the Death Canyon Trailhead.

This hike follows Open Canyon into the high sedimentary peaks at the south end of the Teton Range. It begins at the Death Canyon trailhead with a gradual climb through a lodgepole forest underlain by huckleberry bushes. Turn left (south) on the Valley trail, which traverses to an overlook atop the lateral moraine above Phelps Lake. This deep lake was gouged out of the wooded forelands by the glacier that carved Death Canyon, and the glacier's terminal moraine became a natural dam.

Watch for pikas as the path descends toward the granite portals of Death Canyon. After passing the head of the lake, the trail climbs to a timbered ridgetop that represents another lateral moraine. Turn right onto the trail that runs west along the ridgetop, then enters the mouth of Open Canyon. Here, a large stream tumbles through a series of turbulent waterfalls.

After crossing the stream, the path climbs steadily along the timbered south side of the valley. Massive peaks rise to the west, with granite bases and topped by thick walls of limestone. The trail visits assorted vista points along the creek, then zigzags upward through meadows of larkspur and columbine. It crests the Mount Hunt divide at the base of imposing limestone cliffs, and offers southward views of Granite Canyon and the ski lifts beyond it.

Backpack

Death Canyon Loop

Distance: 25.0 miles total.
Difficulty: Moderately strenuous.
Starting and maximum elevation: 6,790 feet, 10,270 feet.
Topo maps: Grand Teton, Mount Bannon.
Getting there: The hike begins at the Death Canyon Trailhead (see *Mount Hunt Divide*, above).

This loop trip travels from the granite depths of Death Canyon to the sedimentary peaks at the south end of the Teton Range, then turns north and visits the Alaska Basin and the high granite summits that surround Grand Teton. The hike begins on the Valley Trail, which wends its way southward through lodgepoles to reach an overlook of Phelps Lake. The route then leads down to the head of the lake, where it adopts the Death Canyon Trail. This trail runs west through the towering granite portals of Death Canyon. After a brief journey through spruce bottoms, a series of switchbacks leads upward across slopes of broken rock.

At the top of the grade is a hanging valley where a lazy stream winds through shady groves of spruce and fir. This broad valley bears the characteristic "U" shape of its glacial origins, and towering summits of granite flank it

Sedimentary cliffs at the south end of the Teton Range.

on both sides. As the valley bends south, a great palisade of sedimentary cliffs rises to the west. The woodlands now give way to meadows of tall forbs and wildflowers. The trail runs to the valley's head, where it climbs briskly to Fox Creek Pass. A lone limestone tower guards the pass to the south and offers views across the tundra plateaus and isolated summits of the Jedediah Smith Wilderness. To the north, the granite fang of Grand Teton rises above the intervening peaks.

Hike north on the Teton Crest Trail, which follows the narrow and meadowy terrace known as the Death Canyon Shelf. The path follows this narrow ledge beneath 500-foot limestone cliffs that have calved off the immense boulders that litter the shelf. At the far end is Mount Meek Pass, which leads into the Jedediah Smith Wilderness. After a brief tour of the high meadows, the Sheep Stairs lead down into the Alaska Basin. The path leads across plates of exposed granite interspersed with a few wind-torn trees. The lone tooth of Buck Mountain rises above the head of the basin, while great reefs and ziggurats of limestone rise to the north and west.

Rockbound tarn high on the shoulders of Static Peak.

At the far side of the valley, turn right on the Alaska Basin Trail. It winds upward among rocky meres and then follows Teton Creek to the pass at the head of the valley. A barren wasteland of rock lies ahead, dominated by the spire of Buck Mountain and the blocky limestone cliffs of a nameless summit. Watch for Rimrock Lake high on the far wall of Death Canyon as the trail charts a cliff-hanging course to the divide below Static Peak. It's an easy scramble to the summit of Static Peak, but the main trail snakes down the dizzying precipices and pinnacles of the divide to reach a low saddle. After dropping southward into an open stand of whitebark pine, it traverses southeast to an overlook above Phelps Lake. The mountain views continue as a long series of switchbacks leads down to the floor of Death Canyon. Turn left at patrol cabin to return to the trailhead.

Jedediah Smith Wilderness   9

Location: 10 miles east of Driggs, Idaho.
Size: 196,740 acres.
Administration: Targhee National Forest (Ashton District, Teton Basin District),
Bridger–Teton National Forest (Jackson District).
Management status: Jedediah Smith Wilderness (123,451 acres), unprotected roadless
lands (73,289 acres).
Ecosystem: Douglas fir forest, western spruce-fir forest, lodgepole pine, and sagebrush
steppe, with extensive aspen woodlands.
Elevation range: 6,560 feet to 11,105 feet.
System trails: 180 miles.
Maximum core to perimeter distance: 7.2 miles.
Activities: Hiking, backpacking, horseback riding, fishing, spelunking.
Best season: July–early September.
Maps: Teton Ranger District travel map; Jackson Lake and Yellowstone National Park South
1:100,000. See map on page 63.

TRAVELERS ADVISORY:
GRIZZLY COUNTRY, SUDDEN STORMS

The Jedediah Smith Wilderness covers the western slope of the Teton Range,
forming a wilderness complement to Grand Teton National Park. Although it
lies entirely within Wyoming, the easiest access is from the Idaho side of the
range. Unlike the granite spires at the height of the range, the peaks within the
Jedediah Smith Wilderness are sedimentary, and they form long reefs with
east-facing cliffs. A number of small creeks offer avenues into the heart of the
mountains, where vast meadows teem with wildflowers. From the inner recesses of the wilderness you can enjoy superb views of the high Teton spires.

The sedimentary strata of the Jedediah Smith Wilderness slope upward
from the Snake River Plain to form long reefs and cliff bands capped by massive limestone peaks. The drainages have carved deep canyons into the monocline, and between them stretch vast, sloping plateaus mantled in rolling alpine
meadows. The limestone bedrock forms a kind of natural pavement in places.
The porosity of the limestone means that many of the alpine soils have very
little groundwater, resulting in a kind of alpine desert in some locales. Preserved in the limestone are fossilized algae heads, known as *stromatolites*.

Housetop Mountain guards the meadows of Fox Creek.

The foothills are home to an extensive aspen belt. The persistence of aspen is stimulated by periodic fires, which wipe out the shade-tolerant conifers that would otherwise shade out the aspens. High populations of elk also suppress the spread of aspens, and the relative scarcity of elk has allowed aspens to proliferate here. A coniferous forest dominated by Engelmann spruce and subalpine fir is found at higher elevations. Moose is the most common large animal, while the high country is home to wolverines, pikas, marmots, and nesting raptors.

The Shoshone and Bannock tribes moved into this area around 1,500 A.D., migrating up from the deserts east of the Sierra Nevada. Archeological evidence points to summer usage of the western slope of the Teton Range by indigenous peoples for hunting and gathering, and rock shelters have been found high on the peaks of the Jedediah Smith Wilderness.

RECREATIONAL USES: Because the area is relatively small and high-profile, crowds are common in the Jedediah Smith Wilderness, and some managers are concerned that it is being "loved to death." The southern half of the wilderness, particularly near Grand Targhee Resort and in the Alaska Basin area, is the most crowded. It is hard to find a horse trip long enough to be worthwhile, and you can reach any place in the wilderness on a day hike. The Teton Crest Trail follows the length of the range from north to south, and although it may be hard to follow in places, it offers the best possibility for an extended trip. Wind Cave and nearby Ice Cave, in the Darby Canyon area, offer very technical spelunking featuring coral and brachiopod fossils, as well as small crystalline growths. The area is not known for its fishing, and hunting is reported to be mediocre as a result of poaching and lax game law enforcement in the past.

ACCESS: To access most of the trails that run into the Jedediah Smith Wilderness, it is necessary to start in Idaho and follow poorly marked gravel roads eastward from Idaho 32. The Grand Targhee ski resort, located northeast of the town of Driggs, provides the fastest and easiest access to the west side of the wilderness. US 26 runs along the southern boundary of the wilderness, and there are several trailheads along it on the Idaho side of Teton Pass. The wilderness shares its eastern boundary with Grand Teton National Park, and trails from Death Canyon and Granite Canyon link up with the Jedediah Smith trail system.

Day Hike

Wind Cave

Distance: 3.4 miles
Difficulty: Moderate.
Starting and maximum elevation: 7,050 feet, 8,400 feet.
Topo map: Mount Bannon.
Getting there: For the Darby Canyon Trailhead, drive south from Driggs on Idaho 33, then turn left (east) on Road 300 South. Follow this good road to the base of the mountains, then jog right (south), following signs for Darby Canyon. A narrow dirt road, often deeply pot-holed, follows Darby Creek to end at the trailhead some 4.5 miles from the highway.

This trek follows a popular trail to the mouth of a large cave. Like many trails on this side of the Tetons, it receives heavy pressure especially from church groups during July and August, and provides more solitude in June and autumn. The hike begins on the heavily traveled Wind Cave trail, which crosses Darby Creek and begins a lazy ascent up the South Fork. At first, the trail passes a narrow limestone cleft, staying in the shade of spruce groves. It then breaks out into overgrown meadows, winding upward between ledges of limestone. A pretty waterfall can now be seen emerging from the arched portal of Wind

The high Tetons as seen from the Alaska Basin.

Cave. The trail now climbs westward to the portal of the cave; do not attempt to enter the cave without technical spelunking gear such as wetsuit and crampons. The upper end of the valley is managed for primitive recreation, and offers opportunities for off-trail exploring.

Day Hike

Dead Horse Pass

Distance: 5.5 to 6.3 miles one way.
Difficulty: Moderately strenuous.
Starting and maximum elevation: 7,500 feet, 9,710 feet.
Topo map: Rammel Mountain, Ranger Peak.
Getting there: To reach the Indian Meadows Trailhead, take Idaho 32 to Felt, then drive east from "town" on an unmarked gravel trunk road. It soon bends north-northeast, and 2 miles later you will turn right on the Pinochle Road, which departs eastward near an old railroad siding. After 3.5 miles it enters the Targhee National Forest and becomes FR 266. Follow it for 6 more miles, then turn right on FR 254. After 3 miles, swing left onto the Rammel Mountain Cutoff (FR 656), which leads 1.7 miles to the Indian Meadows Trailhead and the South Badger Creek Trail.

Barren peaks above Bitch Creek.

This trail penetrates the north end of the Teton Range, and with some extra scrambling you can gain superb views of Moran Canyon and the high peaks of the Tetons. The hike begins on the South Badger Creek trail, which descends steadily through scattered Douglas fir and aspen-studded meadows. Upon reaching the floor of the South Badger valley, the trail enters the wilderness and is joined by a cutoff trail from Dry Ridge. Bear left for 2 miles of easy traveling up the bottomlands through verdant meadows and copses of tall spruce. Frequent avalanches have cleared the slopes above the trail.

The gradient steepens as you approach the head of the valley, which is guarded by a rocky peak. The path peters out at a heavily used campsite; turn straight uphill to reach the Teton Crest trail. A long series of switchbacks leads up the open slopes to crest the divide above Dead Horse Pass. The barren, sedimentary summits that guard Bitch Creek can now be seen to the north. Adventurous souls can scramble southeast along the divide to climb a nearby summit that offers superb views of the Teton crags.

Winegar Hole Wilderness   10

Location: 20 miles west of Flagg Ranch and 25 miles east of Ashton, Idaho.
Size: 13,438 acres.
Administration: Targhee National Forest (Ashton District).
Management status: Winegar Hole Wilderness (10,715 acres); Winegar Hole Wilderness Study Areas (2,723 acres).
Ecosystem: Douglas fir ecosystem, characterized by stands of lodgepole pine interspersed with riparian habitats along ponds, lakes, and streams.
Elevation range: 5,800 feet to 7,360 feet.
System trails: 0.8 mile.
Maximum core to perimeter distance: 2.0 miles.
Activities: Cross-country hiking, hunting, fishing, wildlife viewing.
Best season: Mid-June–September.
Maps: Ashton Ranger District travel map, Yellowstone National Park South 1:100,000.

TRAVELERS ADVISORY:
GRIZZLY COUNTRY

The Winegar Hole Wilderness covers a small patch of forested plateau on the south boundary of Yellowstone National Park. The gently rolling terrain is glacial in origin, resulting from the outwash of the Pleistocene ice cap that once covered the Yellowstone plateaus. It is robed in stands of lodgepole pine, and scattered here and there are groves of aspen, spruce, and subalpine fir. The entire area is shot through with marshes, ponds, and sluggish streams, and much of the wilderness falls into the category of riparian habitat. Small lakes choked with lily pads are favorite haunts of moose and waterfowl.

The Winegar Hole Wilderness was set aside primarily to safeguard critical grizzly bear habitat, which is abundant in this area. Moose are commonly spotted along the lakes and streams, where they feed on willows and aquatic plants. Elk, deer, and black bear move through the area on a periodic basis, but they are rarely seen. The wetlands provide nesting habitat for loons, sandhill cranes, and the endangered trumpeter swan.

To the west is a Wilderness Study Area that extends to the Falls River. Some small-scale logging is occurring along the fringes of this WSA, but the lodgepole that dominates the forest is of very little value as timber. This forest has a heavy infestation of pine bark beetle, which has grubs that tunnel beneath the

10   WINEGAR HOLE WILDERNESS

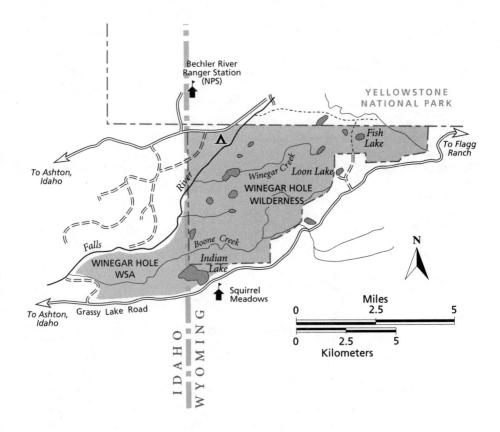

tree bark, eating its living cambium layer and ultimately killing it. Bark beetles and fire are part of a natural cycle in lodgepole pine forests that leads to the elimination of old stands and thus regenerates the forest. Several oil and gas leases are pending here as well. It seems likely that the area will be accorded wilderness status.

RECREATIONAL USE: The short Fish Lake Trail receives moderate use from hikers on their way to destinations within Yellowstone National Park. Otherwise, the Winegar Hole Wilderness and the neighboring roadless areas receive only a small amount of dispersed use, most of which comes during the fall hunting season. Swampy terrain hampers off-trail travel, and the flat and timbered landscape offers few landmarks to assist in navigation. If you visit the remote parts of this area, be certain that someone in your party has strong map-and-compass skills, and make plenty of noise while traveling to warn grizzly bears of your presence. Trout can be found in the lakes and larger streams within this area, although boggy banks make it difficult to approach the water without waders.

ACCESS: From the east, you can reach this small wilderness by driving the Grassy Lake Road west from Flagg Ranch at the south boundary of Yellowstone National Park. It can be approached from the Idaho side by driving east from Ashton on ID 47, and after the highway turns north, turning east onto Grassy Lake Road. This road is prone to mud and potholes, and may be closed early in the summer. About 20 miles west of Flagg Ranch, a spur road runs north to the Fish Lake trailhead. The South Boundary trail once intersected the Grassy Lake Road farther east, but it has long since disappeared. Trail-less access to the wilderness can be had farther west on the Grassy Lake Road, in the marshy country between Loon Lake and Indian Lake.

Day Hike

Fish Lake

Distance: 0.6 mile.
Difficulty: Easy.
Starting and maximum elevation: 6,460 feet, 6,488 feet.
Topo maps: Hominy Peak, Cave Falls.
Getting there: Drive US 191 north from Grand Teton National Park to the Flagg Ranch, then head west on the Grassy Lake Road. This gravel byway can be quite muddy in wet weather, but is otherwise passable for most cars. Follow it west for 20 miles, over the divide beyond the reservoir, and turn right on the first road that runs north. This unmarked road also visits Loon Lake, and it features deep potholes and muddy traveling following wet weather—high clearance is a must. Drive it for about 2 miles, bearing right at the lone intersection to reach the Fish Lake trailhead.

This short, well-trodden trail follows rounded hilltops sparsely wooded in lodgepole pine and aspen. After 0.6 mile, it reaches an overlook of Fish Lake, ringed with lilypads and backed up against the rhyolite bluffs to the east. Watch for trumpeter swans and moose, which are often sighted here.

Day Hike

Winegar Lake Loop

Distance: 4.1 miles round trip.
Difficulty: Moderate (map and compass required).
Starting and maximum elevation: 6,460 feet, 6,525 feet.
Topo maps: Hominy Peak, Cave Falls.
Getting there: The hike starts at the Fish Lake trailhead (see *Fish Lake* above).

Moose are abundant in the Winegar Hole Wilderness.

This trek follows good trails and then departs for a bushwhacking route through the Winegar Hole Wilderness. It requires excellent wilderness skills and map and compass ability. The hike begins by following the Fish Lake trail across rolling, open country with views of the bluffs to the east. After passing Fish Lake, the trail enters Yellowstone National Park. Turn left on the South Boundary Trail and follow it west through the lodgepole. It becomes more primitive as the Mountain Ash Trail splits away, and passes Junco Lake before veering northwest.

After 2.1 miles, a sign identifies Winegar Lake. From the east side of its outlet stream, hike due south through the lodgepole forest, following clearings on the hilltops as you pass the east shore of the lake. Continue south on the hilltops above the lake's head, taking advantage of dry meadows where the volcanic bedrock shows through. If your aim is good, you will arrive atop a low cliff of basalt. Veer southeast to pass the cliffs, then descend to a circular pond in the midst of a broad, marshy meadow. Turn due east here, crossing rolling country before emerging on the Fish Lake Trail near the parking area.

2

Western Ranges

The smaller and lesser-known ranges of western Wyoming have a unique charm all their own. They lie far from the beaten path and are free from the crowds that plague the marquee wilderness areas. Surrounded by sagebrush desert, these sedimentary ranges rise to colorful peaks robed in forests of aspen and conifer. They stand at the eastern edge of the Columbia Basin, and the moister locales share ecological ties with the spruce-fir and tall forb communities commonly found in the Pacific Northwest.

These are the mountains of Wyoming's overthrust belt: Here, massive strata of sedimentary bedrock have been pushed eastward over the top of younger formations, resulting in a series of long, sedimentary cliffs that have a north-south orientation. In some places, the rock strata have been folded skyward, exposing the seams between strata to erosion. Weaker, easily eroded shales have been carried off by erosion, leaving long *strike valleys* between palisades of more resistant limestone. Subterranean reservoirs of oil beneath the overthrust have long attracted the attention of oil companies.

Gros Ventre Wilderness

Location: 5 miles east of Jackson.
Size: 414,848 acres.
Administration: Jackson, Big Piney, and Pinedale Districts, Bridger–Teton National Forest.
Management status: Gros Ventre Wilderness (287,000 acres); Shoal Creek WSA (32,400 acres), adjacent roadless lands (95,448 acres).
Ecosystem: Douglas fir forest, western spruce-fir forest, lodgepole pine, and sagebrush steppe.
Elevation range: 6,890 feet to 12,936 feet.
System trails: 232 miles.
Maximum core to perimeter distance: 6.7 miles.
Activities: Hiking, backpacking, horseback riding, big game hunting, fishing.
Best season: Late June–mid-September.
Maps: Bridger-Teton National Forest map (Buffalo and Jackson Ranger Districts), Jackson and Jackson Lake 1:100,000.

TRAVELERS ADVISORY:
GRIZZLY COUNTRY, FAINT TRAILS

The Gros Ventre Range represents the forgotten mountains of Jackson Hole, rising to the east of the valley in a jumble of sandstone peaks. There is plenty of room to roam here, particularly in the remote eastern end of the range. Though not as lofty as the Tetons, the Gros Ventre Range makes up for it with color-splashed summits rising above verdant alpine meadows. Wilderness status was conferred upon the range in 1985.

The high peaks of the range are made up of sandstone, limestone, and dolomite laid down in ancient seas. The south faces are tinted with streaks of red and yellow that result from iron and sulfur laid down within the marine sandstone of the Nugget formation. Faults crisscross the range in all directions, and frequent earthquakes make it geologically unstable. The foothills on the northern end of the range are made up of loose conglomerates that are prone to landslides. The most famous slide occurred in 1925, damming the Gros Ventre River at the northern end of the range to form Slide Lake. The dam of rubble and debris burst two years later, wiping out the town of Kelly.

The northern side of the range is mantled in a lush forest of conifers, which rises into tidy alpine meadows bordered by stands of whitebark pine. Along the south-facing ramparts, the timberline areas along the western end of the range

11   GROS VENTRE WILDERNESS

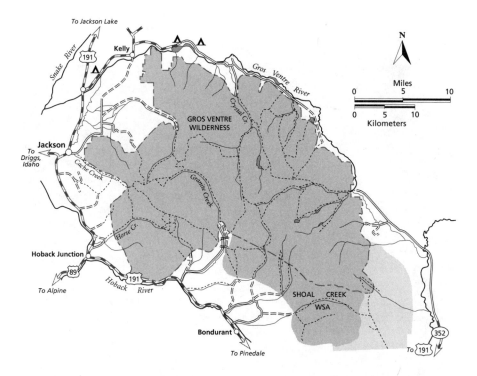

are typified by a tall forb community that thrives on abundant precipitation and creates jungle-like thickets. The tall forb meadows are associated with copses of aspen and Engelmann spruce. Farther east, drier conditions favor sagebrush in the subalpine meadows, and the forest is a mix of Douglas fir and lodgepole pine.

The wilderness is an important summer range for elk that winter in Jackson Hole. A native population of bighorn sheep inhabits the timberline meadows surrounding Sheep Mountain. Once numbering over 1,000 animals, this herd began its decline with the advent of domestic sheep grazing in the area, and it now numbers around 300 head.

Some of the rarer inhabitants of the Gros Ventre Range include the lynx, wolverine, northern goshawk, flammulated owl, great gray owl, and three-toed woodpecker. The Gros Ventre Range is also a grizzly bear recovery area, and bears have established themselves in the Tosi Creek drainage at the southeastern end of the wilderness and have begun to disperse into the Wind River Range. These bears are wary and reclusive, and they are not easily approached as are the Yellowstone grizzlies. The boreal draba is among the rare plants native to the range. This endemic wildflower is a cushion-forming plant.

Alpine meadows at the head of Little Granite Creek.

As the Ice Age fauna of steppe bison and woolly mammoth went extinct at the end of the Pleistocene ice ages, prehistoric hunters shifted their activities from the low basins into the mountains. The warmer climate made for abundant game in the high country, and the Gros Ventre Range entered a period that would see continuous human habitation for the next 9,000 years. The indigenous people found an abundance of bighorn sheep, and supplemented their diet with the nuts of the limber pine. They left circular rock shelters atop the highest peaks, and tipi rings and petroglyphs at their camping areas. A prominent Indian trail ran up the Gros Ventre River and then followed Warm Springs Creek to Union Pass for access to the Wind River Basin.

The range was named for the Gros Ventre tribe, a fragment of the Arapaho nation that drifted northward into the Yellowstone area. The name translates from French as "Big Belly," a reference to the fact that tribal members often invited themselves into the camps of white trappers in hopes of securing a meal. However, the tribe that inhabited the range during the early history of the American West was the Sheepeater tribe. These horseless and secretive mountain dwellers hunted bighorn sheep with the help of stone driveways that led to traps or passes where the animals could easily be killed.

The first white man to record a visit to the Gros Ventre Mountains was John Colter, who ventured over Union Pass and down the Gros Ventre River in 1807. The range became an important ground for fur trappers between 1825 and 1840. In 1832, Captain William Bonneville established an outpost along the Green River that came to be known as "Fort Nonsense," and from here he made excursions into the high peaks of the Gros Ventre Range.

Grazing allotments cover three regions of the wilderness: The ridges to the northeast of Sheep Mountain, the foothills to the west of Granite Creek, and the half of the wilderness that lies east of Crystal Creek. Heavy cattle grazing in the tall forb meadows of upper Boulder Creek has led to severe trampling and erosion as well as the degradation of hiking trails.

RECREATIONAL USES: The Gros Ventre Range receives much less visitor pressure than its neighbors, although Turquoise Lake and Goodwin Lake are popular and heavily impacted. Many of the more remote trails exist in a primitive and poorly maintained state, requiring route-finding skill to follow. The soils in this area have a high clay content and turn into slippery mud when it rains. There are good hunting opportunities for elk and bighorn sheep. The fishing is fair to good in the larger streams and alpine lakes within the range. Granite Creek Hot Springs lies at the southern end of the wilderness. Some of the pools have been developed into a day-use resort, while other pools across the creek remain natural.

ACCESS: The western end of the Gros Ventres receives the greatest amount of use, with the closed road up Cache Creek receiving heavy use. County roads run up Flat Creek, linking up with FR 30440, a rocky gravel road that climbs to the Goodwin Lake trailhead. The Gros Ventre Road runs east from US 191 north of Jackson and provides good access to a number of trails along the northern edge of the wilderness. In the upper reaches of the Gros Ventre River, this road becomes primitive and difficult in wet weather. Along the southern end of the range, a spur road runs up Granite Creek from the Hoback Canyon to reach the Granite Creek trailhead. Rough logging roads, used mostly by hunters, access the range's eastern end.

Backpack

Granite Highline

Distance: 24.0 miles total.
Difficulty: Moderate (W to E); moderately strenuous (E to W).
Starting and maximum elevation: 7,960 feet, 9,700 feet.
Topo map: Gros Ventre Junction, Blue Miner Lake, Granite Falls, Turquoise Lake, Bull Creek, Cache Creek.
Getting there: The hike begins at the Goodwin Lake Trailhead. Drive to the east end of Jackson, then turn north on the Flat Creek Road, following signs for the elk refuge. The road bends east and then turns north to reach the junction with the Curtis Canyon Road (FR 30440). Follow this road past the campground, and bear right at the split after 3.7 miles to stay on FR 30440 to reach the well-marked trailhead. To reach the Granite Creek end of the hike, drive east from Hoback Junction on US 191 for about 7 miles. After passing through Hoback Canyon, turn left on the Granite Creek Road (FR 30500). Follow this wide but sometimes pot-holed gravel road for 7 miles to park near the trail sign opposite the second junction with FR 30521.

This long trail follows the timberline along the southwestern palisade of the Gros Ventre Range. Close proximity to the high peaks prevents mountain views in most places, but the tall forb meadows offer fine scenery and the potential for wildlife viewing is high. It requires a two-car shuttle to get between the widely separated trailheads.

After a brisk climb up open slopes with views of the Tetons, the trail strikes the top of a timbered ridge. It follows the ridge crest to the wilderness boundary, then contours across the slopes to reach Goodwin Lake, sited in a pretty cirque. The path then climbs into a timberline community of whitebark pine and low-growing meadow plants. Striking views of Cache Peak unfurl as the trail crosses a drainage divide and follows the high benches above the Flat Creek basin.

Upon reaching the head of the valley, follow signs for Cache Creek as the trail slips through a gap and then drops onto steep, south-facing slopes. A vigorous growth of tall forbs lines the path as it descends 1,200 feet to a junction with the Cache Creek trail. Turn left onto the Granite Highline, which surmounts a pass to begin its long, up-and-down journey along the timberline. Stick with the northernmost (and highest) of the multiple trails at all times.

The traveling is difficult at first, with uneven footing leading through a waist-deep jungle of flowering plants. About halfway up the Horse Creek drainage, the plants thin out and the trail tread improves. The high peaks begin to appear as the path crosses the Horse Creek divide and descends into the Little Granite drainage. Multicolored crags rise to the north as the trail rounds an endless series of false divides. It finally reaches the Boulder Creek valley, where signs of cattle are everywhere. Follow the cairns, always choosing

High mountain landscape at the head of Flat Creek.

the high route as the path rounds a series of grassy hillsides. Magnificent ranks of summits stretch eastward as the trail crosses the final ridgetop and makes the long descent to the Granite Creek Road.

Day Hike

West Miner Creek

Distance: 3.8 miles one way.
Difficulty: Moderate.
Starting and maximum elevation: 7,010 feet, 8,100 feet.
Topo map: Grizzly Lake.
Getting there: From U.S. Highway 191, drive the Gros Ventre River Road past Slide Lake. The trail starts opposite from the Red Hills Campground.

This hike follows an obscure drainage into the Gros Ventre Range. Parts of the trail are primitive, and route-finding skill is helpful. The hike begins at the Red Hills Campground sign, offering superb views of the Red Hills, Tetons, and

Gros Ventres as it works its way around the Red Hills Ranch. Watch for signs of beaver as the path crosses Miner Creek and then West Miner. After crossing the second creek, climb onto the high shelf and then turn left (south) on the faint and unmarked trail as the main path heads downhill.

This is the West Miner trail. It is poorly maintained but easy to follow as it winds upward through sagebrush meadows. West Miner Creek tumbles through meadowy hillocks, and as ridges rise up on either side, the major peaks appear at the valley's head. The trail passes several pretty ponds before terminating as shaly hillocks block the valley.

Day Hike or Backpack

Blue Miner Lake

Distance: 6.5 miles one way.
Difficulty: Moderately strenuous.
Starting and maximum elevation: 7,010 feet, 9,760 feet.
Topo map: Grizzly Lake, Blue Miner Lake.
Getting there: From U.S. Highway 191, drive the Gros Ventre River Road past Slide Lake. The trail starts opposite from the Red Hills Campground.

This good trail accesses a remote lake in the northwestern flank of the Gros Ventre Range. The hike begins at the Red Hills Campground sign and offers views of the Red Hills, Tetons, and Gros Ventres as it rounds the Red Hills Ranch. After fording Miner and West Miner Creeks, the trail climbs and then makes a substantial descent to meet the Blue Miner trail above a swampy pond. Turn left as the Blue Miner trail carries you up a tall and timbered ridge, visiting an exposed scarp high above the West Miner drainage.

The trail dips across a grassy opening, then climbs onto a high plateau where it enters an aging forest of whitebark pine and subalpine fir. The trees thin out into flower-strewn meadows as the path crosses the final distance to crest the escarpment above Blue Miner Lake. A cairn marks the trail's descent across steep and flower-strewn slopes. At the bottom is Blue Miner Lake, an alpine gem set at the foot of soaring peaks and surrounded by snowfields and talus slopes.

The Palisades

Location: 10 miles southwest of Jackson.
Size: 331,630 acres.
Administration: Targhee National Forest (Palisades District); Bridger–Teton National Forest (Jackson District).
Management status: 129,000 acres in Palisades WSA in Wyoming; 202,630 acres of unprotected roadless area in Idaho.
Ecosystem: Douglas fir forest, western spruce-fir forest, lodgepole pine, and sagebrush steppe, with tall forb meadows at timberline.
Elevation range: 5,900 feet to 10,115 feet.
System trails: 247 miles.
Maximum core to perimeter distance: 6.3 miles.
Activities: Horseback riding, hunting, hiking, fishing, heli-skiing.
Best season: Mid-June–mid-September.
Maps: Palisades Ranger District Travel Map, Jackson and Palisades 1:100,000.

TRAVELERS ADVISORY:
FAINT TRAILS, GRIZZLY COUNTRY

The Palisades roadless area encompasses the rugged mountains to the north of the Snake River Canyon. This area receives lots of rainfall, which sustains a lush tangle of brush and trees reminiscent of the Pacific Northwest. These mountains, known as the Snake River Range, are among the steepest and most inaccessible in the Rockies. Traveling is often difficult, as many trails are poorly signed and maintained. The core of the roadless area lies on the Idaho side of the border, and has been recommended for wilderness in the Forest Plan, but as yet has received no official protection. The smaller Wyoming portion has been designated a wilderness study area. Here, rolling foothills are crisscrossed with abandoned logging roads, and many of the south-facing slopes are robed in extensive grasslands.

The Palisades form an important biological link between the Teton Range and the more southerly ranges of the Overthrust Belt. Bald eagles and peregrine falcons nest along the Snake River Canyon and among the high peaks of the interior. Grizzly bears have been reported in the area, and they are expected to increase in number here. Mountain goats have been released on the Idaho side of the Palisades and have become an established herd. Individuals are spot-

12   THE PALISADES

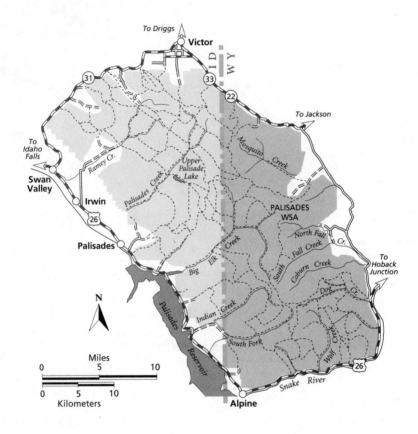

ted occasionally in their Snake River Canyon winter range. Elk are also present in the Snake River Range.

Domestic sheep graze in some of the tall forb meadows found near timberline at the southern edge of the wilderness study area. The sheep do a considerable amount of damage to the native vegetation and pose a significant threat for disease transmission to native herds of bighorn sheep in Grand Teton National Park.

RECREATIONAL USES: Most trails within this extensive roadless area are little used during the summer season. Heavier use occurs along Dog Creek, Mosquito Creek, and Black Canyon, and the trail corridor to Upper Palisades Lake is extremely popular. Most visitors arrive in the fall, using horses to pack in to hunting camps. For the most part, trails are maintained only by hunters and stockmen for their own use, and many of the trails that appear on Forest Service maps are badly overgrown. Stream fords are the rule rather than the ex-

View from the slopes of Wolf Mountain.

ception, and crossings can be dangerous during times of high water. There are good opportunities for mountain biking in the Mosquito Creek and Fall Creek drainages on the Wyoming side of the border. The mountains on the Idaho side are a focal point for winter heli-skiing.

ACCESS: A gravel trunk road runs south from Wilson along the eastern edge of the mountains, and from it a network of old logging roads stretches west to the edge of the roadless area. US 26 follows the Snake River Canyon and Palisades Reservoir, accessing short spur roads that lead to trailheads on the south side of the area. The western boundary is Idaho 31, which links Swan Valley, Idaho, with Victor. On the north side, there are a handful of trailheads along Idaho 33 near Teton Pass, while trails farther west can be accessed via county roads south of Victor.

Day Hike

Wolf Mountain

Distance: 3.5 miles one way.
Difficulty: Moderately strenuous.
Starting and maximum elevation: 5,960 feet, 7,220 feet.
Topo map: Munger Mountain.
Getting there: Drive east from Hoback Junction on US 26. Some 0.5 mile past the Fall Creek–Wilson Road, then turn right on the unmarked gravel road just beyond the Targhee National Forest sign. Follow it north, then turn left across the bridge to reach the Dog Creek Trailhead at its end.

This trail climbs to the timberline on the shoulders of a high peak that guards the Snake River Canyon. The route of the trail has been changed and topo maps are out of date; ignore the maps and follow the signs. The hike begins by following Dog Creek up into the hills, timbered on the north-facing slopes, with tall grass and sagebrush on the south-facing side. Continue past the mouth of Beaver Dam Canyon, and follow the main trail as it tracks Dog Creek farther up the valley.

After the first crossing of Dog Creek, veer left onto the Cabin Creek trail, which ascends along a small tributary that flows through overgrown meadows. After a mile, turn right at the sign for Wolf Mountain. This rarely used path ascends a shallow vale, plugging along through a shoulder-deep jungle of wildflowers. The trail peters out high on the shoulders of Wolf Mountain; you can easily climb the bald hilltop to the north for broad views of the surrounding ranges and a glimpse of the Tetons. Those with the "summit or die" mentality can scramble up the steep slopes for about a mile to reach the top.

Hoback Peak   13

Location: 15 miles south of Jackson.
Size: 264,542 acres.
Administration: Bridger–Teton National Forest (Big Piney, Jackson, and Greys River Ranger Districts).
Management status: Unprotected roadless area.
Ecosystem: Douglas fir forest, western spruce-fir forest, lodgepole pine, and sagebrush steppe, with extensive aspen stands.
Elevation range: 5,575 feet to 10,845 feet.
System trails: 268 miles.
Maximum core to perimeter distance: 4.0 miles.
Activities: Hunting, hiking, horseback riding, fishing.
Best season: Late June–mid-September.
Maps: Bridger–Teton National Forest (Big Piney, Greys River, Kemmerer Districts); Afton and Jackson 1:100,000.

TRAVELERS ADVISORY:
FAINT TRAILS, SUDDEN STORMS

The Hoback Peak roadless area encompasses the northern end of the Wyoming Range and associated lowlands to the south of the Hoback River. The western half of the area is composed of low, rolling foothills where patches of aspen and lodgepole pine are intermingled with sagebrush meadows in a mosaic of vegetation that is some of Wyoming's best elk habitat. In the center, two tall, north-south hogbacks rise high above the neighboring valleys. The eastern portion of this de facto wilderness is a jumble of jagged, red peaks that are nearly impenetrable.

During 1811, John Jacob Astor's party of fur traders passed this way en route to establish a trading post on the Oregon coast. They were led by John Hoback, a well-known mountain man for whom many of the local landmarks have been named. During the decades that followed, mountain men snowshoed along the streams of the northern Wyoming Range in their quest for prime beaver pelts. A major trapper's trail became established along Bailey Creek, crossed through Telephone Pass, then swung west up Meadow Creek before descending Strawberry Creek in the Salt River Range en route to the salt deposits of the Star Valley. The trappers then returned to Fort Hall in the Snake River Basin to resupply. During this same period, bands of Shoshone Indians made summer forays into the Hoback Peak area in search of game and wild plants.

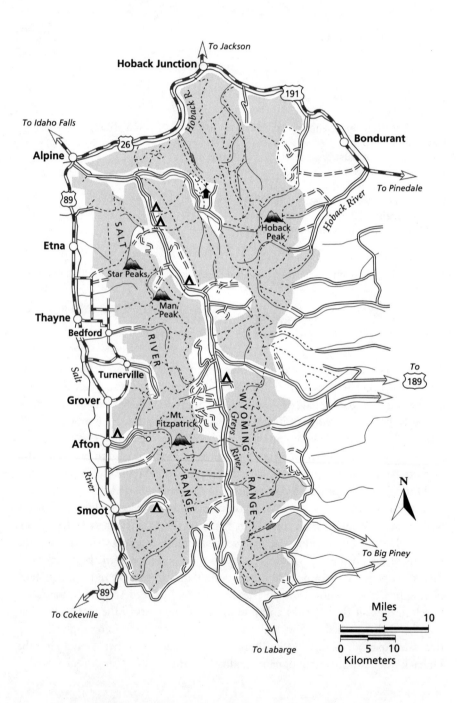

To Jackson

Hoback Junction

191

To Idaho Falls

Bondurant

Alpine

26

To Pinedale

Hoback River

89

Etna

Hoback Peak

Star Peaks

SALT

Man Peak

Thayne

RIVER

Bedford

Salt

Turnerville

To 189

Grover

Afton

Mt. Fitzpatrick

WYOMING RANGE

Greys River

River

RANGE

Smoot

To Big Piney

N

To Cokeville

89

To Labarge

Miles
0   5   10

0   5   10
Kilometers

In the 1880s this region was under consideration for federal protection, and President Theodore Roosevelt was invited to visit the area for an elk hunt. Roosevelt enjoyed his visit so immensely that he created the Bridger National Forest by executive order in 1908. His camping spot near the head of the Little Greys River came to be known as Roosevelt Meadows. When the Bridger National Forest was newly created, the Little Greys basin was designated as an elk preserve, and hunting was prohibited until the 1950s.

RECREATIONAL USE: This little-known area receives few visitors during the summer, and many of the trails have become overgrown and indistinct. Bailey Lake and the lower reaches of the Willow Creek trail are popular in the summer; Bailey Lake is home to a thriving population of pan-sized trout. Most of the visitor use occurs in the autumn, when the area becomes a world-famous elk hunting destination. During the winter, some parts of this area are closed to all access (motorized and non-motorized) to minimize disturbance to wintering game animals.

ACCESS: The Little Greys River Road penetrates the western end of the area and is suitable for passenger cars. It can be accessed by driving east from Alpine on the Greys River Road. The bridge at Astoria Hot Springs provides the only access to the south side of the Snake River Canyon, and a road that runs south from it leads to several trails. U.S. Highway 191 parallels the lower Hoback River, providing access to the Willow Creek and Cliff Creek areas. To the east, a good gravel trunk road follows the Hoback River to its headwaters.

Day Trip on Foot or Horseback

Grayback Ridge

Distance: 3.0 miles one way.
Difficulty: Strenuous.
Starting and maximum elevation: 7,240 feet, 9,510 feet.
Topo map: Bailey Lake.
Getting there: Drive east from Alpine on the Greys River Road, and as the valley bends south, turn east up the Little Greys River Road. Follow signs for the McCain Guard Station, turning right at all forks near the end. Turn right on the road marked "commercial outfitter" and park at the south end of Waterdog Lake.

The Big Springs trail provides a steep and sustained climb to the top of a high ridge just west of the main peaks of the Wyoming Range. Trails atop Grayback Ridge are virtually invisible; travelers who seek a longer trip should plan on traveling cross-country.

From Waterdog Lake, hike up the road and through the outfitter's camp to acquire the trail. It soon follows a small brook eastward through a heavy

Looking south along Grayback Ridge.

growth of cow parsnip and nettles, bearing for the base of Grayback Ridge. The gradient increases to a stiff climb as the path follows the watercourse to Big Spring. Beyond this point, copses of subalpine fir dot the open slopes as the path continues up the steep slopes of the upper ridge. Look back for sweeping vistas that include the sawtooth peaks of the Salt River Range and the more compact summits of the Snake River Range farther north.

The trail continues its steep slog to the ridgetop, where it purportedly meets a trail that follows the ridge crest. This trail might be spotted going south, but the northbound leg has been obliterated by time. Ignore the trails and hike southward up the ridgeline, following open meadows to crest a bald summit. From here, you can enjoy top-of-the-world views that encompass Hoback Peak and the jumble of steep red crags that flank it.

Day Hike

Hoback High Line

Distance: 3.2 miles one way.
Difficulty: Moderately strenuous.
Starting and maximum elevation: 7,755 feet, 9,708 feet.
Topo map: Hoback Peak.
Getting there: Drive east from Bondurant on U.S. Highway 191, then turn south on the Upper Hoback Road (FR 30700). Follow this good gravel road to the trailhead at its end.

An eroded spur of Hoback Peak as seen from the High Line.

This primitive trail leads to ridgetop meadows for views of the eroded red summits of the Wyoming Range. The trail is very faint as it crosses the subalpine meadows, making route-finding skill a must. The hike begins on the Upper Hoback Trail, which follows the Hoback River past clearcuts and beaver dams. After 0.5 mile, turn right on the High Line Trail, which wanders northward and then turns east as it snakes up a steep ridge. A ragged forest of spruce blocks out the scenery, but a short bushwhack to the ridgeline allows views of the surrounding mountains. The trail zigzags upward at a steady pace, staying to the east of the ridgetop.

It ultimately reaches tall forb glades, and a reef of buff-colored sandstone can be seen to the west. After crossing a spring-fed trickle, the path turns straight uphill, then resumes its northward traverse. It peters out entirely in an open draw that marks the head of the Jamb Creek drainage. A grassy dome rises ahead; climb it for grandstand views of Hoback Peak and the range of red crags that trails away northward toward the Gros Ventre Range.

Wyoming Range   14

Location: 24 miles west of Big Piney; 40 miles east of Afton.
Size: 76,191 acres.
Administration: Bridger–Teton National Forest (Big Piney and Greys River Ranger Districts).
Management status: Unprotected roadless area.
Ecosystem: Douglas fir forest, western spruce-fir forest, sagebrush steppe, and lodgepole pine, with extensive whitebark pine parklands at timberline.
Elevation range: 8,200 feet to 11,363 feet.
System trails: 133 miles.
Maximum core to perimeter distance: 2.9 miles.
Activities: Hunting, horseback riding, fishing, hiking, mountain biking.
Best season: Mid-June–mid-September.
Maps: Bridger-Teton Travel Map (Big Piney, Greys River, Kemmerer); Afton 1:100,000. See map on page 94.

TRAVELERS ADVISORY:
SUDDEN STORMS, FAINT TRAILS

The Wyoming Range is a long chain of sedimentary peaks crowned by brilliant red summits. Eclipsed in height and grandeur by the neighboring Tetons and Wind Rivers, this minor range has charms all its own. Hidden from major highways by intervening foothills and vast sagebrush plains, the Wyoming Range escapes the notice of most tourists. Its vast subalpine meadows dotted with whitebark pine were once the site of large-scale sheep grazing, but now livestock use has been scaled back and the high meadows are home to elk and deer. Its primitive trails are well suited to long forays into the wilderness, and the rolling country at the foot of the peaks is ideal for off-trail exploration. Solitude can be found almost anywhere in these remote mountains.

The Wyoming Range is rich in wildlife, and its elk and mule deer populations are quite dense. Bighorn sheep have been reintroduced at Darby Mountain and Fish Creek Mountain, two summits on the eastern flank of the range. The sheep herd has stabilized at a population that fluctuates between 200 and 300 head. The mountains hold a stable but sparse population of lynx, and wolf tracks have also been confirmed in the area. Ecologically, the range is dominated by Douglas fir–lodgepole pine forests on its flanks and whitebark pine savannas at the timberline. Spruce grow along some of the major watercourses, and subalpine fir can be found in moist timberline basins.

Krummholz fir high in the Wyoming Range.

One of a pair of enormous radio antenna sits atop Coffin Mountain, in the heart of the roadless area. This enormous, obsolete array is an eyesore, and detracts mightily from the wild character of the roadless area. Despite the fact that the radio antennas are no longer in use, Qwest (the owner) is reluctant to give them up and the Forest Service has thus far lacked the resolve to order them dismantled. There has been some wildcat drilling for oil along the Blind Bull Road at the north end of the range, but oil was not found in profitable quantities. *Tie-hacking* to produce railroad ties occurred in the Cottonwood Creek drainage around the turn of the twentieth century, but logging activity has been light otherwise due to low-grade timber and long distance to markets.

RECREATIONAL USE: Most of the trails that thread their way through the Wyoming Range receive little (if any) maintenance, and route-finding challenges are the rule rather than the exception. Along the crest of the range, vast grasslands swallow trail treads in short order, and travelers must navigate using cairns, posts, blazes, and dead reckoning. Trails that receive regular maintenance include Box Canyon, Marten Creek, Middle Piney Creek, and the trail that climbs to Wyoming Peak from the west. This entire area is excellent terrain for horses, and the high meadows and rolling topography of the timberline lend themselves well to off-trail hiking. The Wyoming Range is a more or less undiscovered destination, and it contains no areas that receive heavy summer use.

Motorized vehicles are permitted on many of the trails within the Wyoming Range roadless area. However, the narrow tread of most trails precludes the passage of anything but narrow-gauge dirt bikes, and thus motorized use of the area is uncommon. The trail that receives the only measurable ATV use is the North Piney Creek Trail as far as its junction with the Wyoming Range National Scenic Trail. Beyond this point, the spur trail to Roaring Fork Lakes is closed to motorized traffic. Motor vehicles are also prohibited on the Wyoming Range Trail north of the Marten Creek pass.

For hunters, the Wyoming Range offers a chance to encounter trophy mule deer, although the density of deer is lower here than elsewhere. The elk herd is healthy and productive, but large racks are the exception rather than the rule. Blue grouse can also be found on the high hogbacks during the hunting season. Although the Wyoming Range is not known for trophy-sized trout, there is some angling to be had in the many lakes and larger streams along the eastern side of the range.

ACCESS: From the east, the area can be reached by driving west from Pinedale on US 191, then turning south on US 89. After 3 miles, the McDougal Gap Road (County 116) runs west to access the north end of the area. From Big Piney, Wyoming 350 runs west, splitting into the South Piney Creek and Bare Pass roads. The Bare Pass Road runs along the Wyoming Range front, accessing many major trailheads, while the South Piney Road runs around the south end of the range to link up with the Greys River Road. This latter trunk road runs the length of the western edge of the range, accessing trails at Wyoming Peak, Box Canyon Creek, and Marten Creek en route to the village of Alpine. All of these trunk roads are susceptible to potholes, but are passable to all but low-clearance vehicles.

Multi-Day Backpack or Horse Trip

Wyoming Range National Recreation Trail

Distance: 36.2 miles.
Difficulty: Strenuous.
Starting and maximum elevation: 8,020 feet, 10,860 feet.
Topo maps: Park Creek, Triple Peak, Box Canyon Creek, Mount Schidler, Wyoming Peak, Mount Thompson, Poison Meadows.
Getting there: To reach the north end of the trail, drive east from the Greys River Road on the McDougal Gap Road (FR 10125) for about 6 miles. In the grassy basin just below the west side of McDougal Gap, park at a turnoff to the left; the trail starts across the road at a "no motorized" post.

The south end of the Wyoming Range trail is reached by driving west from Big Piney on Wyoming 350. After 10.4 miles, turn left on the South Piney Road (County 142), a gravel thoroughfare that runs west into the mountains, reaching the Lander Cutoff Crossing after 12.4 miles. Just beyond this bridge, turn right and drive through the Snider Basin Ranger Station and down a two-track road to park beside South Piney Creek. Adventurous drivers can cross the creek and continue up the very muddy and badly rutted road for 1.5 miles to the sheep camp at its end, but it is wiser to walk this last part of the road.

This trail follows the crest of the Wyoming Range, linking alpine basins guarded by the deep red summits that are the hallmark of the area. The trail is virtually invisible in places; be prepared to navigate by infrequent cairns or blazes and make frequent map consultations. From McDougal Gap, the trail follows the headwaters of Sheep Creek, first through meadows guarded by tall cliffs and then through a deep forest of spruce. Soon after crossing Sheep Creek, the trail splits. Turn right, following a tributary valley along grassy slopes and past a pretty little waterfall. Big meadows open up as the stream bends south, and the trail climbs briskly to cross a pass at the valley's head.

Contour south, following a faint track that climbs the steep slopes high above the valley of Cottonwood Creek. Red summits range to the east as the path skirts around one grassy summit, then follows the ridgeline to surmount two others. It then descends to a pass at the foot of a rocky peak; turn northeast and follow blazed trees down a sparsely wooded draw. Upon reaching a dependable spring, the trail turns east and is well defined as it rounds a timbered mountainside. It soon descends to an alpine basin, then climbs to the first of two saddles in spur ridges.

After the second saddle, the path descends into the valley of the South Fork of Cottonwood Creek. It crosses the creek in an alpine basin, then climbs steeply up the grassy ridge to the east. The trail tracks the ridge southward, then drops into a broad and grassy pass where it meets several other trails. From the signpost, hike southwest up through a grassy gap, following posts and cairns to Martin Creek. The trail visits the low pass at its head, then climbs southward through the trees. A well-beaten spur soon leads to the tiny Roaring Fork Lakes, set in a sparsely wooded basin at the foot of low cliffs.

The main trail continues south, beginning a long traverse. Soon it crosses the grassy slopes of several rounded plateaus. It then plays out onto rolling meadows dotted with copses of whitebark pine. The trail then climbs over a divide and descends to the pond in Box Canyon Pass. Seek out the trail that climbs steeply southward across slopes of shattered rock. A long ascent leads to the top of a lofty summit. The path then skirts the rim of a red-walled cirque as it follows a rounded ridgetop across a wind-blasted alpine desert.

Wyoming Peak (at left) as seen from the Wyoming Range trail.

After crossing two saddles, the path climbs across a slope and then drops steeply eastward, following a grassy spine down to a subalpine basin. It follows the basin downward, then doglegs southwest, traversing across gladed slopes and beneath mounds of talus. The trail crosses Lake Creek near the head of its valley, and a difficult grade leads up to the next divide. From the top, superb views encompass the red peaks that guard Straight Creek as well as the cliffs to the north. A brief but steep drop leads into the next valley, where the trail passes through well-groomed meadows and charming groves of whitebark pine and subalpine fir.

The path ultimately reaches the alpine bowl guarded by Coffin and Wyoming Peaks, and it makes for the low saddle at the base of the latter summit. An old trail once climbed to the summit, but our route drops into basin beyond, then bends west toward the head of Middle Piney Creek. Park-like shelves high above the valley floor lead to a windswept pass, where the trail turns south to surmount a bald peak. The route levels off near the top, providing expanding views of Wyoming Peak and the Salt River Range.

The trail adopts the first spur ridge leading west and follows its crest as it bends northward. A foot-pounding descent through the sagebrush leads to the East Fork of Greys River; cross the watercourse and hike downstream to strike the trail as it climbs along a fold in the hills. A rocky ravine soon leads up to an open saddle. Continue south along the draw that bears the Middle Fork South Piney Creek. A good trail takes form to carry you down to the forks, then along the beaver ponds of South Piney Creek to reach the trail's end.

The upper valley of North Cottonwood Creek.

Salt River Range   15

Location: 5 miles east of Afton; 5 miles south of Alpine.
Size: 259,270 acres.
Administration: Greys River Ranger District, Bridger–Teton National Forest.
Management status: Unprotected roadless area.
Ecosystem: Douglas fir forest, spruce-fir forest, lodgepole, and sagebrush steppe, with extensive aspen communities.
Elevation range: 6,550 feet to 10,770 feet.
System trails: 212 miles.
Maximum core to perimeter distance: 3.1 miles.
Activities: Horseback riding, hiking, backpacking, hunting, fishing.
Best season: Late June–mid-September.
Maps: Bridger-Teton Travel Map (Big Piney, Greys River, Kemmerer); Afton 1:100,000. See map on page 94.

TRAVELERS ADVISORY:
FAINT TRAILS, SUDDEN STORMS

The Salt River Range is a monocline made up of long, sedimentary reefs that rise into blocky, glacier-carved summits at the crest of the range. The strata produce an oddity of hydrography: The lakes below the eastern faces of the high peaks actually drain westward through underground channels, emerging as springs and upwellings on the western side of the range. Periodic Spring is the most remarkable of these upwellings. It flows heavily for a period of 18 minutes, then dries up completely for a period. Periodic Spring provides the municipal water supply for the Star Valley and is also bottled commercially for sale throughout the country under the Geyser label.

On the western side of the range, Douglas fir and sagebrush meadows dominate the lower elevations, while lodgepole pine and aspen skirt the range to the east. The uplands are timbered in subalpine fir and Engelmann spruce, with whitebark pine on the drier and more windswept exposures on the high ridges. To the west of the divide, upland forests are a mixture of spruce and aspen, while lodgepole pine and Douglas fir dominate the lower elevations. Extensive tall forb meadows are the hallmark of the range. Composed of such plants as cow parsnip, broad-leafed bluebells, and arnica, these meadows occur near timberline on the windward (western) side of the range, which receives more rainfall.

Long fault scarps typical of the Salt River Range.

The roadless country within the Salt River Range is eligible for wilderness consideration, but local land managers fear wilderness status would be accompanied by an influx of visitors that would destroy the solitude that can now be found in the range. The Greys River and the Salt River are eligible for protection under the National Wild and Scenic River Act. The Salt River Range includes two Research Natural Areas, identified for their pristine and unimpacted plant communities. Between the high peaks and the Greys River, rolling hills robed in aspen and spruce provide a critical calving area for local elk. Mule deer are also abundant, although heavy hunting pressure has culled out most of the big bucks.

This mountain range is of historical significance to the livestock industry. At the turn of the twentieth century, the Salt River Range was the first leg of an annual cycle of sheep grazing: The range's tall forb meadows were prized as summering grounds, and Basque drovers herded as many as 300,000 sheep through Sheep Pass each summer en route to the verdant meadows of the high country. These "mountain maggots" ate everything in sight, creating a blighted wasteland of denuded slopes. The result was a rapid erosion of the topsoil and the destruction of over half of the tall forb meadows in the Salt River Range. Up to 5 feet of soil washed away in places before the driveways were closed in 1969.

Today, domestic sheep are still grazed throughout the Salt River Range, particularly on the Greys River side. Although their numbers are much lower than they once were, the sheep still destroy the fragile meadow vegetation in places where they are allowed to graze for long periods without moving. Upper Corral Creek and the headwaters of the Salt River receive the highest levels of sheep grazing, while few (if any) sheep will be found north of Strawberry Creek. The watershed of Swift Creek has been closed to sheep grazing to prevent damage to some of the last undisturbed communities of tall forb meadow left in the range.

The benches above the Greys River were the site of heavy logging activity from the 1940s through the 1960s. There is only limited timber activity today, which occurs along existing roadways. An abandoned, obsolete antenna stands atop one of the high peaks. During World War II, vanadium mines were dug into the bedrock along the western flank of the range. Vanadium is a strategic metal that is used in the hardening of steel for armor plate. Now that the Cold War has come to a close, it is unlikely that the demand for vanadium will be such that these mines will be reopened. In any case, most lands to the west of the Salt River divide have been rated as too steep for mineral or oilfield development, and it is unlikely that the Forest Service will ever grant permits for such activities.

RECREATIONAL USES: Since the Salt River Range is so narrow, there are few (if any) areas that cannot be reached in a day hike. A network of trails runs along the crest of the range, allowing for longer backpacks. Trail maintenance is minimal, and trail junctions tend to be poorly marked. Many of the little-used segments have been swallowed up by meadow vegetation. Map and compass skills will be required in many areas. Horsemen should be aware that the disappearance of trail tread on some of the steeper slopes tends to make riding along the crest of the range a difficult and hazardous proposition.

The Salt River Range has gained considerable notoriety for producing trophy mule deer. As a result, the mountains are aswarm with hunters each autumn, hoping to track down a big buck. The end result of this hunting pressure has been to eliminate most of the mature bucks from the herd, and as of this writing, few trophy animals were being taken. The Salt River Range is also home to a burgeoning elk population, though it is not known for heavy-antlered bulls. At the time of this writing, the elk were so abundant that hunters were allowed to take an animal of either sex. During winter, a herd of some 2,000 elk gathers at two supplemental feeding grounds along the Greys River, where they can fuel up on hay. Lake Barstow receives rather heavy fishing pressure, but otherwise the fishing is only fair in the small streams and lakes.

ACCESS: U.S. Highway 89 follows the western side of the Salt River Range, and from it a number of county roads run east to become rough-and-ready forest roads that lead into the mountains. The long, gravel ribbon of the Greys River Road begins in the southern part of Alpine and winds around the north side of the Salt River Range and then bends south to follow the eastern flank of the mountains. This road is plagued with potholes and washboards in places, but is passable to most passenger cars. From it, you can use old sheep bridges and logging roads to cross the river and reach most of the trails; trails leading to Pearson and Henderson Creeks require fording the Greys River and are used mostly by horsemen in late summer and autumn.

Day Hike or Backpack

Bear Creek Loop

Distance: 14.5 miles overall.
Difficulty: Moderately strenuous.
Starting and maximum elevation: 7,070 feet, 9,420 feet.
Topo maps: Park Creek, Rock Lake Peak.
Getting there: To reach the Bear Creek Loop Trailhead, drive south on the Greys River Road from its junction with the road over McDougal Gap. Turn right (west) on the Bear Creek Road, veering right at the "Road Closed Ahead" sign and taking the right fork on the far side of the creek. The hike begins on the closed road.

This loop trail climbs to the alpine basins at the head of Bear Creek. The trail becomes quite primitive in its upper reaches, with faint tread that poses route-finding challenges. The steep and unstable footing in this area makes the alpine traverse impassable to horsemen.

The hike begins on an old road that parallels the north bank of Bear Creek. After 0.8 mile, the road veers uphill, while the route follows the blazed trail that continues up the valley floor. Riparian wetlands and sagebrush meadows dominate the early going, while timber increases as the trail proceeds upstream. After passing below a talus slope, the trail climbs steeply as the valley bends northward. Gaps in the trees reveal a succession of majestic peaks that rise at the crest of the range.

The mountain views dwindle as the path follows verdant glades toward the head of the valley. Here, the headwaters of Bear Creek tumble over a band of cliffs and flow into broad subalpine meadows. Turn right to climb toward a

Alpine meadows and cliffs at the head of Bear Creek.

pass, then left as the loop trail runs below the foot of the cliffs and surmounts a spur ridge. It will cross three such ridges, visiting nearly identical alpine basins robed in a verdant carpet of wildflowers. The final basin is ringed with majestic peaks. The trail disappears here; you can hike to one of the small cirque lakes below the cliffs at the head of the basin, or continue the loop as described by hiking down the meadowy benches to the north of the creek that drains the basin.

After passing a grassy avalanche slope, pick up the good trail that descends into a bottomland flat filled with bluebells. This well-beaten track soon drops steeply down the timbered slopes beyond, eventually adopting a neck of land between two cataracts. It fords the northern one at the confluence, then fords Bear Creek itself. The trail on the far bank doesn't look like much, but faithful as an old dog, it leads up to a grove of aspen just below the Bear Creek Trail. Turn right and retrace your steps to complete the hike.

Day Hike

Wagner Lake

Distance: 3.5 miles one way.
Difficulty: Strenuous.
Starting and maximum elevation: 7,514 feet, 9,720 feet.
Topo maps: Red Top Mountain, Mount Wagner.
Getting there: Drive south from Afton on U.S. Highway 89. Just beyond the settlement of Smoot, turn left (east) on County 153. The pavement ends after 1 mile, and the road becomes the rough, all-weather Forest Road 10208. Follow it 5 miles to Cottonwood Lake Campground, driving through the campground and around the north shore of the lake to reach the trailhead at road's end. There is no fee to park at the trailhead.

This steep trail visits a high lake in the south end of the Salt River Range. After the footbridge over Timber Creek, the wide path follows Cottonwood Creek through a forest of ancient spruce. Avalanche paths have opened a broad meadow beside the immense rockslide that formed Slide Lake, and the trail climbs the steep slopes to the west to avoid the rubble. It emerges beside the lake, which has water in early summer but drains itself in early July to become a grassy meadow.

Continuing up the valley, the trail passes through a dense growth of tall forbs beneath the avalanche chutes of the mountainsides. At the valley's head, the path turns west, climbing steeply up an open couloir. After a brief respite on an open shelf, the path continues to climb beneath the great, gabled cliffs of Mount Wagner. It ultimately levels off, traversing eastward through a forest of tall spruce and subalpine fir. Another steep couloir slopes up to the narrow gap that leads to the headwaters of the Salt River.

The ecological contrast is marked here, with spacious meadows of low-growing plants dotted at intervals with copses of whitebark pine and subalpine fir. Our trail splits away to the right, traversing westward through open country that bears obvious scars of overgrazing. Soon it returns to the mountainsides for the final trek to Wagner Lake. This small cirque lake occupies a rocky shelf at the foot of Mount Wagner.

Commissary Ridge

16

Location: 40 miles south of Afton; 20 miles west of Labarge.
Size: 163,385 acres.
Administration: Bridger–Teton National Forest (Kemmerer District).
Management status: Roadless area currently managed as non-motorized.
Ecosystem: Douglas fir forest, western spruce-fir forest, and sagebrush steppe.
Elevation range: 7,380 feet to 10,330 feet.
System trails: 464 miles.
Maximum core to perimeter distance: 4.0 miles.
Activities: Horseback riding, hiking, backpacking, hunting, fishing.
Best season: Mid-June–September.
Map: Fontenelle Reservoir 1:100,000.

TRAVELERS ADVISORY:
FAINT TRAILS

Commissary Ridge is a long, north-south monocline with a continuous cliff escarpment that faces toward the east. The ridge was named for the commissary wagons that kept early sheepherders provisioned during the early 1900s. A series of tiny cirque lakes lies at the foot of these cliffs like a string of gems on a necklace, and subalpine meadows offer pleasant camping spots. The only major body of water to the west of the Commissary Ridge divide is Lake Alice, which formed thousands of years ago when an enormous slab of Lake Mountain slid down to block Poker Creek.

The main ridge is flanked by rolling uplands and plateaus where stands of subalpine fir, spruce, and whitebark pine are interrupted by ridgetop parks and wet meadows in the headwater basins. Along the eastern edge of the roadless area, the edge of the plateau drops away into steep slopes that have been dissected by deep canyons. A forest of Douglas fir and lodgepole pine dominates this area, grading into sagebrush steppe at the edge of the mountains. Stands of aspen grow in moist pockets and on slopes where groundwater seeps to the surface.

Commissary Ridge is a key summer range for mule deer, moose, and elk. The deer and elk move out of the high country during the winter, when they feed on serviceberry, mountain mahogany, and bitterbrush in the lowlands that

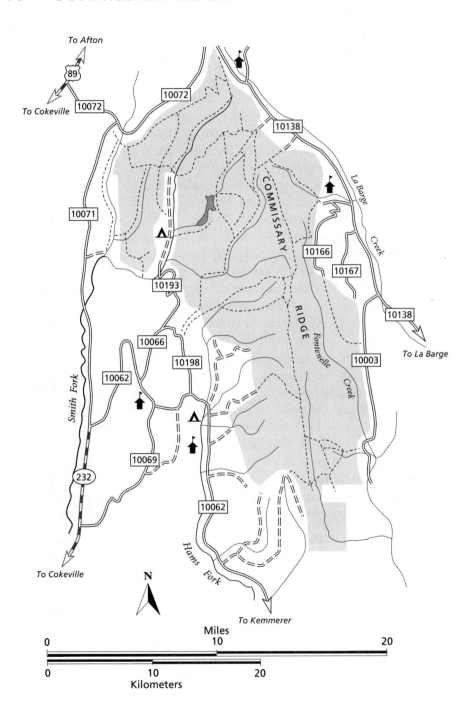

To Afton

89

To Cokeville

10072

10072

10138

COMMISSARY

La Barge

10071

10166

10167

Creek

10193

10138

To La Barge

10066

RIDGE

10198

10003

10062

Smith Fork

Fontenelle

Creek

232

10069

10062

To Cokeville

Hams Fork

N

To Kemmerer

Miles
0   10   20

0   10   20
Kilometers

surround the roadless area. The moose are particularly abundant, and range throughout every drainage as they concentrate their browsing on aspen and subalpine fir. Some of the bulls attain impressive sizes by Rocky Mountain standards. The riparian areas along streams and marshes are rich in willows, which provide the primary staple for the beaver that are abundant throughout the area.

Though never abundant, black bear and mountain lion populations have been increasing in recent years, and Commissary Ridge provides superb habitat for these large carnivores. Pine martens and bobcats are common (though seldom seen) residents, and lynx also roam this area in low numbers. There has been a verified wolf sighting on the eastern slopes of Commissary Ridge, although this area is not known to have a resident pack.

The Emigrant Trail runs through the northern tip of the roadless area. This old wagon road was once part of the Lander Cutoff, an alternate to the main Oregon Trail that was blazed by General F.W. Lander in 1857 to bypass the arid and treeless deserts to the south and to offer a shortcut to the Snake River Plain. Lander boasted that his route was "so abundantly furnished with grass, timber, pure water, with mountain streams abounding with fish, plains thronged with game . . ." that immigrants "may move with their families and herds of stock to the Pacific Coast in a single season, without loss." But modern visitors will find old graves beside the wagon ruts that mark the passing of pioneers who never got so far as to set eyes on the lush pastures of the Oregon country.

At the turn of the twentieth century, Commissary Ridge was the site of large-scale sheep grazing each summer. Herds were wintered in the Red Desert, then driven up into the meadowy pastures of Commissary Ridge for the lambing season. Great flocks of thousands of sheep, driven by Basque herders, made a circuit through the Salt River and Wyoming Ranges before the summer was out. Stockmen still graze much smaller bands of sheep in the high meadows near the crest of the ridge. The Labarge oilfield, just east of Commissary Ridge, has been a center for oil production since 1924. There is some possibility that oil exploration may take place on Commissary Ridge in the future.

RECREATIONAL USES: The trails that crisscross the highlands of Commissary Ridge were principally blazed and maintained by stockmen and hunters. As a result, some trails are well-worn, while others have disappeared entirely through disuse. Commissary Ridge is an excellent place for hikers and horsemen to find solitude. The grassy parks at the base of the cliffs offer abundant opportunities for dispersed camping with ample graze for horses. Blue and ruffed grouse are found within the highlands, although this area is not known for producing high densities of game birds. Big game hunters will find strong populations off moose, elk, and mule deer here.

The Colorado cutthroat trout is native to the eastern slope of Commissary Ridge, while the Bonneville subspecies is found to the west of the divide. LaBarge Creek and many of the small lakes within the roadless area have been stocked with brook and rainbow trout in the past, to the detriment of the native cutthroats. The Wyoming Department of Game and Fish is now actively trying to restore the native cutthroats that have been pushed out by the introduced game fishes. The small Fontenelle Lakes are known as steady producers of pan-sized brook trout, and the oddly titled Nameless Creek is also known to offer good fishing for brookies. Lake Alice, to the west of the divide, is noted for having an outstanding fishery.

ACCESS: The north side of roadless area can be reached by driving south from Afton on US 89 to reach the Smiths Fork Road (Forest Road 10138). This all-weather gravel road eventually links up with the Labarge Creek Road, which runs along the eastern side of the roadless area and provides trail access at numerous points via old logging roads. To reach the western side, take US 30 to Cokeville and follow Wyoming 232 up the Smiths Fork, or start from Kemmerer and drive north a mile on US 189 to Wyoming 233 and follow this road northwest past Viva Naughton Reservoir and up the Hams Fork. Many of the logging roads in this part of the state are falling into disrepair and may offer difficult traveling.

Day Hike

Indian Ridge

Distance: 4.5 miles one way.
Difficulty: Moderately strenuous.
Starting and maximum elevation: 7,860 feet, 9,900 feet.
Topo maps: Coal Creek, Devils Hole Creek.
Getting there: Drive south from Labarge to reach the Labarge Creek Road (County 315). This road is paved for the first 9 miles of its westward journey, after which it becomes a gravel trunk road susceptible to potholes and even minor fords. Ten miles past the end of the pavement, turn left onto Forest Road 10003, which is marked with a sign for Fontenelle Creek. Warning signs notwithstanding, this road is passable to most cars for the 5.5 miles to the ford of Fontenelle Creek. The trailhead is just beyond the ford.

This route leads up to the top of Indian Ridge, a prominent spur to the east of Commissary Ridge. It begins by following an abandoned road west along Fontenelle Creek. After a shallow ford of Bear Trap Creek, turn left (south) and follow this tributary past willow-choked bottoms where beaver make their homes. Stay right at the junction as the main fork of Bear Trap Creek bends

Beaver pond on Bear Trap Creek.

westward. The trail now crosses south-facing sagebrush meadows and passes through extensive stands of aspen. After entering the forest, there is a confusing intersection where the main trail crosses the stream.

If you miss it, don't worry: You can catch the official trail as it climbs steeply northward to the ridgetop. Here it turns west again, snaking up the ridgeline through a subalpine forest. The trees thin out as the trail reaches the base of Indian Ridge. It climbs aggressively at first, then swings south to surmount Indian Ridge via a low gap. All traces of a trail end here. Turn left (south), climbing moderately through an open woodland of whitebark pine and subalpine fir. At the top of the grade, the rocky brow of Indian Peak looks eastward over the timbered slopes and ridgetop parks that stretch toward the Green River.

Day Hike or Horse Trip

Red Park

Distance: 1.7 to 4.3 miles one way.
Difficulty: Moderate.
Starting and maximum elevation: 8,980 feet, 9,900 feet.
Topo maps: Devils Hole Creek, Mount Thompson, Graham Peak.
Getting there: Drive up the Labarge Creek Road as for the Indian Ridge hike. Turn left on FR 10013 five miles beyond the Forest boundary, following signs for the Scaler guard station. Turn left at the guard station and follow FR 10166 up a series of switchbacks, parking at a marked trail sign at the head of Schafer Creek.

This trip starts high and passes the tiny Fontenelle Lakes before making a climb to the top of Commissary Ridge and following it south to Red Park. The trail begins by slipping through a deeply timbered gap in Absaroka Ridge and descending to the headwaters of Fontenelle Creek. Here, open parks are bordered

Along the crest of Commissary Ridge.

with stands of spruce and fir, and small ponds dot the woodlands. The trail passes two junctions with the South Labarge trail, then grows faint as it runs southwest across a wet meadow. The path becomes obvious as it climbs vigorously through open timber en route to the southernmost of the Fontenelle Lakes. This shallow mere sits at the base of Commissary Ridge, and brook trout cruise its clear waters.

From the lakeshore, the trail angles southward for the stiff ascent of Commissary Ridge. Open slopes and scattered whitebark pines allow fine views across the parks of Fontenelle Creek to the distant summits of the Wyoming Range to the north and Deadline Ridge to the east. As the trail drops over the top of the ridge, turn left (south) at a junction and follow a good path along a strip meadow just west of the ridgetop. The trail ultimately crests the ridgeline again, and a cliff-top perch just ahead overlooks the emerald waters of the Twin Creek Lakes.

Meanwhile, the main trail slips behind the ridge crest again, following an open lane in the pines. As another cliff-girt promontory looms ahead, the path drops into a grassy saddle. Thirty yards up the far slope, the well-camouflaged main trail descends southwest into the timber, while a dead-end path continues up the ridgeline. Our route follows the descending trail as it arcs downhill to Red Park. Here, numerous trails converge in a broad and grassy basin surrounded by slopes of reddish soil.

Raymond Mountain

Location: 3 miles north of Cokeville.
Size: 41,350 acres.
Administration: BLM (Rock Springs District).
Management status: Raymond Mountain WSA (32,936 acres), 8,140 acres of unprotected roadless area.
Ecosystem: Douglas fir forest, sagebrush steppe.
Elevation range: 6,300 feet to 9,313 feet.
System trails: 18 miles.
Maximum core to perimeter distance: 1.4 miles.
Activities: Hiking, backpacking, hunting, fishing.
Best season: June–September.
Map: Fontenelle Reservoir 1:100,000.

The steep slopes of the Sublette Range rise from the gentle grasslands to the east in a single, lofty hogback 19 miles long with a low gap at its center. Douglas fir forests mantle the eastern slopes of the range and encircle the higher summits. The western slopes are drier, with grasslands dominant at low elevations and scattered timber on the higher slopes. Brakes of twisted hardwoods are found on windswept ridgetops throughout the range. At the foot of the mountains, sagebrush steppe is interspersed with juniper, and aspens cluster around seeps and dry watercourses.

Ecologically, this range has more in common with the arid ranges of the Columbia Basin and the Great Basin than it does with the Rocky Mountains. Critical winter range for elk, moose, and mule deer is found here. Huff and Raymond Creeks, which drain from the Sublette Range, harbor a pure strain of the rare Bonneville cutthroat trout.

The Sublette Range lies within the Overthrust Belt, and has a moderate potential for oil and gas. However, more favorable geologic structures for petroleum production can be found in the neighboring basins, and the steep terrain of the Sublette Range is unfavorable for drilling. There are no current oil and gas leases, and two wells drilled within the WSA were capped as unproductive.

RECREATIONAL USES: Visitation is very light within the Raymond Mountain WSA. The steep terrain makes for difficult cross-country travel, and there are only a few miles of trail in the area. Remote parks and high shelves within

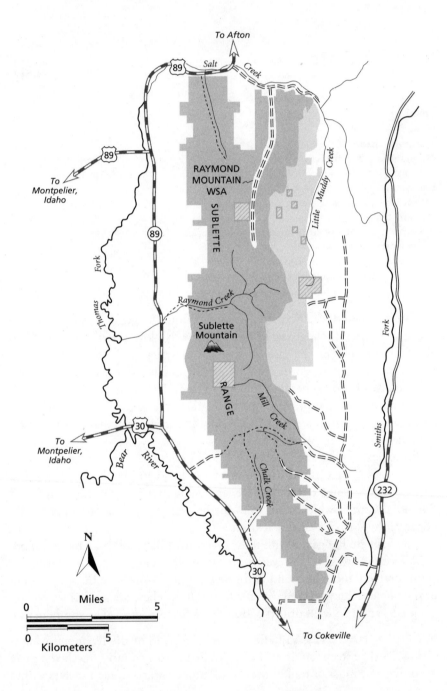

Sagebrush valley on the east side of the Sublette Range.

the Sublette Range are favorable for primitive camping, and the entire area is good terrain for big game and upland bird hunting.

ACCESS: U.S. Highway 89 and Wyoming 89 run along the western base of the range, but private lands between the highway and the WSA make access difficult. On the north side, Huff and Salt creeks provide the best public access. To the east of the range, a confusing network of largely private roads runs through the hills above the Hams Fork. Legal public access is lacking in this area.

Day Hike

North Crest Loop

Distance: 7.7 miles round trip.
Difficulty: Moderately strenuous.
Starting and maximum elevation: 6,350 feet, 8,160 feet.
Topo map: Giraffe Creek, Geneva, Huff Lake.
Getting there: Drive north on US 89 from Geneva, Idaho. After 3.7 miles, the highway turns east into Salt Canyon. Follow the highway another 2.1 miles and park at the first major side valley that comes in from the right (south). The hike begins on the old jeep road that runs up this valley.

This route follows a good trail southward along the base of the Sublette Range, then follows game trails up steep slopes to reach the crest for a one-day loop trip. The country is very rough, and the descent crosses steep and sometimes unstable slopes. Wear boots with lots of ankle support.

To begin, follow an old jeep road as it fords Salt Creek and then heads south up a narrow draw. The roadbed, now a cattle trail, runs through sagebrush flats guarded by an occasional stand of aspen. The valley's west-facing slopes have an arid aspect, and are dominated by sage and juniper. The east-facing slopes represent the northern tail of the Sublette Range, and are timbered in Douglas fir. As the route follows the draw upward, aspen groves become more prevalent and conifers crowd the valley floor. The draw soon narrows to a tight ravine; drop into the wash to regain the roadbed beyond the narrows. It ends in a broad sagebrush meadow where the drainage splits into three forks.

The route now follows game trails west, climbing steeply across slopes of grass and shaly scree. You will soon strike the crest of a spur ridge, where elk tracks lead up through a sparse growth of Douglas fir and hardwoods. Views now open up to the northwest, where the most prominent peak is Red Top Mountain of the Salt River Range, with the crimson summits of the Wyoming Range gracing the skyline farther south. At the top of the grade is a level, brushy meadow. Cross it on a westward heading and pass through the timbered flats beyond it. The mountainside soon slopes upward again; traverse north along the clearing to gain the crest of the range.

As a rolling divide of grass and shrubs slopes away to the north, views sweep north and west to take in the Gannett Hills and the Thomas Fork Valley. Follow the ridgeline over a grassy knob, then down the increasingly bald hilltops to reach a high point crowned with ragged Douglas firs. Turn east down a spur ridge for the final, steep descent across sparse grasslands and loose rock to return to the mouth of the draw and complete the loop.

3

Wind River Range

The Wind River Range is a 120-mile-long anticline, or upfolding of the earth's crust. This high and sawbacked stretch of the Continental Divide boasts 48 summits that rise above 13,000 feet, including Gannett Peak, the tallest mountain in Wyoming. The Bridger, Popo Agie, and Fitzpatrick Wilderness Areas along with the Wind River Tribal Wilderness cover all but the foothills of the range, preserving it from industrial exploitation. Almost a thousand miles of trail wind along the elevated pediment of the Winds and penetrate its inner recesses. Even so, many drainages are completely trail-less, offering possibilities for fresh explorations. Over half of the annual precipitation falls as snow, but there is a major peak of rainy weather in May and June.

When the range was created some 55 million years ago, the upthrust pushed the bedrock of the Wind Rivers over 60,000 feet above the same strata in the neighboring basins. During this period, Wyoming lay close to the equator, with a warm tropical climate and lush jungle foliage. There were no intervening ranges between the Wind Rivers and the ocean, and as a result the Winds received heavy quantities of rainfall. The sedimentary rocks that once capped the range wore away under the onslaught of coastal storms, exposing the hard Precambrian core of the range. The sediment from all of this erosion piled up along the flanks of the range, burying all but the highest peaks in a mantle of sand and silt.

Much later (about 10 million years ago), the landmass that was to become Wyoming rose over 5,000 feet in elevation, steepening the watercourses and setting erosion to work once more. The rejuvenated waters carried the sediment to the sea, effectively excavating the buried Wind River Range. At the north end of the range, flat plateaus some 12,000 feet in elevation are all that remain of the original sediment fill that once buried the range.

The range's core rock is migmatized gneiss, with granite and diorite. Migmatized gneiss is a metamorphic rock that has been subjected to super-heated water which melts the rock and reconstitutes it into a hard substance similar to granite. To the east the foothills are sedimentary, while to the west they are made of tuff, conglomerate, and rhyolite of volcanic origin. At its core, the summits have been sculpted by glacial erosion into horn peaks and saw-tooth ridges. The range contains seven active glaciers, and the Dinwoody Glacier is the largest glacier in the Rocky Mountains. To the west of the range, a thrust fault dips eastward beneath the range. The range is surrounded on three sides by synclinal basins, caused by the down-warping of the earth's surface: the Green River Basin to the west, the Wind River Basin to the east, and the Great Divide Basin to the south.

The Wind River Range has been a summer hunting and gathering area for indigenous peoples for over 10,000 years. These first explorers built circular rock shelters and traps and drive lines for bighorn sheep. Shoshone Indians arrived in the Green River Basin in the 1500s, and they were there when the first mountain men explored the area. The modern trails over Indian Pass and Washakie Pass were traditional Indian travel routes through the mountains.

The list of trappers and explorers who plied the Wind River Range during the early 1800s reads like a who's who of prominent mountain men: Jim Bridger, Kit Carson, Jedediah Smith, William Sublette, Thomas Fitzpatrick, and Lieutenant John C. Frémont. In 1833, Captain William Bonneville was the first recorded explorer to penetrate into the heart of the range. During this time, a number of annual fur rendezvous were held in the upper Green River, just west of the modern site of Pinedale. Great company wagon trains laden with supplies to trade for the furs were driven out to this remote corner of Wyoming, and a great festival was held for trappers and Indians alike. A typical rendezvous was replete with whiskey, gambling, horse races, and general debauchery.

Although the wagon trains streamed over South Pass between 1843 and 1865, white settlement in the cold basins that bordered the Wind Rivers was minimal until the cattle and sheep ranching boom in the 1870s. The friction between cattleman and sheepherders reached many flashpoints during the early years, and cattle ranchers killed huge numbers of sheep and even killed herders along the New Fork River and in the meadows beside Raid Lake. In modern times, sheep and cattle still graze within the wilderness areas of the Wind River Range under permits that predate the wilderness act.

The Wind River Range's high lakes are renowned for their excellent trout fishing. Most of these lakes did not originally have fish, but were planted with trout during the mid-1900s and these trout have established self-sustaining populations. Many of the high lakes of the Wind Rivers have basins of granite bedrock, which makes them highly susceptible to poisoning by acid rain and snow. They have become indicators of environmental degradation; recent reports indicate that these high lakes are headed inexorably for acidification and

An alpine pond high on the Green River divide.

thus extinction for their trout populations. In addition to acid rain, airborne fluorine released by trona mines to the southwest threatens the health of forests of the Wind River Range.

The Wind River tribal roadless area covers 180,387 acres of virgin country along the east side of the Wind River Divide. It is open to hiking and backpacking on a permit-only basis. The fishing permit covers both hiking and fishing pursuant to tribal regulations. You are required to purchase a fishing permit and conservation stamp to enter this area *even if you start and end your trip on Forest Service land.* These permits can be purchased from the tribal headquarters in Fort Washakie and in many sporting goods stores in neighboring towns, both on and off the reservation. The Shoshone and Arapaho manage the lakes and streams in the Wind River tribal roadless area as trophy fisheries. Be aware that some reservation waters will be closed to public fishing even if you hold a tribal permit. Visitors are encouraged to engage a licensed guide when traveling in this area.

Bridger Wilderness   ![18]

Location: 5 miles east of Pinedale.
Size: 646,144 acres.
Administration: Bridger–Teton National Forest (Pinedale District), BLM (Lander District).
Management status: Bridger Wilderness (428,169 acres), Scab Creek Primitive Area (6,680 acres), unprotected Forest Service lands (208,295 acres), unprotected BLM lands (3,000 acres).
Ecosystem: Douglas fir ecosystem, with Douglas fir—lodgepole and aspen communities in the foothills and spruce-fir and whitebark pine parks at the timberline.
Elevation range: 7,380 feet to 13,804 feet.
System trails: 600 miles.
Maximum core to perimeter distance: 12.4 miles.
Activities: Backpacking, horseback riding, mountaineering, fishing, hunting, cross-country skiing.
Best season: July–early September.
Maps: Pinedale Ranger District Forest Map; *Earthwalk Wind River* (North and South); *Handy Maps Wind River.*

TRAVELERS ADVISORY:
ALTITUDE SICKNESS, SUDDEN STORMS, GRIZZLY COUNTRY

The western slope of the Wind River Range was designated a primitive area in 1931. It was one of the first roadless set-asides in the nation, spearheaded by the work of environmentalist Robert Marshall. Today, this vast wilderness stretches over 100 miles from north to south, with enough elbowroom for wilderness trips that last for weeks on end.

The western foothills are characterized by open slopes of big sagebrush and bunchgrasses interspersed with extensive stands of aspen and groves of Douglas fir and limber pine. A level shelf extends from the top of the foothills to the base of the high peaks, up to 10 miles wide in places. This area was buried deep beneath glacial ice during the Pleistocene Epoch, and the glaciers planed off the granitic bedrock in some places and deposited deep beds of glacial till in others. It is now robed in a mixed woodland of lodgepole pine, Engelmann spruce, and subalpine fir. Whitebark pine stands commonly grow atop the windswept bluffs and on dry, south-facing exposures. Prior to 1900, major fires swept through the wilderness every 20 to 30 years. The fires were much more prevalent at lower elevations due to drier conditions found there. Above

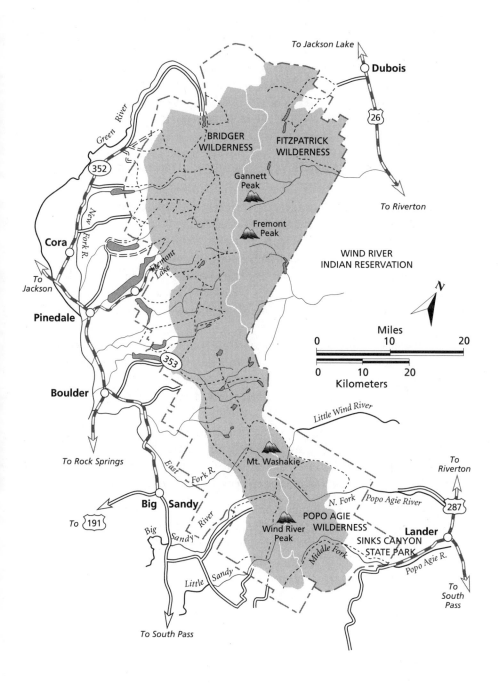

10,000 feet, ecologists have found spruce-fir stands that have not burned in over 750 years.

During the Pleistocene ice ages, major valley glaciers carved deep canyons into this plateau as they moved southwest into the Green River Basin. As the ice stagnated at the basin's edge, it left behind huge mounds of debris that had been pushed down from the mountain heights. These mounds, called *terminal moraines*, dammed the streams that occupied the glacier-carved canyons to create natural reservoirs at the foot of the Wind River Range. Active rock glaciers are present along some of the north-facing canyon walls. Made up of deep drifts of rocky rubble with a core of ice, they creep down hill by *solifluction*, a gradual downhill flow of the ice in the rock interstices.

The highlands at the base of the peaks are summer range for mule deer, elk, and bighorn sheep. At the timberline, moose browse on diamondleaf and grayleaf willows, the same species that are the staples of the moose diet in the mountains of interior Alaska. Above the timberline, mountain avens, arctic willow, and sedges populate the extensive meadows. There have been confirmed sightings of grizzly bears here, and black bear, mountain lions, and lynx are well-established residents. The high peaks provide aeries used by nesting peregrine falcons, bald and golden eagles, and red-tailed hawks. Rare and endangered plants of the alpine zone include several species of milkvetch, the purple Weber's saussuria, a species of cushion draba, and an androsace. Williams' rockcress, found in the Wind River Range, is thought to be endemic to Wyoming.

Commercial grazing of livestock is allowed in areas where grazing occurred prior to the creation of the wilderness. Sheep herds graze the subalpine meadows in the southern two-thirds of the range, from the Bald Mountain Basin south. Concentrations of sheep are often found in the high grasslands surrounding Dream Lake and Raid Lake, which are known to opponents of livestock as "The Sheep Desert." Cattle graze in the high meadows of the northwestern corner of the range, particularly around Round Lake. Visitors who don't want livestock to interfere with their wilderness experience can contact the Pinedale Ranger District for current locations of stock herds.

RECREATIONAL USE: A number of special regulations are in effect for the Bridger Wilderness. Camps must be away from trails, lakes, and streams. All horse parties and organized groups staying overnight in the Bridger Wilderness must first get a special permit (no charge) at the ranger station in Pinedale. Hikers, backpackers, skiers, and snowshoers do not need a permit. The Bridger Wilderness has a group size "limit" of 15 people and 25 head of stock, ensuring that solitude-seekers are free to encounter small armies of outfitters and their clients. Fires are not permitted above the tree line.

Elkhart Park, with its paved access all the way to the high country, receives heavy use by both hikers and horse parties. Expect crowds all the way up to the divide, particularly in the Titcomb Basin. Trails originating from the Big Sandy Opening also receive heavy pressure from hikers and backpackers and moderate stock use, with heavy crowds at Big Sandy Lake. The Green River Lakes area receives heavy use from hikers but only light stock use; the tight canyon makes legal campsites scarce before Trail Creek Park. Other trailheads that receive moderate stock use include Willow Creek Guard Station, Boulder Lake, and Scab Creek.

Bridges occur only in places where there is no safe crossing during low-water periods. Elsewhere, fords are the rule, and as a result many trails are impassable until the spring runoff has subsided. (This usually occurs by the second week in July). The highest trails may have snowfields that linger into August, and an ice ax may be required to cross the high passes of the Continental Divide. Wise travelers check at the Pinedale Ranger Station for current trail conditions before setting out. Mosquitoes are present in murderous numbers during the height of summer, and due to the abundance of mountain wetlands found here, visitors are encouraged to carry repellant and perhaps even head nets.

Hunting season begins in mid-September in the Bridger Wilderness, and hikers who visit the range during this season should wear blaze orange at all times. Elk and moose are the primary game species, and blue grouse provide plentiful opportunities for upland bird hunters. Beware of the severe snowstorms common in the Winds from late September onward.

The granite peaks of the Winds offer excellent mountaineering opportunities that rival those of the Tetons. Gannett Peak is such a popular destination for mountaineers that alpinists can expect crowds and little solitude on its routes. Fremont Peak also receives heavy use from mountaineers. Hundreds of other peaks offer mountaineering challenges in a more primitive setting.

There are over 2,300 lakes and ponds in the Bridger Wilderness, and 90 percent have been stocked with trout at some point in time. Some populations have become self-sustaining, while others are supplemented by aerial plantings on a periodic basis. Golden, cutthroat, and rainbow trout commonly attain record sizes in these rich aquatic environments, while brook trout tend to become overpopulated and dwarfed by malnutrition in the lakes where they occur. Even remote lakes far from the trail system often have fish.

ACCESS: Major highways follow the Green River along the foot of the Wind River Range, and from these a series of all-weather, gravel roads runs eastward into the mountains. These roads are passable to most vehicles, although they are prone to potholes and washboards. The road to Elkhart Park, which leads

One of the Firehole Lakes, typical of the Fremont Shelf country.

from Pinedale past Fremont Lake to a trailhead high on the forelands, is paved. In the southern marches of the range, long drives on gravel roads are necessary to reach the Big Sandy Opening and Little Sandy Creek Trailheads.

Multi-Day Backpack or Horse Trip

Dream Lake—Boulder Canyon

Distance: 26.0 miles total.
Difficulty: Moderate.
Starting and maximum elevation: 8,200 feet, 9,940 feet.
Topo map: Scab Creek, Raid Lake, Halls Mountain, Horseshoe Lake.
Getting there: To reach the Scab Creek Trailhead, take U.S. Highway 191 to Boulder, then drive east on Wyoming 353. After 6.5 miles, turn left on Scab Creek Road. It is a wide gravel thoroughfare at first, but at mile 1.4 you will bear left onto a lesser, somewhat bumpy road (marked "Scab Creek Campground"). This road leads 7 miles north and then east to reach the Scab Creek Trailhead just before the campground. For the Granite Canyon Trailhead, drive east from Boulder on Wyoming 353 for 2.4 miles, then turn north on the Boulder Lake Road. This is a good-quality county road up to the National Forest boundary, but is fraught with potholes and washboards beyond it. Drive past Boulder Lake and the guest ranch to reach the trailhead at mile 10.2.

This semi-loop travels along the elevated forelands at the foot of the Wind River Range, visiting numerous lakes and affording views of the high peaks. From the Scab Creek Trailhead, the path climbs steeply up open slopes of sage and bitterbrush, interspersed with aspen clumps. It levels off as a shady vale filled with pines and leads to an old cabin and the entrance to the BLM's Scab Creek WSA. A second grade leads upward through the granite to reach the top of the wooded shelf that stretches along the base of the high peaks.

The next 8 miles is an up-and-down journey among granite knobs, through stands of lodgepole and spruce, and past grassy glades and marshy lakes. Bear left as the route runs around the north shore of Little Divide Lake; the vast spread of Divide Lake lies just to the south. The trail surmounts the next minor divide to gain the first glimpse of the high peaks, then descends to the rockbound Lightning Lakes. More ups and downs lead to the valley of South Boulder Creek, where vast meadows lead east toward the jagged summits of Mount Bonneville and Raid Peak. A broad stretch of crags is now visible to the north.

Follow signs for Dream Lake as our trail splits away from the Scab Creek trail and crosses the South Fork. It winds among the outcrops to reach Dream Lake, at the north end of broad pastures that are a summer range for domestic sheep. From the signpost at the foot of the lake, hike northeast, following cairns across the open grassland. The route crosses a major trail, then descends into the trees where it gathers into a footpath that follows a small brook down to Junction Lake. The trail skirts the rocky highlands north of this marshy lake, then makes a knee-deep ford of Middle Boulder Creek. It then visits the north shore of the lake for views of the peaks.

A rift in the granite leads to Full Moon Lake with its rocky islands. The trail then climbs over lofty domes to reach the Firehole Lakes. The path crosses Pipestone Creek at the foot of rockbound Vera Lake, then turns west to traverse out over its yawning chasm. The trail descends among steep mounds of granite, passing through stony gaps on the way down to Dugway Lake. A bridge spans the North Fork of Boulder Creek in its granite gorge below the lake, and the trail descends along the cataracts of North Fork Falls. The grade eases as the other forks of Boulder Creek join in.

Glassy pools and runs alternate with boulder-choked cascades as the trail descends into a bottomland forest of spruce. The arid slopes above are populated by aspen, Douglas fir, and juniper. The trail ultimately passes behind a granite summit to visit a swampy lake, then tracks the sagebrush bottoms to the first of three bridges over Boulder Creek. Follow signs for the trailhead and campground as the trail bypasses the Boulder Lake Ranch to reach its terminus.

Multi-Day Backpack

New Fork—Doubletop Mountain

Distance: 29.5 miles overall.
Difficulty: Moderately strenuous.
Starting and maximum elevation: 8,200 feet, 10,840 feet.
Topo map: New Fork Lakes, Kendall Mountain, Squaretop Mountain, Gannett Peak, Fremont Lake North.
Getting there: Drive west from Pinedale on U.S. Highway 191, then turning north on Wyoming 352. After 14.3 miles, turn right on the New Fork Lakes Road and follow it around the north shore of the lake to reach the trailhead at its terminus.

This long loop travels to the windswept tundra at the north end of the Wind River Range, providing spectacular views of Gannett Peak and other lofty summits. From the New Fork Trailhead, the hike begins by passing Upper New Fork Lake, staying inland among the aspens. Halfway up the lake, it surmounts an old moraine for views of the water and New Fork Canyon to the east. The trail soon courses up this broad canyon, flanked by big walls and towering spires. The trail alternates between shallow grades and level stretches as it passes above beaver ponds and small granite gorges carved out by the New Fork River.

Patches of lodgepole give way to burned-over slopes as the river approaches its great northward bend. Here, the trail makes two shallow fords before proceeding into the long and spruce-dotted meadows of New Fork Park. The jagged pinnacles of Dome Peak now soar to the west, and ahead is the impressive face of granite that guards the mouth of Palmer Canyon.

At the head of New Fork Park, the path crosses Dodge Creek, meets the Palmer Lake Trail, then zigzags up a finger ridge to the north of Dodge Creek. After a long ascent, follow the trail to Clark Lake as it splits away from the Porcupine Pass route and traverses across steep mountainsides. It soon switchbacks upward beside the foaming tumult of a tributary stream, yielding aerial views of New Fork Park and the cliffs that guard it. Ultimately the trail enters a hanging valley, all broken granite and timberline meadows. It follows the brook upward, then climbs east through a high gap that yields the first views of the peaks along the Continental Divide.

The path dips down across the headwaters basin of the New Fork, visiting Lozier Lakes on its way to a high pass that leads to the Green River valley. From these heights, a jaw-dropping panorama of jagged peaks crowds the horizon, stretching from the fan-shaped crest of Gannett Peak to the sawtooth crags of Brimstone Mountain. The trail zigzags down to Clark Lake, filled with brook trout but lacking a legal campsite. It then follows the outlet stream down to Trail Creek Park, where the route turns right to run south on the Green River Trail.

Gannett Peak (left distant) and other high peaks along the crest of the Wind River Range.

This path leads up Trail Creek through a forest of ancient spruce and a marked spur path makes an optional side trip to Vista Pass for close-up views of the high peaks. The main trail continues up the valley, following timberline meadows to the windswept tundra of Green River Pass. Two shallow meres lie atop the divide, and beyond them is Summit Lake. Turn right at the first marked junction to acquire the Doubletop Mountain Trail.

This footpath climbs westward between granite domes, linking a series of alpine lakes via low gaps in the bedrock. Swards of wildflowers bloom beside sparkling brooks, and to the east are occasional glimpses of the crags. After passing the Cutthroat Lakes, the path descends into lush parks where spruce and whitebark pine stand guard over meadows and marshy ponds. The trail bottoms out at the foot of Palmer Lake, which is guarded by bulky granite faces and offers views of the Dome Peak cliffs beyond New Fork Canyon.

Climb the grassy benches on the far side, then turn south briefly to spot the western leg of the Doubletop trail as it climbs southwest across grassy slopes. High on the shoulder of Doubletop Mountain, look east for the most extensive panorama of high peaks on the hike. The trail then winds across moun-

New Fork Canyon.

taintop grasslands with long westward views toward the Gros Ventre and Wyoming ranges. At the second junction with the Bluff Creek Trail, a grassy gap offers an easy side trip to the rim of New Fork Canyon.

The main trail tops a final rise, then descends along grassy alleyways between the outcrops. Rainbow Lake marks the upper limit of the forest, beyond which the trail follows Willow Creek downward. It ultimately swings northwest to seek the ridgetop, then drops off the south side of the ridge to reach a junction in an aspen-lined meadow. Turn right and climb through a clearcut to surmount the ridge and make the long descent to the ford at the head of the New Fork Lakes.

Popo Agie Wilderness

Location: 15 miles west of Lander.
Size: 187,431 acres.
Administration: Shoshone National Forest (Washakie District).
Management status: Popo Agie Wilderness (101,991 acres), unprotected roadless lands (85,440 acres).
Ecosystem: Douglas fir forest, lodgepole pine, western spruce-fir forest, with whitebark pine parklands at timberline.
Elevation range: 7,380 feet to 13,192 feet.
System trails: 135 miles.
Maximum core to perimeter distance: 6.6 miles.
Activities: Hiking, backpacking, horseback riding, fishing, hunting, mountaineering, rock climbing.
Best season: July–early September.
Maps: Shoshone National Forest South Map, *Earthwalk Wind River South*, *Handymaps Wind River*. See map on page 125.

TRAVELERS ADVISORY
ALTITUDE SICKNESS, SUDDEN STORMS

The Popo Agie Wilderness covers the southeastern corner of the Wind River Range, including the headwaters of the Popo Agie, Little Popo Agie, and Little Wind rivers. *Popo Agie* (pronounced po-PO-zhyuh) means "head of the river" in the Shoshone dialect. It derives from the fact that the Popo Agie River sinks into a subterranean passage in the foothills of the range, only to emerge again in a swirling pool known as "the Rise," just downstream. The high country of the Popo Agie was a well-known trapping ground of the early mountain men, and a fur rendezvous was held along the banks of the Popo Agie in 1829.

Foothills of weathered granite form the outer cordillera of the range, while soaring spires and cliffs guard the Continental Divide. This side of the range also saw extensive glaciation during the Pleistocene, and the ice carved out horn peaks, aretes, and vertical walls from the granitic rocks at the core of the range. Large lakes lie against the divide, occupying the rock basins and cirques carved out by the ice. Most of the Popo Agie Wilderness lies near or above timberline.

The woodlands of the Popo Agie are the legacy of a natural cycle of wildfire that has been going for thousands of years. The skirts of the peaks are wooded in a lodgepole pine forest, while at the timberline the whitebark pine is the dominant tree. Whitebark and lodgepole pines require low-intensity wildfires to clear the soil of debris so that their seedlings can take root. Sometimes whitebark seedlings get their start in buried caches forgotten by squirrels. In addition to elk and mule deer, the wilderness is home to the Temple Peak herd of bighorn sheep. Alpine areas are home to abundant pikas and marmots, which in turn attract raptors.

RECREATIONAL USES: The Stough Lakes basin receives heavy visitor pressure, and the Cirque of the Towers and Lonesome Lake have received such heavy use in recent years that special restrictions may soon be implemented. As it is, all campers must pitch their tents at least 200 feet from trails, lakeshores, or streams. Fords are required at many of the major stream crossings, and some trails will be impassable during the spring runoff. Backpackers should note that the Forest Service ranger station in Lander has a few bear-resistant food containers to lend to visitors who will be camping in the Popo Agie Wilderness.

Each summer, nearby Lander is the site of an international climber's festival. The big walls and towering peaks found in the Popo Agie country offer some of the best face climbing and mountaineering in the Rockies, and rival that of Yosemite. Climbs typically require at least a day of approach hiking, and the remote wilderness character of the area makes rescue a self-help proposition.

ACCESS: There are 2 primary arteries that provide access to the Popo Agie Wilderness. The Sinks Canyon-Louis Lake Road (FR 300) runs from Lander to the high country, and ultimately joins Wyoming 28 near South Pass. It accesses the Worthen Meadow Reservoir, Popo Agie River, and Fiddlers Lake Trailheads. The Dickinson Park Road begins at the south end of Fort Washakie and climbs to the Dickinson Park Trailhead, just outside the Wind River Indian Reservation. Both gravel roads are suitable for passenger cars, but are prone to potholes.

Day Hike

Silas Canyon

Distance: 3.3 to 5.0 miles one way.
Difficulty: Moderate.
Starting and maximum elevation: 9,420 feet, 10,600 feet.
Topo maps: Cony Mountain, Christina Lake.
Getting there: From Lander, drive west on Wyoming 131, following signs for Sinks Canyon. The pavement ends after 9 miles, becoming FR 300, a good gravel trunk road. Follow it up a major grade and then westward for 19 miles to reach the trailhead just beyond Fiddlers Lake Campground.

Big granite faces above Smith Lake.

Island Lake.

This trail offers a quick route to several alpine lakes at the south end of the Wind River Range. The hike begins on the Christine Lake Trail, which runs past the shore of Fiddlers Lake. After an old spur trail from the campground joins in, the path runs southwest to cross Fiddlers Creek. The rolling bench country found here is dotted with granite outcrops and boulders, and robed in a woodland of lodgepole pine. The trail winds past kettle ponds and wet meadows where former lakes have silted in.

After 1.5 miles, turn right onto the Silas Canyon Trail, which climbs into the Popo Agie Wilderness via a wooded finger ridge. Upon reaching Silas Creek, a spur path descends southward into the wooded basin of Lower Silas Lake. Turn right as our route makes a rocky stream crossing that poses a barrier for most horsemen. The path continues up the increasingly rocky ridgetop as the lodgepoles give way to the multiple trunks of whitebark pines. The country ultimately levels off as streamside meadows of wildflowers and willows border the meandering watercourse.

Trail maintenance ends at Upper Silas Lake, at the base of a granite spur of Roaring Fork Mountain. A primitive footpath continues upward into Silas Canyon, a deep and glacier-carved trough guarded by craggy cliffs. A modest ascent through timberline woodlands and across bands of bedrock leads to Island Lake, with its rocky peninsulas and large cutthroat trout. From here, you can make off-trail excursions across the durable granite surface to reach the cirque lakes at the head of the basin.

Backpack

Bears Ears Trail

Distance: 11.3 to 14.4 miles one way.
Difficulty: Moderately strenuous.
Starting and maximum elevation: 9,300 feet, 11,900 feet.
Topo maps: Dickinson Park, Lizard Head Peak.
Getting there: From the south end of Fort Washakie, drive west from the Wind River Trading Post on Trout Creek Road. The pavement ends after 5 miles; then swing right onto a gravel trunk road, following signs for Moccasin Lake. Stay right at the next junction to climb the long grade up the foothills. After a total of 19 miles, turn left as the road to Dickinson Park splits away from the Moccasin Lake road. Drive 1.5 miles through Dickinson Park, then turn right at the ranger station and follow the rocky road to the trailhead.

This trail starts high and climbs even higher over a divide that offers expansive views of the Wind River Range, then descends to the headwaters of the Little Wind River to visit several subalpine lakes. From Dickinson Park, the trek begins with a slow climb through the forest, first lodgepole and then whitebark pine, as the path seeks a ridgetop of granite outcrops. The trees fall away altogether in a high alpine basin, and great tors of rock rise from the surrounding ridges. The trail soon turns north to cross a pass and contours high around the headwaters of Ranger Creek for views of Funnel Lake.

After Adams Pass leads into the Sand Creek valley, Bears Ears Mountain and the pyramid of Mount Chauvenet rise to the west, while to the north are massive and nameless domes of granite. Broken rock and patches of tundra lead to the nameless divide at the valley's head, where eye-popping views of the sawtooth crags and the Little Wind valley stretch away to the west. Grave Lake is guarded by sharp horns to the north, while Washakie Lake is nestled between half domes farther south.

The trail now climbs across high and windswept country, mostly exposed bedrock. It soon turns south, ultimately navigating through a gap in the formation to descend to a low pass. A deep chasm drops away to the east, while the trail descends westward along an alpine valley. It passes Little Valentine Lake in an open pocket, then skirts onto steep, south-facing slopes as the first whitebark pines crop up. After 11.3 miles, the trail bottoms out at Valentine Lake, a large mere that reflects the distant glacier on Camels Hump.

Looking across the Little Wind basin at Grave Lake and the high peaks of the Continental Divide.

After crossing the outlet stream, the path descends across a lateral moraine. It passes through Ranger Park, a boulder-dotted meadow on a high shelf, before dropping to the valley floor. A knee-deep ford of the Little Wind River leads to the Washakie trail; turn left for a brief climb through spruce groves and timberline meadows to reach Washakie Lake at the 13.7-mile mark. This lake occupies a broad basin flanked by sheer cliffs and jagged peaks. It offers good fishing along with the neighboring lakes to the west, and Macon Lake, 0.7 miles farther, also yields views of the Washakie Glacier.

Fitzpatrick Wilderness   **20**

Location: 5 miles southwest of Dubois.
Size: 199,012 acres.
Administration: Shoshone National Forest (Wind River District).
Management status: Fitzpatrick Wilderness (198,525 acres), Whiskey Mountain
Wilderness Study Area (487 acres).
Ecosystem: Douglas fir forest, western spruce-fir forest, with whitebark pine parks and
open tundra at timberline.
Elevation range: 7,550 feet to 13,804 feet.
System trails: 105 miles.
Maximum core to perimeter distance: 12.8 miles.
Activities: Hiking, backpacking, horseback riding, hunting, fishing, mountaineering, wildlife
viewing.
Best season: Late June–mid-September.
Maps: Shoshone National Forest South Map, *Earthwalk Wind River North, Handymaps Wind
River*. See map on page 125.

TRAVELERS ADVISORY:
SUDDEN STORMS

The Fitzpatrick Wilderness covers the northeastern corner of the Wind River
Range. Here, sedimentary reefs hide an interior fortress of glacier-carved granite peaks and sparkling lakes. There are 44 active glaciers in the Fitzpatrick
Wilderness. The largest is the Dinwoody Glacier, with a surface area of over
1,200 acres (almost 2 square miles). The scenery is as striking as anywhere in
the range. Its comparatively few trails make off-trail mountaineering in the
Fitzpatrick Wilderness a rewarding experience.

The first white explorers to explore the northern Rockies found the Wind
River Basin occupied by the Shoshone tribe. The Shoshone were closely relat-
ed to the Paiute Indians of the Great Basin deserts, and migrated north and
east from their ancestral homeland in Death Valley between 1200 and 1800
A.D. Before the arrival of the Shoshone, the foothills of the Wind Rivers were
the home of other indigenous hunter-gatherers with a history of continuous
habitation going back to 10,000 years before the present. During the early
years of western exploration, the Wind River Basin was a hunting ground
much prized by the Shoshone, Crow, and Blackfoot tribes, spurring a series of

bloody battles that took place between them. The foothills that border the Fitzpatrick Wilderness bear hundreds of petroglyphs that date from the first years of white exploration in the region.

Wyoming's largest herd of bighorn sheep summers in the high meadows of the Fitzpatrick Wilderness and winters along the grassy slopes of Whiskey Mountain to the southeast of the wilderness boundary. The herd numbers around 1,000 head, and serves as a reservoir for bighorn sheep reintroduction efforts throughout the Rocky Mountains. The Fitzpatrick Wilderness has special enabling legislation that allows the use of motorized equipment inside wilderness boundaries for the enhancement of sheep habitat. Lands along the southeastern boundary of the Fitzpatrick Wilderness were closed to mineral leasing in 1970 in order to protect bighorn habitat.

The rutting season for bighorns runs from late November into December. This is the best time to view and photograph the sheep, which can be found above Trail Lake, on BLM Ridge, and on the slopes above the Jakeys Fork. View the sheep from a distance using binoculars, spotting scopes, and telephoto lenses to avoid disturbing them during this sensitive time of year. The Foundation for North American Wild Sheep staffs a full-scale visitor center in the town of Dubois, where detailed information on the latest sheep movements and population status can be found.

The Whiskey Mountain Wilderness Study Area encompasses a little more than one square mile of BLM land along the southern boundary of the Fitzpatrick Wilderness. Over 900 head of bighorn sheep winter on the slopes of Whiskey Mountain. Sheep are most commonly spotted above Trail Lake and above the mouth of Jakeys Creek. Stands of whitebark pine were once present here, but they burned during 1931 when a wildfire coursed across the slopes of Whiskey Mountain. In the wake of the blaze, the open grasslands became accessible to the sheep, which used the area to move between vast pastures. Some horse-based logging has been proposed for this area in order to open up the woodlands and maintain the migration corridors. The Whiskey Mountain WSA has not been recommended for wilderness status by the BLM.

RECREATIONAL USES: The Dinwoody Glacier Trail is the main route into the Fitzpatrick backcountry, and it connects to the Bridger Wilderness on the far side of the divide via Dinwoody Pass. As a result, visitor use (both foot and horse) is heavy on this trail. Other trails receive lighter use, and the trail-less reaches of the Fitzpatrick Wilderness also offer good hiking opportunities. If you stay in the backcountry overnight, you must site your camp at least 100 feet from streams, lakeshores, and trails.

ACCESS: The best public access to the Fitzpatrick Wilderness is the Dinwoody Glacier Trailhead. It can be reached via the Whiskey Basin–Trail Lakes Road,

Gjetetind and Ross Lake.

3.5 miles southeast of Dubois. The Dinwoody Creek Trail begins on the Wind River Indian Reservation, and a tribal permit (which comes at a hefty cost) is mandatory to access its trailhead. The upper reaches of this trail do not require a permit, and can be reached by backpackers via the Dinwoody Glacier Trail. The trails to Jakeys Fork begin on private lands owned by the CM Ranch. Hikers must park at the Game & Fish trailhead and walk the road for 2.5 miles to reach this trail.

Day Hike

Whiskey Mountain Loop

Distance: 11.1 miles round trip.
Difficulty: Strenuous.
Starting and maximum elevation: 7,800 feet, 9,540 feet.
Topo maps: Torrey Lake, Simpson Lake.
Getting there: Drive east from Dubois on U.S. Highway 26 for 3.6 miles, then turn right (south) at signs for the Whiskey Mountain Habitat Management Unit. Bear left at the first junction, following a well-built road past Trail Lake and then on to the Dinwoody Glacier Trailhead at the end of the road.

This trail climbs into the high and windswept tundra atop one of the outer peaks of the Fitzpatrick Wilderness. It offers splendid views of the high peaks in the heart of the wilderness and a good chance to spot elk and bighorn sheep. The trail's upper reaches are faint; be prepared to navigate by cairns. The initial ascent is hot and dry; avoid it during the mid-day heat.

The hike starts on the Dinwoody Glacier Trail, which climbs through a folded landscape of glacier-scoured granite. Soon the Whiskey Mountain Trail veers away to the right, climbing steeply across arid slopes. Eventually some Douglas firs provide a bit of shade, and by the top of the grade the subalpine forest is interspersed with sunny glades. Be sure to check your water supply before the trail enters the alpine zone.

Turn right at the junction with the Lake Louise Trail as our route follows the cairns up through the limitless tundra. After cresting a saddle, an old jeep track runs downslope to a much lower pass. Turn left and follow the trail along the timberline to meet the Lake Louise Trail once more. Take a side trip to the lake, or turn left to complete the loop and descend to the starting point.

Dubois Badlands

21

Location: One mile east of Dubois.
Size: 10,553 acres
Administration: BLM (Lander Field Office).
Management status: Dubois Badlands WSA (4,520 acres); unprotected state, BLM, and private lands (6,303 acres).
Ecosystem: Wyoming Basin wheatgrass-needlegrass shrub steppe.
Elevation range: 6,720 feet to 8,179 feet.
System trails: 0.5 mile.
Maximum core to perimeter distance: 1.0 mile.
Activities: Hiking, horseback riding, bird watching, big-game hunting.
Best season: March–June; September–October.
Maps: Mason Draw 1:24,000.

TRAVELERS ADVISORY:
FLASH FLOODS, BAD WATER.

The Dubois Badlands are a maze of colorful sandstone fins and canyons near the headwaters of the Wind River. The badlands have been eroded from the Wind River formation, a series of mudstones and sandstones interbedded with thin sheets of conglomerate, and derived from alluvial stream deposits. These conglomerates are embedded with fossil algae colonies that grew from the sediments of small ponds. The formation dates from 55 million years ago, when the first mammals roamed the continent. The red layers within the badlands are eroded sediments that originally came from the iron-rich Chugwater sandstone, which crops up along the highway just south of the WSA.

The vegetation found here is an arid steppe community of saltbush, greasewood, rabbitbrush, and sagebrush. In the badlands the plants are very sparse, forming a high desert landscape. Threadleaf sedge grows colonially among the shrubs, forming mats that spread outward from a central origin. The rare Dubois milkvetch, a member of the pea family, can also be found here. Above the rims are extensive flats of bunchgrasses, dominated by bluebunch wheatgrass and western wheatgrass. A few scattered limber pines grow along the rims of the buttes. The deeper canyons in the eastern part of the badlands have cottonwoods growing along their washes.

21   DUBOIS BADLANDS

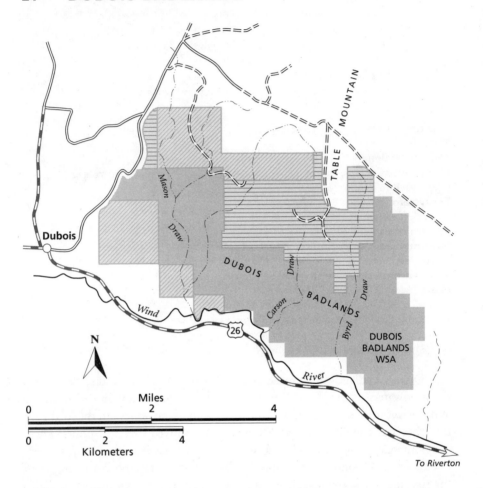

The area provides year-round habitat for a herd of around 50 bighorn sheep. During severe winters, the badlands also offer shelter and forage for elk. Mule deer are permanent residents of the breaks, and antelope are sometimes spotted on the uplands above them. Coyotes and bobcats are common, and the tracks of grizzly bear have been recorded within the badlands during springtime. Although this is a high desert community, rattlesnakes do not inhabit the area. The short-horned lizard (also called the "horned frog") is the badlands' only reptile. Prairie falcons, golden eagles, red-tailed hawks, and American kestrels nest and hunt within the Dubois Badlands. Cliff-nesting swifts and swallows also find suitable nesting habitat among the sheer walls of sandstone.

Although the Dubois Badlands are designated as an Area of Critical Environmental Concern, the area has not been recommended for wilderness by the

BLM. The Dubois Arch, a known producer of oil, is not far distant from the wilderness study area, and the area is thought to have moderate potential for oil and gas development. Several abandoned wells within 2 miles of the WSA have had shows of oil from the Phosphoria formation. Because of the special designation that already exists, oil and gas development may only occur here with a "no surface occupancy" restriction, which means that future wells and associated roads may not be sited within the badlands.

Perhaps the greatest threat to the Dubois Badlands derives from uncontrolled development along its margins. Subdivisions, the scourge of the American West, are beginning to encroach along the southern boundary of the WSA. The town dump of Dubois is located along the western edge of the WSA, and inconsiderate residents have also dumped trash at random in the surrounding areas. These western reaches of the badlands are also the site of concentrated off-road vehicle activity. Up to the time of this writing, widespread violation of WSA boundaries by off-road vehicles has been an ongoing problem.

RECREATIONAL USES: The proximity of the Dubois Badlands to Yellowstone and Grand Teton National Parks makes them a potential focal point for outdoor recreation on a national scale. With the exception of a nature trail at the western edge of the WSA, the Dubois Badlands have no official trails. In the gentler country surrounding Mason Draw, a number of impromptu horse trails and game tracks make for easy traveling along the watercourses, which are linked by low saddles. Hikers should note that domestic cattle graze in Mason Draw during the spring months.

There is no surface water in the badlands, so visitors will need to carry a sufficient supply of drinking water. Clay pans in the soil lead to high levels of surface runoff, and as a result, flash floods are common in the Dubois badlands. Make your exit quickly if you sense that a cloudburst is on its way. Hiking is difficult following a rainstorm, as the clay soils found in some locales turn into sucking mud. At the eastern end of the WSA, the landscape is typified by steeper country and narrow canyons, where tall ledges and pour-offs often block passage.

A limited drawing hunt for bighorn sheep has produced several trophy rams over the past years. Mule deer also are found in the badlands, although they do not receive much attention from hunters.

ACCESS: A county road runs east from Dubois, traveling along the western edge of the roadless area. From it, jeep trails descend eastward toward the badlands. Gravel roads also access Table Mountain at the northern edge of the badlands, but private lands block all public access, and landowner permission is required to visit this area.

Buttes and window rocks above Mason Draw.

Day Hike

Mason Draw

Distance: 5.0 miles round trip.
Difficulty: Easy.
Starting and minimum elevation: 7,300 feet, 6,920 feet.
Topo map: Mason Draw.
Getting there: From the crossroads at the center of downtown Dubois, leave the highway and drive east on the main street. It soon bends north; just after the bend, turn right on Marciana Street and continue to follow the broadest route as it zigzags up to the base of an escarpment. It soon becomes a county road that climbs to the top of the scarp, passing a water tower and then a spur road to the town dump. Drive straight ahead here, following the main road another 2 miles. Turn right at the first primitive road, which descends 0.7 mile to reach the dry wash of Mason Draw.

This route follows horse trails down the major wash that drains the western end of the badlands. Begin the hike by following the wash down Mason Draw through arid and rolling hills. The orange and buff bedrock rises through the dun-colored vegetation in places, but the truly dramatic formations will appear to the east of the draw: window rocks, fins, and monoliths of banded siltstone or massive sandstone. As the cottonwoods that flank the Wind River appear ahead, watch for a trail that runs east through a low gap beside the badlands. This path leads to the east branch of Mason Draw. Follow the streamcourse downward as tall breaks rise to the east. As you approach the suburban sprawl of Dubois, turn west and cross the ridge at a low spot, then follow the main wash of Mason Draw up past fretted cliffs and back to your vehicle.

Banded breaks above Byrd Draw.

One view of Bighorn Basin.

4

Bighorn Basin

The hinterlands of the Bighorn Basin are filled with desert badlands. The scorching heat of summer and the lack of surface water have protected these areas from human settlement, and the rugged terrain and erosive bedrock are quick to reclaim roadways. The Bighorn Basin badlands are home to a cold desert ecosystem not currently represented in the national wilderness system. A number of BLM wilderness study areas found here have excellent wilderness potential.

Some 52 million years ago, volcanic eruptions in the Absaroka Range carpeted northern Wyoming with a thick layer of rhyolite ash. Runoff and swift-flowing streams carried the ash down from the mountains and deposited it in the Bighorn Basin to form the Willwood formation. During this time, aprons of volcanic debris filled the basin completely, sometimes attaining a depth of 3,000 feet. Modern uplifts have elevated the Willwood formation, and now it forms the highest points in the Bighorn Basin. Exposed to wind and water, the banded sediments erode rapidly. The elements are constantly sculpting this friable layer into spires, buttes, and canyons, forming the clay badlands for which the region is noted.

During Pleistocene times, the Bighorn Basin was filled with a windswept steppe that was underlain by permafrost. Conditions must have been similar to those found in modern Siberia, with subterranean ice wedges pushing up polygonal hummocks in the treeless tundra. A suite of exotic mammals roamed the steppes, including woolly mammoth, steppe bison, camels, and cave lions. Prehistoric man arrived in the Bighorn Basin about 12,000 years ago, and the area has been a focal point for human activity ever since.

Access to the more remote quarters of the Bighorn Basin has always been a dubious proposition. Graded gravel roads built to supply oilfields and pipelines have high clay content and turn into a slippery and deep gumbo when wet. Secondary roads and jeep trails have the tendency to wash out as the wilderness reclaims its own. The best time to visit is in the cooler months of spring and fall. If rain threatens, get to the pavement immediately or plan on staying put for a while.

Bighorn Canyon National Recreation Area

22

Location: 15 miles northeast of Lovell.
Size: 17,920 acres.
Administration: National Park Service, Bureau of Land Management (Cody Resource Area), Crow Tribe.
Management status: Roadless backcountry managed by NPS (9,600 acres), BLM (2,560 acres), and Crow Tribe (5,760 acres). Motorboats currently allowed on Bighorn Lake.
Ecosystem: Wyoming Basin sagebrush steppe.
Elevation range: 3,610 feet to 4,593 feet.
System trails: None.
Maximum core to perimeter distance: 0.8 mile.
Activities: Hiking, canoeing, spelunking, scuba diving, fishing.
Best season: April–October.
Maps: Bighorn Canyon N.R.A. map; Powell and Bridger 1:100,000.

TRAVELERS ADVISORY:
RATTLESNAKES

The wild and treacherous canyon of the Bighorn River was originally impassable to human visitors. The Bad Pass Trail was originally blazed 10,000 years ago by indigenous hunter-gatherers to bypass the canyon above its western rim. It was later used by fur trappers to pack their goods around Bighorn Canyon. Fur trader Charles Laroque was the first white explorer to visit the region when he met the Crow Indians at the mouth of Bighorn Canyon in 1805.

Bighorn Lake was created in 1968 with the construction of Yellowtail Dam in Montana. This reservoir is 71 miles long, stretching through the entire length of Bighorn Canyon. The fact that the lake level approximates the river course through the wilds of upper Bighorn Canyon lends an essentially wild and pristine character to this awe-inspiring landscape. The reach of the canyon between Horseshoe Bend and Barry's Landing retains its wild and untamed character.

The Pryor Mountain Wild Horse Range borders the area to the west, where a herd of 120 feral horses roam free on BLM lands. Bighorn sheep ply the upper reaches of the canyon and are commonly spotted by waterborne travelers. The side canyons are home to mule deer and black bears, and elk winter here as well. Peregrine falcons have been reintroduced in Bighorn Canyon, and a number of other raptors also find nesting habitat among the sheer cliffs and

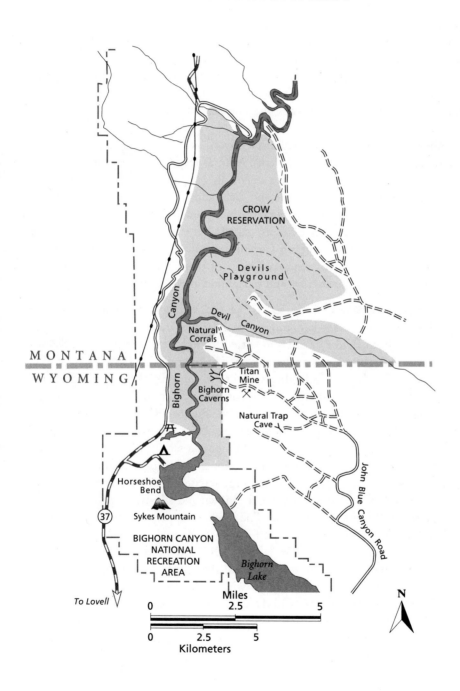

CROW
RESERVATION

Devils
Playground

Canyon

Devil Canyon

Natural
Corrals

MONTANA
WYOMING

Bighorn

Titan
Mine

Bighorn
Caverns

Natural Trap
Cave

John Blue Canyon Road

Horseshoe
Bend

37

Sykes Mountain

BIGHORN CANYON
NATIONAL
RECREATION
AREA

Bighorn
Lake

To Lovell

N

Miles
0   2.5   5

0   2.5   5
Kilometers

towering pinnacles. Numerous species of waterfowl can be found on the waters of Bighorn Lake.

The wild character in the upper reaches of the canyon is well worth preserving. It would be beneficial for the Park Service to designate Bighorn Lake south of Horseshoe Bend and Bighorn Canyon north of Barry's Landing as motorboat areas, and allow the stretch of canyon between them be designated nonmotorized. Navigation markers could be removed along this stretch, since they offer no advantage to visitors who can read a map. These steps would minimize conflicts between users and enhance the opportunity for primitive recreation in the canyon.

Above the eastern rim of Bighorn Canyon, near its confluence with Devil Canyon, is a suite of limestone caverns. Natural Trap Cave is a vertical sinkhole in the limestone that has become a major dig for paleontologists. Many Pleistocene mammals fell into the hole and died, and their remains have become a paleontological treasure chest. Among the bones are the remains of woolly mammoth, steppe bison, primitive horses, camels, American lion, and dire wolves. Horsethief Cave and the Bighorn Caverns system are thought to have over 10 miles of interconnected passageways, most of them unexplored. They feature dripstone features like stalactites and stalagmites as well as crystal growths.

RECREATIONAL USES: Water sports are the highlight of Bighorn Canyon N.R.A. Canoeing and sea kayaking are popular pastimes on the lake. The still waters of Bighorn Reservoir offer no current to fight, but afternoon winds can be an issue at the upper end of the canyon. The reservoir is a favorite haunt of a small cadre of freshwater scuba divers, and snorkeling can also be rewarding. Be prepared to share the water with motorboats and jet skis on the weekends. Drift logs brought down from the mountains by the Bighorn River are a common occurrence in Bighorn Reservoir. These logs may be so waterlogged that they float invisibly below the surface. These drift logs pose a serious threat to waterskiers and boat propellers, and as a result the National Park Service recommends that all motor boaters carry spare propellers and exercise extreme caution.

Anglers will find big-water fishing for brown and lake trout, perch, crappie, catfish, sauger, burbot, and walleye. The canyon's upper reaches are also noted for ice fishing in winter. Fly fishing for trout is possible in areas where clear-flowing tributaries empty into the lake, which is often turbid. Be sure that you have the fishing license for the appropriate state. Inside Bighorn Canyon, the border is marked from both directions with signs.

The rims above Bighorn and Devil Canyons are well suited to cross-country hiking through the high desert scrub. Elevation changes are minimal, but sheer drop offs at the overlook points are a hazard. Boaters who venture to the mouth of Devil Canyon will find that it is possible to bushwhack up the

Limestone butte reflected in the still waters of Devil Canyon.

Looking into Devil Canyon from the rims.

bottoms of this canyon for many miles, until the canyon enters National Forest lands at the Wyoming border. Spelunkers who want to explore Horsethief Cave and Bighorn Caverns require a special permit that can be obtained at the BLM office in Cody. Natural Trap Cave is open only to researchers.

The park headquarters can be found just east of Powell on US Alternate 14. There is a toll station on the access road that runs along the western side of the reservoir. A "user fee" is required of all visitors, and the Golden Eagle Pass is not accepted for admittance. This entrance charge covers all boat launching and campground fees. There is no fee in effect for the eastern side of the reservoir at this time.

ACCESS: A paved road runs north from US 14A along the west side of the reservoir and then above the canyon rims. It allows access to the boat launches at Horseshoe Bend and Barry's Landing along the way. The John Blue Canyon Road follows the east side of the reservoir. This rough gravel trunk road soon climbs into the uplands, accessing the jeep roads that visit Devils Canyon, the Natural Corrals, and nearby caves.

One-Day Paddle by Canoe or Sea Kayak

Devil Canyon Paddle

Distance: 6.8 miles one way.
Difficulty: Moderate.
Topo maps: Natural Trap Cave, Sykes Spring, Hillsboro.
Getting there: From Lovell, drive east on US 14A for 3 miles, then turn north on Wyoming 37, followings signs for Bighorn Canyon N.R.A. This paved highway leads about 9 miles to the turnoff for the Horseshoe Bend campground. Begin from the Horseshoe Bend boat launch.

This trip follows the narrows of the Bighorn Canyon as far as the mouth of Devil Canyon, providing a breathtaking day of paddling among towering walls and pinnacles. From the Horseshoe Bend boat ramp, turn away from the red sandstone buttes and follow the bayshore east toward the old river channel. As you turn north, low walls of limestone rise on either side, pocked with caves, grottoes, and slot canyons. With northward progress, the walls rise hundreds of feet above the water, the limestone stained red in places by oxidized iron that has seeped down from the overlying strata. By the time you reach the Montana border, the cliffs tower 1,000 feet overhead.

The Natural Corrals are now visible ahead, a low gap in the eastern wall of the canyon. This unique geological feature was carved by the Bighorn River early in the uplift; later, the river cut a new channel, eroding deeply

The collared pika is a common resident of talus slopes and boulder fields.

into the bedrock and leaving the shallow canyons of the Natural Corrals high on the rim of the main canyon. A long and looping oxbow leads to the mouth of Devil Canyon, equally deep but narrower than Bighorn Canyon. You can paddle up Devil Canyon for 1.5 miles, enjoying views of isolated pinnacles, craggy buttes, and towering walls all the while. Upon reaching the clear-flowing waters of Porcupine Creek, turn around and retrace your route to complete the trip.

McCullough Peaks

23

Location: 10 miles east of Cody and 8 miles south of Powell.
Size: 54,000 acres.
Administration: Bureau of Land Management (Cody Field Office).
Management status: McCullough Peaks WSA (25,210 acres); unprotected roadless lands (28,790 acres).
Ecosystem: Wyoming Basin Province, sagebrush steppe and wheatgrass-needlegrass shrub steppe.
Elevation range: 4,395 feet to 6,546 feet.
System trails: None.
Maximum core to perimeter distance: 2.7 miles
Activities: Hiking, horseback riding, rockhounding, hunting.
Best season: March–June; September–November.
Maps: Powell 1:100,000.

TRAVELERS ADVISORY:
BAD WATER, FLASH FLOODS

The north slope of the McCullough Peaks has been weathered away into a spectacular maze of buttes and canyons. The badlands are comprised of volcanic ash beds of the Willwood formation that are 2,800 feet deep. The rock is primarily tan in color but has occasional bands of reddish sediment. The ash layer is interbedded with thin layers of shale that resist erosion and form hoodoos and gooseneck formations. The McCullough Peaks have long been known as an important area for the study of paleontology. Mammal, reptile, and bird fossils have all been found within the strata of the Willwood formation.

Between 300 and 400 mule deer can be found in the McCullough Peaks badlands, and the area is also home to mountain lions, swift fox, and wild horses. Antelope and cottontail rabbits are also common residents at the lower elevations. Nesting birds include prairie falcons, merlins, golden eagles, and sage grouse. Intermittent watercourses have deposited alluvial flats within the badlands, and these have become hidden pastures of grama grass and prickly pear cactus. Some of the major washes have a riparian vegetation of willow and cottonwood.

The National Park Service has identified the badlands of the McCullough Peaks as a potential National Natural Landmark. Human imprints on the

23 MCCULLOUGH PEAKS

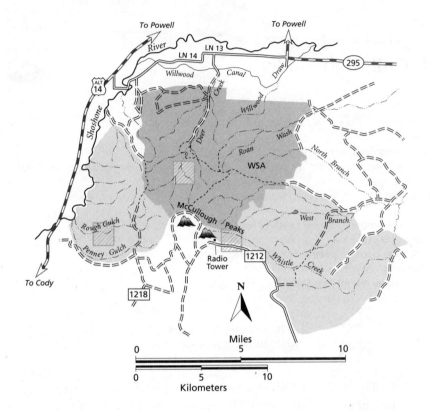

landscape, such as seismograph trails, reservoirs, and drift fences, are small and widely scattered. They do not detract from the pristine character of the badlands. The BLM has recommended only 8,020 acres in the center of the roadless area for wilderness designation. The eastern part of the WSA was not recommended because wilderness designation would disrupt vehicular access to rockhounding sites (this will be appreciated by handicapped rockhounds). The eastern portions are also thought to have a moderate potential for oil and gas production. An estimated 2 billion cubic feet of natural gas and 5,000 barrels of oil may lie beneath the WSA. The potential for subbituminous coal production is low since coal beds are thin and enclosed within shale beds. Roadless areas to the east and west that are both spectacular and pristine were ignored by the BLM study.

RECREATIONAL USE: The WSA receives about 500 visitor days of use annually. Most use comes during the fall and spring and consists of hunters, horsemen, and rockhounds from the local area. The area has outstanding potential for dispersed recreation, and the innumerable draws and canyons could absorb a large number of visitors without losing the feeling of solitude. Although there are only a handful of trails, the badlands are generally conducive to cross-country hiking. Horsemen are advised to stick to the lower, northern fringes of the badlands or established trails to avoid the steep and unstable slopes found in the high breaks.

ACCESS: A series of old BLM roads penetrates the northern reaches of the Mc-Cullough Peaks badlands. Rampant erosion is beginning to take its toll on these roads, and in some places they have become completely impassable. High clearance is a must, and four-wheel drive and strong judgment are recommended. From the south, a good graded road leads to the radio towers atop the McCullough Peaks. Jeep trails that descend down the north side of the escarpment from the crest of the mountains have mostly disappeared and are dangerous to attempt even with an ATV. All gravel roads in this area should be avoided during wet weather.

Day Hike

Deer Creek Overlook

Distance: 2 miles one way.
Difficulty: Moderate.
Starting and maximum elevation: 4,800 feet, 5,200 feet.
Topo maps: Vocation, Ralston.
Getting there: Take US Alternate 14 southwest from Ralston, then turn left (south) on County Road 18. Stay on the pavement as the road becomes Lane 15 and then Lane 14. Some 2.5 miles from the highway, the road bends north and then east; at the next curve, turn right (south) on the unmarked BLM 1211. Follow this pot-holed, fair-weather road 1.6 miles to the first split; bear left and park at the stock tank.

This route leads through the lower badlands to the north of the McCullough Peaks and ends at an overlook of the tall breaks of Deer Creek. From the reservoir, follow the stock trail southward as it tracks a shallow draw. After passing a low wall of hoodoos, the path crosses a gap to enter a grassy basin. Heart Mountain rises far to the west as the path adopts an old jeep trail. It follows a wash through hidden pastures and banded, eroded buttes. The draw ultimately narrows, then splits. Follow the beaten track that climbs the hill between the two ravines. It emerges atop an elevated, grassy shelf and follows the base of the banded slopes to reach a high basin. Hike to the southeast edge of the basin, where a low wall offers an overlook of the eroded valley of Deer Creek, which rises into the weathered breaks that form the north face of the McCullough Peaks.

Badlands near Deer Creek.

Day Hike

Whistle Creek Breaks

Distance: 4.2 miles overall.
Difficulty: Moderately strenuous.
Starting and minimum elevation: 5,472 feet, 4,830 feet.
Topo map: Gilmore Hill.
Getting there: Take US 20 east from the edge of Cody for 17 miles to reach BLM 1212, an unmarked gravel road that runs north from the highway. It runs north for 5 miles to the top of the escarpment, then turns west. Drive over the first hilltop to reach a fence-corner gate at mile 5.8. The hike begins by passing through this gate.

This rugged trek requires some elementary scrambling as well as good map-and-compass skills. After passing through the fence gate, follow a good trail eastward along the fenceline. Views from atop the rims take in a vast maze of eroded buttes and canyons. The trail ultimately descends from the high summits to reach a low shelf guarded by banded walls. Upon reaching the fence gate found here, turn sharply northwest, following a faint horse track through a rounded gap along the rims. It soon turns west, traversing across steep slopes to reach a grassy finger ridge. Follow the trails down this ridgetop to reach the canyon floor far below.

The route now follows the wash eastward until it emerges into an open basin. Turn south here, following a trail along the bases of banded buttes and beneath yellow pinnacles. Continue along the base of the hills as the route bends west, following a grassland shelf above a draw bounded by tabletop mesas. The trail passes an old reservoir, then surmounts several rounded humps before reaching a canyon that leads southward into the hills.

Follow this ravine, which ends up in a steep-sided box canyon. The escape is via game trails that lead up to the more southerly of two notches in the east wall. This notch leads to the grassy basin at the head of the hike's original wash. Contour eastward across the high benches to regain the original horse trail that leads back to the starting point.

Whistle Creek breaks.

Sheep Mountain   24

Location: 25 miles northwest of Worland and 20 miles west of Greybull.
Size: 24,835 acres.
Administration: BLM (Worland Field Office).
Management status: Sheep Mountain WSA (23,690 acres); unprotected roadless lands (1,245 acres).
Ecosystem: Wyoming Basin Province wheatgrass-needlegrass shrub steppe and saltbush-greasewood desert.
Elevation range: 4,400 feet to 5,972 feet.
System trails: None.
Maximum core to perimeter distance: 2.2 miles.
Activities: Hiking, horseback riding, hunting, rockhounding.
Best season: March–May, September–November.
Map: Basin 1:100,000.

TRAVELERS ADVISORY:
BAD WATER, FLASH FLOODS

The Sheep Mountain WSA covers the brightly colored badlands at the eastern end of the Tatman Mountain massif. Deeply dissected, irregular draws fan out in all directions from Sheep Mountain, the highest point in the WSA. Ash and sediment beds belonging to the Willwood and Tatman formations are painted in shades of yellow and orange, interbedded in places with narrow ribbons of white and purple. They border the major draws with crenulated walls, and soar to magnificent heights as you approach the summit of Sheep Mountain. The fossils of Eocene mammals found here include ancestral pigs and tapirs.

The vegetation is a mix of sagebrush, crested wheatgrass, and grama on the rolling uplands, while the badlands and wash bottoms support a sparse vegetation of greasewood, snakeweed, and a few cottonwoods along the wash banks. The area is used by the Tatman Mountain wild horse herd. About 150 mule deer and a handful of antelope may be found in the area, and bighorn sheep may occasionally be sighted. The area is home to strutting grounds for sharp-tailed and sage grouse, and bald eagles are known to roost here during their migrations. Hawks and falcons find nest sites on the high cliffs and pinnacles.

The BLM has failed to recommend any of this area for wilderness. Their rationale that the Sheep Mountain badlands do not contain any significant features

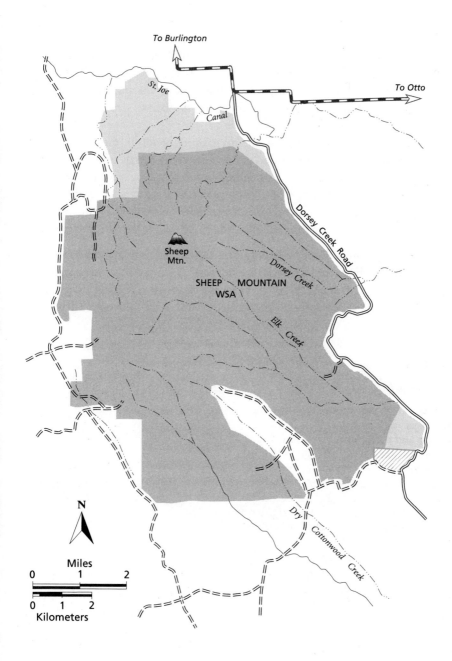

To Burlington

To Otto

St. Joe

Canal

Dorsey Creek Road

Sheep
Mtn.

Dorsey Creek

SHEEP   MOUNTAIN
WSA

Elk Creek

Dry Cottonwood Creek

N

Miles
0   1   2

0   1   2
Kilometers

that would warrant wilderness designation is puzzling. The badlands found here are the most brilliantly colored in Wyoming, the broken terrain offers excellent opportunities for solitude, and the landforms are as spectacular as any existing wilderness in the state. Their BLM's evaluation noted that widely scattered seismograph lines, jeep tracks, abandoned reservoirs, and fencelines did not detract from the area's natural character. Public comments received during the review process overwhelmingly favored wilderness designation. The logical conclusion is that there were back-room politics influencing the BLM's decision that had nothing to do with the public interest.

There is a moderate potential for oil and gas production in the area. An estimated 6 billion cubic feet of natural gas and 100,000 barrels of oil might be recovered. Currently no oil leases are pending in the area. The recommendation of "no wilderness" fits with the BLM's longstanding track record of opposing wilderness in any area where it might interfere with the private profits of corporate interests, and of relegating the interests of the public to a secondary role.

ACCESS: Dorsey Creek Road, a good gravel thoroughfare that links Emblem with Worland via Fifteenmile Creek, provides the best access to this area. The southwestern edge of the WSA also has several roads that provide public access, but these roads are primitive and difficult, even with four-wheel drive.

Day Hike

Dorsey Creek

Distance: 2.2 miles one way.
Difficulty: Easy.
Starting and maximum elevation: 4,360 feet, 4,600 feet.
Topo maps: Wardel Reservoir, Sheep Mountain.
Getting there: Drive south from Emblem on Wyoming 30. After 5.5 miles, the main highway bends west; drive straight ahead on County RD 8. It ultimately bends east, becoming LN 42. It reaches the marked Dorsey Creek Road (BLM 1107) some 4.2 miles from the highway. Follow the fair-weather Dorsey Creek Road southward. After 4 miles it drops to meet the first major wash, which is Dorsey Creek.

This hike wanders through colorful badlands along the edge of the Sheep Mountain WSA. It begins by following an old jeep trail along the canyon's broad floor, passing between painted desert walls eroded by wind and water. The colors intensify as the route passes an old reservoir, and now a stock trail leads upward through the canyon. A low gap soon affords distant views of Sheep Mountain, but the wash swings south into the gullied hills. With upstream progress, the vegetation becomes more lush in the protected pockets of

Sheep Mountain (in distance) and badlands.

the badlands. The desert grassland takes over the slopes as the draw narrows, and now wind-carved pinnacles and goosenecks provide the scenery. The wash ultimately reaches a broad basin where forks converge from the east and west; this is a good turnaround point, as the country ahead grows increasingly drab.

Day Hike or Overnighter on Foot or Horseback

Elk Creek

Distance: 3.5 miles one way.
Difficulty: Easy.
Starting and maximum elevation: 4,390 feet, 4,600 feet.
Topo maps: Wardel Reservoir, Sheep Mountain.
Getting there: Follow the Dorsey Creek Road as in the previous hike. Five miles beyond Dorsey Creek is the wash of Elk Creek, a deep trench that requires high clearance to cross. Park here.

This trip makes a nice leisurely backpack, and making a base camp near the upper basin provides fine opportunities for additional explorations in the badlands. To begin the trip, travel up the broad wash of Elk Creek, which is studded with isolated cottonwoods and guarded by fabulous walls of the painted desert variety. The bottoms offer easy traveling through a sparse growth of desert shrubs, with occasional streambed crossings. After a while, the valley narrows as the channel of Elk Creek snakes its way among rounded hills broken by an occasional outcrop of sandstone. The colorful badlands can still be seen up the side draws, which offer opportunities for further exploration.

Eventually, the main wash breaks out into a long valley flanked by tall buttes, deeply weathered and banded with bright colors. Cottonwoods again rise beside the wash, and the sparse grasslands of the flats make easy traveling. Tatman Mountain's summit can be seen ahead, its gray-green crest rising above the mounting badlands of orange and yellow. You will ultimately reach a major fork. If camping, select an impact-resistant site nearby. The northern fork leads into a circular basin before splitting into many channels that wind into the badlands. The south fork cuts a swath into the tallest of the colorful hills, finally giving out to the east of Tatman Mountain.

Bobcat Draw

25

Location: 10 miles east of Meteetsee.
Size: 29,706 acres.
Administration: BLM (Worland Field Office).
Management status: Bobcat Draw Badlands WSA (17,150 acres plus 1,390 acres of state-owned inholdings); unprotected roadless lands (11,166 acres).
Ecosystem: Wyoming Basin Province, wheatgrass-needlegrass shrub steppe, saltbush-greasewood desert, and sagebrush steppe.
Elevation range: 4,650 feet to 5,620 feet.
System trails: None.
Maximum core to perimeter distance: 2.2 miles.
Activities: Hiking, horseback riding, rockhounding, big game and upland bird hunting, photography.
Best season: March–October.
Map: Basin 1:100,000.

TRAVELERS ADVISORY:
BAD WATER, FLASH FLOODS

Bobcat Draw is home to some of the most extensive desert badlands in Wyoming. Here, the high, rolling grasslands that lead up to the snowy Absarokas fall away steeply into a deeply dissected series of breaks, a maze of cliffs and badlands that rivals Bryce Canyon in grandeur and extent. This painted desert landscape is made up of the Willwood ash beds, splashed with brilliant red, orange, white, tan, and purple. Wind and water have sculpted the rock into fretted cliffs, window rocks, and mushroom-shaped hoodoos. The ash and clay beds are interlayered with thin strata of shale and sandstone that resist erosion and form caprock over the softer ash beds.

The Bobcat Draw badlands have been recognized as an area of national importance in the field of paleontology. Primitive mammal fossils from the early Eocene period have been found in this area. Other vertebrate fossils found here include crocodiles, fishes, and turtles. Plant and invertebrate fossils have also been found here. Bear in mind that vertebrate fossils are protected by federal law, and it is illegal to collect or disturb them.

Along the breaks, deep and narrow gulches wind upward toward the grasslands above the rims. From the heights, visitors gain vast views of the Absaroka

25   BOBCAT DRAW

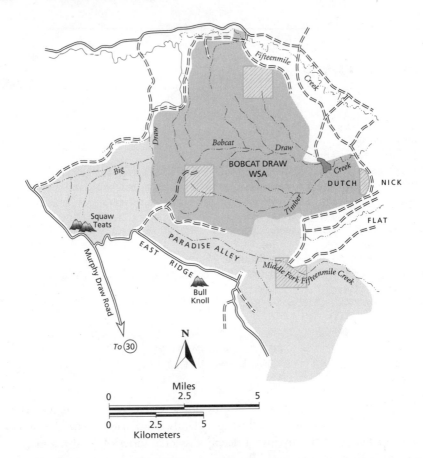

Range to the west and the Big Horn Mountains to the east. Farther to the east and north, a scattering of badland buttes and ridges interrupt the open flats. Bunchgrass and grama are prevalent on the grassy shelves between the badland ridges, and a ragged community of sagebrush and greasewood grows along the breaks and draws.

The Tatman Mountain herd of wild horses ranges throughout the high grasslands above the rims. This herd ranges between 100 and 270 animals, and excess animals are rounded up and auctioned off by the BLM on a 4-year rotation. Below the breaks, the Fifteenmile wild horse herd is managed at a population of about 100 head. The area is also home to about 180 mule deer and around 325 antelope, as well as bobcats, chukars, and burrowing owls.

The BLM has recommended some 18,540 acres of the Bobcat Draw badlands for wilderness status. In addition, the National Park Service has nominated the Gooseberry Badlands and the east ridge of Fifteenmile Creek (along the southern edge of the WSA) as National Natural Landmarks. Evidence of man within the WSA is growing progressively fainter as small reservoirs, fence-lines, and dead-end jeep tracks fall into ruin.

Ranchers currently hold permits to graze sheep within the WSA during winter, but these are the only grazing permits that cover the Bobcat Draw area. There is thought to be a moderate potential for development of about 10 billion cubic feet of natural gas some 20,000 feet below the WSA. Three wells have been drilled in the surrounding areas, and all have been abandoned as dry holes. Recent oil and gas leases have been drawn up for Paradise Alley, and development may proceed there in the near future. There are no existing oil and gas leases within the WSA.

RECREATIONAL USES: Bobcat Draw receives only about 250 visitor days a year. The grassy uplands above the breaks afford easy traveling on foot or horseback, and the rims and peninsulas offer spectacular camping spots. The badlands along Timber Creek and Bobcat Draw are conducive to cross-country hiking, and the flats to the east and north offer no obstacles to cross-country travel. Horsemen will find it safer to approach the breaks from below via one of the primitive roads that border the eastern edge of the WSA.

Although mule deer are not abundant, some trophy bucks are rumored to take residence within the breaks. Antelope are prevalent above the rims and on the low-elevation flats to the east of the breaks. Hunters will find that the broken country of Bobcat Draw furnishes challenging terrain for the chase.

ACCESS: The rims of Bobcat Draw and Timber Creek can be accessed via the Murphy Draw Road, an improved gravel thoroughfare. Farther east, the Platte Pipeline and Dutch Nick roads link up with jeep trails that provide access to the lower badlands of the Bobcat Draw WSA.

Day Hike or Backpack

Bobcat Draw

Distance: 4.6 miles one way.
Difficulty: Moderately strenuous.
Starting and minimum elevation: 5,420 feet, 4,618 feet.
Topo maps: Dead Indian Hill, Dutch Nick Flat NW.
Getting there: From Meteetsee, drive 19 miles south on Wyoming 120, then turn east on Wyoming 431. After 5.7 miles, turn left on Murphy Draw Road. Follow this fair-weather trunk road for 7.6 miles to the base of the Squaw Teats, then turn right (east) on Dutch Nick Road. It drops into a gulch and then climbs to the top of a mesa. After 2.3 miles, Dutch Nick Road veers right as a two-rut road continues straight ahead. Follow this two-track, passable to vehicles with moderate clearance, for 3.2 miles to reach the starting point.

The Bobcat Draw breaks.

This hike descends from the grassy uplands through the massive breaks of Bobcat Draw, then follows the wash out into the badlands of Dutch Nick Flat. Begin by descending from the rolling, grassy ridgetop into the shallow drainage to the north. The traveling is easy at first, but a steep and tricky descent awaits. You must descend along the toe of a steep and eroded ridge to reach the floor of Bobcat Draw. Here in the head of the canyon, steep and dun-colored slopes crowd in, and it will be necessary to alternate between scrambling down the dry wash and traversing onto the vegetated slopes that surround it.

After several miles, the floor of the draw widens enough to accommodate grassy terraces, and now the traveling is easy between eroded walls tinted with pastel shades of red, yellow, and purple. As the wash leaves the highlands behind, the bottoms widen into a broad, grassy plain punctuated by badland buttes and sinuous ridges of deep red and pale green. Window rocks and pillars are commonplace, and side draws entering from the north offer distant views of the high breaks. Eventually, a series of red, chimney-shaped pinnacles appears ahead. These pinnacles make a good destination for the hike.

Red Butte   26

Location: 15 miles northwest of Worland.
Size: 23,500 acres.
Administration: BLM (Worland Field Office).
Management status: Red Butte WSA (11,350 acres); unprotected roadless lands (12,150 acres).
Ecosystem: Wyoming Basin Province saltbush-greasewood and sagebrush steppe.
Elevation range: 4,000 feet to 5,185 feet.
System trails: None.
Maximum core to perimeter distance: 2.2 miles.
Activities: Hiking, horseback riding, geological study, photography, big game hunting.
Best season: March–May; September–November.
Maps: Basin 1:100,000.

TRAVELERS ADVISORY:
BAD WATER, FLASH FLOODS

Red Butte is a tall and eroded summit that rises from the grassy highlands at the head of Fifteenmile Creek. Rugged, colorful badland ridges radiate from its heights toward Elk Creek to the north. Saltbush-grass steppes dominate the high and rolling badlands along the western edge of the roadless area. About 100 mule deer and 50 head of antelope use the Red Butte WSA, providing trophy-hunting opportunities. Mountain lions and bobcats prowl the area, and burrowing owls, ferruginous hawks, and golden eagles are known to nest here. Sage and sharp-tailed grouse have strutting areas in the Red Butte WSA that they use traditionally for mating year after year.

The BLM has failed to recommend any portion of the Red Butte WSA for wilderness status. This decision was based in large part on the small size of the WSA, which was in turn dictated by faulty (or completely lacking) assessments of the status of the roads that surround the area. A major road along Elk Creek is not only impassable today but has disappeared entirely in many places. Cumulative impacts of widely dispersed seismograph trails and jeep roads, fence-lines, and abandoned stock tanks have largely been erased by the rapid erosion of the soft bedrock.

Red Butte has a moderate potential for oil and gas production, and an estimated 4 billion cubic feet of natural gas and 100,000 barrels of oil are thought

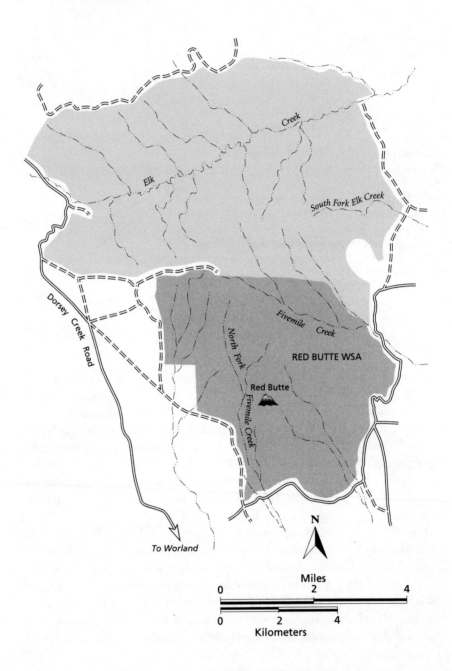

Creek

Elk

South Fork Elk Creek

Dorsey Creek Road

Fivemile Creek

North Fork

RED BUTTE WSA

Red Butte

Fivemile Creek

To Worland

N

Miles
0   2   4

0   2   4
Kilometers

A bushy draw north of Red Butte.

to underlie the area. The Dobie Creek oilfield is 5 miles east of Red Butte, and the Worland anticline is adjacent to the WSA. The WSA is above the deepest structural part of the Bighorn Basin. Three nearby wells were abandoned as dry holes, and there is currently no leasing activity within the WSA. Coal may be present below the WSA at a depth of 4,000 to 5,000 feet, but it is not recoverable using current methods.

RECREATIONAL USE: The Red Butte area receives about 120 visitor days per year, mostly hunters and rockhounds. The Elk Creek corridor is well suited to both hiking and horses, while the badlands leading up to Red Butte offer excellent opportunities for cross-country hiking and scrambling. The badlands contain numerous hidden pockets and remote canyons where visitors can escape from any sign of human activity.

ACCESS: The Dorsey Creek–Fifteenmile Road provides good dry-weather access for all vehicles approaching from Worland. Visitors who approach this road from the north will need high clearance to get across the Elk Creek wash. Only poor-quality jeep roads access the eastern side of the WSA.

Day Hike

Red Butte

Distance: 2.2 miles one way.
Difficulty: Moderate.
Starting and maximum elevation: 4,660 feet, 4,700 feet.
Topo maps: Sucker Dam, Schuster Flats NW.
Getting there: From Worland, drive southwest on US 20. After crossing the Bighorn River at the edge of town, turn right (north) on Wyoming 433. Take an immediate left at signs for the fairground, then follow the Fifteen Mile Road northwest. This broad, gravel road (which turns to deep mud in the rain) leads for about 24 miles to a marked junction with the Dorsey Creek Road. Turn right (north) on this road and drive for 1 mile to reach the crossing of a buried gas pipeline that marks the start of the Red Butte hike.

This hike crosses the tablelands to reach the base of Red Butte. To begin, hike eastward across high desert grasslands dotted with prickly pear and saltbush. Head directly for Red Butte as you cross two shallow drainages and surmount a rolling ridge. Just beyond the next valley, a broad skirt of badlands rises to the base of Red Butte. Select the grassy draw that leads through the low breaks toward Red Butte. When it bends northward, climb onto the tablelands to the east, taking in the eroded ridges of maroon and pale green that flank the main massif. Broken and vegetated country leads through the maze of low mesas; skirt slightly south to cross the North Fork of Fifteenmile Creek and reach the base of Red Butte. Its colored walls rise like sail above the surrounding altiplanos. On the return trip, you will enjoy sweeping views of the high grasslands, punctuated to the northwest by Tatman Mountain, and with the snowy Absarokas on the western horizon.

Day Hike

Red Butte Badlands

Distance: 2 miles one way.
Difficulty: Easy.
Starting and maximum elevation: 4,350 feet, 4,400 feet.
Topo map: Wardel Reservoir.
Getting there: Drive the Dorsey Creek Road north 6.8 miles past the Red Butte starting point, descending into the Elk Creek gulch and turning right on the short jeep road that leads east. The hike starts from the end of this road.

This trek follows the dry canyon of Elk Creek, then ascends a tributary wash into the heart of the badlands. To begin the trek, follow the abandoned jeep

Red Butte.

trail down the north bank of the Elk Creek wash. Its broad bottoms are flanked
on both sides by badlands tinted with orange and yellow. After passing a grove
of cottonwoods, the wash passes through a narrow chokepoint in the eroded
walls. Just beyond it, watch for an inconspicuous draw that leads south beside
high, conical buttes. Follow this wash upward into the badlands to gain excellent views of the taller cliffs that lead eastward to the summit of Red Butte.
Several side draws in this direction offer chances for further exploration. The
main wash continues upward along the edge of the uplands, passing through
low but eroded breaks punctuated by hoodoos. The draw ultimately splits up
to disappear into a maze of hills.

Alkali Creek   27

Location: 10 miles north of Hyattville.
Size: 17,117 acres in two units.
Administration: BLM (Worland Field Office).
Management status: Alkali Creek WSA (10,100 acres), private inholdings (680 acres), unprotected roadless lands (6,337 acres).
Ecosystem: Wyoming Basin Province sagebrush steppe, dominated by juniper scrub and riparian habitat types.
Elevation range: 4,850 to 7,085 feet.
System trails: None.
Maximum core to perimeter distance: 1.6 miles.
Activities: Hiking, wildlife viewing, hunting, rockhounding, scrambling and bouldering.
Best season: March–May; September–October.
Map: Worland 1:100,000.

TRAVELERS ADVISORY:
RATTLESNAKES, FLASH FLOODS

The headwaters of Alkali Creek are a maze of finger canyons and slickrock badlands carved into an upthrust layer of Tensleep sandstone. The desert scrub community, combined with the beauty of the slickrock canyons, creates a landscape reminiscent of the Grand Staircase country of southern Utah. From the rims of the canyons, views encompass the Bighorn Mountains and stretch across the Bighorn Basin, with its red buttes of Chugwater sandstone. Pictographs, rock shelters, and other evidence of prehistoric use point to human habitation dating back at least 9,000 years.

The flora of Alkali Creek is transitional between the Big Horn Mountains and the desert floor of the Bighorn Basin. The rolling uplands above the canyon rims are robed in a steppe vegetation of sagebrush, grasses, and mountain mahogany. Juniper scrub dominates the broken country of the Alkali Creek canyons and is associated with limber pines in a few locales. Cottonwoods, skunkbush, and alluvial swards of grass are found in the canyon bottoms, where springs and seeps offer a little fresh water in an otherwise parched landscape. Wildflowers are particularly abundant and showy in the Alkali Creek canyons in April and May.

27 ALKALI CREEK

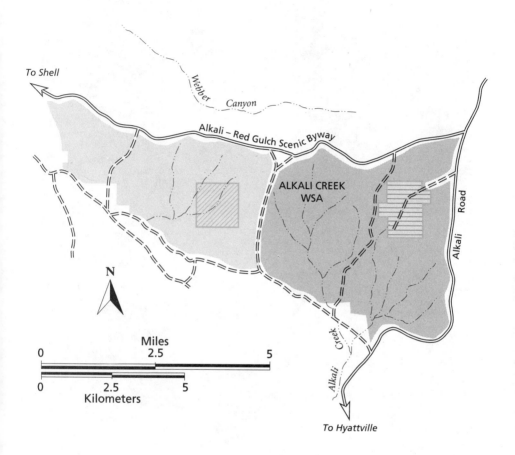

Alkali Creek is a critical winter range for over 300 elk and unknown numbers of mule deer. Resident mule deer and small mammals find water in the springs and seeps within the canyons, and bird life is also abundant here. Golden eagles and other raptors are known to inhabit the WSA. It also contains two sage grouse dancing sites, where the birds gather to breed each spring.

The area has a low potential for oil and gas development, but five deposits of tar sands have been identified within the WSA, and they may be recoverable at some future date. There are a number of unpatented mining claims within the Alkali Creek area, mainly covering deposits of silica sand of low grade and high iron content. These deposits might be suitable for foundry sand. USGS

Slickrock country above the rims of Alkali Creek Canyon.

analysis states these sands are of low economic value; the claimants disagree and believe the sands could be mined economically. The Alkali Creek watershed also shows possibilities for producing small quantities of silver, sulfides, rare-earth elements, and uranium.

RECREATIONAL USES: The many branches of Alkali Creek offer countless possibilities for day hikes and scramble routes, either on the canyon bottoms or along the slickrock ledges of the canyon walls. The multiple canyon forks and hidden pockets in the rock provide unlimited possibilities for solitude. Before this area was withdrawn as a WSA, it received 400 visitor days annually of ATV use associated with hunting, rockhounding, and the livestock industry. There have been problems with illegal ATV and jeep use within the WSA.

ACCESS: The Alkali-Red Gulch Scenic Byway follows the northern and eastern boundaries of the WSA. This well-maintained gravel road runs north from Wyoming 31 just west of Hyattville. From Alkali Flats, a series of fair-quality jeep roads provides access to the many canyon mouths.

Scramble Route

Alkali Creek Canyon

Distance: 1.7 miles one way.
Difficulty: Moderate.
Starting and maximum elevation: 4,950 feet, 5,500 feet.
Topo maps: Bush Butte, Hyatt Ranch.
Getting there: Take WY 31 to the Alkali Road, just west of Hyattville. Follow this fair-weather trunk road 8 miles to Alkali Flats, then turn left onto a jeep road that runs northwest. After 0.3 mile, the jeep trail forks; park here and hike up the right-hand fork.

This route represents one of many possible day hikes into the Alkali Creek canyons. To begin the hike, follow the unsanctioned jeep trail northward through the sage and rabbitbrush of Alkali Flats. This low basin is rimmed to the south and west by red buttes of Chugwater sandstone. Straight ahead, the many branches of Alkali Creek have carved deep canyons into the Tensleep formation. As the route enters the folds of the hills, the flats narrow to level benches beside the wash. Ignore the side canyons as the main streamcourse trends north-northeast into the heart of the hills.

Sedimentary walls soon slant upward beside the streamcourse, ranged in three tiers that form the canyon. Above it all are massive klippes of Tensleep sandstone carved into eerie shapes by wind and rain. Initially, game trails provide easy traveling beside the wash, but as the walls close in, it becomes nec-

Alkali Creek Canyon.

essary to drop into the dry streamcourse. After a brief journey across the slick-rock streambed, the route encounters a stretch of stream where water is often found at the surface. A lush growth of grasses and hardwoods creates a hidden garden here. Near the head of the canyon is a major confluence; travel becomes quite difficult beyond this point. Turn around and retrace your steps to complete the hike.

The Honeycombs 28

Location: 15 miles southeast of Worland and 10 miles southwest of Tensleep.
Size: 52,764 acres.
Administration: BLM (Worland Resource Area).
Management status: The Honeycombs WSA (21,000 acres), unprotected roadless lands (31,764 acres).
Ecosystem: Wyoming Basin Province sagebrush steppe.
Elevation range: 4,800 feet to 5,600 feet.
System trails: None.
Maximum core to perimeter distance: 1.7 miles.
Activities: Hiking, backpacking, horseback riding, rockhounding, hunting.
Best season: March–May; September–November.
Map: Noiwater Creek 1:100,000.

TRAVELERS ADVISORY:
FLASH FLOODS, BAD WATER

The Honeycombs are a vast series of deeply eroded badlands of the Willwood and Fort Union formations. The badlands are banded with colors that range principally in the browns and tans but can vary from bone white to pink and deep red. Sagebrush grasslands dominate the highlands above the breaks, while rabbitbrush and greasewood border the wash drainages. The area is a critical winter range for mule deer and pronghorn antelope. Nesting habitat for sage grouse, golden eagles, and great horned owls can also be found within the Honeycombs.

The BLM has failed to recommend any of the Honeycombs roadless area for wilderness status. Bladed trails dating from oil and gas exploration in the 1950s and reservoirs are scattered throughout the area, but have deteriorated to the point that they can scarcely be recognized. The Honeycombs represent a last remnant of a broad sweep of badlands that has already been overrun by oil wells and roads. It would be wise to preserve this small portion of such an impressive landscape for the enjoyment of future generations.

Just east of the WSA are four underground coal mines that have been worked in the past. Coal deposits within the Honeycombs are characterized by marginal quality and high extraction costs and are not thought to be of much economic value. The WSA may contain deposits of black sandstone that bear

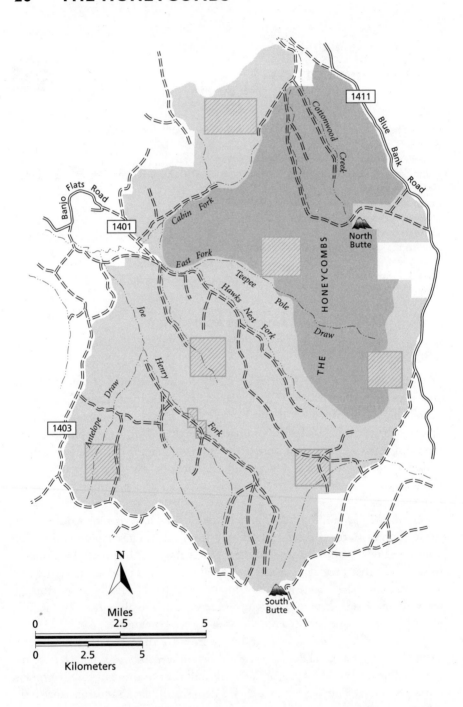

1411

Blue Bank Road

Cottonwood Creek

Banjo Flats Road

1401

Cabin Fork

East Fork

North Butte

THE HONEYCOMBS

Teepee Pole

Draw

Joe

Hawks Nest Fork

Henry

Draw

Antelope

1403

Fork

South Butte

N

Miles
0   2.5   5

Kilometers
0   2.5   5

Looking out across the Honeycombs.

strategic minerals such as titanium, niobium, and tantalum used in making alloys. The area has a moderate potential for oil and gas production, but so far oil exploration in the immediate area has turned up only dry holes. The Cottonwood Creek oilfield lies just west of the WSA. Oil and gas leases that predate the Federal Land Planning and Management Act (FLPMA) cover 2,244 acres of the WSA. If the Honeycombs were to become wilderness, the lease-holders could still drill for oil within the wilderness boundaries.

RECREATIONAL USES: Opportunities for solitude and primitive recreation were rated as outstanding by the BLM. The major drainages offer good horse routes into the heart of the badlands, while the intervening buttes and draws are conducive to cross-country hiking and scrambling. The Honeycombs offer good hunting for mule deer in a challenging and picturesque setting. The extremely rugged terrain and loose soils found here are unsuitable for motorized vehicles and mountain bikes.

ACCESS: The western side of the WSA can be accessed via the Banjo Flats Road, which is lost in a tangle of unmarked oilfield roads. The maze is so difficult to navigate that visitors are advised to use the Blue Bank Road instead. This good gravel trunk road runs south from US 16 and follows the highlands to the east of the Honeycombs. A jeep trail links this road to the top of North Butte, offering another good access point.

Day Hike

Big Cottonwood Ramble

Distance: 6 miles round trip.
Difficulty: Moderately strenuous.
Starting and minimum elevation: 4,950 feet, 4,700 feet.
Topo map: Castle Gardens.
Getting there: Take U.S. Highway 16 to a marked junction 16 miles east of Worland and 9 miles west of Tensleep to reach the Blue Bank Road. It runs south for one mile to join the old highway bed. Turn left, cross the Big Cottonwood wash, then turn right on the hilltop to continue south on Blue Bank Road. After 5.2 miles, park beside the corral on the left (east) side of the road.

This scramble route wanders through the badlands to the north of North Butte, visiting the heart of the Honeycombs. From the corrals, hike west, descending along sagebrush slopes into a depression where badlands topography rises from a level basin. Cross the basin, weaving an up-and-down course among the buttes. A ragged ridge guards the far side, and a northward detour leads around it and into the next northward-flowing draw. Climb over the ridge beyond this wash and pick your way down steep slopes to reach a spot where two flat-bottomed valleys converge.

The more westerly valley bears the dry wash of Big Cottonwood Creek. Follow its streamcourse upward through the sagebrush for easy traveling between the eroded walls of the Honeycombs. As you approach the base of North Butte, a cluster of cottonwoods marks the former location of Chess Reservoir. Turn east from this landmark, climbing the ridgeline toward a crimson summit. Upon reaching the Big Cottonwood divide, continue east down sagebrush slopes into the headwaters of Little Cottonwood Creek. As you follow the streamcourse northeast, isolated buttes rise from the sagebrush steppe. The wash intersects the Blue Bank Road at Green Bug Reservoir; hike north on the road for 1 mile to return to your vehicle.

Cedar Mountain   29

Location: 8 miles southwest of Worland.
Size: 21,560 acres.
Administration: BLM (Worland Field Office).
Management status: Cedar Mountain WSA (21,560 acres).
Ecosystem: Wyoming Basin Province wheatgrass-needlegrass shrub steppe, with significant stands of juniper scrub in the uplands.
Elevation range: 4,200 feet to 5,500 feet.
System trails: None.
Maximum core to perimeter distance: 1.8 miles.
Activities: Hunting, rockhounding, hiking, horseback riding.
Best season: March–May; September–October.
Map: Thermopolis 1:100,000.

Cedar Mountain is a massive outcrop of sandstone, siltstone, and shale that towers above the banks of the Bighorn River. The wilderness study area is characterized by deep, steep-sided drainages flowing north and west into the Bighorn River. Petrified wood and fossilized reptiles are found in the Lance and Meteetsee formations in the southern reaches of the WSA. The Fort Union formation, which is exposed on the northern slopes of the Cedar Mountain massif, has been known to produce mammalian fossils.

The uplands are characterized by a desert scrub community dominated by juniper. The skirts of the upland are robed in a steppe grassland dotted with sagebrush and rabbitbrush. Cedar Mountain was once grazed quite heavily by livestock, but in recent years it has received only light grazing pressure. The area is known to have a strong population of mule deer. The cliffs on the southern and western faces of Cedar Mountain provide nesting habitat for raptors.

The BLM has proposed 10,223 acres of the Cedar Mountain unit for wilderness designation. The potential for oil and gas production is low within the core area recommended for wilderness by the BLM, and moderate along the northern and eastern reaches of the roadless area that the BLM did not recommend for wilderness. It seems unlikely that wilderness designation for the entire area would have any impact on the oil and gas industry.

RECREATIONAL USES: Hiking and scrambling are possible along the ridgelines atop the Cedar Mountain massif and along the barren draws that run

29   CEDAR MOUNTAIN

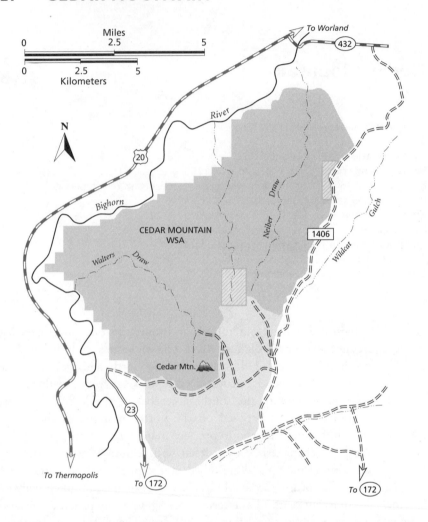

north from its crest. A few abandoned jeep roads offer routes for horsemen. Snowshoeing and cross-country skiing are possible on Cedar Mountain following heavy snowstorms. The Tie Down Flats area is notorious for rampant and indiscriminate off-road vehicle use.

ACCESS: BLM 1406 is a rough jeep road that runs north from Wyoming 172, climbing over the divide along the eastern boundary of the WSA. Public access on this road is blocked at its north end, where it joins Wyoming 432. The Cowboy Mine Road follows the east bank of the Bighorn River, and a section of state land offers the only public access to the southwestern corner of the area.

Cedar Mountain.

Day Hike

Neiber Draw Divide

Distance: 0.9 mile one way.
Difficulty: Moderate.
Starting and maximum elevation: 5,080 feet, 5,110 feet.
Topo map: Cedar Mountain.
Getting there: From Lucerne, drive east on Wyoming 172. After 7.2 miles, turn left (north) on an unmarked two-track road. After 2.7 miles, turn left (west) at the junction. Pass through a gate and drive 0.8 mile, past a corral, then through a second gate before turning north at the next intersection. This road requires high clearance and good torque, and it leads 4 miles up to the top of the Cedar Mountain divide, where the hike begins.

This off-trail scramble runs the ridges toward Cedar Mountain, passing sandstone hoodoos along the way. The hike begins by following the ridgetop westward as views of the Owl Creek and Bighorn ranges crowd the far horizons. The route runs up and down as it surmounts three summits and dips into the intervening passes. Expect easy walking, as the desert pavement is broken only occasionally by junipers and clumps of grass. Small pinnacles and wind-sculpted outcrops line the south-facing cliffs, and the wooded massif of Cedar Mountain rises to the west. The trek ends atop the third summit; from here you can see a fence and jeep trail in the saddle to the west.

Birdseye Creek   30

Location: 20 miles south of Thermopolis, 15 miles north of Shoshoni.
Size: 7,978 acres.
Administration: BLM (Lander Field Office).
Management status: Copper Mountain WSA (6,858 acres); unprotected roadless lands (1,120 acres).
Ecosystem: Wyoming Basin Province wheatgrass-needlegrass shrub steppe with substantial coverage of juniper scrub.
Elevation range: 4,900 feet to 6,621 feet.
System trails: None.
Maximum core to perimeter distance: 1.8 miles.
Activities: Hiking, hunting, geology study.
Best season: April–June; September–October.
Map: Riverton 1:100,000.

To the east of the upper portals of the Wind River Canyon, a collection of rugged summits and pocket basins at the head of Birdseye Creek has been designated the Copper Mountain WSA. With its close proximity to Boysen State Park, it provides excellent opportunities for primitive recreation in a semi-desert setting.

The heart of the WSA is a miniature range of barren, arid peaks, a subset of the Owl Creek Mountains that guards the upper portal of Wind River Canyon. The bare peaks of limestone are dissected by small valleys and basins robed in a juniper scrub community with some sparse grasslands and sagebrush-rabbitbrush meadows on the high flats. Small stands of limber pine grow at the base of the north-facing cliffs. Along the southern edge of the WSA, deeply eroded badlands of the Wind River formation rise in miniature buttes and canyons of crimson, alabaster, purple, and pink. These badlands are characterized by highly alkaline soils, and only a sparse desert vegetation of Utah juniper, prickly pear cactus, saltbush, and yucca grows here.

The WSA is a winter range for mule deer and pronghorn antelope. Chukars, red fox, and bobcats are some of the small animals that are present here. The high and dissected peaks provide nesting habitat for such endangered raptors as peregrine falcons and bald eagles. Small caves are numerous among the peaks, providing roosting habitat for bats.

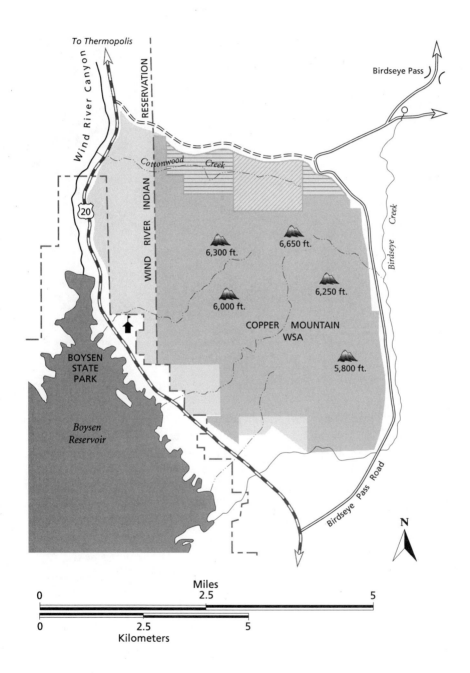

To Thermopolis

Wind River Canyon

RESERVATION

Birdseye Pass

Cottonwood Creek

WIND RIVER INDIAN

20

Birdseye Creek

6,300 ft.

6,650 ft.

6,250 ft.

6,000 ft.

COPPER MOUNTAIN
WSA

5,800 ft.

BOYSEN
STATE
PARK

Boysen
Reservoir

Birdseye Pass Road

N

Miles
0   2.5   5

0   2.5   5
Kilometers

Badlands along the south edge of the Copper Mountain WSA.

The Owl Creek Mountains stretch from the southern tail of the Absaroka Range to the Big Horn Mountains. They rose up during the Laramide Orogeny, which occurred about 55 million years before the present. Only a few million years later, the Absaroka highlands emerged in a cataclysmic burst of intense volcanism. The Owl Creek Range was completely buried beneath volcanic debris that had eroded from the Absarokas, so filling the surrounding country that the Wind River and Bighorn basins merged into a single plain. The waterways were forced to seek new channels as a result of the new topography, and a great river was formed, draining the eastern slopes of the Wind River Range before flowing northward into what is now Montana. About 4 million years ago, a broad regional uplift raised the Owl Creek Mountains once again. The sediments that buried the range washed away, and the Wind River cut down through the emerging bedrock. In doing so, it carved the deep chasm that is now known as Wind River Canyon.

The Wind River Canyon has always been a traditional travel route for native peoples who made periodic visits to the hot springs at Thermopolis. It took a long time for white explorers to discover the passage, as they were not expecting a river to flow through the high mountains between two basins. In modern times, a highway and a railroad run through the length of the Shoshones' sacred canyon, but a small patch of roadless country still remains above its upper end. Known as the Copper Mountain Wilderness Study Area, it encompasses the headwaters of Birdseye Creek and the mountains that rise between Birdseye Pass and the Wind River Canyon. The Birdseye Pass stage road that ran above the eastern rim of the canyon now forms the eastern boundary of the WSA.

The BLM failed to recommend any of the Copper Mountain WSA for wilderness status, citing only marginal opportunities for primitive and unconfined recreation. Their study report indicated that the sights and sounds associated with the nearby highway and reservoir were "unavoidable." In fact, due to the highly dissected nature of both the mountains and badlands and the numerous protected basins, opportunities for primitive and unconfined recreation in a pristine setting are outstanding. This faux pas seems to have resulted from what one government employee termed a "windshield assessment." It is disturbing that the authors of this Environmental Impact Statement did not do their jobs more thoroughly.

Natural gas has been found along the southern fringes of the WSA at a depth of 13,000 feet. The USGS rates potential for production as low, while other sources rate potential as moderate to high. A field with four wells is projected within the southern third of the wilderness study area, although no current oil and gas leases exist. It is likely that the mere presence of natural gas within the WSA has been the primary factor in the BLM's refusal to recommend the area for wilderness status. The southern badlands are considered favorable for the occurrence of uranium, but the market for this mineral collapsed in the wake of the Three Mile Island nuclear disaster, and no mining activity is anticipated in the near future.

RECREATIONAL USES: The Birdseye roadless area is a prime spot for mule deer hunting. The rugged and often steep terrain favors foot travel over horses, with plenty of hidden pockets for primitive camping. Rockhounds will find a wide variety of bedrock types in which to prospect for interesting finds.

ACCESS: The wilderness study area is bounded to the south and east by Birdseye Road, which provides the only public access. Highway 20 lies west of the roadless area, but you must get a special permit to cross Wind River Indian Reservation lands to access the backcountry from this side.

Multicolored badlands of Birdseye Creek.

Day Hike

Birdseye Creek Badlands

Distance: 1.2 miles round trip.
Difficulty: Easy.
Starting and minimum elevation: 5,160 feet, 5,060 feet.
Topo map: Birdseye Pass.
Getting there: Take US 20 north from Shoshoni to Birdseye Road, which leaves the highway 4 miles south of the Boysen State Park headquarters. Follow this improved gravel road 2 miles to reach the start of the badlands hike just behind the first hill.

This short stroll visits the brightly colored badlands just west of the Birdseye Creek Road. The hike begins by running west through a gap in the hills, following a path of sorts to reach a dry streamcourse. Follow the wash westward as it descends through rounded hills to enter a colorful badland where crimson and white buttes rise amid hillocks of pink and ochre. The vibrant green of the junipers lends color to an otherwise drab vegetation of cactus and dried grass. As the wash leaves the badlands and enters round, grassy hills, turn north along a tributary draw. It climbs through colorful formations and onto the dun-colored slopes above. Turn east now, rounding the technicolor badlands to close the loop and follow the original wash back to the trailhead.

Day Hike

West Birdseye Basin

Distance: 1.4 miles round trip.
Difficulty: Moderate.
Starting and maximum elevation: 5,700 feet, 5,980 feet.
Topo map: Birdseye Pass.
Getting there: Take US 20 north from Shoshoni to Birdseye Road, which leaves the highway 4 miles south of the Boysen State Park headquarters. Follow this improved gravel road through a narrow canyon and bear left at the split with the Copper Mountain Road. After passing a ranch, the road passes through a barbed-wire fence without a gate or cattleguard. Pull to the roadside just beyond this fence.

This bushwhacking route climbs through the juniper scrub to visit one of the many pocket basins at the upper end of the WSA. From the starting point, hike west through a fence gate and then cross a juniper-clad draw to reach a bald finger ridge. Follow the ridgeline westward, ascending gradually amid expanding views of the arid and craggy peaks. As the ridge swings north, descend to cross the main wash and climb onto a second open and westward-trending ridge. It leads upward, unveiling views of the summits that ring the head of the basin. Just beyond a rounded saddle, a bald hilltop occupies the center of the basin, offering panoramic views of the high peaks.

Spear Lake in the Bighorn's Cloud Peak Wilderness.

5

Big Horn Mountains

The Big Horn Mountains rise from the High Plains like a great swell on the surface of the sea, over 170 miles long from end to end. The northern half of the range has been preserved for public use within the Bighorn National Forest; the southern half has been carved up into private timber holdings and ranches. The eastern front of the Bighorns is typified by short, rugged chasms that lead to vast grasslands guarded by reefs of sedimentary rock. Along the arid western edge of the Bighorns, you can explore deep canyons and trackless badlands that remain accessible in spring and fall when the rest of the range is locked in snow. The northern end of the range is crowned with rolling alpine meadows that stretch for miles. Crowning it all is the Cloud Peak Wilderness, where the cliff-girt massif of granite rises over 13,000 feet above countless lakes and alpine meadows.

Vegetation in the Big Horn Mountains falls into five major belts. Along the eastern edge of the mountains, ponderosa pine savannas occur between 5,000 and 7,000 feet. Much of this foothills ecosystem falls within private ranch lands. Lodgepole stands occur extensively between 7,500 feet and 9,000 feet and are renewed on a cyclical basis by natural wildfires. Extensive meadows dominated by Idaho fescue grow on limestone soils within this belt because these soils carry little groundwater. Above 9,000 feet, timberline stands of Engelmann spruce and subalpine fir are interspersed with vast alpine meadows. The Big Horn Mountains have more species of rare or endemic wildflowers than any other range in Wyoming except the Tetons. Forests on the mid-slopes of the western face contain almost as much Douglas fir as lodgepole pine, and on the lower slopes arid sagebrush steppe grades into a desert scrub of juniper and saltbush.

The lowlands bordering the Big Horn Mountains were occupied by nomadic hunter-gatherers as early as 12,000 years ago. These earliest explorers are thought to have wintered in the sandstone canyons at the edges of the mountains, and to have made forays into the uplands during the summer months to hunt, gather the bulbs of bitterroot and sego lily, and gather chert and quartzite for making stone tools and points. A kill site found in the northern

Bighorns contained the bones of bison, elk, and bighorn sheep, and dated from 3,000 B.C. Prehistoric peoples left behind pictographs in Medicine Lodge Canyon and built the Medicine Wheel, a large array of cairns and rocks that has been likened to a New World Stonehenge.

During the 1800s, the Big Horn Mountains continued to draw indigenous people, who used the barren peaks as sites for vision quests and religious ceremonies. Several Indian trails from this period follow the mountain crest in the northern marches of the range. The Bighorn Basin was occupied by the Shoshone and Flathead peoples, while to the east of the mountains, the Crow, Cheyenne, and Arapaho tribes ruled the plains. A trickle of white fur trappers came and went, followed by tie hacks who supplied the railroads with wood and later ranchers who drove their livestock to the high meadows for summer grazing. Each group has left a faint but characteristic imprint on the mountains.

Highland Park in the Cloud Peak Wilderness.

Little Bighorn Canyon   31

Location: 40 miles northwest of Sheridan.
Size: 134,760 acres.
Administration: Bighorn National Forest (Medicine Wheel District).
Management status: 134,760 acres currently managed as roadless non-motorized.
Ecosystems: Rocky Mountain Douglas fir forest, lodgepole pine, Palouse prairie.
Elevation range: 4,600 feet to 9,830 feet.
System trails: 55 miles.
Maximum core to perimeter distance: 2.2 miles.
Activities: Hunting, fishing, hiking, horseback riding.
Best season: June–September.
Maps: Bighorn Forest Map; Burgess Junction 1:100,000.

Far in the northeast corner of the Big Horn Mountains, the Little Bighorn River flows down from grassy parks, passes through a narrow and rugged canyon, and wanders out onto the High Plains. This remote patch of roadless country extends all the way from the timberline to the foothills, providing a cross-section of plant communities unique among Big Horn Mountain roadless areas.

There are a number of striking features within this roadless area. Leaky Mountain has a number of large springs that gush from its blank limestone cliffs. The inner gorge of the Little Bighorn is carved through granite over half a billion years old. Bull Elk Park, a meadow perched high above the Dry Fork, is home to a Palouse Prairie grassland, with species normally found in the Columbia Basin isolated here after the retreat of Pleistocene ice sheets.

Black bear are abundant in the canyon of the Little Bighorn, and mountain lions are also present, though seldom seen. The valley of the Dry Fork is an important spring range for up to 400 head of elk, and many of the females drop their calves here each year. The upper reaches of the Little Bighorn watershed are used by elk throughout the snow-free months. Mule deer are also abundant here. Moose are year-round residents of the roadless area and are occasionally seen along streams and at springs.

This area has always been a forgotten backwater, far from human settlement. Placer miners drifted through in the late 1800s but never found enough gold to entice them to stay. Later, stockmen discovered the lush, protected grasslands above the Little Bighorn Canyon and thus found an ideal summer

31   LITTLE BIGHORN CANYON

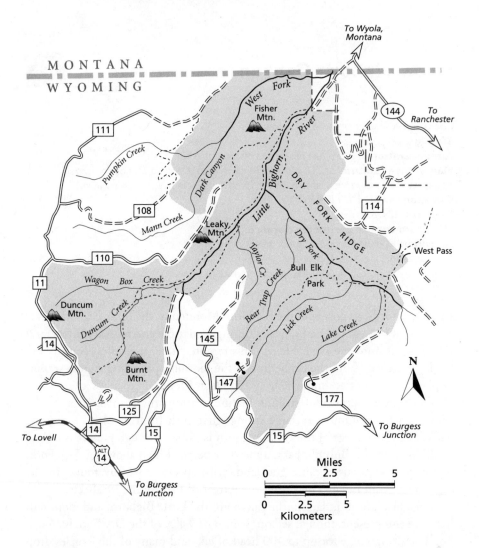

range for their cattle. In modern times, up to 1,900 cattle are driven up the Little Bighorn Canyon each year to summer along the grassy benches above the river. With the cattle have come improved springs, line cabins, and barbed-wire fences.

The Little Bighorn River has been recommended for inclusion in the National Wild and Scenic River system. The lower reaches of the canyon were recommended for Wild and Scenic status, while the upper reaches, where domestic livestock graze in summer, would have received Scenic designation only.

Logging in the southern reaches of the Dry Fork watershed has encroached on the undisturbed forest in recent years.

The greatest threat to the wild character of the Little Bighorn Canyon has come not from cattle ranching but from a proposed water development along the Dry Fork of the Little Bighorn. The proposed dam would flood not only the Dry Fork but also the mouths of the Lick Creek and Lake Creek Valleys. The dam would generate hydroelectric power, and the project might also include a diversion pipe to shunt water away from the Little Bighorn and through the mountains to feed the ranchlands of the high plains. Unnatural water fluctuations would cause a deterioration of downstream trout habitat along the Little Bighorn, and the resulting reservoir would create a significant obstacle to the migrating elk that winter on the Kerns game range. As of this writing, construction of the dam has been at least temporarily defeated.

RECREATIONAL USE: An extensive network of trails makes the Little Bighorn watershed a good choice for extended backpacks and horse trips. Horsemen will find plenty of grazing in the upper meadows of the headwaters streams. Horse use is moderate throughout the area, with many visitors basing themselves out of the vast meadows at the crest of the range. Most of the remaining use comes from knowledgeable anglers.

The Little Bighorn River offers excellent fly fishing in pocket water and rapids choked with enormous boulders. Anglers will find rainbow and cutthroat trout in the faster waters, and brown trout in the calmer stretches. There are long stretches between the Dry Fork and Wagon Box Creek where access to the river is blocked by steep cutbanks that soar hundreds of feet above the water. As a result, an enterprising angler can find plenty of water that receives very little fishing pressure. Brook trout is the predominant species on the Dry Fork as well as the smaller tributary creeks that feed it. Wagon Box Creek and its tributaries also offer fine fishing.

The Little Bighorn Canyon is a prime area for big game hunting as well. Elk, deer, bear, lions, and moose are all abundant. Blue and ruffed grouse and wild turkeys provide bird-hunting opportunities. Because of its size and remoteness, the area receives comparatively light hunting pressure. The protection of large tracts of roadless land such as this one is critical to hunters because they serve as population reservoirs from which elk and deer can expand to repopulate more accessible areas that become depleted by hunting pressure.

ACCESS: From Wyoming 345, County Road 144 runs to the Little Bighorn River, where a primitive secondary road with fords leads to the mouth of the Little Bighorn Canyon. The upper end of the roadless area can be reached from Burgess Junction via Forest Roads 14, 11, and 15. Secondary roads that branch off from the trunk roads can be rough and turn to mud in wet weather.

Forested ridges beyond the Dry Fork.

Day Trip on Foot or Horseback, or Backpack

Bull Elk Park

Distance: 6.0 miles one way.
Difficulty: Moderate.
Starting and minimum elevation: 9,420 feet, 7,750 feet.
Topo map: Bull Elk Park.
Getting there: From US 14A west of Burgess Junction, follow the Dayton Gulch Road (FR 15) northward. After 7.2 miles, turn left (north) on FR 145, then make an immediate right on FR 147. This primitive road climbs through a saddle and continues up a steep ridge for 1.4 miles to reach a closure gate on the ridgetop. The hike starts on the closed road.

This route follows a wooded ridgetop to visit Bull Elk Park, a pristine mountain grassland. At its outset, the route follows a logging road through recent salvage-cuts of the subalpine forest. The road passes the last of the logging activity after about a mile, and now the ridgetop is robed in pleasant glades and stands of subalpine fir. Periodic openings in the trees reveal the valleys of Lick Creek to the southeast and Bear Trap Creek to the northwest. The trail ultimately reaches a large ridgetop meadow, and at this point the subalpine fir begins to give way to spruce. As the ridge loses altitude, these trees in turn are replaced by lodgepole pine and then Douglas fir.

After topping a lofty point of limestone, the path makes a hearty descent. It levels off as the trail enters the Bull Elk Park Natural Area. The trees soon open out into the broad grasslands of Bull Elk Park, and the trail vanishes as it enters the meadow. The cliff-girt mountain to the northeast is Dry Fork Ridge, while the bare summit of Fisher Mountain rises to the north. To reach a spring that makes a good camp spot, follow the tree line along the southeast edge of Bull Elk Park. The route descends gradually along the trees until it reaches a grassy cove. In the corner of this cove, a well-beaten trail leads through the doghair lodgepole to reach the small clearing beyond. There is an outfitter's camp and a pipe-fed spring at the far edge of this meadow.

Day Hike

Little Bighorn Canyon

Distance: 2.4 miles one way.
Difficulty: Moderate.
Starting and maximum elevation: 4,530 feet, 5,100 feet.
Topo maps: Bull Elk Park, Boyd Ridge.
Getting there: Drive northwest from Ranchester on WY 343 (old US 89). After 12 miles, turn left (west) on County Road 144, a gravel highway, and follow it for 16.5 miles. Upon reaching the bottoms of the Little Bighorn River, the county road bends eastward. (This spot can also be reached from Wyola, MT, via County Road 418). Turn left onto a primitive road marked "public access through private lands." This road is rough with some fords, and high clearance is required. Follow it for 2.8 miles, crossing the bridge and parking at the trailhead on the Kerns Wildlife Management Unit. Hike the road to reach the beginning of the trail.

This trail follows the Little Bighorn River through its outer canyon to visit its granite inner gorge. The hike begins by passing several summer cabins in the Douglas fir–ponderosa pine bottoms of the Little Bighorn. Here, the river churns through a long series of rapids punctuated with enormous boulders. The path soon turns a corner, and the soaring, sedimentary cliffs of Fisher Mountain rise above it. The path continues to follow the river along the base of the cliffs, then makes a short climb to surmount a washout.

A meadow shelf above the Little Bighorn valley.

It emerges on a shelf above the valley floor, crossing open country populated by thickets of chokecherry and serviceberry. Soon, the Boyd Ridge trail departs through a gate in the barbed-wire fence that parallels the main path. The Little Horn Trail continues up the broad valley. The imposing reef that can now be seen to the east represents the north end of Dry Fork Ridge. The path soon returns to the riverbank, following it into an inner gorge of ancient granite. Here, a small sand beach lies at the foot of a pretty waterfall. Continue up the trail for cliff-top views of the gorge, then return to the starting point.

Walker Prairie

32

Location: 20 miles west of Sheridan.
Size: 62,980 acres.
Administration: Bighorn National Forest (Tongue District).
Management status: Unprotected roadless lands.
Ecosystem: Rocky Mountain Douglas fir ecosystem.
Elevation range: 4,430 feet to 10,147 feet.
System trails: 58 miles.
Maximum core to perimeter distance: 2.2 miles.
Activities: Horseback riding, hiking, backpacking, hunting, fishing.
Best season: May–October.
Maps: Bighorn Forest Map, Burgess Junction 1:100,000.

Walker Prairie is the largest of the foothills grasslands of the Big Horn Mountains. The meadows stretches for 10 miles from north to south, spanning four major drainage divides. Towering reefs of sedimentary rock rise to the east of the grasslands, guarding steep canyons where the water tumbles across some of the largest waterfalls in the Big Horn Mountains. To the west, granite hills mount up toward the crest of the Bighorns, robed in a dense forest of lodgepole pine.

This vast prairie owes its existence to the bedrock beneath it. This thick layer of shale is quite porous, and rainwater percolates quickly away from the surface of the soil through passageways in the rock. Conifers rely on long taproots to find groundwater at the bedrock level, but here the groundwater flows far beneath the bedrock. Grasses, on the other hand, have dense mats of shallow roots that quickly soak up the water from the brief summer rain squalls as it soaks into the upper layers of the soil. This adaptation allows the grasses to thrive on the open slopes of Walker Prairie.

Coyotes are very common here, and the sedimentary cliffs that loom above the prairie provide nest sites for many raptor species. Walker Prairie is an important year-round range for deer and elk, and also supports domestic cattle during the summer months. Cattle are most prevalent between Big Goose Creek and the Quartz Creek divide. Aside from a few fencelines and some past copper mining activity along Quartz Creek, few humans have intruded into the Walker Prairie area. Logging activity has been heavy in the upper reaches

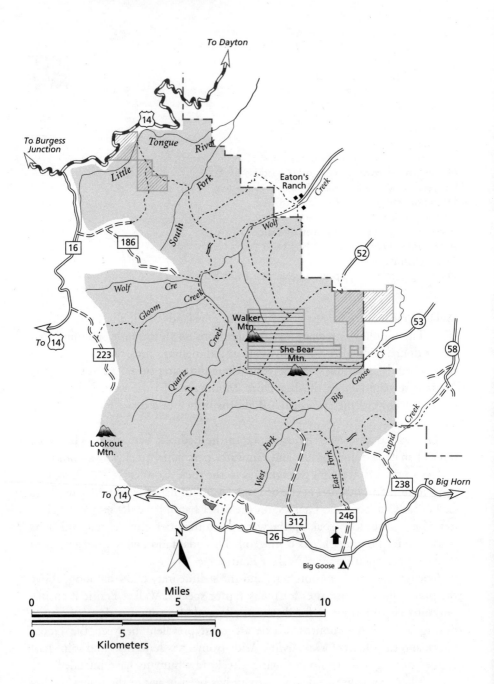

To Dayton

14

To Burgess
Junction

Tongue   River

Little

South   Fork

Eaton's
Ranch

Creek

16

186

Wolf

52

Wolf   Cre

Gloom   Creek

Walker
Mtn.

53

To 14

223

Quartz   Creek

She Bear
Mtn.

Big   Goose   Cr

58

Rapid   Creek

Lookout
Mtn.

West   Fork

East   Fork

To 14

238   To Big Horn

N

312

246

26

Big Goose

Miles

0   5   10

0   5   10

Kilometers

The northern reaches of Walker Prairie.

of Gloom Creek, and clearcuts are steadily creeping into the western end of the roadless area.

RECREATIONAL USES: A network of good trails conducive to both foot and horse travel crisscrosses the Walker Prairie area. Much of the visitation to this area is associated with horse trips from Eatons' guest ranch at the mouth of Wolf Creek. This use is concentrated along the lower and middle reaches of Wolf Creek. The most remote portion of the roadless area lies in upper Quartz Creek, wooded country that receives very few visitors. Elk and deer hunting can be quite productive, although limited access may make for a long haul back out. Although there are no lakes here, major streams like Big Goose Creek, Wolf Creek, and the South Fork Little Tongue offer fly fishing possibilities.

ACCESS: The best access to the area is via the Red Grade Road (FR 26) from Big Horn and US 14 from Dayton. Private lands often block access to trails that penetrate the foothills. The Eatons' guest ranch offers public access up the Wolf Creek Canyon.

Horseshoe Mountain.

Multi-Day Backpack or Horse Trip

Walker Prairie

Distance: 18.2 miles one way.
Difficulty: Moderately strenuous.
Starting and maximum elevation: 7,200 feet, 7,990 feet.
Topo maps: Beckton, Park Reservoir, Walker Mountain, Dayton South.
Getting there: From US 14 south of Burgess Junction (or from the town of Big Horn),
follow FR 26 to Big Goose Park. Turn north on FR 296, following signs for the ranger station.
Drive past the ranger station to reach a junction marked "Schunk Lodge" after 0.8 mile. Turn
right and follow the primitive road (high clearance needed) for one mile. At the end of the
road, drive across the pole bridge over Ranger Creek to reach the south trailhead beside a
cabin. The north trailhead is reached by driving west from Dayton on US 14 for 19 miles.
Just before the S-turns at the base of Steamboat Point, turn left (southeast) on FR 220, an
unmarked, two-rut road that drops to the valley floor. Park at the end of this road.

This route runs the length of Walker Prairie, the largest expanse of grassland within the eastern foothills of the Big Horn Mountains. The trail begins by traveling to the bottoms of the East Fork of Big Goose Creek. Here, the path follows the stream through shady stands of spruce and across a few open glades bordered by lodgepole pine. It makes three slippery fords of the East Fork before reaching a grassy meadow where trail #019 joins in. A fourth ford leads to more extensive grasslands bordered by bald hills.

The trail now starts up the hillside, dipping into an aspen-girt draw before it rises to the top of the hillock. The trail now fades out; hike westward along the edge of the trees, then bear for the saddle to the left (south) of the granite outcrop at the far edge of the meadows. Views encompass the crags of the Cloud Peak Wilderness as well as the rugged canyon of Big Goose Creek. After passing through the saddle, the path descends across a small meadow to join FR 312. (This "road" is really no more than an ATV trail.) Follow the roadbed

Boulders and falls in Wolf Creek Canyon.

northwest for the descent to the West Fork of Big Goose Creek. Upon reaching the creek bottoms, turn downstream to reach a bridge that spans the West Fork just above a striking granite outcrop.

On the far bank, a horse trail climbs steeply into the grasslands, surmounting an open saddle that leads into the Prairie Creek drainage. After passing through a fence, the path descends to cross this stream amid a loose grove of aspen. It then follows Prairie Creek to its confluence with Walker Creek. The trail fords Walker Creek and follows a steep and gullied track high into Walker Prairie. It meets the Big Goose trail on the heights behind a granite knob. From here our route runs northwest, charting a high course across the grassy slopes, staying above the granite knobs that guard Walker Creek. As the path continues across Walker Prairie, a shallow vale descends from the cleft between She Bear and Walker Mountains, bearing a small brook. The Soldier Creek trail follows this stream eastward, and after passing its marked junction, the main trail wanders into the grassy bottoms beside Walker Creek.

The trail passes a primitive cow camp, then passes through a fenceline. Just beyond the fence, the Walker Prairie trail veers northeast to climb vigorously up a grassy draw. Watch for posts that mark the way as the path climbs high beneath the sandstone edifice of Walker Mountain. The trail stays above the trees as it crosses a drainage divide to enter the Quartz Creek watershed. A backward glance reveals the distant summits of the Cloud Peak massif; ahead lie the sandstone reefs of Little and Big Mountains, with the wooded summit of Black Mountain rising to the northwest. The trail now splits in two. The upper path has the gentler gradient and superior scenery, while the lower path offers better access to the grassy bottoms of Quartz Creek. The two trails rejoin near the valley floor, about halfway between Little Mountain and Big Mountain. The path now skirts the upper edge of several tall cutbanks, staying up in the grasslands until it reaches the confluence of Quartz and Wolf Creeks.

Here, it fords both streams and begins climbing along loosely wooded slopes. It crosses grassy balds, passing a spur trail to an overlook of Wolf Falls en route to Bear Creek, where it passes an outfitter's camp. Follow the path down the far bank of Bear Creek. It ultimately turns north, descending to the grassy meadows of Sibley Creek. It reaches a junction beside the stream, then turns left and follows the Horseshoe Mountain Trail over a grassy divide. The route now leads down an open vale at the foot of the Elephants Foot. After a gentle descent, steep slopes lead down to a ford of the South Fork of Little Tongue River, and now the trail climbs through the meadows below the west face of Horseshoe Mountain. The next gap leads down to the Little Tongue, where a rickety footbridge marks the end of the journey.

Cloud Peak Wilderness 　　　33

Location: 30 miles west of Buffalo.
Size: 288,879 acres.
Administration: Bighorn National Forest (Powder River District), Wyoming Game and Fish Department.
Management status: Cloud Peak Wilderness (189,039 acres), Rock Creek roadless area (51,200 acres), other adjacent roadless lands (44,160 acres), state roadless lands on Bud Love Winter Range (4,480 acres).
Ecosystems: Douglas fir forest, lodgepole pine, western spruce-fir forest, sagebrush steppe.
Elevation range: 6,400 feet to 13,167 feet.
System trails: 305 miles.
Maximum core to perimeter distance: 5.7 miles.
Activities: Hiking, backpacking, horseback riding, big game hunting, mountaineering, rock climbing.
Best season: Late June–September in the high country; May–October in the Rock Creek area.
Maps: Bighorn National Forest Map; Burgess Junction, Buffalo, and Worland 1:100,000.

TRAVELERS ADVISORY:
ALTITUDE SICKNESS, SUDDEN STORMS

This wilderness is a wonderland of alpine lakes, sheer cliff walls, and half domes—the Yosemite of the Rocky Mountains. On the eastern side of the Cloud Peak massif, a series of timbered shelves leads up to the foot of the high granite domes. Dotted with lakes and ponds, this part of the Cloud Peak Wilderness is within easy reach of hikers and horsemen alike. From snowfields and alpine meadows, glittering brooks trickle down from the high country to feed the three forks of Clear Creek.

To the west of the Cloud Peak massif, rolling uplands dotted with broad meadows lead to the high peaks. Large alpine lakes are nestled within the deep, glacier-carved valleys of West Tensleep and Paint Rock Creeks. Elsewhere, sparkling streams course down through wet meadows and verdant grasslands en route to the deep rifts of Tensleep Canyon and Paint Rock Canyon. The massive half-domes and sheer granite cliffs that stretch from Bighorn Peak and Cloud Peak dominate the landscape—they are visible even from the distant foothills.

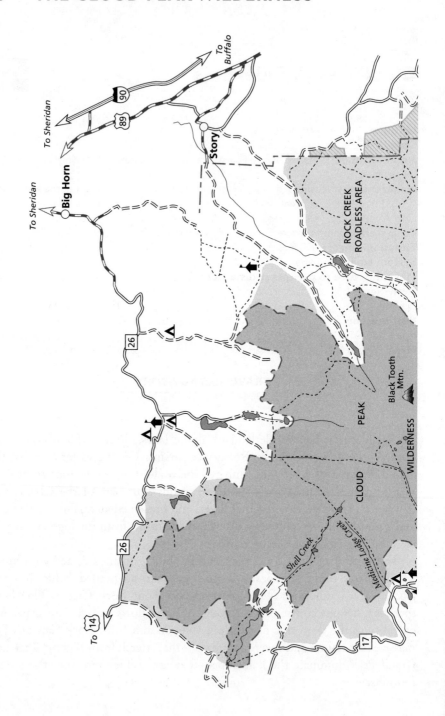

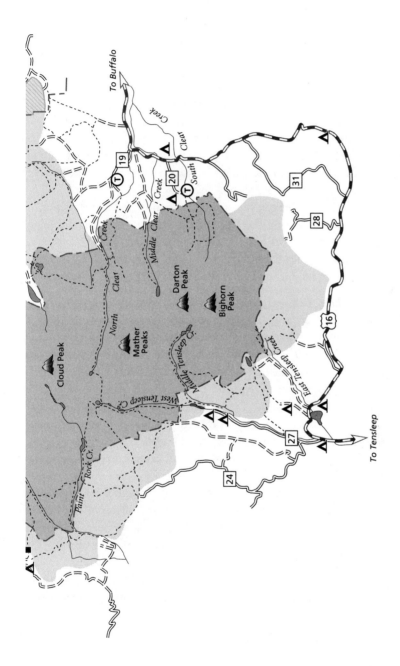

The northern half of the Cloud Peak Wilderness is wilder and more remote than the southern reaches. Fewer trails penetrate into the mountains, and these trails receive less maintenance and thus tend to be more primitive. In contrast to the southern marches of the Bighorns, the northernmost end of the Cloud Peak massif features pyramid-shaped peaks of frost-shattered granite.

The entire Cloud Peak massif is made up of granitic rock that was deeply glaciated during the Pleistocene. The glaciers gouged out myriad cirques and rock basins where meltwaters could collect to form alpine lakes. Since many of these lakes occupy bedrock basins, they are very sensitive to acid rain from air-borne pollutants. The northern leopard frog has been in decline in the Cloud Peak area since the late 1970s, and it is considered a harbinger for disaster that may ultimately claim the area's outstanding fishing.

The Rock Creek roadless area covers a broad swath of the eastern front of the Big Horn Mountains, linking the Cloud Peak Wilderness with the High Plains. It is characterized by short but stunning canyons, tall reefs of sedimentary rock, and broad meadows behind the first range of summits. It is an important winter range for elk and deer, and moose are permanent residents.

RECREATIONAL USES: Although the Cloud Peak Wilderness is vast, most areas can be reached in a day trip. This area is as popular with fishermen as it is with hikers, and solitude is in short supply at the more popular destinations. Mistymoon Lake is the most heavily hammered destination in the wilderness, and it is always crowded on weekends. Florence Pass, Geneva Pass, and Edelman Pass are the only high routes over the crest of the Bighorn divide. The Solitude Trail makes a circuit around the northern half of the massif, offering a 52-mile backpacking route. Battle Park is the hub for backcountry horsemen and receives fairly heavy use. If you are looking for a place in the Cloud Peak Wilderness to find solitude or undertake an off-trail expedition, the northern hinterlands are the best place to start.

Fishing in the lakes of the Cloud Peak Wilderness is legendary. Virtually all of the lakes served by trails have fish in them, and many of the off-trail lakes are also stocked regularly. Closely guarded fishing holes have been known to produce trophy-sized trout, and most of the larger streams offer fast fishing for pan-sized specimens.

The Rock Creek area receives some use by horse parties from the neighboring guest ranches, but it is relatively unknown to hikers. It offers excellent opportunities for long-range backpacks and mountain solitude. It offers better hunting potential than the higher country, which is often vacant of game animals by the autumn.

ACCESS: Major gravel roads from US 16 access the southern end of the Cloud Peak Wilderness at Battle Park, West Tensleep Lake, and Circle Park. On the southeast side, secondary roads that lead to the trails are choked with massive boulders; you can either hike the roads (they're usually short) or drive them in a high-clearance four-wheel drive. A good road runs south from US 14 to Paint Rock Lakes, accessing the west end of the wilderness. Otherwise, the secondary roads that lead to the north boundary are both rocky, may require stream fords, and become impassable in the rain. Access to the Rock Creek roadless area can be had via primitive roads that run north from Hunter Trailhead or by using the public access corridor provided by the HF-Bar Ranch to travel the trail up South Rock Creek. Access to the front is also available at two points within the Bud Love Game Range.

Extended Backpack or Horse Trip

Highland Park

Distance: From Hunter Trailhead, 22.5 miles one way, hiker route; 25.9 miles, horse route.
Difficulty: Moderately strenuous.
Starting and maximum elevation: 7,830 feet, 10,620 feet.
Topo maps: Hunter Mesa, Lake Angeline, Willow Park Reservoir, Cloud Peak.
Getting there: Follow US 16 to mile 79.6, then drive west on the Hunter Creek Road (FR 19). After 2.3 miles, veer left onto FR 394 to reach the Hunter trailhead at the bottom of the grade. Most hikers park here; if you have four-wheel-drive and are looking to abuse your rig, continue up FR 394 to the trailhead beyond Soldiers Park.

This trek runs along the eastern side of the Cloud Peak massif, following good trails and primitive routes en route to spectacular views of the high peaks from Elk Lake and Highland Park. Penrose Creek and Spear Lake make good side trips. Horsemen are advised to ride the old road to Willow Park Reservoir and then follow the Kearny Creek trail to Kearny Lakes Reservoir.

The hike begins by following the Florence Pass trail up the North Fork of Clear Creek. The first views of the mountains come at Trail Park, and just beyond it is a marked junction. Turn right (north) on the trail that climbs over a lofty lateral moraine and into the subalpine basin of South Rock Creek. Follow the cairns across the basin and continue north through a high pass behind the shattered granite of Ant Hill. The trail then descends to Elk Lake, a large and marshy mere set amid broad meadows.

From the west shore of the lake, hikers will head west on the trail to Cloud Peak Reservoir. (Horsemen should follow the trail to Willow Park Reservoir, which runs north from the lake's outlet.) This short trail soon intersects an old road. Turn right on the road, then after 0.2 mile, turn left (west) on the trail that descends to Flatiron Lake. Ford the lake's outlet, then follow the faint track northward along the watercourse. You will emerge at Frying Pan Lake

Elk Lake.

and ford its shallow western arm. On the far bank, follow the good trail beside willow-choked marsh.

At a junction at the north end of the marsh, continue north on the fainter track, which descends along the outlet stream. It soon traverses into the hills to the east, then runs the ridgetops down to the valley floor. Bear left at the next trail junctions to arrive at the extensive swamps at the confluence of Elk and Piney Creeks. Ford the swamp at the cairn to pick up the trail that runs down the west bank of Piney Creek. It ultimately turns northwest across wooded knolls and through small ponds en route to Penrose Creek.

Upon reaching the Penrose Creek Trail, turn left for an initial climb, and then right to reach the grade that zigzags down to the Beaver Lakes. Here, hike around the meadows to cross Kearny Creek on a footlog, then follow the trail west along the north side of the creek. At Kearny Lake Reservoir, climb past the dam and follow the access road northeast for 0.2 mile to strike the Lake Winnie Trail. It climbs heartily to a wooded shelf where Lake Winnie looks out over Penrose Peak and Black Tooth Mountain. The trail then ascends the drainage to reach the timberline plateau where Highland Park stretches vast and waterlogged, high above the Kearny Creek valley.

Marmot at Mistymoon Lake.

Day Hike

Firebox Park

Distance: 2.8 miles one way.
Difficulty: Moderately strenuous.
Starting and maximum elevation: 6,400 feet, 7,060 feet.
Topo map: Stone Mountain (trail not shown).
Getting there: From the west side of Buffalo, drive north on North De Smet Ave., following signs for the Bud Love Wildlife Management Unit. After 2.3 miles, the road splits. Bear right. The pavement ends 6 miles beyond this point. Drive onward for 2.5 miles to reach a sign for the Bud Love Winter Range; turn left onto a dry-weather road. Follow this road 2.4 miles, bearing right at all junctions, to reach the trailhead at its end.

This trail climbs through a steep canyon at the edge of the mountains, then climbs to the elevated grassland known as Firebox Park. The trek begins on the grassy plains of the Bud Love big game winter range. Follow the footpath that descends to a gate in the fence of an abandoned homestead. The trail glides up to the base of the mountains, following North Sayles Creek. Ahead is the mouth of a narrow canyon, flanked by upthrust strata of dolomite and sandstone that have been carved into eerie pillars and pinnacles by the forces of erosion. Upon entering the canyon, the path makes three quick crossings of North Sayles Creek. It then begins an unbelievably steep ascent through a stand of Douglas fir, the gradient precipitous despite the switchbacks. At the top of the grade, the trail surmounts a near-vertical slab of sandstone, then dips and rises as it crosses other rock strata.

It then descends to cross the creek and follow the more open north bank. Here, North Sayles Creek pours down a series of waterfalls linked by quiet pools, and old spruce trees shade the watercourse. At the National Forest boundary, the canyon opens up at the confluence of two stream branches. The trail initially crosses the main branch and follows the more southerly stream, then doglegs sharply to the northeast, climbing to the top of a grassy rise. The path now runs northward through a spruce-aspen woodland beside North Sayles Creek.

It soon makes a final crossing of the stream and climbs into the vast grasslands beyond. North Sayles Creek soon bends west into the mountains, but the path continues north through the grassy vale. There is a low gap at the head of the drainage, but the trail bends northwest to pass through a higher saddle to the west of a rocky hillock. The trail now descends into Firebox Park, a high and verdant meadow with superb vistas of the reefs and foothills in all directions.

Hazelton Peaks   ■ **34**

Location: 35 miles west of Buffalo.
Size: 10,500 acres.
Administration: Bighorn National Forest (Powder River District).
Management status: Unprotected roadless lands.
Ecosystem: Douglas fir forest, lodgepole pine, western spruce-fir forest.
Elevation range: 8,200 feet to 10,534 feet.
System trails: None.
Maximum core to perimeter distance: 1.9 miles.
Activities: Hiking, mountaineering, wildlife viewing.
Best season: June–September.
Maps: Bighorn National Forest Map; Worland 1:100,000.

TRAVELERS ADVISORY:
ALTITUDE SICKNESS, SUDDEN STORMS

The Hazelton Peaks are a miniature range of lofty, pyramid-shapes summits of frost-shattered gneiss that guard the headwaters of the Powder River's north fork. The entire roadless area lies near or above the timberline, with broad meadows and stands of lodgepole pine on the flats and woodlands of spruce, fir, and whitebark pine covering the slopes of the summits. Elk frequent the area during early summer, and their trails make for rapid traveling through the forests.

The higher elevations are a mixture of tundra and frost-shattered granite, where alpine meadows and tundra-clad basins are lit by the blooms of shooting star and alpine forget-me-not. Scattered about are patches of krummholz, which look like evergreen shrubs but are really trees that have been pruned down by winter winds to a prostrate growth form. The alpine zone is home to an abundance of pikas and alpine rodents. The pika spends all summer gathering an immense reserve of dried grass, which it stores beneath the boulders. This "hay" serves as a winter food supply for this tiny relative of the rabbit, which does not hibernate. Raptors are commonly sighted here, soaring on thermals as they search for prey.

In recent decades, clearcutting on the western edge of the roadless area has eaten into the forest. Although these clearcuts were replanted with seedlings, few of the conifers took root, and the damaged area was taken over by grasses.

34   HAZELTON PEAKS

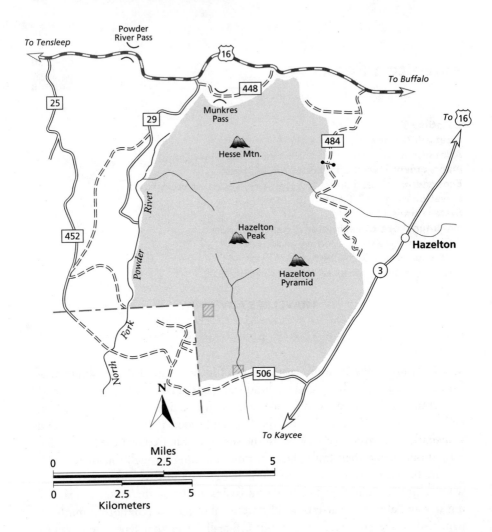

This form of succession following logging is common on the ranges that border the Great Plains. Stands of conifers may take hundreds of years to regenerate on dry sites, where grasses have the advantage of a dense mat of roots just beneath the soil that sucks up all available rainwater before it can reach the deeper roots of the trees. Because conifers cannot regenerate following logging on dry sites, clearcutting them has been labeled "timber mining." These forests are most accurately seen as a non-renewable resource.

RECREATIONAL USES: The Hazelton Peaks are an ideal place for trail-free recreation at and above the timberline, with good bushwhacking and peak-bagging routes. Surface water occurs only at a few springs and streams, limiting the potential for backcountry camping. The alpine tundra found here is quite fragile—walk on exposed rocks whenever possible. The summits command views in all directions. The granite domes of the Cloud Peak massif loom to the north, and to the south are the meadowy highlands at the tail of the Bighorns. Westward views stretch across the Bighorn Basin toward the Absaroka and Wind River ranges, and far eastward are the high plains of the Powder River basin. The North Fork of the Powder offers good fishing, but game is scarce during hunting season.

ACCESS: The high country can be reached from US 16 via FR 29, a gravel trunk road that runs along the western side of the roadless area. A high-clearance vehicle is recommended for FR 448, which runs through Munkres Pass at the northern boundary. The Hazelton Road (County 3) descends from US 16 farther east, and ultimately provides access to some of the lower slopes along the southeastern corner of the area.

Off-Trail Day Hike

Hazelton Peak

Distance: 3.2 miles one way.
Difficulty: Moderately strenuous.
Elevation gain: 1,674 ft.
Starting and maximum elevation: 8,860 feet, 10,534 feet.
Topo map: Hazelton Peak.
Getting there: FR 29 leaves US 16 just east of Powder River Pass. Follow this route, which starts out as a trunk road and deteriorates into a primitive, fair-weather road, for 4.8 miles to the roundabout at its end. The route follows the closed logging road that runs northeast from the far bank of the stream.

This off-trail route leads to the top of one of the major summits in the Hazelton Peaks roadless area. The hike begins by following a closed logging road northeast across the headwaters of the Powder River's North Fork, which is merely a mountain brook. On the far bank, follow the roadbed northeast as it climbs gently up a grassy hillock. Bear left at the first unmarked split in the road. Our road now runs atop a low finger ridge. There is a second junction atop the ridge. Stay right on FR #4011, which runs out into a clearcut above a grassy park. At the far edge of the clearcut, follow an overgrown jeep trail southeast as it charts a level course across a long meadow. The route now leaves established pathways as it heads up the meadow to reach the ridgeline.

The summit of Hazelton Peak.

On the ridgetop is an uglier and more recent clearcut; hike to its upper edge and follow elk trails southeast up the ridgeline. It climbs gently at first, passing through meadows and uncut stands of timber. The pitch ultimately steepens, and soon the first outcrops of gneiss break through the spine of the ridge. The forest then gives way to a timberline meadow studded with dwarfed conifers. Continue up the ridgeline toward the point marked 10,201 feet on your topo map. Knife-edged outcrops of bedrock rise from the ridgetop near the summit. At first you can find a grassy passage through the midst of the slabs, but it soon becomes necessary to traverse onto north-facing talus slopes and contour across the mountainside. Stringers of spruce rise at the far edge of the talus; hike upward through the trees to regain the ridgetop.

The route passes just to the south of point 10,201. It crests the mountaintop to reveal Hazelton Peak's summit, with a grassy bowl spread out below it. Chart an eastward course down past a spring at the upper edge of a stand of timber. From here, follow the upper edge of the meadow toward Hazelton Peak. At the far side of the bowl, climb straight up to reach the ridgetop just above a sharp outcrop of stone. From here, easy ridgeline traveling leads to a spot just below the summit. To attain the top, it becomes necessary to traverse rocks to the east of the summit, then scramble up the loose boulders to reach an old Geodetic Survey marker.

Trapper Canyon   35

Location: 5 miles southeast of Shell.
Size: 7,200 acres.
Administration: BLM (Worland Field Office).
Management status: Trapper Canyon WSA (7,200 acres).
Ecosystems: Wyoming Basin sagebrush steppe and Rocky Mountain Douglas fir forest.
Elevation range: 4,100 feet to 8,360 feet.
System trails: None.
Maximum core to perimeter distance: 0.8 mile.
Activities: Cross-country hiking, fishing, hunting, rockhounding, rappelling, spelunking.
Best season: April–June; September–November.
Maps: Burgess Junction and Worland 1:100,000.

TRAVELERS ADVISORY:
RATTLESNAKES

Trapper Canyon is the wildest and most remote of the major canyons at the western edge of the Big Horn Mountains. Here, the thousand-foot walls stretch for ten miles or more, guarding a seldom-breached fastness that harbors one of the most rich and diverse riparian communities in Wyoming. The canyon walls effectively prevent entry and exit except at the mouth and the headwaters. The cliffs are graced with natural arches in several places, and hanging canyons are host to slender waterfalls following cloudbursts.

The presence of reliable water and abundant game animals have attracted man to Trapper Canyon for over 9,000 years. The slopes along the canyon's lower reaches have patches of desert vegetation, with yuccas and prickly pear scattered amid the mountain mahogany and sagebrush. Above the canyon rim, rolling country slopes upward toward the crest of the Bighorns, mantled in sagebrush grasslands. Stands of Douglas fir are prevalent on north-facing slopes, particularly in the inner recesses of the canyon.

The canyon is truly one of Wyoming's birding hotspots. The towering walls provide nesting habitat for golden eagles, bald eagles, prairie falcons, and peregrine falcons, as well as other raptors. Rock doves (the common pigeons often seen in city parks) have colonized the canyon as well. Flocks of them are commonly seen as they flutter aimlessly through the still air of early evening. Along the waterway, water ouzels flit from boulder to boulder, occasionally diving

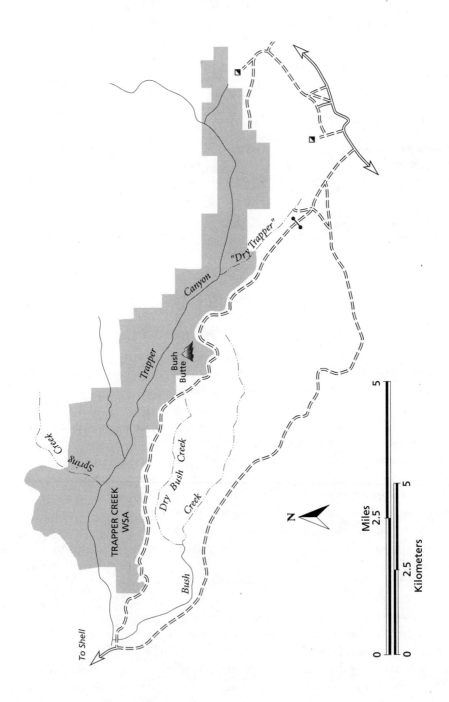

into the turbulent rapids to hunt for aquatic insects before emerging to perform their characteristic "push-ups" on a rock or log.

Mink and raccoons haunt the riparian underbrush along Trapper Creek, hunting for fish and aquatic invertebrates. Black bears are common visitors to the Trapper Canyon bottoms when the chokecherries and gooseberries ripen in late summer. As winter sets in, herds of up to 500 elk and 300 mule deer and even the occasional moose take up residence. The upper reaches of the canyon are an important calving area for elk. Bobcats and mountain lions are year-round residents, and wild turkeys inhabit the cottonwood groves at the canyon's mouth. Trapper Canyon has been identified as having high potential for the reintroduction of bighorn sheep and peregrine falcons.

The vertical rock faces of Trapper Canyon are so forbidding that a road could not be built into the area without prohibitive expense. Trapper Canyon has a low potential for the occurrence of oil and gas. There is some possibility of tar sand deposits, but none have been located so far. Small quantities of silver, uranium, and rare-earth metals may occur here, but they're not considered to be economically significant. Industrial-grade silica sand has also been located in the area, with one active mine pit south of the canyon. There are about 1,500 acres of commercially harvestable timber within the WSA, but no timber sales are anticipated in the near future. The BLM has recommended the entire WSA for wilderness status.

RECREATIONAL USES: Trapper Canyon is one of the most remote and challenging landscapes for primitive recreation. However, for the lure of the solitude, wildlife, grandeur, and outstanding fishing, there is a stiff price to be paid: The canyon is guarded by choking vines and brambles, rockfalls, rattlesnakes, stinging nettles, loose talus, and countless other obstacles. Not only is this wilderness travel, it is travel through a *hostile* wilderness, and all the skills and experience in the world won't make it an easy trip.

Trapper Creek supports a burgeoning population of native Yellowstone cutthroat, as well as browns and rainbows. The few anglers who manage to penetrate the depths of the canyon are typically rewarded with fast fishing in the pocket water. Brush that crowds the stream prohibits long casts and makes it difficulty to find a good place to get into and out of the water. Although game-rich, the country below the rims receives little hunting pressure because of the difficulty of getting downed animals out of the canyon. Chukar, sage grouse, and blue grouse tempt upland bird hunters.

The limestone walls of Trapper Canyon are the site of one of the nation's major cave systems. The lower entrance of Great Expectations Cave lies within the WSA. This cave has at least 4 miles of known passages, and is the third deepest cave in the United States. Cave explorers expect to find many miles of new and uncharted passages in Trapper Canyon in the future.

ACCESS: The Trapper Creek Road runs southeast from Shell to the mouth of Trapper Canyon. Private lands of the Hunter Ranch block the canyon entrance, but permission is often granted to travelers who wish to emerge from the canyon here after entering in its upper reaches. A rough jeep road travels up beside the south rim of the canyon to reach an upper drop-in point at a drainage known locally as "Dry Trapper Creek." This road is a brutal one, with steep grades and substantial sills of bedrock that will turn back all but the most hard-core driver.

Off-Trail Backpack

Trapper Canyon

Distance: 9.1 miles from top to bottom.
Difficulty: Strenuous.
Starting and minimum elevation: 7,330 feet, 4,600 feet.
Topo maps: Black Mountain, Bush Butte, White Sulphur Spring.
Getting there: From the south end of Shell, follow the paved Trapper Creek Road. The pavement ends after 3 miles; bear right at the split and follow a primitive road around the irrigated fields of the Hunter Ranch. Turn left atop the next rise, and either park here and walk or drive the primitive, steep, and rocky track that runs eastward, climbing to reach a gate above the Dry Trapper watershed about 9 miles above the junction. Plan on at least two days to hike down through the canyon, plus a third day if you park at the lower end and hike up the road to start the trip.

For those who hike the access road, the crossing of the Bush Creek wash leads to a steep climb through a desert scrub of rabbitbrush and prickly pear. The ascent eases as the road reaches the rolling grasslands of the uplands. The first canyon views are at mile 4.0, as the road crosses a parcel of private land. The track then passes behind the tree-clad summit of Bush Butte before ascending the ridgeline behind it. Follow the road for another 5.2 miles to reach a fence gate on the ridgetop. This marks the drop-in point to a valley known locally as "Dry Trapper Creek" and the beginning of the wilderness route.

Angle downstream as you drop into this tributary canyon, descending through the Douglas firs to avoid a beetle-killed and brushy area farther east. Upon reaching the bottomlands, you can either hike the streamcourse or try the wooded slopes that face north, or the grassy, south-facing exposures. Whatever your choice, it will eventually become necessary to descend to the streambed to avoid the cliffs that guard the lower reaches of the valley. Here, you must tangle with the thorny brush and stinging nettles whenever boulders block the way. Take time to notice the astonishing diversity of butterflies and birds that call this canyon home.

Looking into Trapper Canyon from the south rim.

After a difficult slog, Dry Trapper joins the much larger declivity of Trapper Canyon itself. A good camp spot at the confluence is typical of the good spots to be found wherever tributary canyons join the main chasm. The slopes to the south of Trapper Creek are timbered in Douglas fir, while those to the north are open and arid. The stream itself is clogged with a tangle of brush that features thorns and stinging nettles. Pick your poison: cliffs and downed logs on the timbered slopes, rattlesnakes and rockfalls on the open exposures. Changing your mind here is expensive, with each trip through the riparian wall of thorn scrub a tedious and time-consuming battle.

In the initial stretch of Trapper Canyon, you can see a small arch up Dry Trapper as well as a much larger span down the main canyon. The big walls appear as you reach the first major side canyon on the north. In the heart of Trapper Canyon, the Douglas firs give way to a scattered growth of mountain mahogany and other desert plants. A second, lower tier of cliffs now appears beside the creek, forcing additional stream crossings. After a short distance, the cliffs sink back into the valley floor, and for a time you will enjoy hassle-free traveling along grassy flats beside the creek.

Big walls in the heart of Trapper Canyon.

Natural arch in Trapper Canyon.

Once you reach Spring Creek, a trail of sorts starts on the north side of the canyon floor and leads down past an overhanging cave. The neck-stretching walls run all the way to the mouth of the canyon. Here, they sink abruptly into the earth, and the bottoms are filled with a jungle-like growth of hardwoods and vines. The best course here is to splash down the shallow riffles until you reach the irrigation headgate, where you can pick up a dirt road across private land for faster traveling. Follow it to an intersection, then turn left and hike the jeep track up the wash of Bush Creek to intercept the original access road.

Medicine Lodge   36

Location: 5 miles north of Hyattville.
Size: 28,500 acres.
Administration: BLM (Worland Field Office), Bighorn National Forest (Medicine Wheel—Paintrock District).
Management status: Medicine Lodge WSA (7,740 acres); unprotected BLM and National Forest lands (20,760 acres).
Ecosystem: Wyoming Basin Province sagebrush steppe; Rocky Mountain Province Douglas fir forest, lodgepole pine.
Elevation range: 4,920 feet to 9,186 feet.
System trails: 6 miles.
Maximum core to perimeter distance: 1.2 miles.
Activities: Hiking, fishing, big game hunting, wildlife viewing, spelunking.
Best season: April–June, September–October.
Maps: Bighorn National Forest Map; Worland 1:100,000.

TRAVELERS ADVISORY:
RATTLESNAKES

The two branches of Medicine Lodge Creek have carved deep canyons into the western slopes of the Big Horn Mountains. This is arid country, and during the summer the streams may disappear under the gravels for long distances before emerging once more. The canyon walls are composed of Madison limestone, which contains the fossils of brachiopods, corals, bryozoans, and crinoids. This roadless area offers a truly primitive experience for folks who want to try their hand at off-trail canyoneering.

Medicine Lodge Canyon has always been a magnet to indigenous hunter-gatherers. The canyons derive their names from the "medicine lodge," a circular structure traditionally built by Plains tribes for religious ceremonies. At the mouth of Dry Medicine Lodge Canyon is the Medicine Lodge Archaeological Site. This well-known landmark features a wall covered in pictographs of shield figures that were made by Plains Indian tribes just before the arrival of white explorers. Archaeological evidence for this area suggests that this area was inhabited continuously for 10,000 years before the arrival of the white man, and the canyons are thought to contain a rich wealth of archaeological sites that have yet to be cataloged.

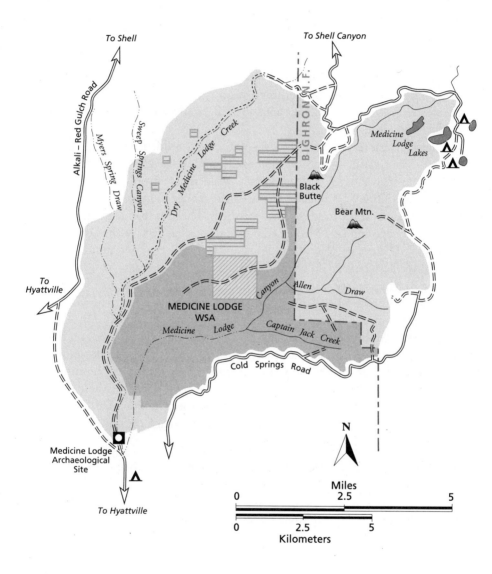

To Shell

To Shell Canyon

Alkali – Red Gulch Road

Myers Spring Draw

Sweep Spring Canyon

Dry Medicine Lodge Creek

BIGHORN N.F.

Medicine Lodge Lakes

Black Butte

Bear Mtn.

To Hyattville

Canyon

Allen

Draw

MEDICINE LODGE WSA

Medicine   Lodge

Captain Jack Creek

Cold   Springs   Road

Medicine Lodge
Archaeological
Site

N

To Hyattville

Miles
0   2.5   5

0   2.5   5
Kilometers

Medicine Lodge Canyon is crisscrossed with game trails, and the grassy slopes above the rims are a winter range for thousands of mule deer and elk. The sloping steppes between the canyons are robed in sagebrush and grasses. Slopes and ledges of mountain mahogany and bluebunch wheatgrass within the canyons are important winter range. The Wyoming Game and Fish Department has bought out all of the private inholdings in this area and is managing them as big game winter range. Cool locales on north-facing slopes and at higher elevations support stands of Douglas fir. The canyon bottoms have extensive riparian groves of cottonwood and other hardwoods. Substantial tracts of juniper scrub grow on the rolling desert foothills along the western edge of the roadless area, forming an important year-round habitat for mule deer.

The BLM has recommended only 3,600 acres for wilderness designation. The rugged terrain naturally restricts motorized travel in the area, and livestock use in the canyon has never been important. Wilderness advocates would include not only the entire WSA but also Dry Medicine Lodge Canyon and roadless Forest Service lands at the heads of the watersheds. The jeep road that separates the Medicine Lodge and Dry Medicine Lodge canyons has been washed out near its lower end. There is no plan to rebuild it, and if it were closed to motor vehicles, the two roadless areas could be unified into a single wilderness.

The BLM's primary reason for recommending such a small area for protection was a supposed need for motorized access to allow for maintenance of range developments like fences, springs, and pipelines above the rims. The author would humbly submit that any cowboy who can't do his work on horseback ought to look for another career. Opportunities for solitude above the rims are limited at certain times of year, particularly during the hunting season. This argument does not detract from the importance of these pristine shrub steppes from a habitat and ecosystem perspective. Potential for oil and gas drilling and hard rock mining are low, and the area faces no known threat from the mineral extraction industry.

RECREATIONAL USE: Medicine Lodge Canyon has no trails and offers rugged and sometimes brushy traveling cross-country. An old roadbed follows Dry Medicine Lodge Canyon along its entire length. It has reverted to a primitive trail, with loose boulders in some places and thorny brush in others. Cave passageways of the P-Bar cave system are found in Medicine Lodge Canyon, and during times of high water, they carry the entire flow of the creek.

The eastern reaches of the roadless area and the desert foothills region receive an estimated 250 visitor days of ATV use, principally associated with hunting and livestock management. The area is very popular with big game hunters, and chukars, partridge, sage grouse, and turkeys are also present here. There are cutthroat trout in Medicine Lodge Creek, but low water conditions make them spooky during the height of summer.

ACCESS: Good gravel trunk roads run from Wyoming 31 to the Medicine Lodge Archaeological Site near Hyattville. The Archaeological Site, at the mouth of both canyons, is staffed by the Wyoming Game and Fish Department and offers developed camping. The Cold Springs Road runs up the highlands above the south rim of Medicine Lodge Canyon and is passable to all but low-clearance vehicles. The Paint Rock Lakes Road (FR 17) runs south from US 14 at the head of Shell Canyon, providing good access to the upper reaches of the area. It gets muddy when wet. The Black Butte Road, a jeep road that climbs the slopes between Medicine Lodge and Dry Medicine Lodge canyons, is closed to motor vehicles from December through June to protect winter range of elk and deer.

Day Hike

The Arch

Distance: 1.3 to 4.3 miles one way.
Difficulty: Moderate.
Starting and maximum elevation: 5,220 feet, 6,950 feet.
Topo maps: Allen Draw, Hyatt Ranch.
Getting there: Drive east from Manderson on WY 31. After 22 miles, turn left on the Alkali-Cold Springs Road. Turn right after 0.3 miles on Cold Springs Road. Follow the signs for the Medicine Lodge Archaeological Site, following farm roads through hayfields and then through the campground to reach the pictograph site. From here, drive or hike north up the jeep track that runs through the parking lot and up the canyon for 3 miles. Park at the spot where the road begins its climb out of the canyon.

This route follows an abandoned roadbed through the bottoms of Dry Medicine Lodge Canyon. At the outset, the old roadway follows the course of Dry Medicine Lodge Creek between low walls of brittle rock. Early on, a lush growth of cottonwood, box elder, and other canyon hardwoods crowd the dry wash of the creek. The walls soon rise to impressive heights as the canyon cuts into the western slope of the Bighorns. Just below the mouth of Sheep Springs Canyon, watch for The Arch, an enormous natural bridge that graces the western wall of the canyon.

The Arch, which guards Dry Medicine Lodge Creek.

Off-Trail Canyon Scramble

Medicine Lodge Canyon

Distance: 6.4 miles overall.
Difficulty: Moderately strenuous.
Starting and minimum elevation: 7,700 feet, 5,000 feet.
Topo maps: Allen Draw, Hyatt Ranch.
Getting there: Drive east from Manderson on WY 31. After 22 miles, turn left on the Alkali-Cold Springs Road. Turn right after 0.3 miles on Cold Springs Road. The pavement ends just beyond the cutoff to the Medicine Lodge Archaeological Site. Follow the main road, which climbs into the hills for 9.6 miles to reach a jeep road that runs north just before the main road makes a major swing to the south. This jeep road marks the hike's beginning. The trek ends 1 mile up the Dry Medicine Lodge Road from the Medicine Lodge pictograph site (see *The Arch*).

This route penetrates one of the major western canyons in the Big Horn Mountains, traversing a wild and remote area that lacks trails. The canyon walls extend upstream to Black Butte, but the route described here covers only

Looking into the upper reaches of Medicine Lodge Canyon.

the more accessible lower reaches of the chasm in a challenging through-hike that can readily be completed in a single day. From the starting point, follow the jeep trail north to the edge of the valley of Captain Jack Creek. The road soon descends gently toward the floor of this vale. After passing through a fence, follow the livestock trail that leads westward to the bottomlands. Here, lush swards of grass provide easy traveling, with slopes of Douglas fir to the south and outcrops of limestone to the north.

After 1.3 miles of easy traveling, the descent steepens and the route leads around a small, overhanging pour-off. Here, elk trails replace the cattle paths. The cliffs rise in several tiers above Captain Jack Creek, which now flows at the surface. The creek bottoms are choked with brush and brambles, making for a laborious passage down the steep streamcourse. As the walls rise higher on both sides, the canyon of Captain Jack Creek joins with Medicine Lodge Canyon, and spectacular scenery unfolds ahead. Drift onto the slopes of mountain mahogany to the north of Captain Jack Creek, then work your way down the divide to reach the floor of Medicine Lodge Canyon.

The canyon's limestone walls rise to staggering heights, and below them are steep slopes. Elk trails crisscross these slopes and can be followed for long stretches. Hike along the north-facing slopes of mountain mahogany or the south-facing slopes, which bear a sparse growth of grasses. The streamcourse itself is also a potential corridor for travel, but it is bordered by a dense tangle of brush and vines that is practically impenetrable. Select a route and follow the canyon downward. Eventually the walls begin to dwindle, and it becomes possible to follow game trails along the grassy benches beside the stream.

As the canyon bends southward, watch for a rounded gap in the cliffs on the right (west) side of the canyon. Climb through this gap, which leads into the canyon of Dry Medicine Lodge Creek. Next, descend to the canyon floor to reach the jeep road on the far side of the wash. This road leads to the Medicine Lodge pictograph site after 1.3 miles.

Paint Rock Canyon   **37**

Location: 5 miles northeast of Hyattville.
Size: 16,038 acres.
Administration: BLM (Worland Field Office); Bighorn National Forest (Medicine Wheel–Paintrock District).
Management status: Unprotected BLM lands (11,588 acres) and National Forest lands (4,480 acres).
Ecosystem: Wyoming Basin sagebrush steppe, Rocky Mountain Douglas fir forest, lodgepole pine.
Elevation range: 5,120 feet to 9,400 feet.
System trails: 16.3 miles.
Maximum core to perimeter distance: 1.7 miles.
Activities: Hiking, horseback riding, fishing, hunting.
Best season: April–June, September–October.
Maps: Bighorn National Forest Map, Worland 1:100,000.

TRAVELERS ADVISORY:
RATTLESNAKES

The many forks of Paint Rock Creek descend through a grassy basin before joining forces to carve a deep chasm in the limestone just east of Hyattville. The towering and multicolored walls rise above sparkling riffles and shady woodlands. Prehistoric hunter-gatherers camped along the canyon and it is considered to be rich in archaeological sites.

Vegetation varies from desert scrub of juniper near the canyon mouth to arid sagebrush steppe above the rims and in the interior meadows. Stands of Douglas fir grow on the north-facing canyon slopes and extensive forests of lodgepole pine robe the uplands at the east end of the proposed wilderness. Along the watercourses, a rich riparian woodland of hardwoods and shrubs is home to a diverse array of birds. Paint Rock Canyon and the grasslands above it are a critical winter range for elk and deer. Bighorn sheep were reintroduced to the Paint Rock Canyon area in the 1980s, but the population is not doing well.

The roadless area encompasses both BLM and Forest Service Lands. The canyon was once considered for wilderness status during the RARE II process in the 1970s, but for reasons unknown it was dropped from consideration in the BLM's wilderness EIS in 1984. The BLM lands are closed to motor vehi-

37   PAINT ROCK CANYON

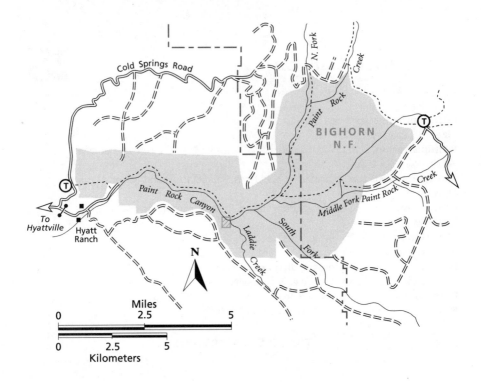

cles, but ATVs are allowed on the Forest Service portion of the roadless area. The potential for mining and petroleum exploration is low for this entire area. Cattle are grazed on the meadows within the Bighorn National Forest, but otherwise there is little economic activity here.

RECREATIONAL USES: An abandoned roadbed follows the stream through Paint Rock Canyon, then links up with trails that are well-suited to both horses and hikers. Paint Rock Creek itself is a blue-ribbon trout stream, and a majority of the visitors to this roadless area have fishing on their itinerary. Paint Rock Creek features a charming mixture of pools, runs, and pocket water that will challenge any fly fisher. Rainbow and cutthroat trout are the principal species found here. Hunting potential for elk and deer is also high, although access to the lower canyon is difficult during the rifle season. Access to the area via Forest Service roads remains open during this time.

ACCESS: A connecting trail leads from the Cold Springs Road toward the mouth of Paint Rock Canyon. You must then hike eastward up the road through the private lands of the Hyatt Ranch to reach the mouth of Paint Rock

Canyon, where motorized travel ends and the public lands begin. When passing through the Hyatt Ranch, stay on the approved roadway and exercise the utmost courtesy so that the ranch allows travelers to pass this way in the future. This access trail is open only from May 11 to September 30.

To reach the Lone Tree trailhead, drive up the Cold Springs road for 6 miles, then turn right (south) on the primitive jeep road that descends to the Lone Tree trailhead. This trailhead has no seasonal restrictions. The upper end of the canyon can be reached by driving the Cold Springs Road to the top of the range, then following FR 349 down a hair-raising and primitive grade that leads to the Hyatt Cow Camp.

Day or Overnight Trip on Foot or Horseback

Paint Rock Canyon

Distance: 12.8 miles one way.
Difficulty: Moderate.
Starting and maximum elevation: 5,430 feet, 7,500 feet.
Topo maps: Hyatt Ranch, Bush Butte.
Getting there: Drive east from Manderson on WY 31. After 22 miles, turn left on the Alkali-Cold Springs Road. Turn right after 0.3 miles on Cold Springs Road. The pavement ends just beyond the cutoff to the Medicine Lodge Archaeological Site. Follow the main road as it climbs into the hills to reach the well-marked trailhead on the left side of the road, 5.8 miles from the highway. To reach the upper trailhead, follow the Cold Springs Road all the way to the crest of the range, about 15 miles. Turn right onto FR 352 and follow it for 0.6 mile. Turn left onto FR 349. Park at the top of the hill, or (if you have four-wheel-drive) make the perilous descent of 3.2 miles to reach the bridge over North Paint Rock Creek. The end of the trail joins this road 0.2 mile beyond the bridge.

This trail follows Paint Rock Creek through its deep chasm, then climbs into a meadowy basin where it enters the Bighorn National Forest. The trek begins on low, arid hills covered in juniper scrub. As the path wanders down to cross the first wash, it enters an area that burned in 1996. After a short southwestward climb, the path descends into a second draw, this one untouched by fire. After crossing it, the trail follows the watercourse downward and soon drops into the lush, pastoral bottomlands of Paint Rock Creek. The route now enters private land owned by the Hyatt Ranch and follows a dirt road past irrigated hayfields and verdant pastures. Rocky cliffs rise on both sides of the valley, low at first and then rising to great heights. As the valley constricts to form a narrow canyon, the trail returns to BLM lands. Motor vehicles are prohibited beyond this point.

The tall limestone cliffs now rise above sagebrush slopes, and a verdant ribbon of cottonwood shades the stream banks. The green waters of Paint Rock

Limestone cliffs in Paint Rock Canyon.

Creek hurry downward through an endless series of riffles and pocket water. As the trail reaches the first big bend in the canyon, watch for a small natural arch high on the north rim. Douglas firs now stud the north-facing slopes across the creek, and soon they rise along the streamcourse as well. The canyon walls maintain an impressive height as the trail continues eastward, climbing at a modest pace. The old road crosses a small tract of private land at the mouth of Laddie Creek; here, the south walls of the canyon are robed in a climax forest of Douglas fir.

As the trail continues upward, it enters a broad, grassy basin guarded by The Island, a sphinx-like butte that rises between South and Middle Paint Rock Creeks. Upon reaching a fence, follow it downward to reach the gate at a section corner. Pass through the gate and continue westward beside the tumultuous, boulder-choked rapids of Paint Rock Creek. A grove of mature aspen grows at the confluence of Middle Paint Rock and the main fork. Here, the trail crosses a sturdy bridge over the main fork and climbs through muddy seeps along its east bank.

The next part of the journey crosses open sage meadows, following the great northward bend of Paint Rock Creek as the canyon falls behind. Now a pack trail, the route dips into the bottoms, then rises again to cross a long flat beneath a timbered mesa. At the far edge of the clearing, the trail leaves BLM land and enters the Bighorn National Forest.

It now becomes an ATV trail, which winds gently upward across open benches. The streamside woodland now takes on a montane character, with spruce and lodgepole pine replacing the cottonwoods of the lower elevations. At the confluence of the main fork and North Paint Rock Creek, the trail crosses a bridge over the main fork and follows North Paint Rock. On the far side, a sustained climb leads up to gentler country where tawny grasslands stretch eastward from the stream. The trail emerges onto FR 349 at a ragged grove of aspen, marking the end of the trek.

Another view of Paint Rock Canyon.

The Thunder Basin National Grassland contains some of the High Plains' finest roadless areas, such as the Miller Hills pictured here.

6

Powder River Basin and High Plains Region

Two centuries ago, a vast and empty plain stretched east from the Rocky Mountains, a high and semi-arid grassland that was home to vast herds of wild animals and the indigenous people who hunted them. Herds of buffalo that numbered in the millions migrated across the face of the grasslands, eating the grasses down to their roots and then moving on. Antelope followed in the wake of the bison, foraging on the forbs that sprang up from the bare ground. Herds of elk and deer wandered freely across the plains, and wolves and grizzly bears hunted along the fringes of the great bison herds. The Plains tribes called this region *Wyoming*, or Large Plains.

All of this changed soon after the first white explorers pushed west through the region. In an insatiable quest for land, the American government undertook a systematic campaign to acquire the ancestral homelands of the Plains Indians by negotiation whenever possible and by force if necessary. When the U.S. Army failed to conquer the superior fighting forces of the northern Plains tribes, President Grant initiated a campaign to starve the Indians into submission by killing off the buffalo. Aided by hide hunters and the building of the railroads, the bison were driven extinct by the 1880s, and the frontier had changed forever. Soon thereafter, the remaining free tribes were forced to accept small reservations made up of lands that the white settlers didn't want.

By the time the first American and Canadian settlers pushed westward into the Plains, the bison were gone, market hunters had eliminated the Plains elk, and wolves and grizzly bears had been driven into the mountains. Spurred on by the "rain follows the plow" myths perpetuated by land speculators, railroads, and other boosters, immigrants filed for homesteads of 160 acres and started farming. But as explorer John Wesley Powell wisely pointed out at the time, all of Wyoming is in fact a desert. Frequent droughts and prairie fires made farming extremely difficult, and few of the settlers were able to outlast the vagaries of the climate.

Meanwhile, herds of cattle were being driven up from Texas to establish vast ranches backed by English financial interests. What law there was could be bought, and the open range owned by the U.S. government could be controlled by anyone who had enough manpower and guns to enforce his will. Many of the big ranchers sent paid flunkies to stake out fraudulent homesteads around the scarce water sources, then bought the homesteads for a pittance. These were freewheeling times—a rope and a running iron were all that was needed to start a cattle outfit, cattlemen and sheep herders engaged in open gun battles, and farmers and smaller ranchers were burned out by the big outfits.

But the winter of 1881 forced many to leave the ranching business, and when the U.S. Army put an end to the Johnson County Range War in 1892, it signaled an end to the open range. Barbed-wire fences sprang up everywhere, and ultimately the federal government instituted a program of grazing leases for public lands. Today, about half of Wyoming's rangelands are publicly owned and are administered by the U.S. government. Ranchers who hold grazing leases count federal lands into the total acreage of their ranches, and often hold a proprietary view of these lands.

Modern visitors will find that the High Plains are divided up into ranches, overrun by oilfields, and in some places strip-mined for coal. Public lands are a minority of the holdings in this region, and these have been fragmented in many areas. Roads both major and minor crisscross the landscape, connecting oil wells, windmills, stock tanks, and remote ranches. On public lands, there are scarcely any large areas that have remained roadless and natural. The few remaining wild areas are that much more precious, representing the last remnants of a grassland ecosystem that has almost entirely disappeared.

North Fork of Powder River

38

Location: 30 miles northwest of Kaycee.
Size: 19,486 acres.
Administration: BLM (Buffalo Field Office)
Management status: 10,089 acres in North Fork WSA; 9,397 acres of unprotected BLM, state, and private lands.
Ecosystem: Rocky Mountain Douglas fir forest, dominated by ponderosa pine savannas.
Elevation range: 5,710 feet to 8,155 feet.
System trails: None.
Maximum core to perimeter distance: 1.75 miles.
Activities: Horseback riding, hiking, big game and upland bird hunting, fishing, rock climbing.
Best season: May–October.
Map: Kaycee 1:100,000.

The North Fork of Powder River flows through the rolling forelands at the eastern edge of the Big Horn Mountains. The river and two of its tributaries have carved deep canyons into the rolling savannas of the foothills. This spectacular landscape is transitional between the Great Plains grasslands and the forests of the Big Horn Mountains. As such, it provides a rich and diverse assemblage of plants and animals. The eastern half of the WSA is an important winter rage for elk from the southern Bighorns. Golden eagles and prairie falcons are known to nest within the confines of the canyons. Bald eagles roost in the area during the wintertime.

The potential for economic development in this area is low. Cattle already graze the uplands, and this activity would continue under wilderness designation. The WSA contains 2,900 acres of commercially harvestable timber. Packsaddle Canyon is the only planned cut in the foreseeable future, and timber yields would be low. This foothills region has a low potential for oil and gas exploration. In short, Wyoming's economy has nothing to lose by designating this parcel as wilderness.

RECREATIONAL USES: The North Fork of the Powder River is rated as an outstanding trout fishery, with rainbows, browns, and brook trout. The rolling meadows and open timber above the rims are ideal horse country and would offer many highly scenic camp spots along the tops of the cliffs. The deep canyons of the North Fork and Packsaddle Creek offer fine opportunities for

38   NORTH FORK OF POWDER RIVER

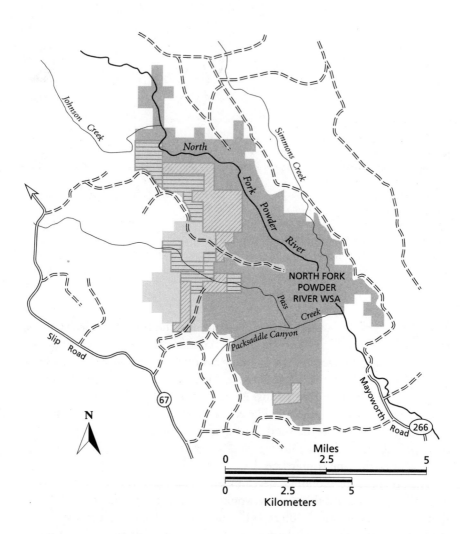

rock climbing, although the area is little known as a climbing destination. The only trails found here are made by game, so travel within the canyons is a wilderness canyoneering proposition.

ACCESS: The North Fork WSA is an island of public land surrounded by privately owned parcels, and not a single road provides legal public access. The Mayoworth Road is an improved gravel road that runs to within 2 miles of public lands before NO TRESPASSING signs bar the way. The Slip Road runs

Hogbacks of Chugwater sandstone lead to the north of the North Fork Canyon.

along the headwaters of Packsaddle Canyon, but again private lands must be crossed to reach the roadless area. It is theoretically possible for an experienced wilderness traveler to start at the end of BLM 6207 and hike south along the steep slopes of the Big Horn Mountain front, following a narrow strip of public lands with the aid of a Global Positioning System (GPS) for 10 miles to reach the north end of the WSA. In practice, this route is not feasible without a developed trail.

The BLM has an avowed policy to provide public access to its lands. Despite the fact that the North Fork is a wilderness study area with blue ribbon fishing and outstanding hunting, travel easements or land swaps that would provide public access are not in the works. Even a trail down the public corridor from the north would be helpful, but as yet there are no plans to construct one. This lack of resolve is perhaps indicative of BLM antipathy toward wilderness, inasmuch as the lack of public access has been used as an excuse to recommend the North Fork for non-wilderness status.

Gardner Mountain   39

Location: 35 miles northwest of Kaycee.
Size: 21,025 acres.
Administration: BLM (Buffalo Field Office).
Management status: 6,423 acres in Gardner Mountain WSA; 14,602 acres of unprotected roadless lands.
Ecosystem: Rocky Mountain Forest Province; Douglas fir forest with extensive ponderosa pine savannas.
Elevation range: 5,300 feet to 8,398 feet.
System trails: 8 miles.
Maximum core to perimeter distance: 1.3 miles.
Activities: Big game and upland bird hunting, fishing, hiking, horseback riding, spelunking.
Best season: May–October.
Map: Kaycee 1:100,000.

The Gardner Mountain WSA encompasses the rolling country where the Red Fork of Powder River emerges from the Big Horn Mountains. Gardner Mountain itself is a long scarp of high, roadless country with all the attributes of wilderness but no special land use designation. The wilderness study area identified by the BLM lies across Cottonwood Creek from this peak. The landscape is a mix of grassland and loose stands of conifers that is ideal for cross-country hiking and horseback riding.

The steep country of Fraker Mountain is interspersed with forests and grasslands. The uplift is cut by the canyons of the Red Fork and Beartrap Creeks, with sheer walls that rise 600–800 feet above their respective streams. The southern portion of the WSA is characterized by lower elevations and drier conditions, with sagebrush and mountain mahogany. Some 750 acres are rated as commercial forestland, and should the WSA be released from wilderness consideration, this timber is slated to be harvested.

Gardner Mountain provides habitat for elk, mule deer, black bear, and mountain lions. It is also home to 500 resident mule deer and about 100 head of elk. During winter, the WSA serves as a range for up to 700 mule deer. Both peregrine falcons and bald eagles use the area during their spring and fall migrations, and prairie falcons and red-tailed hawks nest on the cliffs and canyon walls within the proposed wilderness. Oil and gas are not present beneath the WSA, and recreation is its most valuable asset.

39   GARDNER MOUNTAIN

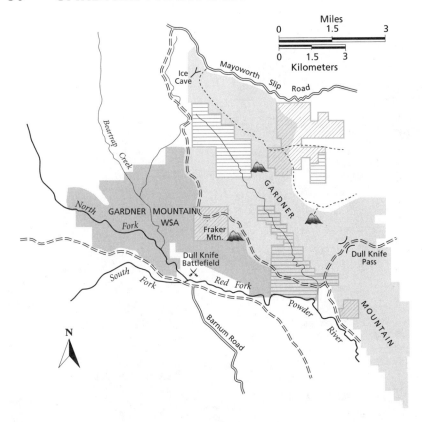

The Dull Knife Battle occurred along the southern edge of the WSA. During this fight, the U.S. Army captured the Cheyennes' horses and burned their lodges, but then the tribal warriors fought them to a standoff. After the battle, the Northern Cheyenne fled through the WSA to make their escape in the mountains. Lacking food or shelter, the tribe wintered with the Sioux tribe before surrendering to the Army and being escorted to their present reservation in Montana.

RECREATIONAL USES: Both the Red Fork and Bear Trap Creek are known to offer excellent fishing for rainbow, brown, and brook trout. Hunters who ply this area enjoy a high rate of success when pursuing elk and mule deer. Turkeys, chukars, and blue grouse are some of the game birds that can be found here. Access is problematic, however: local landowners are known to charge access fees or even deny access to the public lands that lie beyond their ranches.

Cliffs on the west face of Gardner Mountain.

ACCESS: The Slip Road is a rough and washed out county road that climbs from Mayoworth to the crest of Gardner Mountain. From here, a new trail has been built southward along the mountain crest, and one can descend southwest from this trail to hike across public lands to legally reach the WSA. A dirt road follows Cottonwood Creek down from the Slip Road along the western boundary of the WSA. Since public access on this road is blocked by private land, there is no public interest in keeping it open. The BLM should permanently close this road and obliterate it, linking roadless lands on Gardner Mountain with the WSA.

Day Hike or Horse Trip

Gardner Mountain Trail

Distance: 6.2 miles one way.
Difficulty: Moderate.
Starting and minimum elevation: 8,120 feet, 7,310 feet.
Topo map: Fraker Mountain
Getting there: Drive south from Buffalo on I-25 to the Reno Road exit (exit 365). Drive west to Wyoming 196, and follow this highway north for 2.7 miles. Then turn left on Mesa Road, a gravel trunk route that leads west and then south for 10 miles to the Mayoworth crossroads at the end of Wyoming 191. Turn right (west) at this junction and follow the gravel Mayoworth Road west for 2.6 miles, then turn left on the Slip Road. While this road is a county road, the grade up Gardner Mountain is extremely rocky and high clearance is required. Drive up the main grade, across a basin and past a reservoir, and up a second hill. After 6 miles, turn left at a post marked "trail" and park down in the hollow.

This newly created trail follows the crest of Gardner Mountain for aerial views of the WSA. It is faint along much of its length, presenting many route-finding challenges. The trek begins on a jeep road that curves south and then west to reach the ridgetop. Here, a fence guards Ice Cave, with its gaping limestone maw leading down into the depths of the Earth. The hike follows the ridgetop southwest to the main ridgeline, where limestone reefs jut out above the head of Cottonwood Creek. Follow the ridge southward through shady groves of pine and high grasslands where balsamroot blooms.

The country becomes progressively more open as you travel southward, and in the middle reaches of the route you will have views of the low canyon walls of Cottonwood Creek, the steep cliffs at the base of Gardner Mountain, and a broad sweep of the High Plains, punctuated by crimson buttes of Chugwater sandstone. The track ultimately descends eastward, but our route follows the ridgetop to a high, pine-girt summit known as Eagles Trap. Thread your way through low walls of limestone to reach the top, where mountain mahogany crowns a lofty cliff with sweeping westward views.

Fortification Creek

40

Location: 25 miles northwest of Gillette.
Size: 20,109 acres.
Administration: BLM (Buffalo Field Office).
Management status: Fortification Creek WSA (13,059 acres); unprotected roadless lands (7,050 acres).
Ecosystem: Great Plains Shortgrass Prairie Province; wheatgrass-needlegrass shrub steppe with extensive juniper scrub communities.
Elevation range: 3,800 feet to 4,680 feet.
System trails: None.
Maximum core to perimeter distance: 1.6 miles.
Activities: Hunting, horseback riding, hiking, backpacking.
Best season: March–June; September–October.
Maps: Echeta and Livingston Draw 1:24,000.

TRAVELERS ADVISORY:
FLASH FLOODS

Fortification Creek flows through a series of rugged hills and breaks to the east of the Powder River. It is grazed very lightly, and as a result the grassland community found here is composed of a mix of native grasses that represents an island of short-grass prairie. This roadless area is home to a herd of elk that ranges between 100 and 250 animals, the only plains elk remaining in the United States. There have always been resident elk in this broken country, and in 1952 the area was planted with additional animals to supplement the local herd. Their principal calving area lies within the Fortification Creek WSA. The endangered bald eagle and peregrine falcon both use this area during their winter migrations.

On the north-facing slopes of the hills, stands of Rocky Mountain juniper are quite dense in places. Some 1,000 acres of these junipers have been opened to post and firewood harvest. The Amos Draw formation, a known producer of oil and gas, stretches to the east and south of the Fortification Creek WSA. There is a possibility of oil and gas development within the WSA in the Muddy Sandstone formation. Giving wilderness designation to Fortification Creek would add an ecosystem that is missing from the current wilderness system.

40 FORTIFICATION CREEK

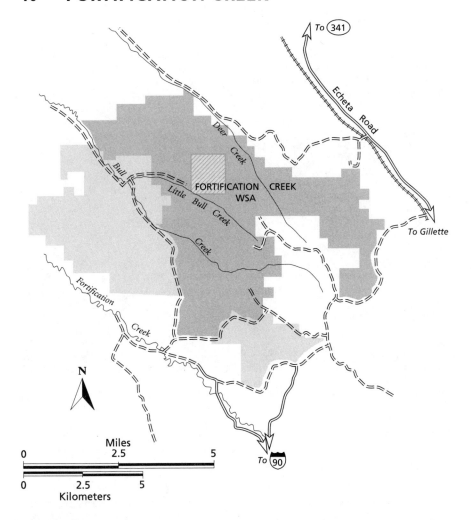

RECREATIONAL USES: This wilderness has more value as an untrammeled ecosystem than it has for recreation. Were public access to be provided, the area would offer excellent opportunities for horseback riding and good possibilities for hiking as well. The elk herd is hunted every other year on a permit basis, but due to the limited public access, neighboring landowners control the hunt. Sage and sharp-tailed grouse use the WSA as a nesting ground, although sage grouse have been on the decline in recent years. Surface water is in scarce supply here; a few water wells and a windmill on Little Bull Creek represent the only reliable sources.

Big, arid buttes typical of Fortification Creek.

ACCESS: There is no public access to this area, despite its size and importance to hunters. You can take the Kingsbury Road north from I-90 to link up with the Fortification Road, which approaches its south boundary. The Echeta Road follows the railway and approaches to within 3 miles of the WSA. From here, access is contingent on landowner permission. The BLM is currently negotiating a public access corridor along this route.

South Fork of Powder River   `41`

Location: 35 miles northwest of Casper.
Size: 33,900 acres.
Administration: BLM (Casper Field Office).
Management status: Unprotected roadless lands.
Ecosystem: Great Plains Shortgrass Prairie Province, wheatgrass-needlegrass shrub steppe.
Elevation range: 5,300 feet to 6,380 feet.
System trails: None.
Maximum core to perimeter distance: 1.7 miles.
Activities: Horseback riding, hiking, big game and upland bird hunting, rockhounding.
Best season: April–October.
Maps: Lysite and Midwest 1:100,000.

TRAVELERS ADVISORY:
FLASH FLOODS, BAD WATER

This open country near the headwaters of the Powder River's south fork is made up of clay buttes and tablelands dissected by broad coulees, with some eroded badland features to the east of Cottonwood Creek. It is dominated by vast grasslands of big bluestem and blue grama. Cheatgrass, an annual invader that takes over following overgrazing, forms extensive swards in the riparian draws, along with sagebrush and greasewood. A series of sandstone hills rises along the western edge of the roadless area, wooded loosely in juniper, ponderosa pine, and limber pine. This is an area of rock hoodoos and miniature canyons carved out by intermittent streams.

This area is a summer range for pronghorn antelope, and mule deer can be found along the wooded margins and in the badlands. Prairie falcons and northern harriers are also common residents. A few old fencelines and vehicle two-tracks are scattered across the area, but they do not detract from its wild character. There has been oil development along the sandstone domes farther south, and there is some possibility of future oil development within the roadless area. Cattle and sheep have grazed this area for over a century, and the practice would continue if the area is granted wilderness status.

RECREATIONAL USES: This open country is ideal for unconfined horse travel, and gives a real feeling of the old west. Hiking and backpacking are also easy

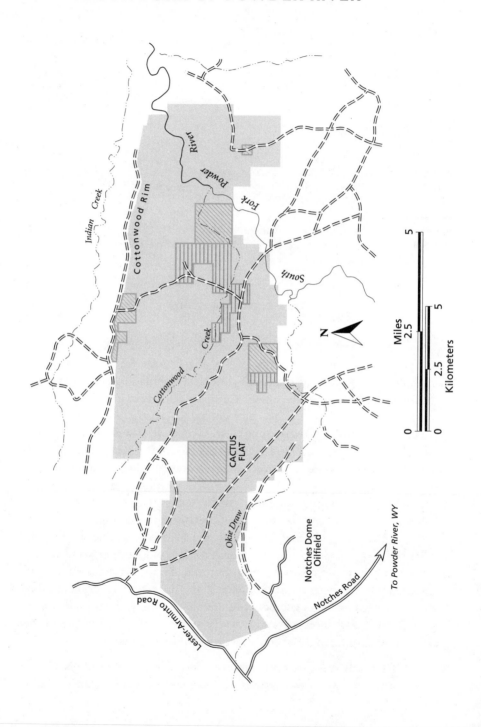

High Plains buttes guard Cottonwood Creek.

across the open grasslands, but there are no supplies of good water. Rockhounds can search the dry washes for interesting finds. There is fine potential for big game and upland bird hunting here, with antelope being especially prevalent.

ACCESS: The western edge of the roadless area can be accessed from the town of Powder River via the gravel Notches Road or the Lester-Arminto Road. From the east, the area can be accessed by traveling west from the Twentythree Mile Road near Merino.

Day Hike

Cottonwood Notch

Distance: 11.7 miles round trip.
Difficulty: Easy.
Starting and minimum elevation: 5,900 feet, 5,520 feet.
Topo maps: Notches Dome, Cave Gulch Reservoir.
Getting there: Drive west from Casper on US 20 to the settlement of Powder River, then drive north on County 106. Follow this gravel trunk road for 6 miles, then go straight at the forks and continue another 7.4 miles. Turn right on the gravel road just beyond the sandstone hoodoos. Follow this graded but pot-holed road 1.2 miles, then swing left onto a two-track road. Bear right at the first split and left at the second to park atop a promontory between two small canyons.

This off-trail hike visits small, rocky canyons and vast grasslands where buttes and scarps swell from the lowlands. To begin the trek, drop northward into the low canyon of Okie Draw and follow it east until it emerges from the hills. When gentler slopes appear, ascend onto the tableland to the north and hike along its rim. Note the unusual buttes to the south, demarcating the edge of Notches Dome. You will pass through several fence gates and beneath a telephone line before an old jeep trail leads down to Cactus Flat.

Follow the northern edge of the flat to a fenceline and follow it east to reach a gate. After passing through, you will have entered the vast and trackless reaches of the South Fork highlands. Bear east for a notch in the flatirons ahead, crossing several clay-banked washes beyond Cactus Flat. Hike into the notch to meet an old jeep track, then follow it north along the bench tops for fine views of the Cottonwood Creek basin and the dissected buttes beyond it. Then return westward along the rims to complete the trek.

Cow Creek Buttes Complex   **42**

Location: 15 miles east of Bill, Wyoming.
Size: 34,960 acres in 3 units.
Administration: Thunder Basin National Grassland.
Management status: Unprotected primitive area.
Ecosystem: Great Plains Shortgrass Prairie ecosystem, wheatgrass-needlegrass grassland.
Elevation range: 4,500 feet to 4,900 feet.
System trails: None.
Maximum core to perimeter distance: 1.9 miles.
Activities: Horseback riding, hiking, bird watching, hunting.
Best season: March–May; September–November.
Maps: Thunder Basin National Grassland Map; Bill and Lance Creek 1:100,000.

TRAVELERS ADVISORY:
FLASH FLOODS, SUDDEN STORMS

It is hard to find a stretch of High Plains grassland open to the public that remains in its essentially wild state. The Thunder Basin National Grassland has, through a program of land swaps, cobbled together a few such tracts of pristine grassland. The Great Plains call to mind images of featureless flatlands and treeless wastes. But far from being a low, flat expanse, the prairies of the Thunder Basin rise in undulating swells, punctuated by odd buttes and collections of low, wooded mesas.

This remote corner of Wyoming has always been sparsely populated. A few homesteaders tried their luck at dry-land farming and small-time ranching here at the turn of the century, but homestead allotments were too small for ranching and the climate was too dry for farming. The last of the settlers were driven out during the Dust Bowl years of the 1930s, and the federal government closed the area to homesteading. In the 1960s, these empty prairies were turned over to the Forest Service for management as the Thunder Basin National Grassland.

A series of uplands in the heart of the Thunder Basin National Grassland remain in a primitive state. Isolated among tracts of private ranch lands, these areas have been largely protected from motorized intrusions by their remoteness and difficulty of legal access. The Miller Hills is the northernmost unit, a

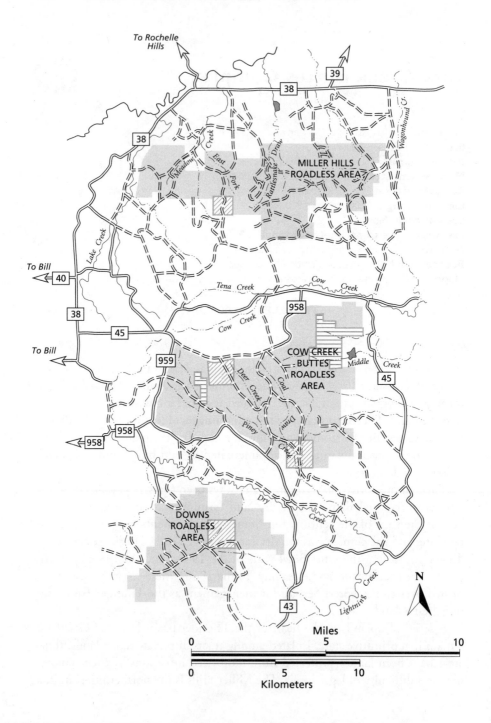

high tableland wooded in ponderosa pine and dissected into innumerable hill-tops and valleys by seasonal streams. The Cow Creek Buttes lies within the central unit, a collection of sparsely wooded mesas and badlands bordered by sloping grasslands. The Downs unit is farthest south, featuring low, rolling grasslands and shrub steppes. Together, these areas represent the finest remaining tracts of primitive grassland in Wyoming.

The high buttes and mesas found in this area are composed of reddish scoria, a hard rock created when clay beds are baked by underground fires in the coal beds underneath. These underground fires are a common natural occurrence, and result from lightning strikes or prairie fires igniting bands of coal that lie exposed in stream banks or badlands. The resulting fires can smolder underground for years.

The Cow Creek Buttes represents a complete microcosm of the High Plains ecosystem. The lower elevations at the fringes of the roadless areas have grassy flats where black-tailed prairie dogs make their homes. The sloping grasslands are a mix of wheatgrass-needlegrass prairie and sagebrush grassland where the meadowlark and the rare mountain plover nest. Along the watercourses, a riparian community is dominated by tall cottonwoods. The trees provide nesting habitat for red-tailed hawks and other raptors, and bald eagles roost here in great numbers during the winter. The uplands are wooded in a ponderosa pine savanna, providing nesting habitat for owls and songbirds. A number of livestock tanks are scattered throughout the area and provide fine habitat for waterfowl.

The Cow Creek Buttes is used by a herd of 400 elk that range far across the uplands of the High Plains from Laramie Peak. The grasslands offer year-round habitat for pronghorn antelope, the most common of the large animal species. Mule deer are prevalent among the hills and pine woodlands of the Miller Hills and Cow Creek Buttes. Just to the north of this area is a vast complex of prairie dog towns, where federal biologists are planning to reintroduce the endangered black-footed ferret.

While many of the grassland plant species found here are native, these grasslands have changed substantially since the arrival of white settlers. When the bison were driven extinct and later replaced by cattle, the short-grass communities of grama and buffalograss were gradually pushed back by mixed-grass communities of wheatgrass and needlegrass. The earliest settlers reported free-flowing streams where beavers built their dams. But the coming of trappers, farmers, and ranchers fundamentally changed the hydrology in this region, and now there is little permanent surface water. With cattle also came exotic invaders like cheatgrass, which thrives in overgrazed areas. Prairie fires were once a key component of the natural ecosystem, but during the last century these fires have been aggressively suppressed by county fire departments. By pursuing a let-burn policy in this area, land managers could push back sagebrush, prickly pear, and cheatgrass, rejuvenating the grasslands and improving the range for both livestock and wildlife.

The Cow Creek Buttes unit was once recommended for wilderness status by the Forest Service, and the other two units are managed for primitive back-country recreation. All three units are underlain by coal beds, but commercial values of this coal are believed to be low. There are known oil deposits under parts of the primitive areas, and oil wells are currently sited along the western boundary of the Cow Creek Buttes unit. Oil and gas leases are pending in this area, and might be developed in the future. However, the relatively compact size and shape of these areas makes them conducive to directional drilling and subsurface development on a "no surface occupancy" basis.

A number of vehicle two-tracks within these primitive areas receive very little use, and many of them are washed out in places or have become overgrown already. Those that remain within the primitive areas will rapidly disappear with closure to motorized vehicles, leaving these areas in a completely roadless state. Fencelines, water developments, and stock tanks are scattered widely throughout the three units, and do not detract significantly from the essentially pristine quality of the landscape. All in all, these three areas are excellent candidates for wilderness status, representing an ecosystem that is lacking in the current wilderness system.

RECREATIONAL USES: The open country of all three areas is ideally suited to cross-country horse trips and backpacks. Old jeep roads make excellent trails for hiking or horseback riding, and the open prairies and sparse woodlands are conducive to cross-country travel. Map and compass skills are necessary, as it is easy to become lost amid the open swells of prairie or in the wooded maze of the Miller Hills. The prairie blooms in May, and the green swards of grass make a particularly striking landscape at this time of year. The grasses dry out during summer, when scorching temperatures and violent thunderstorms discourage visitation.

Bird watchers will find an outstanding assemblage of ground-nesting birds, shorebirds, waterfowl, and raptors in the area. In the autumn, this area receives a limited amount of hunting use. Antelope and mule deer hunting can be good, and a limited drawing of elk tags is available. Upland bird hunters will find chukars here as well as sage and sharp-tailed grouse.

ACCESS: These units are approached via gravel county roads that are passable for passenger cars in dry weather and impassable for any vehicle in wet weather. Primitive roads radiate toward the primitive areas from all sides, but access is blocked by private lands in some cases and springs or washouts in others. The

Cow Creek Buttes can be reached from Bill by taking County Roads 38 and 45, then driving south on a primitive road (FR 958). A jeep trail runs along the north side of the primitive area, while the west boundary is accessed via FR 959, which is passable for most cars. The Miller Hills can be reached via a primitive road which runs south from County 38 along Lake Creek. The Downs unit has no legal public access at this time, but the National Grassland is pursuing land swaps to provide an access corridor to it.

Day Hike or Horse Trip

Owl Creek Loop

Distance: 6.0 miles round trip.
Difficulty: Moderate.
Starting and minimum elevation: 4,855 feet, 4,585 feet.
Topo map: Esau Spring, Pinnacle Rocks.
Getting there: From Bill, follow the Dull Center Road (County 38) as it jogs east and north across the plains. After 10 miles, turn right (east) on County 45. Follow this road for 7.3 miles, then turn south on FR 958, following signs for Cow Creek Buttes. High clearance is recommended for the final 3.5 miles; park at a hilltop crossroads beside a stand of pines.

This loop trip follows jeep trails through the eastern end of the Cow Creek Buttes area, offering good views of the buttes and of the Owl Creek badlands. The trek begins by following the jeep road that runs south past several stock tanks and then onto the rolling divide between Deer Creek and Coal Draw. The Owl Creek Buttes rise on the eastern skyline, while to the west the vast and undulating prairies stretch all the way to Laramie Peak.

After a gentle descent, the route reaches a pyramid-shaped butte of eroded clay. Turn left at the junction just north of it as the route follows a fainter track down a grassy rise. At the bottom of the grade is Coal Draw, where veins of coal are exposed in the cutbanks. Follow the track up the next divide to reach a junction beside a windmill. Turn left as the route leads northeast along the Owl Creek divide. This old roadbed yields close-up views of the Cow Creek Buttes and the eroded badlands below.

At the head of the drainage, continue north at a crossroads on a track marked 1437B. It leads to the Middle Creek divide, where the road turns northwest and gradually fades out. Hike along the butte tops, then descend westward to skirt along the eastern edge of a stand of ponderosa pine. Once you reach the upper edge of the stand, turn north again and climb to the top of the divide. Follow game trails among the buttes until you strike an overgrown roadbed that leads northwest to the starting point.

Ponderosa pine savannas are typical of the Miller Hills.

Off-Trail Day Hike or Horse Trip

Miller Hills

Distance: 6.0 to 8.0 miles one way.
Difficulty: Moderate.
Starting and maximum elevation: 4,553 feet, 4,900 feet.
Topo map: Esau Spring, Pinnacle Rocks.
Getting there: From Bill, drive north to County 40 and follow this gravel thoroughfare north and then east for 12 miles to meet the Dull Center Road (County 38). Turn left on this road and follow it for 5 miles, then turn right on a primitive road marked 1420C. This road leads 1.5 miles to a junction with an eastward running road, which marks the start of the trip.

This trip represents the legal way to gain access to the Miller Hills. Once there, the landscape offers superb opportunities for further off-trail exploration. To begin the journey, ford Lake Creek and follow the old road northeast to the tops of scoria hills. A scattering of ponderosa pines crowns the hilltops as the road winds southeast, ultimately dropping into the grassy drainage of Meadow Creek. The route now abandons the roadbed, skirting around the head of eroded gullies as it crosses the valley floor on an eastward heading. Climb to a grassy divide south of a wooded butte to meet a fenceline, and follow it south to reach a gate that leads into the East Fork valley.

The route now crosses this drainage and wanders up into wooded hills. Slip through a narrow gap and contour around the next north-flowing drainage. After passing a stock tank, continue east over the next divide, then descend to cross a deep ravine. A short but vigorous climb leads southeast to the top of the next ridge. Follow this ridgetop eastward to gain a bald promontory above the broad basin of Rattlesnake Draw. The Miller Hills rise beyond, and it is an easy trip across the rolling lowlands to reach them.

Bennett Mountain.

7

Oregon Trail Country

n 1843, the first wagon train rolled through South Pass, with 120 wagons and 1,000 emigrants en route to promising farmlands in the Oregon Territory. They were followed by a flood of settlers, some in well-outfitted and highly organized parties, others in poorly prepared, ragtag bunches. The Sweetwater River was the obvious choice for the route, with the potable water of the river (surrounding streams are strongly alkaline), availability of graze for the draft stock, and easy crossing of the Continental Divide at South Pass.

The Oregon Trail soon became a rutted and dusty swath across the empty plains, lined with shallow graves and the skeletons of draft animals. Camping spots sprang up beside every watering hole, which soon became so fouled with human and animal wastes that they turned into festering breeding grounds for contagion. The ruts of the wagons and the grave markers of those who died can still be found along much of the route.

With the establishment of the Mormon state of Deseret in 1847, a new wave of emigrants passed along the trails of the Sweetwater River. Most were foreign immigrants, recruited by Mormon missionaries from among the dispirited lower classes in industrial Europe. They were told of a glorious kingdom being built in the lush paradise of the Salt Lake valley, where they could work as free men and earn a passage into the Celestial Kingdom. The Mormon parties were organized along military lines into cohesive companies for the passage across the plains. Some companies pushed all of their possessions in man-powered, two-wheel handcarts for the entire distance of the journey.

Despite their tight organization, several Mormon parties met with disaster along the Sweetwater River. In 1856, two handcart companies that set out too late in the year were caught in separate blizzards and faced horrible fates. The Martin handcart company was trapped just beyond Devils Gate, in a small basin within the Granite Mountains that came to be known as Martins Cove. Over 150 of the settlers died of exposure and starvation, while the remaining 425 were rescued with varying injuries and frostbite. The same blizzard caught up with the Willies handcart company in the open highlands east of South Pass, and more than 70 died before the relief wagons arrived.

Split Rock was a famous landmark for Oregon Trail pioneers.

As a steady stream of immigrants crossed through the Indian country on their way to Oregon, California, and Utah, the U.S. Army established a chain of military posts along the Oregon Trail. They became supply points for the Pony Express and the Wells Fargo stage, which followed the emigrant trails and were the main bearers of news and mail before the advent of telegraph lines. Wagon traffic slowed in 1869 with the completion of the Union Pacific transcontinental railway, but the last recorded wagon did not creak through South Pass until the summer of 1912.

The mountains that rise above the Sweetwater River belong to a landform known as the Sweetwater Arch, a chain of granite-cored hills that stretches from the southern tail of the Wind River Range to the Freezeout Mountains above the town of Medicine Bow. To the south of the Sweetwater Arch is the Emigrant Gap Thrust fault, which extends northwest from Muddy Gap for 50 miles. The northward thrusting of the Seminoe and Shirley Mountains has buried the younger sediments of the Sweetwater Basin.

Bennett Mountain 43

Location: 35 miles northeast of Rawlins.
Size: 11,549 acres.
Administration: BLM (Rawlins Field Office).
Management status: Bennett Mountains WSA (6,003 acres); 5,546 acres of unprotected roadless lands.
Ecosystem: Wyoming Basin sagebrush steppe and Douglas fir forest.
Elevation range: 6,300 feet to 8,281 feet.
System trails: None.
Maximum core to perimeter distance: 1.4 miles.
Activities: Hunting, hiking, horseback riding, trapping.
Best season: May–October.
Map: Shirley Basin 1:100,000.

The Seminoe Mountains are a rather small scarp of granite that rises steadily from the plains to the north. The Bennett Mountain WSA encompasses the eastern end of the range. Its slopes are interrupted at frequent intervals by knobs and spires of deeply seamed granite, rendering a picturesque landscape out of what would otherwise be a rather drab set of foothills. The steep south face of the massif overlooks Seminoe Reservoir, and triangular slabs of vertically tilted limestone provide a southern palisade that makes the range instantly recognizable from afar. The massif is cut by several streams that flow north from the crest of the range, and these waterways have carved steep-walled canyons that are interrupted periodically by portals of massive granite.

The skirts of the mountains are robed in sagebrush grasslands, with some mature stands of cottonwood and aspen in the northward-flowing drainages. At higher elevations, a savanna of ponderosa pine covers the slopes. The Seminoe Mountains are inhabited by both deer and elk, which must share the range with a multitude of domestic cattle. The cattle concentrate along the northward-flowing streams, impacting the sensitive riparian areas of this mountain ecosystem.

The BLM has recommended the removal of the Bennett Mountains WSA from wilderness consideration. These mountains are thought to have a low potential for ore-bearing rocks, and the potential for oil and gas development is likewise low. It is likely that the area will retain its wild character even if wilderness status is denied.

43   BENNETT MOUNTAIN

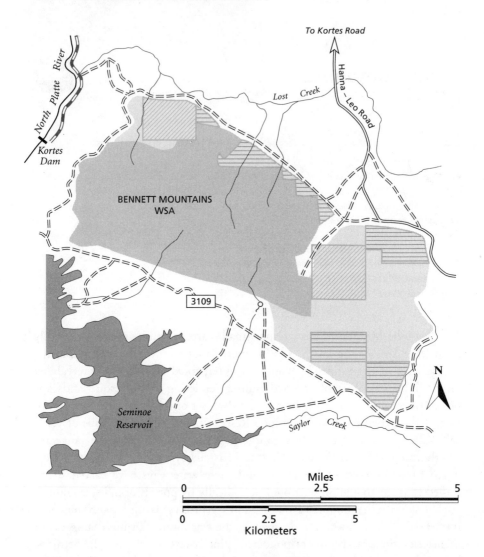

RECREATIONAL USES: The crest of the range is almost level, making an ideal camping area for folks who are willing to tote a supply of water up from the drainages to the north. The springs and streams to the north of the Seminoe crest carry good water, but it is fouled by domestic livestock and must be thoroughly treated before it becomes potable for humans. Bennett Mountain is popular for mule deer hunting, which accounts for the lion's share of visitation to the backcountry.

ACCESS: This area was once easy to access by driving over the Seminoe Dam to access a trunk road that runs along the southern base of the mountains. Public access across Seminoe Dam was closed in the early 1970s, however, a move that drastically reduced the number of visitors to the Bennett Mountain area. There is now a single access road from the Kortes Dam area (described below), and the northeastern corner of the roadless area can be accessed via the short stretch of the Hanna-Leo Road (County 26) that crosses through BLM lands.

Day Trip on Foot or Horseback

Number Two Gulch

Distance: 3.0 miles one way.
Difficulty: Moderately strenuous.
Starting and maximum elevation: 6,530 feet, 7,640 feet.
Topo map: Seminoe Dam NE.
Getting there: Take I-80 to Sinclair, departing at the western exit (exit 219). Drive northeast on the main highway, and bear left at the split on the north edge of town to get on the Seminoe Road. Follow this paved highway for 30 miles, then continue straight ahead as a steep gravel road climbs over the Seminoe Mountains. On the far side, the road descends to cross a bridge over the Platte River. On the far bank, turn right on the road to Kortes Dam. Follow this paved road 1.7 miles to a large pile of rubble left over from the Kortes Dam project.

Turn left on BLM 3109 just beyond the rockpile, following signs for Bennett Mountain. This road is fairly primitive but can be negotiated by most cars. Follow it east for 0.8 mile to a split, then turn right and follow the road up a canyon for 1.6 miles. Park at the head of the cottonwood grove—the road beyond is quite rough, even for a four-wheel-drive vehicle.

This pleasant trip leads up the valleys on the north side of the range to reach the tabletop meadows at the top. To begin the journey, travel up the road to reach the ridgeline, then turn northeast down the draw to intersect the bottoms of Number Two Gulch at a grove of cottonwood. Follow the livestock trail along the fenceline on a southward heading toward the heart of the mountains. As you move up the valley, mature cottonwoods shade the stream. Weathered spires of granite rise all around, and soon the stream snakes through a series of tall, knife-blade walls of stone. Watch out for thorny brush as the path makes its way to a major confluence shaded by a stand of cottonwood.

Follow the trail up the east fork as its valley bends around to an eastward heading. After crossing a wide basin, the stream jogs south again, passing through massive portals of granite. Follow the trail along the main streamcourse as it winds through sage-clad hills, then enters a narrow canyon where cathedral spires of granite rise on both sides. At first the cleft seems impassa-

Seminoe Reservoir as seen from the top of Bennett Mountain.

ble, but with a little bushwhacking you will strike the cattle trail as it climbs steeply along the west bank of the watercourse. Once through, a lush basin beckons, and a spring marks the head of the stream.

Turn south along the flats to strike the deeply entrenched trail that climbs the hill between two draws. The path soon swings into the eastern draw, following it upward and ultimately petering out. A gently sloping grassland now leads south for a surprisingly short distance to the crest of the range, with northward views of Pathfinder Reservoir and the Pedro Mountains. Continue south across the crest to reach a granite promontory that juts southward from the range, offering superb vistas of Seminoe Reservoir and the lowlands that surround it.

Pedro Mountains

44

Location: 27 miles southwest of Alcova.
Size: 12,345 acres.
Administration: BLM (Rawlins Field Office).
Management status: Unprotected BLM lands.
Ecosystem: Rocky Mountain Province Douglas fir and sagebrush steppe ecosystems.
Elevation range: 6,100 feet to 8,316 feet.
System trails: None.
Maximum core to perimeter distance: 1.2 miles.
Activities: Hiking, horseback riding, scrambling, rock climbing, rockhounding, big game hunting.
Best season: June–September.
Map: Shirley Basin 1:100,000.

The Pedro Mountains are a chain of low but impressive granite peaks that rises to the east of Pathfinder Reservoir. The granite is almost continuous in the uplands, and plants must grow from small swaths of sandy soil or chinks in the bedrock. Among the rocky summits, the vegetation consists of loose stands of limber pine, Rocky Mountain juniper, and ponderosa pine. The draws are less arid, with ample groundwater that supports hardwoods like aspen and cottonwood. Surrounding the mountains are high sagebrush grasslands dotted with such desert plants as yucca and prickly pear cactus.

The Pedro Mountains are a focal habitat for up to 800 elk, and mule deer are also abundant in the area. The sagebrush plains that surround the range are home to pronghorn antelope. The high granite balds are nesting habitat for bald eagles and whippoorwills. During winter, the Pedro Mountains are an important roosting area for bald eagles, and up to 20 individuals have been spotted here at one time. The mummified remains of a prehistoric human were found in a cave within the Pedro Mountains in the 1920s.

This area was evaluated during the RARE II process, but was excluded from consideration as a WSA as a result of private land subdivisions around the base of the mountains. The roadless core of the range is naturally resistant to development due to its steep and rocky terrain.

RECREATIONAL USES: The rugged nature of the peaks precludes horsemen on all but the most outlying ridges. Hikers will find many challenging off-trail routes that may require non-technical scrambling. For rock-climbing enthusiasts, there are lots of opportunities for bouldering, and even a few vertical faces

44   PEDRO MOUNTAINS

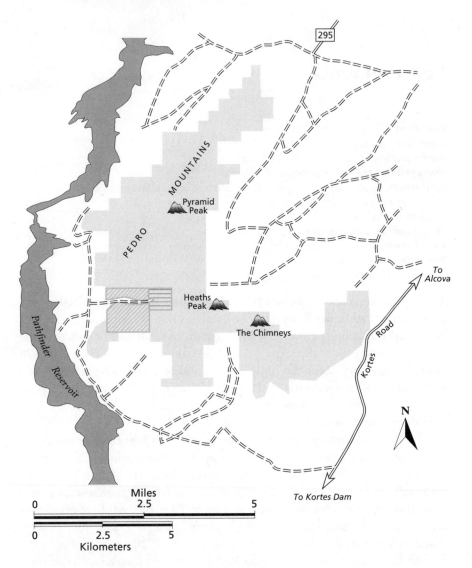

of more than 100 feet within the range. Mule deer are abundant here, and the hunting is considered to be excellent. Rockhounds will find agates and the elusive black jade in this area.

ACCESS: Principal access to this range is provided by the Alcova Road, which runs from Alcova Reservoir to Seminoe Reservoir. The Pedro Mountains are surrounded on almost all sides by private lands. Jeep trails run up to the base

Pyramid Peak from the foot of the Pedro Mountains.

of the mountains from all directions, but for most of them public access is blocked by private holdings. The only legal access is via a thin strip of state land that follows a ridgetop east from Pathfinder Reservoir. You can hike or ride this ridgetop eastward across state land to reach the BLM lands of the Pedro Mountains.

Day Hike and Scramble Route

Heaths Peak

Distance: 4.0 miles one way.
Difficulty: Strenuous.
Starting and maximum elevation: 5,980 feet, 8,125 feet.
Topo map: Pathfinder Reservoir SW, Leo.
Getting there: Drive south from Alcova on County 407. The pavement ends after 15 miles, giving way to a fair-weather gravel route that leads south for 12 miles. After crossing Sage Creek, turn right and follow the gravel road to the shore of Pathfinder Reservoir. Turn right (north) here, fording Sage Creek and following a high-clearance road up the shore of the reservoir for one mile to a major junction. The main road swings northwest here; instead, continue straight ahead, following the road to park at the base of a granite ridge.

The Chimneys.

This route runs the ridges to the crest of the range, then requires some scrambling to surmount one of its highest peaks. To begin the trek, climb across the arid grassland to the base of the granite ridge, passing among cactus and yucca as well as the ever-present sagebrush. A broad couloir leads to the ridgetop, where easy traveling leads eastward among granite tors and scattered pines and junipers. Toward the middle of the ridge, it becomes necessary to descend and climb to dodge the granite that impedes progress on the ridgeline. The ridge ultimately leads to a broad saddle at the base of a much higher knob. Traverse northeast across its slopes to a saddle at the head of a nameless valley.

From here, chart your course to the high summit to the northeast, which is Heaths Peak. The best route climbs steadily as it traverses across open slopes, staying well below the ridgetop but above the big outcrops of the midslopes. Ultimately, it leads up a timbered couloir filled with boulders to reach a stand of conifers on the south face of the peak just below the summit. Continue through this stand and climb up a narrow rift to reach a notch just east of the summit. A sheltered camp spot lies just below this notch. To reach the top, traverse west across terraces of bare granite, then scramble east along the ridgetop. From the peak, panoramic views are highlighted by The Chimneys to the east and Pyramid Peak to the north, with the low and distant ranges rising like islands from a sea of sagebrush.

Ferris Mountains

45

Location: 30 miles north of Rawlins.
Size: 27,444 acres.
Administration: BLM (Rawlins Field Office)
Management status: Ferris Mountains WSA (22,245 acres); private inholdings (160 acres); unprotected roadless lands (5,199 acres).
Ecosystem: Wyoming Basin Province Douglas fir ecosystem.
Elevation range: 6,890 feet to 10,037 feet.
System trails: None.
Maximum core to perimeter distance: 1.8 miles.
Activities: Cross-country hiking, horseback riding, hunting, fishing, bird-watching.
Best season: May–October.
Maps: Bairoil 1:100,000.

The Ferris Mountains are a small and forested range at the northern edge of the Great Divide Basin. The core of the range is granite, forming two great east-west ridges (synclines in their geologic structure) that are separated by the rounded gap of the Youngs Pass Anticline. The high peaks are flanked to the north and south by vertical beds of Madison limestone that rise to form the series of tooth-shaped palisades that give the range its distinctive appearance. The south face of the range makes a steep drop of 2,000 feet to reach the alkali deserts of Separation Flat, within the Great Divide Basin. Here, great sand dunes migrate eastward at the foot of the palisades, and greasewood and saltbush grow between salt pans that fill with water when it rains.

This small range has steep slopes leading up to a narrow spine with many miniature summits. The top of the range is dotted with ancient tree-trunks, laid bare by the elements and then scoured by wind-blown snow and ice. Views from here stretch from the Big Horn Mountains to the Wind River Range and southward across the Great Divide Basin. To the north of the range, sloping grasslands rise to become timbered reefs.

Long, east-west meadows occupy the flanks of the range, growing atop vertically bedded sedimentaries that hold no groundwater. Conifers have deep taproots that seek out water at the bedrock; here, there is none, favoring grasses with their mats of shallow roots that soak up rainwater before it can sink deep into the soil. The mountainsides are robed in dense "doghair" stands of lodgepole

45   FERRIS MOUNTAINS

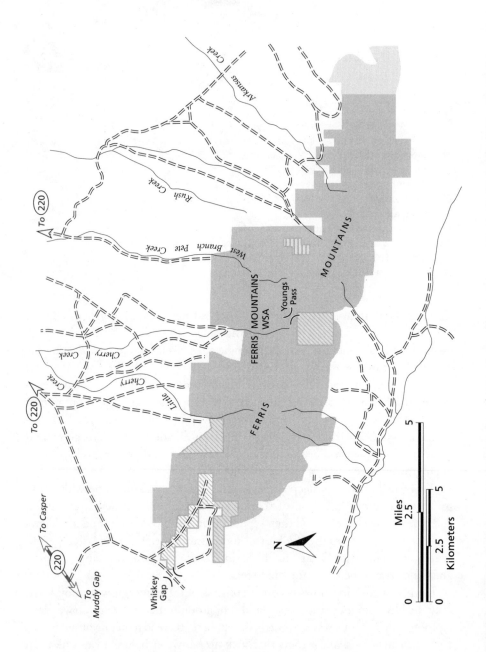

pines that grew in the wake of intense lightning fires in the 1940s. Several permanent streams course down the northern slopes of the range, flanked by willow thickets and stands of subalpine fir. Small stands of Douglas fir and ponderosa pine can be found on some of the drier slopes.

In the winter of 1963, the Wyoming Game and Fish Department transplanted 25 elk into the Ferris Mountains. The population has thrived, summering on the high ridgetops and wintering at the base of the mountains between Cherry and Pete Creeks. Mule deer are also present. Pine marten and mountain lions inhabit the deep forests and high peaks, but are rarely seen by visitors. The Ferris Mountains offer nesting habitat for prairie falcons, northern goshawks, and golden eagles.

Before the arrival of white settlers, a herd of the now-extinct Audubon's bighorns pursued a seasonal migration that encompassed the Ferris Mountains, Green Mountain, the Sweetwater Rocks, and the Seminoe Mountains. It is believed that the settlement of the Sweetwater River basin interrupted their natural migrations and caused the decline of the herd, which went extinct around 1900. Transplants of Rocky Mountain bighorn sheep in the Ferris Mountains first occurred in 1958, and supplemental plantings took place in 1967, 1976, and 1980. The current population has declined from a high of 80 animals to a current population of around 30, principally through the low survivorship of newborn lambs.

There is some cattle grazing here, organized into two separate allotments that are divided by Youngs Pass. The Babbs Mine, just west of Youngs Pass, was the site of some mineral prospecting between the late 1950s and the early 1970s. Two *adits*, or horizontal shafts, were blasted into the rock, and a bulldozer pit was excavated in an unsuccessful quest for copper and tungsten. The mine never produced enough ore to be patented, and recently the access road to the mine site was "rehabilitated," inasmuch as the road has been completely plowed up into a jumbled ribbon of debris that is difficult even to walk on. The Spanish Mines consist of 5 adits and numerous glory holes dug into the eastern base of the range. They once produced commercial quantities of silver, lead, talc, and tungsten, and the patents are still valid. The Ferris Mountains have been officially recommended for wilderness status, and in the absence of any industrial interests, it seems likely that they will ultimately get it.

RECREATIONAL USES: The Ferris Mountains receive an estimated 1,000 visitor days annually, most of which comes during the autumn hunting season. The elk herd is the subject of a limited quota hunt, and the area is known for producing trophy-quality racks. There is plenty of dense lodgepole for the animals to hide in, making hunting a real challenge in this steep and heavily timbered range. Brook trout are present in Cherry and Pete Creeks, providing a rather lim-

Wooded reefs on the north slope of the Ferris Mountains.

ited fishery for pan-sized trout. Off-road vehicles currently account for about 10 visitor days annually. The deep, secluded canyons are a haven to many species of songbirds and are a good destination for the adventurous birdwatcher.

For the wilderness hiker, the Ferris Mountains offer a supreme challenge in trail-less bushwhacking. The range's eastern marches are characterized by deep canyons that offer limitless possibilities for solitude. The high peaks of the range can be reached via scramble routes, and they offer sweeping views in all directions. The total lack of trails makes for the ultimate wilderness experience—each visitor will have to discover a unique pathway through the steep and rugged country and will need to use ingenuity to surmount obstacles along the way. For the most part, the Ferris Mountains are too steep and rugged for any but the most hard-core backcountry horseman.

ACCESS: The Cherry Creek Road is a rough jeep road that runs south from Wyoming 220 to access the western half of the Ferris Mountains. The eastern reaches of the range can be reached by similar jeep roads that follow Arkansas and Sand Creeks up from County Road 410, which leaves WY 220 about 3 miles northeast of Independence Rock.

Day Hike

Youngs Pass

Distance: 2.5 miles one way.
Difficulty: Moderate.
Starting and maximum elevation: 7,650 feet, 8,750 feet.
Topo map: Youngs Pass.
Getting there: To reach the Cherry Creek trailhead, drive northeast from Muddy Gap Junction on Wyoming 220 for about 9 miles to reach the North Ferris Road, a broad gravel strip marked only with a sign for the Bar-V Ranch. Drive south on this road for 2 miles, then turn right on Cherry Creek Road (BLM 3147). This primitive road is quite rocky in places, and it turns to a morass during wet weather. Follow it 4 miles, then bear right to ford Cherry Creek. The road is full of boulders as it climbs to the bench beyond and continues upstream. There is a second ford 4 miles beyond the first; park on the near bank.

This off-trail route leads to a low and grassy pass between the major ridges of the Ferris Mountains. From the second road crossing of Cherry Creek, hike east on the jeep road to surmount a grassy rise, then turn south along the next draw that leads up into the mountains. Open meadows to west of the wooded watercourse soon offer a game trail that leads upward between vertical slabs of limestone. On the far side of the narrows, the gully bends east and the route follows trails through the timber along its south bank. Bear left as the wash forks, and you will soon be able to climb northward onto open savannas dotted with limber pine. Adopt a zigzagging upward course as you climb the steep hillside.

At the head of the drainage, hike south to identify a grassy tabletop straight ahead, then circle the next valley to reach it. From the grassy rise, descend eastward down the meadows for several hundred yards, then swing through a narrow band of timber to reach a larger grassland. An old jeep track leads eastward down the clearing, and upon entering the trees, it passes a series of springs. Swing left on a cattle trail that passes the springs, then traverses through the trees to reach the west end of the final meadow. From here you can follow the clearing eastward across rolling country until finally a narrow strip of meadow leads up to Youngs Pass. A buck-and-pole fence delineates the pass, which offers superb views of the angular slabs of limestone that form the south palisade of the Ferris Mountains.

Sweetwater Rocks   46

Location: 10 miles northeast of Jeffrey City.
Size: 34,470 acres in 4 units.
Administration: BLM (Lander Field Office).
Management status: Lankin Dome WSA (6,316 acres), Split Rock WSA (12,789 acres), Savage Peak WSA (7,041 acres), Miller Springs WSA (6,429 acres); unprotected roadless lands (1,895 acres).
Ecosystem: Wyoming Basin Province grama-needlegrass-wheatgrass steppe.
Elevation range: 6,230 feet to 8,360 feet.
System trails: None.
Maximum core to perimeter distance: 1.8 miles.
Activities: Rock climbing and bouldering, rockhounding, hiking, hunting.
Best season: March through May; September through November.
Maps: Bairoil and Rattlesnake Hills 1:100,000.

TRAVELERS ADVISORY:
RATTLESNAKES

The Sweetwater Rocks are the high points along the Granite Mountains, a range of small, rocky summits that rise some 1,800 feet above the surrounding sagebrush basins. In some locales the granite takes a deeply seamed appearance, while elsewhere, great exfoliating domes of granite rise from the jumbled boulders and outcrops. The Granite Mountains were once as tall as the modern Wind River Range. During the Pleistocene Epoch, a massive ice sheet pushed southward across the region, scouring off the sedimentary layers that once topped the Granite Mountains and exposing the 2.5 billion year old Precambrian granite and gneiss that form the core of the range. Green Mountain, the wooded scarp that can be seen to the south of the Sweetwater Rocks, is the terminal moraine that was pushed up by the Pleistocene ice sheet.

Before the coming of white explorers, the Sweetwater Rocks were used continuously by indigenous people for 12,000 years. The untainted, or "sweet" water of the river was an important magnet for aboriginal hunters as it was for the trappers and settlers who blazed the Oregon Trail just south of the Sweetwater Rocks. The rocks, and Split Rock in particular, became landmarks to the wagon trains of westward-bound pioneers.

The granite massifs are surrounded by a sea of sagebrush, where bluebunch wheatgrass, grama, Sandbergs bluegrass, and needlegrass grow sparsely between the shrubs. Prickly pear cactus can be found on the well-drained sites. This High Plains ecosystem is unique to the Sweetwater Rocks and is not represented elsewhere in the national wilderness system. The flats are underlain by interbedded layers of sandstone, argillite, and tuff. These sedimentary strata are part of deep beds of erosional debris that once buried most of the major mountain ranges in the state.

The sagebrush flats surrounding the Sweetwater Rocks are the domain of the pronghorn antelope, which roams in compact herds across the flats and ventures up into the grassy coves amid the rocks. Prairie dogs dig their colonial warrens on these flats, and sage grouse gather at communal strutting grounds during their mating season. Water is absent on the flats that surround the mountains, and during rainstorms the runoff is strongly alkaline.

Amid the granite, limber pine and Rocky Mountain juniper are the prevalent tree species, while isolated groves of aspen and cottonwood can be found in spots where groundwater seeps to the surface. Rock spiraea, wax currant, and Woods rose are the primary shrub species that can be found in the rocky uplands. Mule deer and bobcats can be found among the rocks. The highest pinnacles form an important nesting habitat for golden eagles, red-tailed hawks, and prairie falcons.

A small resident herd of elk inhabits the Sweetwater Rocks, and the much larger Green Mountain herd winters here in some years. Moose range down the Sweetwater River from their summer haunts in the Wind River Range, and an occasional moose may be found here year-round. Audubon's bighorn sheep inhabited the Sweetwater Rocks when white settlers first arrived in the area, but they went extinct at the turn of the twentieth century. Fourteen bighorns were reintroduced in the 1940s, and a herd of up to 40 animals was established, only to go extinct by 1980. Biologists attribute the decline to poaching, drought, and inbreeding caused by the small number of sheep originally planted here. The Wyoming Game and Fish Department and BLM have plans to reintroduce about 120 of these animals to the Sweetwater Rocks to restore some of its original biodiversity, but this effort is being opposed by neighboring landowners.

Cottontail rabbits are abundant amid the rocks, and golden eagles cruise the thermals hunting for them. Rocky Mountain bluebirds, magpies, and ravens are other commonly seen denizens of the rocky vastnesses. Lizards are common in the Sweetwater Rocks, an unusual sight in such a cold climate. Numerous waterpockets have been weathered into the granite through chemical erosion. They fill up during rainstorms and provide a source of potable drinking water for birds and mammals in the midst of the arid plains.

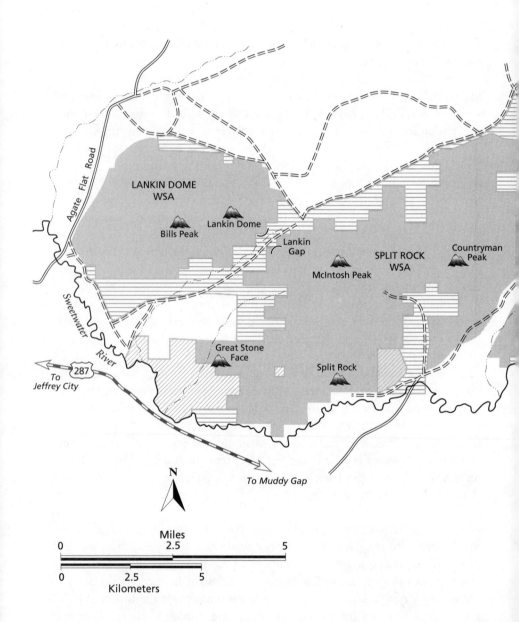

LANKIN DOME
WSA

Agate Flat Road

Bills Peak

Lankin Dome

Lankin
Gap

McIntosh Peak

SPLIT ROCK
WSA

Countryman
Peak

Sweetwater River

To
Jeffrey City

287

Great Stone
Face

Split Rock

To Muddy Gap

N

Miles
0   2.5   5

Kilometers
0   2.5   5

Beef
Gap

MILLER SPRINGS
WSA

SAVAGE PEAK
WSA

Soda Lake

Sweetwater

River

The USGS has reported moderate to high occurrences of jade in the Lankin Dome area, primarily within igneous veins and dikes within the Precambrian granites. One active jade claim within the Lankin Dome WSA produces small quantities of this semiprecious stone each year. The Moonstone formation underlies part of the WSA and has a moderate potential for uranium, for which there is currently no market. Oil and gas leases within the wilderness study area were filed after the passage of the Federal Lands Planning and Management Act, and would be automatically nullified by wilderness designation.

The primary consideration in the BLM's failure to recommend any of the Sweetwater Rocks units for wilderness was the scarcity of public access points. With wilderness designation, the BLM would be faced with a choice of either actually doing something about its avowed policy to provide legal public access to all large tracts of federal lands, or inviting an increase in trespassing on the lands of neighboring ranchers. Of course, as soon as the BLM provides public access in accordance with its own directives, this "problem" will disappear.

The Environmental Impact Statement also makes the dubious claim that hunting and rockhounding within the WSA is "vehicle-dependent" recreation, and assumes that if these areas become wilderness, hunters and rockhounds will be unable to make the maximum trek of one mile across open and level ground to reach any vehicle-accessible corner of the WSA.

RECREATIONAL USES: The Sweetwater Rocks offer outstanding opportunities for hiking and scrambling across trail-free terrain, and the many small pockets amid the granite offer excellent opportunities for solitude. Both Lankin Dome and Split Rock have been nationally known destinations for rock climbers since the 1950s, and have been featured in magazines such as *Summit*. The National Outdoor Leadership School (NOLS) has been using the area as a training ground for would-be rock jocks for years. Rockhounds have long known this area for its production of moss agates and jade.

The mule deer population is known to produce an occasional trophy animal, although the rocky terrain makes for challenging hunting. Antelope are present in huntable numbers within the Wilderness Study Areas, but the limited amount of sagebrush flats that actually falls within these areas precludes them from becoming a destination for "speed goat" hunters. Small-game hunters will find an abundance of cottontail rabbits, mourning doves, and sage grouse in the area.

McIntosh Peak and the core of the Granite Mountains.

ACCESS: The four wilderness study areas of the Sweetwater Rocks are bordered in many places by private lands, making public access a troublesome proposition. Local landowners have suffered though a fair amount of trespassing in the past as a result of the poor access, and the BLM would do well to acquire more public easements to access this outstanding recreation area.

The Savage Peak unit can be accessed via jeep roads that run south from the Dry Creek Road (County Road 321). The northeastern corner of the Split Rock unit can be reached by the jeep road that runs south from the Dry Creek Road through Barlow Gap. The best public access to the Lankin Dome and Split Rock units is via the Agate Flats Road (BLM 2404), a fair-weather gravel trunk road that leaves US 287 some 6 miles east of Jeffrey City. At the time this book was written, you could also continue up the Agate Flat Road to Sage Hen Creek, make two right turns at the junction, and follow a jeep road open to the public by landowner agreement around the north end of Lankin Dome to reach Lankin Gap, between the Lankin Dome and Split Rock units.

Scramble Route

Split Rock

Distance: 1.3 miles one way.
Difficulty: Moderately strenuous.
Starting and maximum elevation: 6,145 feet, 7,180 feet.
Topo map: Split Rock.
Getting there: Follow US 287 to Cranner Rock, between Jeffrey City and Muddy Gap Junction. Just east of the BLM picnic site, an unmarked road runs north just beyond the Natrona County line. Follow this road for 2 miles to reach the Cross-L Ranch, where you will need to ask permission to proceed further across private land. After getting permission, drive across the bridge beyond the ranch compound and turn left to follow a fence along the river. After 1.7 miles, bear right at the split and drive to the top of the rise to find a parking roundabout at the base of Split Rock.

This route leads up across the weathered granite of Split Rock, ending high on its eastern shoulder. From the parking area, follow the trail northeast along the base of the granite. A broad draw soon leads north; hike upward between its two branches. As the rock steepens, scramble upward along the eastern watercourse. Near the divide, you will reach a pocket of moist soil that supports a cluster of tall cottonwoods. Turn west here, following a grassy slope that seeks out a westward-trending gully. Follow this gully to its head, then skirt south onto a ridge of bare granite. The traveling is easiest on the inclined shelves to the south of the ridgeline. After cresting a dome to reach a sandy notch, skirt northward for the final ascent. One can scramble to a spot just below the northeast summit of Split Rock. From here, views encompass the Great Stone Face to the west, Lankin Dome farther north, and McIntosh Peak to the east. Technical chimney or crack climbing is required to gain the summit.

Day Hike

Nolen Pocket

Distance: 4.2 miles one way.
Difficulty: Moderate.
Starting and maximum elevation: 6,300 feet, 6,850 feet.
Topo map: Lankin Dome.
Getting there: Drive east from Jeffrey City on US 287. After 6 miles, turn north on the Agate Flat Road and follow it across the Sweetwater River. A telephone line crosses the road 2 miles past the river, marking the starting point for the Nolen Pocket hike.

The Moonstone (left distant) and other granite formations east of Nolen Pocket.

This off-trail route skirts around the northern side of the Lankin Dome massif. From the starting point, hike due east for a mile, climbing across the sloping sage steppes to reach a rocky gap in the mountains. After passing through, continue east, descending to the level floor of Nolen Pocket. The bald dome of granite marked "7158" is your objective. As you cross the flats, note the tall growth of sagebrush along the washes and the tall limber pines that rise at the base of the granite. These plants are indicators of groundwater below the arid surface. At the midpoint of the basin, Lankin Dome appears, a seamless tower of granite. The route runs to the south of some low ridges, following the watercourse that leads to the gap to the south of dome 7158. Easy walking up inclined granite leads to the pass for superb views of Lankin Dome as well as The Moonstone and McIntosh Peak to the east. An easy northward stroll leads to the top of dome 7158 for even broader views.

Sweetwater Canyon

47

Location: 15 miles southeast of Atlantic City.
Size: 10,016 acres.
Administration: BLM (Lander Field Office).
Management status: Sweetwater Canyon WSA (9,056 acres); unprotected roadless lands (960 acres).
Ecosystems: Wyoming Basin wheatgrass-needlegrass shrub steppe and Douglas fir forest.
Elevation range: 6,800 feet to 7,612 feet.
System trails: None.
Maximum core to perimeter distance: 1.2 miles.
Activities: Hunting (antelope, mule deer, sage grouse), fly fishing, hiking, camping, recreational gold panning.
Best season: Late June through October.
Maps: South Pass 1:100,000.

TRAVELERS ADVISORY:
FORDS, TICKS

Sweetwater Canyon is a low but craggy defile in the southern foothills of the Wind River Range. The landscape is dominated by arid hills mantled in a steppe grassland, punctuated by crumbly outcrops of bedrock. The upper reaches of the canyon are composed of Precambrian greenstone of the Miners Delight formation. This metamorphic mix of schist and hornblende is dark and shaly, decomposing into rough, angular shards. It is the ore-bearing formation that accounts for the gold deposits that gave rise to South Pass City. The eastern reaches of the WSA are dominated by pale granites that weather into rounded outcrops.

Within the canyon, limber pines grow in scattered stands on the north facing slopes and along the riverbanks in places. The riparian vegetation beside the river is dominated by cottonwood, willow, and water birch, creating a brushy habitat that borders the extensive alluvial flats robed in sagebrush. Aspen is locally common in moist habitats, while stands of juniper can be found on some of the rocky, south-facing slopes. Lupine, cinquefoil, and snakeweed are abundant amid the sage, creating a colorful display of blossoms in late spring.

47 SWEETWATER CANYON

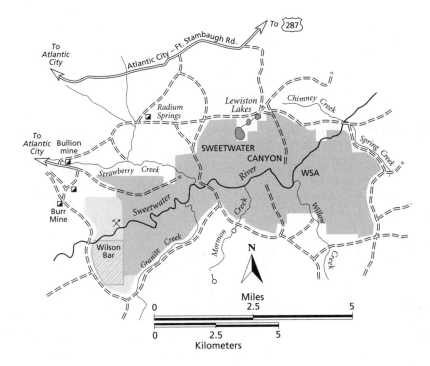

Sweetwater Canyon is an important spring range for elk, and a sagebrush herd makes its home in the draws surrounding the Canyon on a year-round basis. During severe winters, elk move down from the Wind River Range to shelter in the protected defile of the canyon. During such winters, Sweetwater Canyon becomes critical for the survival of these elk herds. It is also a critical winter range for moose, and mule deer are abundant in this area throughout the year. Pronghorn antelope are commonly sighted on the hilltops and uplands flanking the canyon during the summertime.

Sweetwater Canyon also hosts an abundance of smaller animals. Beaver build their dams and lodges in many of the tributary canyons. Other small mammals found here include the red fox, bobcat, and muskrat. Waterfowl use the quiet pools of the Sweetwater River as stopovers on their annual migrations. The canyon walls form nesting and perching habitat for an abundance of raptors. Among the species commonly seen are the prairie falcon, red-tailed hawk, and golden eagle. The rare sharp-tailed grouse uses the WSA for nesting and lekking habitat. Sweetwater Canyon also counts among its residents the rare ferruginous hawk, thirteen-lined ground squirrel, and boreal toad.

Sweetwater Canyon is rich in frontier history. Jedediah Smith, the famous mountain man, stopped here with his company of fur trappers in 1824 en route to their spring trapping grounds on the Green River. They were forced to take shelter in an aspen grove within the canyon for several weeks while a spring snowstorm howled across the uplands. Their subsequent discovery of South Pass would eventually provide the key to West Coast settlement, and their campsite is listed on the National Register of Historic Places. The Oregon Trail and the Mormon Pioneer Trail run along the northern edge of the WSA, and the Seminoe Cutoff of the historic California Trail lies just south of Sweetwater Canyon. Concrete posts mark these routes for easy identification.

The western half of the canyon as well as the uplands stretching to the north and west contain a lode-bearing formation that ignited several gold rushes during the 1800s. Placer gold was found at Strawberry Creek in 1842, but it was not until 1865 that soldiers from Fort Bridger made the first big gold strike: the Carissa Lode, some 20 miles west of the WSA. The gold rush really took off in 1867, and within two years the town of South Pass City sprang up and rose to such prominence that it soon became the principal city in Wyoming. Neighboring towns like Atlantic City and Miner's Delight arose along the eastern end of the mining district.

The easily mined gold had played out by 1873, but a second boom occurred in 1880 with the influx of miners from Park City, Utah. During this time, the gold-mining camp of Lewiston was established just north of Sweetwater Canyon, with its numerous mineshafts and scattered cabins. The gold industry then went into a steady decline, and most of the mines shut down by 1895. According to one estimate, 310,000 ounces of gold were removed from the South Pass area through 1926.

There were brief flurries of activity in the 1930s, when draglines were used to mine gold from the remaining stream gravels. By 1943, the dredging shut down and the last family had moved away from South Pass City. The ghostly skeletons of cabins and mining camps began to sag gracefully into ruin. Several *adits*, or horizontal mineshafts, can be found within the WSA, while many more mine ruins are scattered across the uplands to the north of the river.

The upper reaches of the canyon surrounding Wilson Bar receive heavy grazing from domestic cattle. Cattle have been excluded from the river bottoms in the bulk of the WSA in an attempt to preserve rare and indigenous plants like meadows pussytoes that are found on the canyon floor. Current plans allow for some light seasonal grazing in the future. The BLM anticipates some minor conflicts between grazing and recreation as Sweetwater Canyon grows in popularity, but no major problems are anticipated.

The primary threat to this small patch of wild country comes from the mineral extraction industry. The western third of the WSA has a number of exist-

Riparian vegetation along the Sweetwater River.

ing placer and lode claims, although no mining activity has occurred here for decades. Particularly worrisome are 720 acres of active placer claims along the river bars. Both tin and tungsten can be found in this area, but the USGS rates its potential for commercial extraction as low. Nephrite jade also occurs in the surrounding uplands, but no occurrences of this semi-precious stone have been recorded within the WSA.

Some 5,538 acres along the core of the canyon have been recommended by the BLM for wilderness status. Opportunities for solitude are excellent within the canyon, although human artifacts such as roads, fences, and abandoned mines can be seen on the rolling country above the rims. Illegal vehicle use within the WSA has been a problem on the rolling uplands and at the Strawberry Creek crossing, particularly during hunting season.

RECREATIONAL USES: The upper end of the canyon in the immediate vicinity of Wilson Bar receives moderate use, while visitors are few elsewhere. Use of the area is heaviest during summer weekends, and the fall hunting season also draws a substantial number of visitors. The mule deer that inhabit this area are fairly numerous and offer fine opportunities for hunting. Sage grouse are numerous enough in the uplands to sustain a bit of hunting, while blue grouse and chukars are more rarely found in the lands that surround Sweetwater Canyon.

Although there are no maintained trails in this area, livestock paths line both sides of the river and are easily passable for both horses and hikers in most places. Fords of the river will be necessary where cliffs block the way; during spring runoff you can avoid the fords by climbing to the gentle slopes above the cliffs. Sweetwater Canyon is the site of an irruption of blood-sucking ticks each spring, and visitors who venture here from May through June are well-advised to check themselves frequently for these annoying parasites. The sagebrush steppes above the canyon rims offer unlimited possibilities for cross-country travel on foot and horseback.

The clear waters of the Sweetwater River support a thriving population of trout, drawing anglers from as far away as Utah and Colorado. Rainbow trout can be found in the riffles and pocket water of the fast sections, while brown trout are abundant in the quiet water of the glides and pools. The tributary streams are inhabited by brook trout, although they rarely attain "keeping" size.

The stream gravels of the Sweetwater River are known to produce small quantities of placer gold, which can be recovered with traditional panning methods. If you plan on panning for gold, be certain to contact the BLM to get the exact location of existing mining claims, because it is illegal to pan for gold on claimed areas. Be sure to practice gold panning in such a way that your prospecting efforts are invisible to other wild country visitors, and avoid in-stream siltation as much as possible.

ACCESS: A network of jeep roads runs south from the Lewistown and Hudson–Atlantic City roads. High clearance is required on these roads, which access Sweetwater Canyon at its upper end (Wilson Bar), its midpoint (Strawberry Creek), and its lower end (above Chimney Creek).

Day Hike or Backpack

Sweetwater Canyon

Distance: 4.1 to 9.3 miles one way.
Difficulty: Moderate.
Starting and minimum elevation: 7,260 feet, 6,750 feet.
Topo maps: Radium Springs, Lewiston Lakes.
Getting there: The head of Sweetwater Canyon can be reached by driving to Atlantic City and continuing south on the Lewiston Road. After a mile, veer left at the split. Three miles later, turn left, following signs for the Willies Handcart Site. Follow the main road another 7.3 miles, then turn right opposite a road marked "750," which descends to two private cabins. Our road, a two-track passable to most vehicles, climbs south to the hilltop, where you will bear left (east), then swing right following the more well-beaten two-track. Within a mile you will pass the ruins of the Burr Mine; go straight at the crossroads here as the road now makes a deeply rutted descent (high clearance is a must here). Bear left at all junctions for the remaining 1.3 miles to reach Wilson Bar, where the Sweetwater River enters its canyon.

An aerial view of Sweetwater Canyon.

The canyon can also be accessed at its midpoint as follows. From the east end of Atlantic City, follow the Fort Stambaugh Road east for 2.5 miles to reach the Hudson–Atlantic City Loop Road (BLM 2302). Follow it 4.3 miles, then bear right at the split to stay on 2302. After another 7 miles, turn right (south) on a primitive road marked only with a sign for BLM 2302. Follow this road (suitable for cars with high clearance) downhill for 1.3 miles, then turn left (east) on a two-track marked with posts for the Oregon Trail. This road will soon take you past the mine ruins at Radium Spring; drive around the spring and continue east for 0.9 mile to reach a split marked by a cairn. Turn right at this split, following this road 2 more miles down past a fence gate to park above the rim of the canyon, just east of Strawberry Creek.

This hike follows livestock trails down the Sweetwater Canyon, offering good fishing and wildlife viewing opportunities along the way. There are many fords along the way; if you visit during spring runoff you should be prepared for lots of climbing to avoid the cliffs.

From Wilson Bar, follow the stock trails downstream along grassy sandbars dotted with willow. The route passes the sealed shaft of an old mine before entering the WSA. Great outcrops of greenstone crowd the river at periodic intervals, forcing travelers to choose between fording the shallow river or climbing around the cliffs. The fords become infrequent as the river passes a long gooseneck of land, and by the time it reaches the dry wash of Granite Creek, the dark and jagged outcrops are replaced by deeply jointed knobs of pale granite.

The hills become gentler as the river approaches a broad flat where Strawberry Creek enters from the north. This makes a good turn-around point for day hikers. Soon thereafter, faces of granite rise from the slopes, and by the time the river reaches Mormon Creek, the canyon is flanked by unbroken walls of granite pinnacles. Here, the steep and boulder-choked watercourse is shaded by abundant pines and junipers. The valley widens as it approaches Willow Creek, and the cattle trail crosses a broad flat punctuated by a few young cottonwoods.

As the river turns northeast, it enters an arid reach guarded by tall, parched hills. The bottomlands are now choked with brush, and the easier traveling is along the sagebrush slopes above. After passing a spring shaded by aspens and cottonwoods, the traveling gets marshy beside beaver-dammed wetlands that are a haven for migrating waterfowl. After rounding a flat rim, the river finally winds onto the broad sage flat where Chimney Creek bears the old Oregon Trail down to the river.

8

The Red Desert

T he Red Desert stretches across the southwestern reaches of Wyoming, a vast and trackless stretch of empty country. This is one of the largest undeveloped tracts of cold desert that remains in North America. Feral horses, pronghorn antelope, and desert elk roam free across the arid flats. Burrowing owls, pocket mice, and kangaroo rats are among the smaller desert inhabitants. Average annual precipitation is around 10 inches, most of which falls in a few storms. There are few permanently flowing streams in the Red Desert. Evaporation concentrates the salts that are leached out of the soil by runoff, and when the streams do run, the water is strongly alkaline.

The Great Divide Basin is the centerpiece of the Red Desert, where the Continental Divide splits around a perfect bowl with no outlet to either the Atlantic or Pacific Oceans. The waters flow into the center of the basin to evaporate—when there is water at all. Much of this high basin lies above 7,000 feet. The summers are hot and dry, while the winters are long and bitter cold, with constant winds that whip across this low gap in the Continental Divide. A long procession of active sand dunes runs across the heart of the basin.

Well-drained flats and uplands are robed in a sagebrush steppe that is associated with western and bluebunch wheatgrass, Sandberg and mutton bluegrass, and prairie junegrass. This habitat type is favored by pronghorn antelope. Among the outcrops of bedrock, a scrub vegetation of Utah juniper is interspersed with low-growing mountain mahogany, black sagebrush, and antelope bitterbrush. These areas are important habitat for mule deer. Limber pine may occur on the highest of the rocky prominences, but is rare elsewhere.

The basins are shot through with saline soils and alkaline seeps and watercourses. These areas are dominated by greasewood and saltbush, which are specially adapted to living in chemical-tainted soils. Snakeweed, with its globe-shaped domes of tiny yellow flowers, grows throughout the Red Desert in overgrazed sites. It contains resins that are offensive to herbivores, and thus it escapes being eaten.

Desert camouflage, put into practice by a horned lizard (also known as a horned frog or horny toad).

In the southwestern corner of the state, basin down warping occurred between 59 and 46 million years ago, at the same time that new ranges of mountains were rising to the east. Rivers changed their courses, and waters now flowed westward to pool at the base of the overthrust ranges. The result was Ancient Lake Gosiute, a playa lake over 15,000 square miles in area. Sediments deposited in this vast lakebed accumulated over the millennia to a depth of 2,000 feet to form the Green River formation of southwestern Wyoming. Sediments deposited by lakeside streams form the colorful and variegated beds of the Wasatch formation, which later would form colorful badlands. When the lake dried up, its beach sands began migrating eastward across the Great Divide Basin, forming the active dune fields of Killpecker Creek and the Alkali Basin.

There are already extensive oil developments throughout the Red Desert, and few remote areas have not seen the encroachments of drilling rigs and seismic roads. Despite the all-time low price in crude oil when this book was written, oil exploration continued at a frenetic pace. The Jim Bridger coal-fired power plant near Point of Rocks sends a plume of poisonous sulfur dioxide and nitric oxide over the Great Divide Basin, forming a brown haze where once was some of the most pristine air on the continent. It is certain that acid rain and snow from this source is responsible for sickness and death within the desert plant community; only the magnitude of the damage is in question.

The oil shales found beneath the southwestern corner of Wyoming contain more oil than all of Saudi Arabia. Due to the high expense of wringing the oil from the rock, however, it has heretofore been prohibitively expensive to pursue oil shale as an energy source. There is no guarantee that future technologies will not make oil shale extraction profitable, and the possibility that large-scale oil shale mining may occur at some time in Wyoming's future deserves serious consideration and forethought. Because of the aggressive development of petroleum resources, the roadless areas of the Red Desert contain the most endangered *de facto* wilderness in the state, and they are in urgent need of protection.

The jagged walls and pinnacles of Adobetown.

Oregon Buttes

48

Location: 40 miles southwest of Lander and 25 miles east of Farson.
Size: 22,024 acres in 2 units.
Administration: BLM (Rock Springs Field Office).
Management status: Oregon Buttes WSA (5,700 acres), Whitehorse Creek WSA (4,002 acres), unprotected roadless lands (8,320 acres).
Ecosystem: Wyoming Basin saltbush-greasewood shrub steppe.
Elevation range: 7,314 feet to 8,612 feet.
System trails: None.
Maximum core to perimeter distance: 1.9 miles.
Activities: Rockhounding, hiking, horseback riding, big game hunting.
Best season: April to October.
Maps: South Pass 1:100,000

TRAVELERS ADVISORY:
BAD WATER

The Oregon Buttes guard the low gap of South Pass that leads across the Continental Divide. To pioneers on the Oregon Trail, the Oregon Buttes marked the halfway point on their long journey, The northern butte marks a triple divide at the exact point where the Continental Divide splits to go around the Great Divide Basin, where the streams run nowhere when they run at all. To the northwest are the pale green siltstones and mudstone of the Wasatch formation, which form the badlands of the Whitehorse Creek WSA.

Extensive stands of limber pine grow along the eastern slopes of the Oregon Buttes, and some of the north-facing slopes are moist enough to support aspen groves. Sagebrush and bitterbrush are common on the south-facing slopes of the buttes. During early summer, the slopes are abloom with lupine and snakeweed. The buttes themselves are flanked by a series of clay benches that are so arid that the vegetation is an extremely sparse assemblage of saltbush and grasses. The many saline seeps and springs near the base of the buttes create miniature salt marshes in the midst of the barren desert.

A herd of desert elk haunts the wooded slopes of the buttes, emerging to feed on the open grasslands at dawn and dusk. The Oregon Buttes are one of the few remaining calving areas for this herd. Mountain lions prowl the rocky

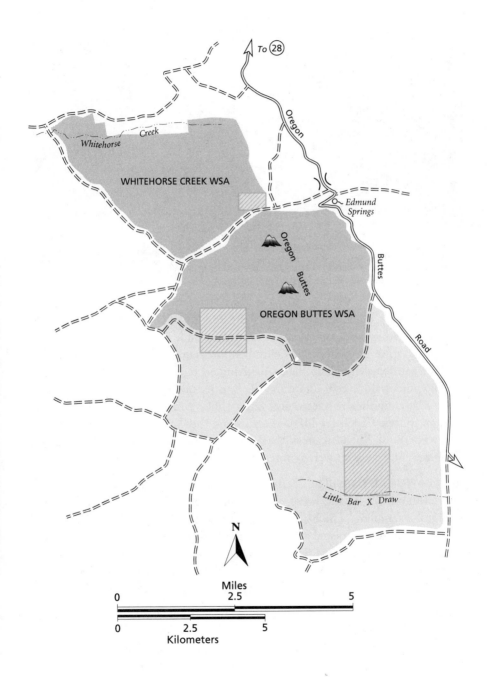

To (28)

Oregon

Whitehorse Creek

WHITEHORSE CREEK WSA

Edmund Springs

Oregon Buttes

Buttes

OREGON BUTTES WSA

Road

Little Bar X Draw

N

Miles
0   2.5   5

0   2.5   5
Kilometers

Looking south from the top of North Oregon Butte.

heights. Golden eagles are a common sight, and northern harriers are also quite abundant. Other raptors that nest in the area include prairie falcons, red-tailed hawks, and great horned owls. The limber pine stands provide forage for flocks of Clark's nutcracker, which makes its living on pine nuts and other seeds.

The potential for coal, uranium, oil, and natural gas in this area has been rated as low by the US Geological Survey. The BLM has recommended the Oregon Buttes WSA for wilderness status and the Whitehorse Creek WSA for non-wilderness. Roadless areas that stretch south from the Oregon Buttes along the Joe Hay Rim were ignored by the BLM.

RECREATIONAL USES: The open nature of the country makes it conducive to off-trail travel by foot and horse, and the buttes offer the opportunity for non-technical scrambling. The badlands of Whitehorse Creek are deeply dissected, with a multitude of isolated ravines and draws that offer fine opportunities for solitude. Rockhounds may find petrified palm wood, agates, and fossil snails and clams to the west of the buttes. The elk of Oregon Buttes are open to a limited permit hunt, and antelope and sage grouse can be hunted down on the flats.

ACCESS: The Oregon Buttes Road is a fair-weather gravel trunk road that starts at Wyoming 28 near the Sweetwater River bridge and runs along the eastern boundary of the Oregon Buttes roadless area, providing the best access. The Whitehorse Creek WSA is reached via jeep roads that run west from Oregon Butte Road farther north.

Off-Trail Scramble

North Oregon Butte

Distance: 2.3 miles one way.
Difficulty: Moderately strenuous.
Starting and maximum elevation: 7,460 feet, 8,612 feet.
Topo map: Dickie Springs.
Getting there: Drive east from Farson or west from Lander on Wyoming 28 to reach the South Pass rest area beside the Sweetwater River. Just west of the rest area, follow the wide gravel road that runs south. This is Oregon Buttes Road (County 445) and it is passable only during dry weather, when it is suitable for most cars. After 9 miles the road tops a rise at the base of the Oregon Buttes. Continue down the far side and park at a pulloff just beyond the ponds of Edmund Spring.

This route climbs the highest of the Oregon Buttes for views that stretch deep into the Great Divide Basin. From the starting point, hike west atop clay benches, bearing for a clump of dark-green shrubs. Upon cresting the rise, a many-channeled watercourse lies ahead. Cross its deeply eroded washes and follow the southernmost ravine westward into the shallow basin that lies southeast of the butte. From here, you can ascend northward across steep slopes of sparse grasses and loose pebbles.

Surmount the top of the butte just behind its eastern promontory. A grassy tabletop yields excellent views eastward toward Continental Peak and north across the green-tinted badlands of Whitehorse Creek to the distant Wind River Range. Turn west, crossing a shallow gap and then turning south across grassy tablelands high above the limber pine woodland of the east face. The southernmost promontory has superb views of the monumental buttes to the south, with rumpled, patterned lowlands between them.

Honeycomb Buttes

49

Location: 38 miles southwest of Lander and 26 miles east of Farson.
Size: 55,528 acres.
Administration: BLM (Rock Springs Field Office).
Management status: Honeycomb Buttes WSA (41,188 acres), unprotected roadless lands (14,440 acres).
Ecosystem: Wyoming Basin saltbush-greasewood ecosystem.
Elevation range: 6,980 feet to 8,431 feet.
System trails: None.
Maximum core to perimeter distance: 3.4 miles.
Activities: Hiking, backpacking, horseback riding, hunting, rockhounding, geological study.
Best season: March through November.
Maps: South Pass 1:100,000

TRAVELERS ADVISORY:
BAD WATER

Along the northern rim of the Great Divide Basin, the tall ziggurat of Continental Peak presides above a maze of badlands and eroded buttes known as the Honeycomb Buttes. Here, the clay-rich shales of the Wasatch formation take on hues that range from deep maroon and purple to salmon, gray-green to livid ochre. Although the relief within the badlands is relatively low (most buttes are less than 100 feet high), their steep walls and craggy spires lend them an aspect of grandeur. Extensive mud caves and sinkholes can be found within the Honeycomb Buttes due to a hydraulic phenomenon called *piping*. This process occurs in soft, clay-rich rock as groundwater carries off dissolved clay particles to form subterranean tunnels.

Trees are almost entirely absent within these desert badlands. Saltbush and grasses grow sparsely on the uplands, while the low washes are bordered by sagebrush and greasewood. Pronghorn antelope are abundant on the rolling uplands that flank Continental Peak, and wild horses roam the lowlands among the buttes themselves. The rugged topography found in the heart of the badlands makes fine nesting habitat for raptors. This area provides winter range for mule deer, although population numbers have been low in recent years. The Sands elk herd has been known to graze in this area year-round.

49 HONEYCOMB BUTTES

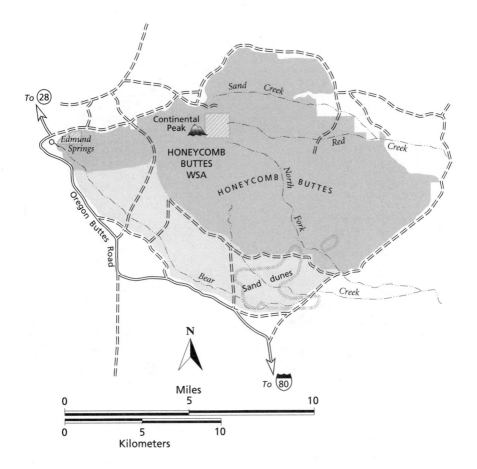

The potential for primitive and unconfined recreation in these spectacular desert badlands is far more valuable that any one-time benefit that could be gained from mining or oil extraction. Potential for oil and gas exploration is rated moderate, and there is also some potential for low-grade placer gold to be found in the terrace gravels of the area. The BLM has recommended the entire area for wilderness status, with the exception of the Sand Creek drainage to the north of Continental Peak.

Continental Peak.

RECREATIONAL USES: Hikers will find that the quickest route to the badlands comes by scrambling down from the Continental Peak escarpment at the
northern edge of the roadless area. Once in the Honeycombs, be sure to consult topo maps and compass often, because it is easy to get lost amid the maze
of colorful ridges. For horsemen, the easiest and safest way to approach the
badlands is via old jeep trails that lead up from the sandy basin to the south.
The varied and diverse terrain offers plenty of solitude, and you could wander
around the Honeycomb Buttes for days and never cross your own tracks.

ACCESS: The northern part of the WSA is best reached by driving south from
Wyoming 28 on the Oregon Buttes road, then following jeep roads east along
the crest of the divide. The Oregon Buttes Road continues south from the divide, bending east to offer access to the southern end of the roadless area as well.

Day Hike

Continental Peak

Distance: 1.5 miles one way.
Difficulty: Moderately strenuous.
Starting and maximum elevation: 7,520 feet, 8,431 feet.
Topo map: Continental Peak.
Getting there: Drive east from Farson or west from Lander on Wyoming 28 to reach the South Pass rest area beside the Sweetwater River. Just west of the rest area, follow the wide gravel road that runs south. This is Oregon Buttes Road (County 445) and it is passable only during dry weather, when it is suitable for most cars. After 9 miles the road tops a rise at the base of the Oregon Buttes. At a hairpin atop the pass, the jeep road to Continental Peak runs eastward atop the divide. Follow it for 5.6 miles to a 4-way crossroads; turn right here for the final 2 miles to park at a breached reservoir.

This short off-trail hike leads to the summit of one of the few tall peaks along the rim of the Great Divide Basin, and it offers aerial views of the Honeycomb Buttes. From the old reservoir, take a straight-line approach to the summit, climbing across inclined slopes of sagebrush grassland. Banded badlands pass by to the east as you climb. Head for the eastern face of Continental Peak for the final ascent, where a worn pathway offers easy access to the summit. From the top you will have views so vast that you can see the curvature of the Earth. The Honeycomb Buttes stretch away to the south, their low and multicolored mazes lying far below on the basin floor. The Oregon Buttes dominate the western skyline, and looking north across South Pass are the distant crags of the Wind River Range. Travel to the western edge of the summit to view Continental Peak's own crimson cliffs and spires.

Day Hike or Backpack

Honeycombs Loop

Distance: 14.8 miles round trip.
Difficulty: Moderate.
Starting and minimum elevation: 7,520 feet, 6,950 feet.
Topo Maps: Continental Peak, Bob Jack Well.
Getting there: Starts and ends at the same reservoir as the Continental Peak hike.

This route penetrates the heart of the Honeycomb Buttes, and requires strong route-finding skills. Bring your own water, as there is none to be found along the way. To begin the trip, hike eastward across the arid steppes at the base of Continental Peak. No climbing is needed to round these hills and emerge on a rolling ridgetop. From here you can see the valley of Bear Creek's North Fork

Inside the Honeycomb Buttes.

arcing southeast into broken country dominated by tall buttes. Drop south-ward down to a major wash and follow it through rolling hills.

Soon the first bands of green clay appear in the hillsides, and a short dis-tance farther the streamcourse enters the Honeycomb Buttes. This maze of low badlands has been whittled by wind and water into solitary pinnacles and miniature ranges of crags. The buttes are banded with greens and reds, creat-ing surreal color combinations. A good horse trail now leads down the drainage, and with southward progress the walls of buttes are broken by broad gaps. As the formations dwindle away, an old two-track leads past sand dunes stabilized by greasewood and other desert shrubs.

Once the buttes play out, turn around and hike north 2.5 miles to the mouth of the second big valley that enters from the west. Follow it into the heart of the Honeycomb Buttes, bearing for the summit of Continental Peak. The valley ultimately splits; follow the northern branch and take advantage of the first opportunity to climb over the rounded ridge to the north. Then con-tour west and north around the heads of several drainages to reach the North Fork divide. Angle northwest to cross the North Fork valley, then follow the altiplano around the high hills to return to the starting point.

The Pinnacles   50

Location: 30 miles northeast of Rock Springs.
Size: 42,510 acres.
Administration: BLM (Rock Springs Field Office).
Management status: Alkali Draw WSA (16,990 acres), South Pinnacles WSA (10,800 acres), unprotected roadless lands (14,720 acres).
Ecosystem: Wyoming Basin sagebrush steppe ecosystem.
Elevation range: 6,850 feet to 7,500 feet.
System trails: None.
Maximum core to perimeter distance: 3.2 miles.
Activities: Rockhounding, geology study, hiking, backpacking, horseback riding, hunting.
Best season: March through October.
Map: South Pass 1:100,000.

TRAVELERS ADVISORY:
BAD WATER

The Pinnacles area offers the last roadless stretch of the high desert escarpments and shrub steppes so typical of the Great Divide Basin. The roadless area encompasses the low canyon of Alkali Creek, with its striking rims of blue-tinted rock. Out on the flats, the cone-shaped clay buttes known as The Pinnacles are a well-known desert landmark. This area is an excellent place to find the vast emptiness and solitude that could once be found throughout the Red Desert.

The open flats and well-drained canyon slopes are robed in sagebrush-saltbush grasslands, with greasewood growing along the dry watercourses. Pronghorn antelope are year-round residents, and the Sands elk herd winters here. Wild horses of the Divide Basin herd wander through the area from time to time. Fossils of snails, clams, and leaves can be found in the sedimentary formation that forms the rimrock of the draw and the buttes. The old Point of Rocks—South Pass Stage Road, dating from the 1860s, runs through the western end of this area.

The BLM has recommended both Alkali Draw and South Pinnacles for non-wilderness. The potential for gas production is considered high in Alkali Draw, particularly in its headwaters. Parts of this area are covered by pre-FLPMA leases, and one well is already in operation within the WSA. Some 27 wells are projected for this WSA if it does not receive wilderness designation.

50   THE PINNACLES

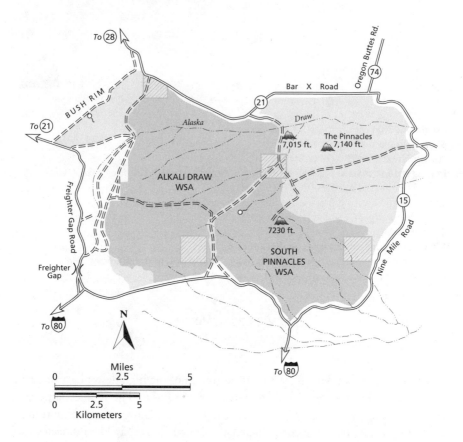

The Pinnacles area is believed to have a high potential for natural gas production, with up to 25 billion cubic feet of natural gas trapped underground. If the South Pinnacles area is not granted wilderness status, a gas field of 17 wells is projected to sprawl across this pristine area. Oilfield roads and pipelines cover a vast majority of the Red Desert already. It is difficult to justify the loss of the remaining pristine areas to accommodate yet another oilfield.

RECREATIONAL USES: The Pinnacles roadless area offers outstanding opportunities for hiking and horseback riding. Solitude can be found easily among the hidden draws and pockets in the rimrock, and the vast empty spaces that surround the Pinnacles lend a feeling of isolation even on the flats. Alkali Draw has rugged buttes and escarpments that give it the flavor of the untamed West. The area receives about 25 hunter-days of use each fall, mostly associated with antelope hunting.

Rugged country within the Pinnacles.

ACCESS: The Bar X Road (County 21) runs along the north boundary of the roadless area and provides the easiest access. The South Pinnacles can be reached via Nine Mile Road (County 15), which visits the southern and eastern parts of the area. The road that once ran between the South Pinnacles and Alkali Draw WSAs is washed out at Alkali Creek, and the desert has begun to reclaim it.

Day Hike

Pinnacles Loop

Distance: 6.1 miles round trip.
Difficulty: Moderate.
Starting and minimum elevation: 7,190 feet, 6,920 feet.
Topo map: The Pinnacles.
Getting there: From Farson, drive east on Wyoming 28 for 13 miles to reach County Road 21, which is marked "Tri Territory Historic Route." Follow this fair-weather, gravel trunk road southeast for 16 miles to reach a junction with the Freighter Gap Road (County 83). Abandon the "Tri Territory" route here and drive eastward. You will crest the top of the Bush Rim after 8 miles. Continue downhill and onto the flats beyond, and 4 miles beyond the bottom of the grade you will veer right on a primitive road as the main road bends northeast. Follow this spur track for 0.4 mile and park above the rims for both of the hikes featured here.

This off-trail route visits the weathered cones of the Pinnacles at close range, wandering among the most impressive formations. To begin, walk the road down from the rims and across the flats to the wash of Alkali Draw. On the far bank, hike southeast toward the eastern end of the largest mesa. In addition to a close inspection of the Pinnacles, views encompass Steamboat Mountain far to the west. Hike across the basin at the foot of the mesa, bearing east for the low gap that leads to the easternmost Pinnacles. After visiting them, hike north across the gently sloping steppes to reach the wash of Alkali Draw, then follow the wash west to return to the old roadbed that leads back to your vehicle.

Day Hike or Horse Trip

Alkali Draw

Distance: 11.7 miles round trip.
Difficulty: Moderate.
Starting and minimum elevation: 7,190 feet, 6,990 feet.
Topo map: The Pinnacles, Freighter Gap.
Getting there: Follow directions as for the Pinnacles Loop.

This route offers a long trip through barren hill country that has a real Old West feel. The trip begins with a descent down the old road grade to reach the broad bottom of Alkali Draw. Take in views of the Pinnacles before the route leads up the draw, following good livestock trails across the bottoms. A sparse growth of sagebrush and greasewood grows on the flats, and the mesas on either side present ranks of promontories that stretch west toward the Bush Rim. Stay with the main valley, passing several major tributary draws to the south and one to the north. Alkali Draw ultimately bends southward, exposing views of Steamboat Mountain. Seek out the jeep track that follows a tributary draw west toward the Bush Rim before bending north to reach the top of the mesa. From here, you can either hike north to strike the Bar X Road or travel cross-country along the rims to return to your vehicle.

Killpecker Dunes

Location: 10 miles east of Eden and 27 miles north of Rock Springs.
Size: 38,289 acres.
Administration: BLM (Rock Springs Field Office).
Management status: Sand Dunes WSA (27,109 acres), Buffalo Hump WSA (10,300 acres), unprotected roadless lands (880 acres).
Ecosystem: Wyoming Basin sagebrush steppe ecosystem.
Elevation range: 6,700 feet to 7,770 feet.
System trails: None.
Maximum core to perimeter distance: 2.7 miles.
Activities: Hiking, horseback riding, photography, nature study.
Best season: March through June; September through November.
Maps: Farson and Rock Springs 1:100,000.

TRAVELERS ADVISORY:
NAVIGATION CHALLENGES

The headwaters of Killpecker Creek are nestled into a low basin surrounded by arid, sedimentary peaks that rise 1,500 feet above the basin floor. This is a region of active sand dunes, forming an ever-changing landscape as the sands are blown along by unceasing winds. From the floor of the basin rises the Boars Tusk, a craggy butte that stands out amid a landscape of rounded mountains and curving dunes. The Boars Tusk is a volcanic neck, the ancient core of a cinder cone that was exposed when erosion carried away its mantle of ash. Indigenous people who visited this basin before the arrival of white explorers left petroglyphs on nearby White Mountain.

Geologists believe that the sands originated on the beaches of Ancient Lake Gosiute, a vast body of water that once covered much of western Wyoming. The dunes themselves begin on the northwest slopes of Essex Mountain to the northwest of the basin and fill the headwaters of Killpecker Creek. From here, they migrate eastward, blown by prevailing winds for a distance of 100 miles before they finally peter out near Seminoe Reservoir.

During early spring, migrating sand dunes commonly overtake snowdrifts, and the buried snow turns into ice that lasts throughout the year. Ice-cored dunes form reservoirs of groundwater in this arid corner of the West, and as summer warms the dunes, much of the ice melts and the water seeps out of the

51   KILLPECKER DUNES

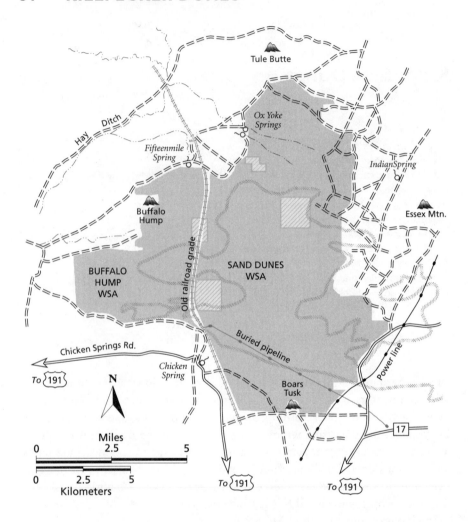

dunes to form small marshes in the midst of the desert. These small wetlands have become focal points for wildlife. Tiger salamanders and spadefoot frogs inhabit the pools, and such shorebird as the sandpiper, snowy plover, white-faced ibis, and avocet stalk the shorelines. Golden eagles and ferruginous hawks nest in the WSA, and desert elk, mule deer, and pronghorn antelope wander across the flats and broken highlands.

The Bureau of Land Management has organized the roadless areas of upper Killpecker Creek into three subunits. The heart of the dunes falls within the Dunes Wilderness Study Area, bounded to the south by Boars Tusk with its

Boars Tusk and the Killpecker Dunes.

primitive access road, to the east by an improved road that serves the oilfield in the northeast corner of the basin, and to the west by the abandoned railroad grade that once ran from Rock Springs to the Iron Mountain mine run by US Steel. The railroad grade was abandoned in the 1960s when the mine closed, and the rails were reclaimed for scrap. The gravel railbed has been overtaken by dunes in several places, but otherwise a few rusting spikes are the only remaining artifacts. This railbed makes an ideal route for mountain bikers and horsemen; a few jeeps still attempt to drive this route despite the shifting sands that render access difficult. The railbed is not officially recognized as a roadway by the BLM.

The western roadless segment has been designated the Buffalo Hump Wilderness Study Area. This is a vast and trackless sea of dunes that have become overgrown by bunchgrass and desert shrubs, and it is pocked with miniature wetlands that have their origins in ice-cored dunes. From an ecological standpoint, this area may be the most important of the three sections due to its diversity of vegetation. It is separated from the Dunes WSA only by the abandoned rail grade. Since the railbed is a historical artifact, it may be included within wilderness, according to the Wilderness Act of 1964. With this in mind, the public interest might best be served by consolidating the Buffalo Hump Unit with the Dunes unit to form a single wilderness. In its wilderness EIS, the BLM has failed to recognize this option.

Wetlands and dunes to the west of Essex Mountain.

Farther east, a roadless unit that encompasses part of the Killpecker Basin has been designated by the BLM for off-road recreation by motorized vehicles. Dune plants have a fragile toehold on life to start with, and thus motor vehicles tend to be extremely damaging to dune plant communities. However, it is unlikely that the eastern subunit would be eligible for wilderness status at any rate, since oil drilling pads blanket its northern half, and the noise from the drilling rigs and the relatively high road traffic degrade the wilderness quality of this roadless area.

The potential for oil within the wilderness study areas is low, with moderate potential for reserves of natural gas. The Nitche Gulch gas field lies just east of the Dunes WSA, and here drilling is proceeding at a frantic pace. The potential for bituminous and subbituminous coal deposits is considered high, and the threat of future strip mining and coalbed methane development hangs over the basin like a pall.

RECREATIONAL USES: This roadless area provides outstanding opportunities for off-trail wanderings through the enormous dunes. Bring a map and compass, because it is easy to get disoriented in the heart of the dunes, and distances are deceiving. Tread lightly around the small pocket wetlands and marshes, which are very sensitive to disturbance. Visitors who ride horses or mountain bikes will find that the old railroad grade is a way to visit the heart of the dunes without stepping off into the soft morass of the sand. Watch out for railroad spikes here.

ACCESS: The Chicken Springs Road offers a good gravel thoroughfare from just south of Eden to the Killpecker dune fields. The Chilton Road (County 17) runs up from the south to access the oilfields on the east side of the dunes. Beware of jeep tracks that lead away from the gravel trunk roads; they cross soft sand where it is easy to get stuck.

Day Hike

Dunes Trek

Distance: Up to 7.0 miles round trip.
Difficulty: Moderate.
Starting and maximum elevation: 6,815 feet, 7,000 feet.
Topo maps: Boars Tusk, Ox Yoke Springs.
Getting there: From Eden, drive south on U.S. 191 for a few miles, then veer left on a gravel trunk road signed with mileages to Boars Tusk and Chicken Springs. Drive past the Boars Tusk to the 3-way intersection, where you will turn left and drive northeast for 3.2 miles. Turn left at signs for the Sand Dunes WSA, and follow the pot-holed trunk road north for 3.5 miles to reach the spot where the road first passes underneath the power lines. Park here for the dunes trek.

This off-trail ramble through the active dunes of upper Killpecker Creek has no set course and few landmarks that do not shift over time. Bring a map and compass, and check the landmarks behind you at frequent intervals so you can easily find your car. The hike can be tailored to any length depending on your time constraints. It is particularly rewarding in early morning, when the tracks of nocturnal animals can be read on the ripples of the dunes.

From the starting point, wander westward toward the heart of the dunes. At first, much of the sand is stabilized by snakeweed, but before long a series of bare, active dunes provides the traveling surface. The sand is not continuous: Between the dunes lie stabilized flats covered with shrubs, and pocket wetlands made green by grasses and rushes. The Boars Tusk rises prominently to the south, while to the north lie the Essex Mountain highlands. The ridge projecting southwest from these heights makes a practical destination for ambitious hikers.

Red Lake Dunes   52

Location: 30 miles northwest of Tipton.
Size: 43,717 acres in 2 units.
Administration: BLM (Rock Springs Field Office).
Management status: Alkali Basin—East Sand Dunes WSA (12,800 acres), Red Lake WSA
(9,515 acres), unprotected roadless lands (21,402 acres).
Ecosystem: Wyoming Basin sagebrush steppe and saltbush-greasewood ecosystems.
Elevation range: 6,590 feet to 6,929 feet.
System trails: None.
Maximum core to perimeter distance: 2.4 miles.
Activities: Hiking, horseback riding, hunting, rockhounding, photography.
Best season: March through October.
Map: Red Desert Basin 1:100,000.

TRAVELERS ADVISORY:
BAD WATER

This roadless region encompasses some of the low-lying areas in the Alkali
Basin. It is divided into two units: The western unit offers views of the volcanic
buttes that rise along the western rim of the Great Divide Basin, while the eastern unit lies at the foot of the Luman Rim, a long scarp with sandstone rims.
The Killpecker Dunes actively migrate through both units from west to east,
the active dunes spaced out at broad intervals between flats of desert scrub.
Here you can find the low, red-bottomed lakes of the Alkali Basin, dry for most
of the year but brimming with runoff during flash floods.

Some of the older dunes have been colonized by greasewood, rabbitbrush,
and sagebrush. This scruffy mantle of vegetation has stabilized the dunes by
protecting the sand from the constant winds that would otherwise keep it
moving. In some cases, stabilized sand dunes have been blown out by fierce
winds, leaving the brush perched precariously atop an unstable haystack of
sand. This is open and empty country, where bands of antelope and feral horses
roam, and jackrabbits hide in the shade of the sagebrush and greasewood.
Prairie falcons and northern harriers are commonly spotted as they fly a
ground-hugging course among the dunes, hunting for rodents and small
birds. Such desert dwellers as kangaroo rats and burrowing owls make their
homes here.

The BLM failed to recommend either of these WSAs for wilderness status, citing conflicts with potential natural gas development. (It is eerie how frequently the federal land management agencies favor corporate profit over the public interest.) Oil boosters believe that there are over 135 billion cubic feet of natural gas trapped beneath the WSAs. Petroleum development is already encroaching along the north side of the Alkali Basin unit, and over 30 wells are projected within the dunes if wilderness status is denied.

RECREATIONAL USES: These roadless areas offer easy access to the dunes, which may be over 50 feet tall in places. Horsemen will find that the dunes are widely spaced, with firmer ground between them that is well-suited to riding. Hikers will find outstanding hiking along the crests of the dunes, and from the heights one can gain long vistas across the Great Divide Basin. Although the roadless corridor is narrow, the tall dunes block out any sign of human encroachments, and one can make a long trip of it by hiking the length of the dunes along an east-west axis.

Prairie falcon hunting over the dunes.

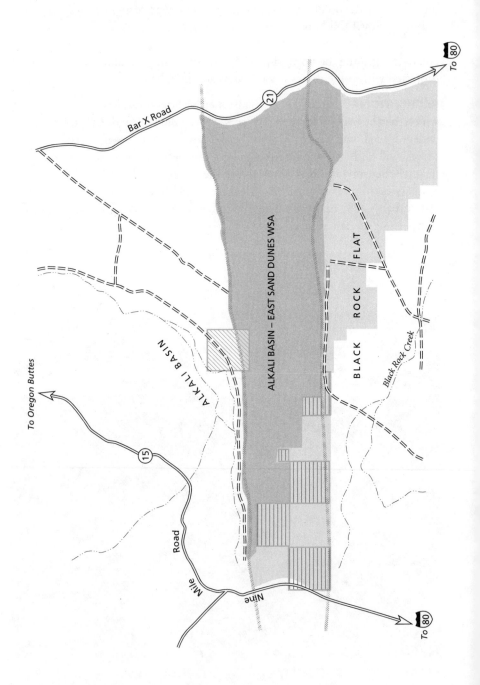

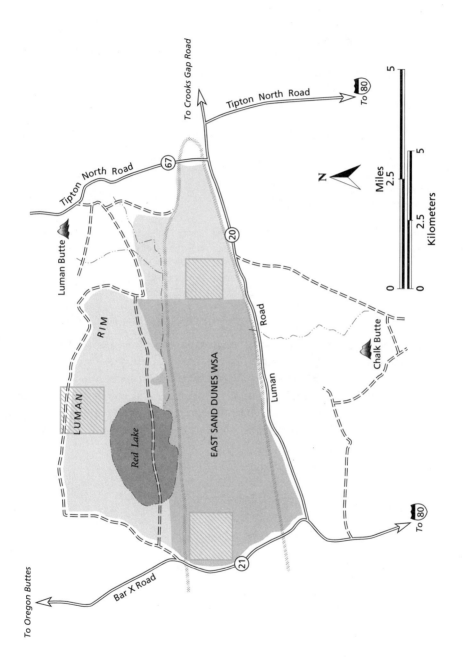

To Crooks Gap Road

Tipton North Road

To 80

Tipton North Road

67

Luman Butte

N

Miles
2.5   5

0

Kilometers
2.5   5

0

20

RIM

Luman

Road

LUMAN

Chalk Butte

Red Lake

EAST SAND DUNES WSA

21

To 80

Bar X Road

To Oregon Buttes

ACCESS: The western unit of the roadless area can be accessed from I-80 via the Bar X Road (County 21) north of its junction with County 20. The western edge of this roadless unit is characterized by checkerboard land ownership, which makes legal public access difficult. The Luman Road (County 20) stretches along the south boundary of the eastern unit. Both roads are suitable for passenger cars, but they turn to soup in the rain.

Day Hike

Luman Dunes

Distance: 4.0 miles or more, round trip.
Difficulty: Moderate.
Starting and maximum elevation: 6,624 feet, 6,650 feet.
Topo map: Red Lake.
Getting there: To reach the starting point for the Luman Dunes hike, take I-80 to exit 152, marked "Bar X Road." After exiting, drive to the north side of the underpass and follow the frontage road west for a short distance to intersect the Bar-X Road. This fair-weather gravel road runs north 23.5 miles to a junction with Luman Road (County 20). Turn right on this road, following it east for 2.5 miles to park at the road's first southward bend.

This off-trail ramble runs through the dunes to the south of Luman Rim. To begin the journey, head north toward the distant cliffs of the Luman Rim. You will cross stagnant dunes stabilized by desert grassland and shrub steppe. Once you reach the active dunes in the heart of the basin, turn east and follow the dunes' axis of migration. You can follow the sand as far as you wish. To return to your vehicle, take a bearing on the collection of low buttes and hills at the edge of a vast flat. Hike to these hills, where you will strike the Luman Road. Follow it westward to your vehicle.

Adobetown   **53**

Location: 50 miles southeast of Point of Rocks.
Size: 85,710 acres.
Administration: BLM (Rock Springs Field Office, Rawlins Field Office).
Management status: Adobetown Wilderness Study Area (85,710 acres including 1,280 acres of state land).
Ecosystem: Wyoming Basin saltbush-greasewood desert and sagebrush steppe.
Elevation range: 6,420 feet to 7,125 feet.
System trails: None.
Maximum core to perimeter distance: 4.2 miles.
Activities: Hiking, backpacking, horseback riding, rockhounding, big game hunting (antelope and mule deer), wildlife viewing, photography.
Best season: April through October.
Maps: BLM 1:100,000 scale Kinney and Baggs.

TRAVELERS ADVISORY:
BAD WATER

Adobetown encompasses a series of arc-shaped rims that rises near the center of the Washakie Basin, sculpted by the intermittent waterways of Sand Creek and its tributaries. The rims rise 500 feet above a low-lying plain of desert brush, sculpted by erosion into a fantastic landscape of spires, balanced rocks, keyholes, and cliffs. Above the rims, a high and windswept plateau stretches westward, covered with stabilized sand dunes and alkali flats that fill with water when it rains.

The bedrock that forms Adobetown is tuffaceous sandstone belonging to the Adobe Town member of the Washakie formation. It is made up of volcanic sediments that were deposited in the Washakie Basin by a long-extinct river that flowed down from the north. Tuffaceous sandstone is soft in character and easily eroded by wind and water. In many places, its surface has been scored with vertical and horizontal grooves that give it the appearance of adobe masonry. Isolated pillars of sandstone rise as much as 2 miles east of the rimrock, and many pinnacles are clustered in groupings reminiscent of long-abandoned cities.

Paleontologists have discovered Pleistocene animal fossils within this area. Among the finds include the titanothere, a giant tapir that reached weights of

53   ADOBETOWN

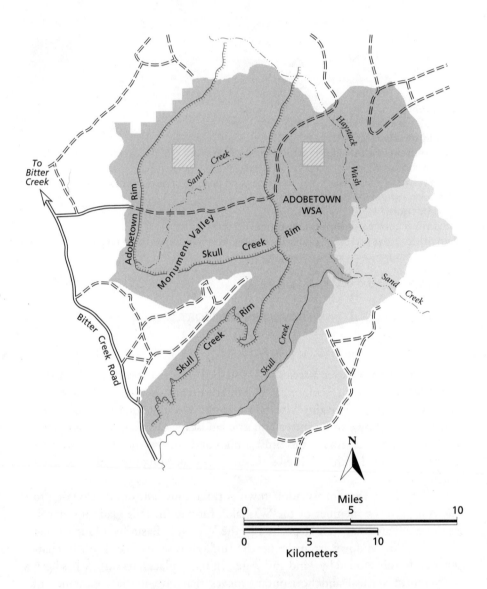

up to 4 tons and could reach a height of 8 feet at the shoulder. Also found here were bones of the uintathere, a woolly rhinoceros. Fossil turtle shells are also common. Archaeologists have unearthed evidence of constant human activity in this area over the course of the last 12,000 years. Adobetown is considered to have an unusually high density of archaeological sites, most of which have yet to be cataloged. Visitors should bear in mind that both vertebrate fossils and human artifacts are protected under the Antiquities Act, and it is a federal crime to collect or disturb them. Fossils and human artifacts are a priceless and irre-placeable record of Wyoming's history, and scientists can only interpret these ar-tifacts within the context of their original position within the rock strata.

The modern mammals of Adobetown feature wild horses, pronghorn ante-lope, and mule deer. The wild horse population ranges between 300 and 500 animals, which can be found both above and below the breaks. In this open country of sagebrush and greasewood, the horses are easy to spot, especially due to their deeply colored white and coal-black pelage, which contrasts sharply with the dun colors of the landscape. The pronghorns belong to the Bitter Creek herd, some 11,000 strong. About 450 antelope summer within the proposed wilderness, while up to 1,200 head can be found here during the winter. Adobetown also offers outstanding habitat for mule deer. The resident population numbers around 200 head, augmented by migrant animals that move in during the winter.

The cliffs and pinnacles of Adobetown offer superior nesting sites for rap-tors, and its diverse array of avian predators is highlighted by golden eagles and ferruginous hawks. The ferruginous hawk has been granted Category II status under the Endangered Species Act—which means that ferruginous hawks are in danger of extinction but scientists lack sufficient population data to list the species as Endangered. The population decline of this hawk has been largely attributed to human disturbance in nesting areas, which has been linked to a nest failure rate of 55 percent in recent years. Scientists estimate that 22 nest-ing pairs of ferruginous hawks call Adobetown home.

If the U.S. Congress follows the BLM's recommendation, only 10,920 acres of Adobetown will be designated as wilderness and 69,430 acres will be released from wilderness consideration. Monument Valley, the Adobetown Rim, and vast acreages of sagebrush flats would be released for industrial exploitation. Views from the resulting shrunken wilderness would ultimately include a maze of drilling sites, roads, pipelines, and other artifacts of the oil extraction industry. Lost in the process would be miles of the most spectacular cliffs, canyons, buttes, and pinnacles in the area, a landscape worthy of National Park status. Due to the wide-open character of this landscape, it would be difficult to find a corner of the recommended wilderness area where the sights and sounds of industrial ac-tivity would be imperceptible. Thus, the preferred alternative presented within the EIS is a boon for the oil industry and a disaster for the American public.

There are almost no signs of past human activity within the Adobetown WSA. Several jeep trails descend from the rims to cross the vast plains of Sand Creek, but these roads would soon be swallowed up by the desert if they were closed. Small reservoirs are scattered across the landscape, built by stockmen to

Pillars near the Adobetown Rim.

retain water from the infrequent cloudbursts that occur here. Most have been abandoned, and their dams are camouflaged by a mantle of sagebrush. Wild horse traps can also be found within the breaks. Cattle and domestic sheep are still grazed throughout the wilderness study area, and this grazing would continue under wilderness designation.

The major man-made intrusions within the proposed wilderness take the form of active and abandoned drilling sites, unimproved roads and jeep tracks, and seismographic lines associated with oil and gas exploration. Major oil reserves have been discovered along the northwestern edge of the WSA, and pockets of natural gas have been located along the western and southern margins. Petrologists estimate that between 1 and 2 trillion cubic feet of natural gas may exist beneath Adobetown, at an average depth of 15,000 feet. Adobetown is underlain by low-grade oil shales, buried beneath 3,000 feet of overburden. It is not economical to mine these oil shales today, but it may become profitable in the decades to come. As for other subsurface minerals, Adobe-town has low potential, and the entire region was withdrawn from development by Executive Order in 1930.

The western half of the proposed wilderness has several oil and gas leases that were filed before the Federal Land Planning and Management Act (FLPMA). By law, the holders of these leases may explore for and develop oil and gas wells despite any future wilderness designation. It is important to note that there is no current oil and gas drilling in the Adobetown area, and many of the neighboring wells have been abandoned as uneconomical. However, according to the EIS, "it is quite probable that development would occur," and gas drilling is currently accelerating in the local area. When the BLM developed its wilderness recommendations, natural gas potential was given priority over public recreation and environmental quality. In short, the Adobetown recommendations are one more in a long line of sellouts in which government officials sacrifice the public interest in the name of corporate profit.

RECREATIONAL USES: Adobetown offers limitless opportunities for off-trail hiking and explorations among the pinnacles and draws of its many rims. The open country both above and below the rims is well suited to horse travel, and it affords access to scenic overlooks and spectacular canyons. The vast extent of this roadless area makes multi-day trips a possibility. Remember that there is no water, and you will need to carry at least a gallon a day per person. The trophy antelope hunting in this area is considered to be of high quality, and trophy mule deer lurk amid the badlands. The Adobetown area receives an estimated 25 visitor days per year from off-road vehicle users, which would be displaced to neighboring areas if Adobetown is granted wilderness status.

ACCESS: Adobetown lies far from any pavement, in the heart of a vast and empty landscape of sagebrush desert. Ranches are few and far between, and there are no services within 50 miles. Carry an extra spare tire, extra fuel, and plenty of water and food in case you get stuck. All roads in this area become completely impassable when wet, and four-wheel-drive and high clearance vehicles are strongly recommended even in dry weather. Clear out if wet weather threatens, and be prepared to effect a self-rescue should you run into trouble.

The Bitter Creek Road runs south from I-80 to Adobetown, providing good fair-weather access for all vehicles. More difficult roads runs southeast to the Adobetown Rim, and the jeep roads that follow the Adobetown and Skull Creek Rims should be attempted only by experienced four-wheel-drive users. The faint jeep tracks that lead to the Sand Creek flats are difficult and dangerous to attempt, even with a tank.

The towering badland breaks of the Skull Creek Rim.

Day Hike and Scramble Route

Monument Valley Loop

Distance: 6.5 miles round trip.
Difficulty: Moderately strenuous.
Starting and minimum elevation: 6,960 feet, 6,840 feet.
Topo map: Monument Valley.
Getting there: Drive I-80 east from Point of Rocks to the Bitter Creek Road, exit 142. Drive south on this broad, gravel road that becomes impassable in wet weather. You will reach the Bitter Creek railway siding after 7 miles; just beyond it, bear left at the split to stay on the Bitter Creek Road. It winds south through empty country for another 21.5 miles to reach the Eversole Ranch. Drive through the ranch compound, then bear left. Continue straight ahead (south) as the Bitter Creek Road bends away to the west. You are now following BLM 4412, which may be deeply rutted and turns to mud when it gets wet. After 3.6 miles, turn left on a major road that leads east 4.4 miles to a pump station on the Adobetown Rim. Park just beyond the pump station.

This off-trail ramble leads through the spectacular pinnacles of the Adobetown Rim. The trek begins by descending eastward from the Adobetown Rim along the roadbed. The road swings south near the bottom of the grade; leave the road here and drop into the wash to the north. Follow the watercourse downward through gabled pillars and pinnacles. When the wash emerges onto the flats, abandon it and hike eastward along the base of the rock formations. As the outcrops subside into sandy slopes, a low and rock-guarded gap appears to the northeast. Cross through the gap and turn northwest, following the base of a sage-clad hill.

You will ultimately strike a wash that runs north through a narrow canyon; follow it through the rocks. It emerges at the base of a low wall of battlements that trend east-west. Hike northwest along the base of the badlands, crossing undulating terrain en route to a long ridge of spires that extends like a bony finger into the basin. Upon reaching this ridge, take time to explore the maze of canyons and spires at its base. Then round the toe of the ridge and begin a westerly climb above a basin crowded with needle-shaped tors. Take advantage of gradual slopes to ascend from one level to the next. Just below the rounded crest of the Adobetown Rim, you will be able to turn southeast along a shelf encrusted with weathered towers. It will soon become necessary to climb atop the rims, and the last leg of the trip follows them southeast with many a westward detour to avoid eroded gullies.

Day Hike

East Fork Point

Distance: 3.4 miles total.
Difficulty: Moderate.
Starting and minimum elevation: 7,055 feet, 6,990 feet.
Topo map: Prehistoric Rim.
Getting there: From Bitter Creek, drive past the Eversole Ranch as for the Monument Valley hike, and continue south on BLM 4412 from the major road junction. After 8 miles, you will see a ranch just ahead. Turn left (east) on a graded road and follow it to the old oil well site at its end. Drive northeast from the drilling pad on a two-rut jeep road that is difficult to find initially but is obvious once you're on it. After 1.4 miles, you will reach a junction near Windy Reservoir. Continue north and drive another 3.0 miles to reach a split. Turn right and drive east for 1.2 miles to park beside an outcrop atop the Skull Creek Rim.

This loop trek stays atop the Skull Creek Rim for aerial views of the colorful breaks and spectacular rock formations. To begin, hike north on the level mesa top. Upon reaching a fence, follow the horse trail that skirts east around its end, then continue north along the rim as pinnacles crowd the draw below. A horse trail soon leads down to the next terrace; hike toward the squat butte that rises to the north (marked "East Fork Point" on the map). From its east side, you will have superb northward views encompassing the Adobetown Rim, as well as the more colorful lower rims that stretch northward to the horizon.

Looking north from the Skull Creek Rim.

After taking in the view, double back to the south, hiking atop a lower rim-rock that demarcates a hoodoo-filled canyon below. Hike all the way around its rim, then continue eastward to visit the many promontories that jut out high above the breaks. You will ultimately arrive at a point farthest east where the mesa dissolves into unattainable pinnacles. From here the views stretch eastward across the vast basin of Sand Creek, whose broad wash can be seen snaking across the plain. The main bulwark of the Skull Creek Rim now stretches to the south, a towering wall of pinnacles and cliffs reminiscent of the Grand Canyon.

After traveling south, turn westward along the rim of the next major canyon. Follow it past the deep chasms of its mouth and the striking pedestals of its headwaters. This rim leads back to the craggy butte at the edge of the higher shelf where you will find your vehicle.

Red Creek Badlands 　　　　　　　　54

Location: 30 miles south of Green River.
Size: 11,420 acres.
Administration: BLM (Rock Springs Field Office).
Management status: Red Creek Badlands WSA (8,020 acres), unprotected roadless lands (3,400 acres).
Ecosystem: Wyoming Basin sagebrush steppe ecosystem, dominated by juniper scrub.
Elevation range: 7,000 feet to 7,900 feet.
System trails: None.
Maximum core to perimeter distance: 1.7 miles.
Activities: Hiking, horseback riding, big game hunting, rockhounding.
Best season: April through October.
Maps: Firehole Canyon 1:100,000; Red Creek Ranch and Richards Gap 1:24,000.

TRAVELERS ADVISORY:
BAD WATER

Red Creek flows through a big basin guarded by lofty breaks that slope down into a maze of minor buttes, ridges, and draws on the basin floor. The badlands are made up of the red sandstones and shales of the Wasatch formation, colorful and highly susceptible to erosion. They offer an excellent landscape for short and medium range forays into the backcountry.

Juniper scrub dominates the badlands and is intermixed with sagebrush, mountain mahogany, and greasewood along the major draws. Cottonwoods can be found beside the major washes, where groundwater is available. Spring willow can also found along some of the major washes. It is not a willow at all, but a flowering shrub whose closest relatives live in the rainforests of Central America. The northernmost stands of piñon pine are thought to occur within these badlands. Red Creek, which runs through the area, is home to the Colorado cutthroat trout, a rare subspecies that is a focus for recovery efforts.

The Red Creek Badlands lies within the Red Creek Area of Critical Environmental Concern, which was established to manage the watershed to reduce its output of salinity and silt. The area was recommended for non-wilderness, primarily because BLM once foresaw a potential need to build erosion control structures that would slow the flow of silt and salts into the Green River. Saline runoff is now recognized as a natural part of the Green River aquatic system,

54   RED CREEK BADLANDS

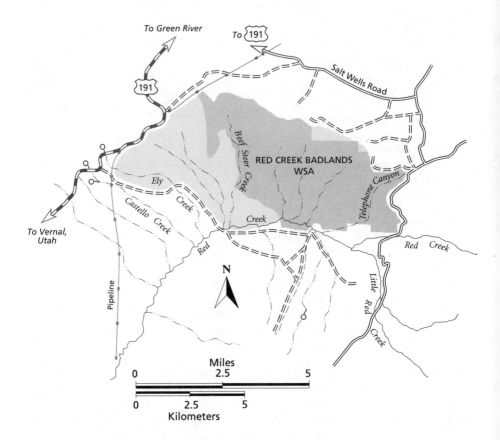

and hydrological developments are now seen as a remote possibility. Cattle graze within the badlands during some seasons, but there is little potential for other economic developments here. It is expected to remain in a wild and pristine state throughout the foreseeable future.

RECREATIONAL USES: The Red Creek Badlands is ideal for off-trail hiking and backpacking trips. Horse trips are possible along the upper rim of the breaks and along most of the major washes that radiate north from Red Creek. Water sources in this area tend to be saline. The Red Creek Badlands is also a popular locale for mule deer hunting.

ACCESS: To visit the Red Creek Badlands, follow US 191 almost to the Utah border. The Salt Wells Road (County 34) runs north of the rims, and the

Aspen Mountain Road (County 27) follows the eastern boundary of the road-less area. These roads are passable to most vehicles when dry but turn into deep mud following wet weather. High clearance is required to drive the primitive road that follows the pipeline for access to the western side of the area.

Day Hike

Telephone Canyon Overlook

Distance: 2.3 miles one way.
Difficulty: Moderate.
Starting and minimum elevation: 7,720 feet, 7,510 feet.
Topo map: Red Creek Ranch.
Getting there: From Green River, follow US 191 south for 30 miles, then turn east on Salt Wells Road (County 34) and follow this rutted, fair-weather road for 6.2 miles. Then turn right on County 27, bearing right at the major split 2.1 miles later. Just 0.2 mile beyond this junction, turn right on an unmarked jeep trail and park.

This off-trail hike visits a promontory on the high rims above the Red Creek Badlands. The hike begins by following a two-track road westward along high, sagebrush uplands above the rims. The roadway climbs over one hilltop, then continues toward the base of a narrow ridge that projects southward over the breaks. Pass through a fence gate and contour to the base of this ridge. Good game trails follow its spine through a sparse woodland of juniper. Views open up of the colorful and eroded breaks as you approach the base of the towering butte that rises at the end of the ridge. Choose a shallow angle to zigzag up the steep, grassy slopes of the butte to gain its top on the northwest side. The finest views come from the cliffs at the eastern edge of this high and isolated flat, looking out over the breaks and badlands of the Red Creek basin.

Day Hike or Horse Trip

Beef Steer Creek

Distance: 3.5 miles one way.
Difficulty: Easy.
Starting and maximum elevation: 6,690 feet, 6,900 feet.
Topo map: Richards Gap.
Getting there: From Green River, follow US 191 south for 34 miles, turn left (south) at the sign for Red Creek Access. After 1.7 mile, turn right on the road that runs due south. It soon gets quite rough; follow the main road to reach the bluffs above Red Creek 4 miles beyond the junction. Park atop the bluffs; the grade down to the creek is brutal for vehicles.

A badland butte along Beef Steer Creek.

This route penetrates the heart of the Red Creek Badlands. The trip begins by following the road down to Red Creek and turning upstream along its broad alluvial gravels. Watch for the second wash entering from the north, which emerges between sandstone buttes only 0.2 mile east of the road crossing. This is Beef Steer Creek, and its sandy wash offers easy traveling among low, red walls interrupted by an occasional outcrop. The surrounding hills bear a sparse growth of juniper, while the bottoms are a mix of sagebrush and greasewood with an occasional young cottonwood along the streamcourse.

Before long, a pretty little draw enters from the east. The first major tributary angles in from the northwest, and it is large enough to permit a side trip. The main channel continues north as the walls become higher and more rugged. Game trails now offer speedy traveling along the terraces above the wash. The draw ultimately widens into a broad basin with high breaks encircling its upper end. This is a good turn-around point or camping area. Beef Steer Spring lies in the wooded draw to the north, while a broader valley leads east to the base of colorful cliffs.

Devils Playground—Twin Buttes   **55**

Location: 28 miles southwest of Green River.
Size: 23,841 acres.
Administration: BLM (Rock Springs Field Office).
Management status: Devils Playground–Twin Buttes WSA (23,841 acres).
Ecosystem: Wyoming Basin sagebrush steppe and saltbush-greasewood desert.
Elevation range: 6,200 feet to 8,012 feet.
System trails: None.
Maximum core to perimeter distance: 2.4 miles.
Activities: Hiking, horseback riding, photography, hunting, rockhounding.
Best season: March through May, September through November.
Map: Firehole Canyon 1:100,000.

Black Mountain is a weathered and arid massif that rises to the west of Flaming Gorge Reservoir in the southwestern corner of Wyoming. Dun-colored terraces of clay lead up to its summit, and to the south are high, rolling steppes that lead up to the base of deeply eroded badlands that are tinted an eerie green. The Devils Playground stretches along the eastern skirts of the massif, an eroded patch of badland topography. Artifacts found near Pine Springs indicate human occupation that dates back 9,000 years.

Extensive stands of Utah juniper are found along the south face of the mountain and sagebrush covers the level forelands here; elsewhere, alkali flats and stabilized dunes are populated with greasewood and saltbush. The vegetation is very sparse throughout the area, and bare ground is prevalent. This is an empty country populated sparsely by pronghorns, coyotes, and jackrabbits. Pocket mice, long-eared bats, midget faded rattlesnakes, and northern tree lizards are some of the rarer desert dwellers found here.

RECREATIONAL USES: Because this roadless area is adjacent to Flaming Gorge National Recreation Area, it provides excellent backcountry recreation potential for visitors to the reservoir. There are fine opportunities for backpacking and horseback riding along the steppes and badlands that ring the base of the high buttes. The buttes themselves offer scramble routes to the high ground, where views stretch southwest to the high Uintas and eastward across Flaming Gorge Reservoir. There is some potential for antelope and small game hunting in the lowlands. Rockhounds will find tiger chert and invertebrate fossils in the uplands.

55   DEVILS PLAYGROUND—TWIN BUTTES

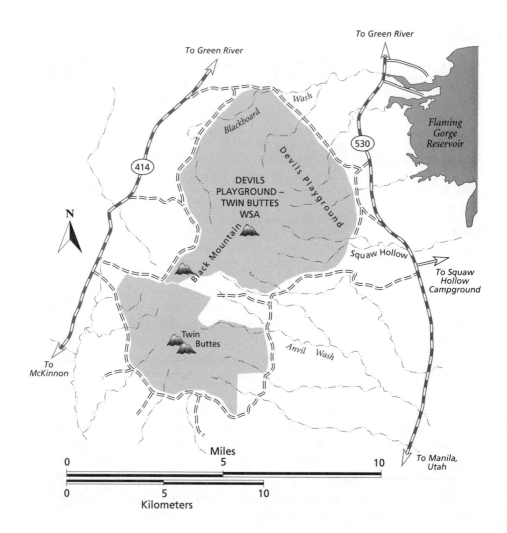

ACCESS: The Devils Playground–Twin Buttes WSA lies to the west of Wyoming 530 between Buckboard Wash and the Haystack Buttes. The McKinnon Road (County 1) is a paved thoroughfare that runs to the west of the roadless area. From these two highways, jeep trails run up toward the bases of the buttes, providing access to the WSA.

Day Hike

Black Mountain Overlook

Distance: 1.5 miles one way.
Difficulty: Moderate.
Starting and maximum elevation: 6,785 feet, 7,100 feet.
Topo map: Devils Playground.
Getting there: From the town of Green River, drive south on Wyoming 530 for 30 miles to reach Flaming Gorge National Recreation Area. Just 0.2 mile beyond the signed road to the Squaw Hollow campground, turn right on an unmarked jeep road. Vehicles with good clearance should be able to follow this road as it runs westward. After 5.7 miles, turn right onto a lesser two-track that veers northwest as the main road swings south. The hike starts at the far edge of the flats.

This trek climbs to a minor summit at the southern end of the Black Mountain massif. From the point where the jeep trail climbs southwest, cross the nearest wash and ascend along a juniper-clad hilltop between two draws. Before long, you can drop into a small amphitheater guarded by badland buttes. The eroded, greenish pinnacles of Black Mountain rise to the north. Climb the grassy ridgetop to reach a bald summit. From here, you will have sweeping views of the lesser badlands of the basin and the high and eroded summits of Black Mountain.

Black Mountain as seen from the Devils Playground.

Day Hike

Devils Playground Ramble

Distance: 2.0 miles round trip.
Difficulty: Moderate.
Starting and maximum elevation: 6,285 feet, 6,350 feet.
Topo map: Devils Playground.
Getting there: From the town of Green River, drive south on Wyoming 530. It ultimately crosses Flaming Gorge Reservoir and turns south along the shoreline. After passing the Buckboard recreation area, turn right (west) on the first jeep road. Bear right at the split and continue northwest for the remaining mile to park at a saddle in the badlands.

This off-trail route wanders among the low badlands at the eastern base of Black Mountain. To begin the trek, hike west down an eroded wash to enter a circular basin flanked with clay buttes. Upon striking the wash that drains the basin, follow it southward into the hills. After a short distance, a shallow draw leads west again. Follow it up to the top of a grassy shelf at the base of the many-tiered terraces that lead up to the summit of Black Mountain. Return via the same route.

The highlands along the south side of Black Mountain.

9

Southern Ranges

The mountain ranges of southern Wyoming are really a northern extension of the Colorado Front Range. The forest communities and their wild inhabitants are separated from the northern Rockies by the Red Desert and High Plains basins, which hinder the dispersal of montane species from range to range. The Medicine Bow Mountains and the Sierra Madre are the tallest of the ranges, while the Laramie Range is a lower swell that borders the Great Plains with granite knobs in its northern reaches and sedimentary ridges in the south.

During the Laramide Orogeny, the Medicine Bow Range was thrust skyward, moved eastward several miles, and denuded of all of its sedimentary overburden. All of this activity occurred within a span of only 10 million years, one of the most rapid mountain-building events in the Earth's geologic history. To the west of the Medicine Bows is the Hanna Basin, where the bedrock is bowed downward in a syncline to create a bedrock basin that is over 40,000 feet deep. Although it is the deepest structural basin in North America, it does not take the form of a great depression because it is entirely filled with sediment.

These ranges are managed by the Medicine Bow National Forest, which oversees forestry on millions of acres of lodgepole and spruce-fir forests. A Timber Supply and Demand Study conducted by the Forest Service itself proved that the aggressive clearcutting strategy employed on the Medicine Bow was unsustainable and therefore illegal under federal law. (When the preliminary results came in, the Forest Service canceled the study and attempted a cover-up). Scientific studies have shown that the Medicine Bow is as badly fragmented as the worst timberlands in the Pacific Northwest, despite the low economic value of Medicine Bow timber products.

The ranges of southern Wyoming offer a broad spectrum of recreational destinations. From the ponderosa pine savannas of the Sherman Range to the deep forests of the Medicine Bows, from the aspen woodlands of the Little Snake River to the windswept tundra and rocky peaks of the Snowy Range, this is a region of diverse landscapes. Although the few roadless areas that have escaped clearcutting are small and offer little opportunity for extended trips, these pocket wildernesses offer all the solitude and primitive quality of larger wildlands.

Laramie Peak

56

Location: 40 miles south of Douglas.
Size: 28,880 acres.
Administration: Medicine Bow National Forest (Douglas District).
Management status: Unprotected roadless lands.
Ecosystem: Rocky Mountain Douglas fir ecosystem, dominated by lodgepole pine forest.
Elevation range: 6,890 feet to 10,272 feet.
System trails: 22.8 miles.
Maximum core to perimeter distance: 2.3 miles.
Activities: Big game and upland bird hunting, hiking, horseback riding, rock climbing.
Best season: Late May through October.
Maps: Medicine Bow National Forest (Douglas District) map; Laramie Peak 1:100,000.

Between Casper and Wheatland, the Laramie Mountains present a long chain of weathered granite peaks rising from a lonesome stretch of the High Plains. Land ownership in this range is about evenly split between private ranches and the Medicine Bow National Forest. The surrounding area is heavily developed, with ranch roads, clearcuts, and summer cabins occupying almost all of the level ground between the steep mounds of granite. Laramie Peak is the tallest summit in the range, and it rises in the midst of the most extensive roadless area in the region. Laramie Peak is the only one of four Forest Service roadless locations in this area that has adequate public access. Even here, the wild character of the landscape is marred by an array of radio antennas atop Laramie Peak and the jarring buzz of all-terrain vehicles.

The slopes of Laramie Peak are covered in a woodland of lodgepole pine, with groves of aspen growing along the draws and streamcourses. Elk, bighorn sheep, and beaver are the most prominent residents. Raptors such as the prairie falcon, golden eagle, and flammulated owl nest in the tall treetops and on the steep faces of rock that stretch westward from the shoulders of Laramie Peak. The lower fringes of the area are home to the Prebles jumping mouse, which may soon be listed as an endangered species. The Ashenfelder Basin is well-known for its old-growth forest of ponderosa pine, one of the last remaining in the region. Laramie Peak was identified as a potential Wilderness during the RARE II process, but now only parts of it are managed for primitive recreation. Some officials in the Medicine Bow National Forest have wrongly contended that the ATV trail to Laramie Peak disqualifies the area from wilderness consideration.

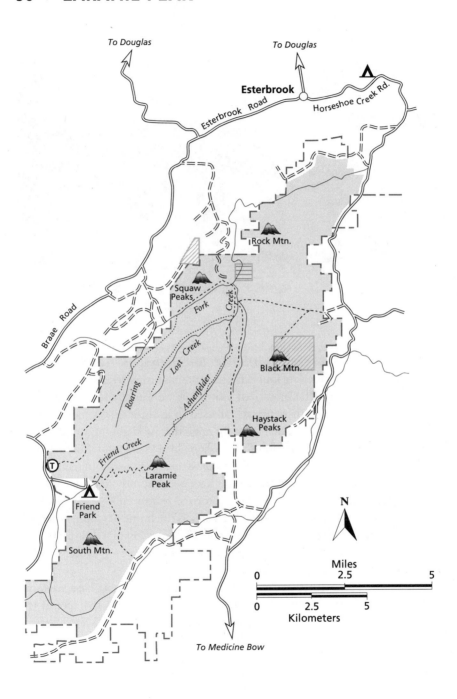

A small waterfall on Friend Creek.

RECREATIONAL USES: The Forest Service has widened the trail to the top of Laramie Peak to accommodate four-wheelers and has promoted the area as a destination for ATV users. The motorized visitors are now as abundant as the hikers on this trail, and horsemen are well advised to avoid it unless their mounts are well-accustomed to the sudden bursts of noise that inevitably accompany trail bikes and other ATVs. Trails along the Ashenfelder Creek and Roaring Fork drainages in the northern reaches of the roadless area were once obliterated by a bark beetle infestation. Many of these trails have been recently rehabilitated, and provide opportunities for primitive, nonmotorized recreation.

Hunters will find that the Laramie Peak area is the home of trophy-sized elk and mule deer, although the steep and rocky country renders hunting quite difficult in the high country, and dragging out your game even more so. Wild turkeys and blue grouse can also be found here.

The granite pinnacles make striking scenery, but solitude is hard to come by, particularly on weekends. The pink granite that makes up the core of the range is abundantly exposed throughout the Laramie Peak environs, particularly to the west of Laramie Peak itself. Though little-known to climbers, this area offers outstanding potential for face and crack climbing, rappelling, and bouldering. Some of the vertical faces exceed 200 feet in height, presenting challenges suitable to climbers of all levels.

ACCESS: Getting to Laramie Peak requires a long drive on gravel county roads that turn muddy in the rain. It can be reached from Wheatland via the Fletcher Park Road (County 133/FR 620), from Douglas via Wyoming 94 and the Braae Road (County 7), from Glendo State Park via the Horseshoe Creek Road (County 59), and from Medicine Bow via the Fort Fetterman Road (County 61) and Esterbrook Road (County 710). Friend Park is the best public access, and there is also trail access from FR 667 near Harris Park. The intermixture of private and national forest lands makes legal access tricky in other areas.

Day Trip on Foot or Mountain Bike

Laramie Peak

Distance: 5.2 miles one way.
Difficulty: Moderately strenuous.
Starting and maximum elevation: 7,500 feet, 10,240 feet.
Topo map: Laramie Peak.
Getting there: From Douglas, drive south on Esterbrook Road (Wyoming 94). After 16 miles, the pavement ends. Bear right onto County 7 and follow it south for 14 miles. Bear right as the Esterbrook Road splits away and drive southwest for 12 miles to a sign for Friend Park Campground. Turn left and drive for 2.3 miles to reach Forest Road 661. Follow this road east for 1 mile to reach the Friend Park Campground. You can park outside the campground and catch the trail that leaves from the campsites or bear left and drive 0.5 mile farther to pay a fee for the privilege of parking at the trailhead.

This trail has become popular with the motorized crowd, and although the scenery is inspiring, it is hard to get a wilderness experience here. The trail begins by making a circuit of the Friend Creek basin, passing beneath low outcrops of granite. After crossing the creek, the path starts switchbacking up through the lodgepole. It passes some small cascades on Friend Creek at the 2 mile mark, then continues uphill as rocky clearings offer views of the magnificent granite faces to the west. After a long and zigzagging climb, the path enters a subalpine woodland for the final ascent. At the summit, a collection of ugly prefabricated buildings and antennae crowds the mountaintop. Panoramic views stretch east across the High Plains and west along the granite peaks of the Laramie Range.

Vedauwoo

57

Location: 17 miles southeast of Laramie; 30 miles west of Cheyenne.
Size: 7,600 acres.
Administration: Medicine Bow National Forest (Laramie District).
Management status: Unprotected roadless lands.
Ecosystem: Rocky Mountains Douglas fir ecosystem with extensive ponderosa pine savannas.
Elevation range: 7,770 feet to 8,831 feet.
System trails: None.
Maximum core to perimeter distance: 1.6 miles.
Activities: Rock climbing, mountain biking, hiking, horseback riding, fishing, photography.
Best season: June–October.
Maps: Sherman Mountains East and West 1:24,000.

The Vedauwoo Rocks are a collection of granite spires, pinnacles, and domes that rises from the High Plains at the southern tail of the Sherman Mountains. *Vedauwoo* (pronounced "VAY-duh-voo") means "earth-born" in the Arapaho dialect. The area got its name from a theatrical play that was performed in the natural amphitheater of Turtle Rock during the 1920s. It is unknown whether this eerie area had special religious significance to the Arapaho; the tribe considers the entire Earth to be sacred.

Here, the high plains lap against the weathered core of an ancient mountain range. The once-lofty range of the Sherman Mountains was planed off by erosion millions of years ago, and its sediments mingled with those of the Medicine Bow Range to fill the Laramie Basin to a depth of thousands of feet. The granitic core of the Shermans was drowned beneath its own sediments, a vast apron of debris that extends all the way into Nebraska. Modern erosion has begun to excavate the range, and now the weathered core of the range rises again above the Plains.

Just to the south of Vedauwoo Rocks, a narrow neck of prairie rises to the top of the Sherman Mountains, linking the High Plains to the crest of the range in a a gentle and unbroken grade. This is the only place in the entire Rocky Mountain Front where one can travel from the plains to the crest of the divide without climbing into the mountains, and as such it became a major migration corridor for the Plains buffalo. The indigenous Plains tribes followed this same route as they pursued the buffalo into the Laramie Basin. Jim Bridger knew of

57 VEDAUWOO

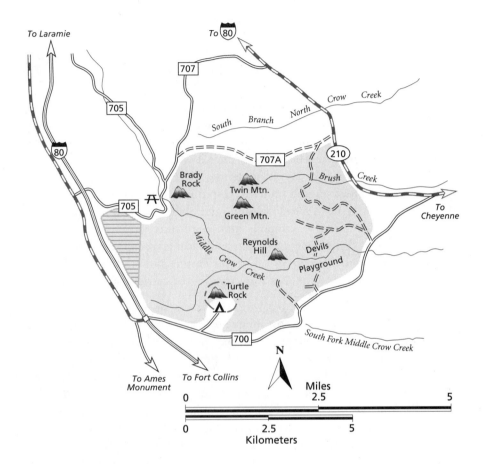

this passageway, but its lack of water and grass made it impractical for the wagons of the westward-bound pioneers. In 1865, it was recognized as the ideal route for the Union Pacific Railroad. Raids of the Cheyenne tribe beset track-laying crews as they pushed west into this area, but they managed to persevere and pave the way for the Iron Horse that was to play such a crucial role in the demise of Plains Indian culture. The track alignment was moved farther south in 1901.

The defining feature of this country is a constant wind that whistles in from the southwest and howls through this low gap in the Front Ranges. The wind blows away surface soil and sand, which results in thin topsoils. The wind is largely responsible for sculpting the rounded domes and pedestals of granite that make up the surreal landscape of Vedauwoo.

The meeting of the mountains and the plains ecosystems makes Vedauwoo one of the most ecologically diverse landscapes on the Medicine Bow National Forest. The granite formations are surrounded by open grasslands and savannas dotted with ponderosa pine. Within the mountains, a maze of miniature valleys and drainages are dotted with meadows and aspen groves and with willow-lined streams that support an abundant population of beaver. Among the rocks themselves, you will find a scattered growth of Douglas fir and limber pine, with sagebrush and bitterbrush growing from patches of sandy soil. These thin soils are derived from decomposed granite and they're poor in the nutrients needed by plants. As a result, this High Plains landscape is highly susceptible to human disturbance, and heals slowly once it is scarred.

The Vedauwoo roadless area is home to a diverse assemblage of wild animals. Golden-mantled ground squirrels, chipmunks, and marmots live among the rocks and in the open meadows, and prairie dogs can also be found here. The rare Preble's meadow jumping mouse inhabits streamside meadows. Beaver build their dams along the streams, and deer graze in the meadows. The granite pinnacles provide nesting habitat for raptors and other birds. The primary ecological threat to the area is overgrazing by cattle that concentrate in vulnerable riparian areas.

RECREATIONAL USES: The most unique recreational feature of Vedauwoo is the rock itself. The weathered granite of the Sherman Mountains is exposed in particularly striking exposures here, with problems in face climbing, crack climbing and chimneying all present. Rock climbers will enjoy opportunities for free climbing and scrambling, belaying, and rappelling. Climbers should be aware that other visitors to the area may be seeking solitude and tranquility just around the corner; be courteous and spare them the victory cries.

The rock and the rolling country that surrounds it provide limitless opportunities for off-trail hiking and scrambling. Hidden alcoves amid the granite provide excellent solitude for primitive camping. Rattlesnakes are entirely absent from the area. A network of livestock trails leads horsemen along most major drainages that are not blocked by naked bedrock. The jeep trails at the eastern edge of the area are popular with mountain bikers. Brook and brown trout inhabit the streams that drain Vedauwoo Rocks, in spite of the siltation and pollution associated with cattle grazing in the riparian areas, and offer some opportunities to fish for pan-sized specimens. From December through March, winter snows bring opportunities for snowshoeing and cross-country skiing.

ACCESS: The Vedauwoo Road (FR 700) is a good gravel road that can be reached from Interstate 80 and follows the south boundary of the roadless area. FR707A forms the north boundary, and can be reached by following the frontage road north from the Vedauwoo exit, then turning right just beyond the Blair Rock picnic area. It leads to Wyoming 210, which runs along the eastern side of the area. Unplanned jeep trails radiate toward the heart of the area, providing motorized access to most of the major rock formations. These ad hoc roads do little to improve access to the area (most of them are less than a mile in length), and since they detract from the wild and primeval character of the area, the Forest Service should block them off with boulders and allow the landscape to heal.

Day Hike

Turtle Rock Trail

Distance: 2.8 miles.
Difficulty: Easy
Starting and maximum elevation: 8,170 feet, 8,240 feet.
Topo map: Sherman Mountains. East, Sherman Mountains. West.
Getting there: Drive I-80 east from Laramie or west from Cheyenne to the Vedauwoo exit (Exit 329). Drive east on FR 700. The Turtle Hill trail can be accessed either from a trailhead in the Vedauwoo Campground (fee required) or via a spur trail from the parking lot at the junction with the Campground road.

This gentle stroll encircles the massive dome of granite known as Turtle Rock. You can start from the day use area in Vedauwoo Campground or, for an extra 0.3 mile each way, avoid the fee and start from the campground entrance road. From the west trailhead, the path glides down through an aspen grove, then follows a stream laced with beaver dams. Inspiring granite outcrops rise along the trail as it rounds the west side of Turtle Rock. Turning east, the trail climbs across sandy country and soon enters a coniferous woodland. The trees thin out in time for views across the flats toward Reynolds Hill and the Devils Playground. Passing east of Turtle Rock, the path strikes a second stream that trickles down through the boulders. It follows this stream to end at the east trailhead.

Day Hike

Reynolds Hill Loop

Distance: 1.9 miles overall.
Difficulty: Moderate.
Starting and maximum elevation: 7,900 feet, 8,050 feet.
Topo map: Sherman Mountains East.
Getting there: From the Vedauwoo Exit, drive FR 700 east to FR 700D, and follow this rough road north to its end.

Granite towers near Turtle Rock.

This primitive hike and scramble route forms a loop in the Devils Playground area. Begin the trek by hiking northwest on the well-beaten cattle path that crosses a small tributary, then makes a muddy ford of Middle Crow Creek. The path then follows a grassy glen beneath the west face of Reynolds Hill. After passing an aspen grove, the route runs past a lesser granite formation before turning east up an aspen-choked draw.

Follow the base of Reynolds Hill through the Douglas fir to reach a low gap, then continue east on an open ridgetop as tortured spires of granite rise all around. Upon reaching Middle Crow Creek, follow the cattle trails upstream. Here, beaver ponds are guarded by the surreal formations of the Devils Playground. Cross the creek and climb over a final hill to return to the starting point.

Day Horse Trip

Twin Mountain Meadows

Distance: 1.5 miles one way.
Difficulty: Easy.
Starting and maximum elevation: 8,260 feet, 8,300 feet.
Topo map: Sherman Mountains East.
Getting there: Drive I-80 east from Laramie or west from Cheyenne to exit 323. From the rest area, drive south on the Blair–Wallis Road (FR 705). After 4.5 miles, turn left (east) on FR 707, follow it for 0.7 mile, and turn right onto FR 707A. This road leads east for 2 miles; then turn right on FR 707AG and park at the base of the hills.

This route explores some of the higher country around Twin Mountain in the northern end of the Vedauwoo roadless area. To begin the trip, ride up FR 707A and turn left at the forks to reach the trail's beginning. The path runs straight toward Twin Mountain at first, but after rounding an aspen grove, it swings east along a sparsely wooded shelf. The path grows faint as it runs out onto a rocky finger, then descends southeast through a sagebrush meadow to reach a fence corner. Pass through and descend to the valley bottom below. Here, an old two-track runs west beside wet meadows and aspen stands. Follow the road up to the big meadow at the base of Twin Mountain. Adventurous souls can dismount and explore westward into the rocky high country.

Sheep Mountain Game Refuge

58

Location: 20 miles west of Laramie.
Size: 18,160 acres.
Administration: Medicine Bow National Forest (Laramie District).
Management status: Game Refuge legislated as roadless/non-motorized.
Ecosystem: Rocky Mountain Douglas fir ecosystem with limber pine and lodgepole woodlands.
Elevation range: 7,710 feet to 9,403 feet.
System trails: 13.1 miles.
Maximum core to perimeter distance: 1.8 miles.
Activities: Hunting, horseback riding, hiking, backpacking.
Best season: August through October.
Maps: Medicine Bow National Forest Map; Saratoga and Laramie 1:100,000.

Sheep Mountain is really its own miniature mountain range that extends from the Medicine Bows, with a chain of rounded summits made up of Precambrian granite. This bedrock is quite friable and crumbles readily into granular crystals. On the tops of the peaks, wind and water have sculpted the granite into the intriguing forms of menhirs and balanced rocks. The crest of the range is robed in a sparse woodland of lodgepole pine, and wind-torn pines and groves of dwarfed aspen are found on the highest peaks. The headwaters of Fence Creek has extensive wetland meadows that are a sanctuary for biting insects. The mosquitoes can be bad throughout the summer, even in late August.

The skirts of the range are robed in an arid grassland punctuated by sagebrush and rabbitbrush. The upper slopes support a loose growth of ponderosa pine and Douglas fir, underlain by juniper, kinnickinnick, and bitterbrush. Bighorn sheep once inhabited the area, but overhunting drove them to extinction in the early 1900s. Antelope and mule deer are commonly seen in the shrub steppes at the base of the range, while the wooded uplands are home to a resident population of elk. During the winter, the range receives an influx of elk and mule deer from the eastern slopes of the Medicine Bow Mountains. The higher elevations provide nesting habitat for northern goshawk, prairie falcons, and golden eagles.

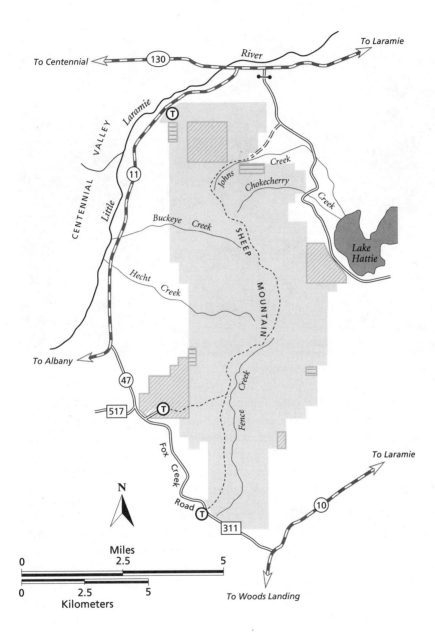

To Laramie

To Centennial

River

130

Laramie

VALLEY

CENTENNIAL

T

11

Little

Johns

Creek

Chokecherry

Creek

Lake
Hattie

Buckeye   Creek

SHEEP

Hecht

Creek

MOUNTAIN

To Albany

47

Creek

517

T

Fence

To Laramie

Fox

Creek

10

N

Road

T

311

Miles
2.5

0   5

0   2.5   5
Kilometers

To Woods Landing

Eroded granite and wind-torn pines atop Sheep Mountain.

The Sheep Mountain Game Refuge was established in 1924 by President Calvin Coolidge to protect big game and game bird habitat. Livestock are not permitted to graze on the refuge, and motorized vehicles have never been allowed. The range is actively managed for forage plants that are important to wildlife. The current management strategy includes a program of prescribed burns to renew brushfields that have grown old and unproductive.

RECREATIONAL USES: Hunting is the primary form of recreation in this area. Although not known for producing trophy animals, it does boast a resident population of around 250 elk and 200–300 mule deer. The few year-round streams support populations of small brook trout. The one trail that runs the crest of Sheep Mountain is suitable for both horses and backpackers, with superb vistas of the Laramie Basin and Medicine Bow Mountains. Camping spots with water are limited to the headwaters of Fence, Chokecherry, and Johns Creeks.

ACCESS: The main Forest Service trailhead is at a marked pulloff on the Fox Creek Road (County 47). A short spur road runs east from this road to reach a Wyoming Game and Fish trailhead at the south end of the Centennial Valley. Access to the north end of the roadless area is limited to a poorly marked trailhead where Wyoming 11 crosses a corner of Forest Service land. This trailhead has no trail, and offers only access for off-trail travel.

Backpack or Horse Trip

Sheep Mountain

Distance: 10.6 miles one way.
Difficulty: Moderate.
Starting and maximum elevation: 7,800 feet, 9,540 feet.
Topo map: Lake Owen, Rex Lake.
Getting there: Drive east from Centennial or west from Laramie on Wyoming 130, then turn south on WY 11, which runs through the Centennial Valley. At the head of the valley, turn left (southeast) on the Fox Creek Road (County 47) and follow this gravel road 5.5 miles to a marked trailhead some 0.8 mile beyond the National Forest boundary.

This trail climbs to the spine of Sheep Mountain and follows it along its entire length. The trail begins by ascending a dry gulch, wooded in Douglas fir on its north-facing slopes. Near the head of the draw, the path climbs onto the open grasslands that crown the ridge above Fence Creek. Watch for pronghorns here, and look back for views of the Colorado Rockies. The trail runs the open ridgetop, joining the rocky mass of Sheep Mountain near an old herder's cabin. Stick with the upper trail, which contours high across granite slopes sparsely wooded in limber pine and Douglas fir.

After joining the trail from the Game and Fish trailhead, the broad track follows a diversion ditch into rolling uplands where scattered lodgepole pines grow. Soon, the swamps and meadows of upper Fence Creek can be seen through the trees, and the trail follows them northward. It ultimately climbs to a ridgetop, where dwarfed aspens and wind-torn pines rise amid outcrops and obelisks of granite. Distant views alternately reveal the Laramie Basin to the east and the Snowy Range to the west. The path threads its way among the summits, and ultimately a broken sign marks the abandoned Buckeye Creek trail.

The main path now begins to lose altitude, once again entering a lodgepole woodland. Aspen-girt marshes mark the headwaters of Chokecherry Creek, and soon the south-facing meadows above Johns Creek can be seen ahead. The trail drops steeply, then enters a lush woodland of aspen and Douglas fir as spring-fed brooks gather to form Johns Creek. There are good camp spots on the grassy shelf to the west, and a sign marks the end of trail maintenance at the base of an open slope.

Snowy Range   59

Location: 35 miles west of Laramie.
Size: 35,090 acres.
Administration: Medicine Bow National Forest (Brush Creek–Hayden and Laramie Districts).
Management status: Unprotected lands managed as non-motorized.
Ecosystem: Rocky Mountain Douglas fir ecosystem, with spruce-fir and alpine tundra communities.
Elevation range: 9,840 feet to 12,013 feet.
System trails: 37.5 miles.
Maximum core to perimeter distance: 2.5 miles.
Activities: Hiking, horseback riding, mountaineering, rock climbing, wildlife viewing, fishing.
Best season: Late June through mid-September.
Maps: Medicine Bow National Forest map (with topographic insert); Saratoga 1:100,000.

TRAVELERS ADVISORY:
ALTITUDE SICKNESS, SUDDEN STORMS

From the rolling, forested uplands of the Medicine Bow Mountains, the Snowy Range rears its cliff-girt summits in stark majesty. While the core of the Medicine Bow Mountains is granite over 2.5 billion years old, the Snowy Range itself is made of pale quartzite. This rock formed 2 billion years ago when sandstones deep within the earth were transformed under great heat and pressure into a harder metamorphic rock. The Snowy Range was extensively glaciated during the Pleistocene ice ages. Cirques and sheer cliffs were gouged out by the glaciers, which left striations on the bedrock to mark the passage of the ice.

It is a strange twist of geography that the Snowy Range sits atop the Medicine Bow Range, and that each mountain chain should have its own separate moniker. Perhaps the early explorers imagined that the pale summits of the Snowy Range were part of a taller massif farther to the west, and that the Medicine Bows were a forested range of foothills in front of them. Regardless, this geographic oddity has a certain credence in the geologic record: Following the uplift of these mountains, the sediment buried them almost completely, so that 20 million years ago only the Snowy Range rose above the surrounding plain, while the long crest of the Medicine Bows lay just below the prairie soil.

59   SNOWY RANGE

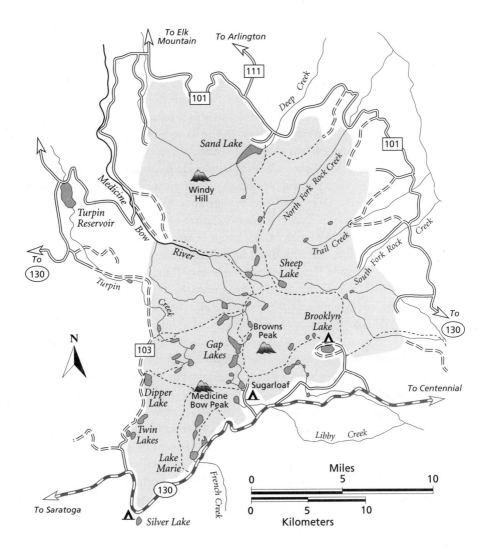

At the crest of the Snowy Range, a combination of high altitude and brisk winter winds have given rise to a true alpine tundra ecosystem. Cushion-forming plants like moss campion and phlox grow in the arid spots where soil is lacking and fractured rock offers the only growing surface. In more protect-ed locales, a rich mixture of alpine grasses and sedges forms a verdant carpet splashed with wildflowers. Such species as snowball saxifrage, American bis-tort, and mountain avens begin their growth before the snow melts away, send-

ing leaves and flowers up toward the sunlight to make the most of the short
alpine growing season. High mountain brooks are lined with mats of diamondleaf willow, the same species of shrub that is found along the streams of
the Arctic Coastal Plain.

Studies in forest ecology have revealed that extensive wildfires swept the
southern flanks of the Snowy Range in 1766 and 1774, and again in 1809. The
timberline forest has been slow to recover from these blazes, and many of the
open meadows and sparse stands of trees in this area are a lingering legacy of
these fires. Old-growth subalpine forest in the eastern end of the roadless area
has trees over 700 years old. At the western edge of the range, bands of "ribbon
forest" have formed just below the timberline. Here, stands of spruce and fir
form natural snow fences, and prevailing winds deposit deep drifts behind
them. The snowdrifts linger late into the summer, killing existing trees as the
soil grows colder and the growing season shorter and preventing young trees
from becoming established. Over time, bands of trees grow in the shallow snow
at the tail of the drifts, and new drifts form behind the new stand of trees.

The alpine meadows that surround the Snowy Range are a critical summer
range for up to 2,000 elk. Mountain lions prowl the high crags and black bears
roam through the timber and meadows to the north of the main peaks. The
rocky meadows and talus slopes are home to an abundance of pikas and marmots, which in turn attract raptors that hunt them from the air. Prairie falcons
and ospreys are among the species that nest here. White-tailed ptarmigans once
roamed the tundra of the Snowy Range, but have not been seen since 1979 and
are believed to be extinct.

The soils of the Snowy Range are extremely fragile, having weathered in
place from the metamorphic bedrock that underlies them. The soil is quite
thin, and sediments are intermixed with frost-shattered boulders. It offers few
nutrients for plants, and cold soil temperatures combined with the short growing season make for marginal growing conditions. Some placer deposits of
kimberlite have been found in the area. This mineral is associated with the
presence of diamonds. The easily eroded soils and fragile plant community led
the Forest Service to close the area to ATVs in 1970.

RECREATIONAL USES: Most of the trails within this roadless area are old
sheep driveways that have been converted to recreational use. In some cases,
trails fade out in open meadows and may be difficult to follow. These meadows erupt into a riot of wildflowers at midsummer, which makes the Snowy
Range a magnet for wildflower enthusiasts. The trails that approach the rocky
peaks often cross jumbles of boulders that make hazardous traveling for horses.
The trails to the north of the main massif cover rolling country that is better
suited to horse travel. Most of the trails within the roadless area are too short

Autumn snows on the south face of the Snowy Range.

for an overnight trip, and there is no spot in the Snowy Range that cannot be reached in a day trip. Because the area is so fragile and heavily traveled, back-country camping is discouraged and commercial guides and outfitters are not allowed.

The only trail that has a high intensity of development is the loop trail to the top of Medicine Bow Peak. This trail receives heavy use from hikers, as does the Sugarloaf area and the Gap Lakes. The Sand Lake trail is popular with horsemen. Other parts of the wildland receive light to moderate use. July and August are the peak months of recreational use. Mountaineers will find fine opportunities for face climbing on the glaciated big walls that face southeast.

There are more than 60 lakes within the roadless area, and although trout are not native to these high lakes, most have been planted with fish. Brook trout is the most common species, and is commonly found in dense populations of pan-sized adults. Golden, rainbow, and cutthroat trout can also be found in some of the lakes. There is no hunting to speak of because game animals migrate to lower elevations before the season opens.

ACCESS: Wyoming Highway 130 runs along the southern edge of the Snowy Range, offering easy access to the roadless area. The primary trailheads are Lake Marie, the Sugarloaf trailhead on its short, paved spur, and Brooklyn Lake, which has a rather pot-holed access road leading up to it. Forest Road 101 provides good gravel access for all vehicles along the eastern side of the area, and it also visits the Sand Lake trailhead, the major northern access point. The western boundary of the roadless area is defined by Forest Road 103, a jeep track so full of mud pits and boulders that even visitors with high-clearance four-wheel drives are compelled to park at Twin Lakes and hike the road to reach trails within the area. The Forest Service would be well advised to close this road entirely to motorized traffic, since most of its use comes from non-motorized visitors.

Day Hike or Backpack

Browns Peak Loop

Distance: 10.5 miles.
Difficulty: Easy.
Starting and maximum elevation: 10,550 feet, 11,000 feet.
Topo map: Morgan, Centennial, Sand Lake, Medicine Bow Peak.
Getting there: Follow Wyoming 130 to the crest of the Medicine Bow Mountains. Turn north on the Brooklyn Lake Road 1.3 miles west of Green Rock Campground or 3.3 miles east of the Sugarloaf area. Follow this paved but pot-holed road 1.7 miles to park at the trailhead on the eastern side of Brooklyn Lake.

This hike combines old sheep driveways for a circuit around Browns Peak, visiting alpine tundra and the pretty tarns and crags of the Gap. From Brooklyn Lake, follow the Sheep Lake Trail as it climbs gently through the subalpine forest. Within a mile, the path passes the first alpine tarn as the forest opens out into rocky meadows. Upon reaching the Twin Lakes, the trail turns west to climb gradually across the gentle north slope of Browns Peak. Here, the open tundra is interspersed with huddled copses of wind-torn fir. These trees take on the shrub-like krummholz growth form, seeking protection from winter gales beneath dependable snowdrifts.

Sheep Lake lies in a shallow depression surrounded by grass, and just beyond it, our route turns left onto the North Gap Lake trail. Follow this faint track across lush meadows and through stately groves of spruce ad fir. It passes several lakes cupped in the rolling country before ascending to the rocky and windswept heights surrounding North Gap Lake. The stark cliffs of a

Klondyke Lake.

northern spur of Medicine Bow Peak provide a striking backdrop for this alpine gem. Watch for pikas as the route follows boulder causeways along the lakeshore, then climbs through the gap and passes South Gap Lake. The well-trodden path now descends toward Lewis Lake, passing gorgeous vistas of Klondyke Lake and the cliffs ranged to the west of it.

Just before reaching Lewis Lake, turn left onto the Lost Lake Trail, which rises through windswept balds and clumps of krummholz fir. The massive bulge of Browns Peak hulks to the north as the trail wanders past lakelets and meres. It circles high around the north shore of the Telephone Lakes, then climbs to Lost Lake, which is backed up against the rocky mass of Browns Peak. The subalpine forest closes in as the trail makes its way to the two Glacier Lakes, beneath a permanent cornice and snowfield. It then descends to return to Brooklyn Lake.

Savage Run Wilderness   60

Location: 50 miles southwest of Laramie; 15 miles southeast of Encampment.
Size: 17,800 acres.
Administration: Medicine Bow National Forest (Laramie District).
Management status: Savage Run Wilderness (15,260 acres), adjacent roadless lands (2,540 acres).
Ecosystem: Rocky Mountain Douglas fir ecosystem.
Elevation range: 7,680 feet to 9,925 feet.
System trails: 14 miles.
Maximum core to perimeter distance: 1.8 miles.
Activities: Hunting, fishing, hiking, backpacking, horseback riding.
Best season: Mid-May through October.
Maps: Medicine Bow National Forest Map, Saratoga 1:100,000.

The Savage Run Wilderness is an island of virgin timber within a sea of clearcuts. The Medicine Bow National Forest pursued an aggressive timber harvest strategy throughout the middle of the twentieth century, cutting down the trees much faster than the forest could regenerate itself. Savage Run Creek is one of the few valleys that survived the onslaught, and in 1978 Congress set aside this roadless remnant as the Savage Run Wilderness. It is known more for its ecological importance than for its scenery and recreation potential.

The valley is underlain by relatively young granite (1.4 billion years old), which decomposes into sand that makes a relatively nutrient-poor soil base. This bedrock is intruded in places with younger igneous rock. The forest is dominated by lodgepole pine, some of which form unusual climax stands over 300 years old. Aspen stands and sagebrush meadows grow in the lower reaches of the valley. In 1970, some 41 bighorn sheep were introduced into the wilderness in hopes of repopulating the Medicine Bow Range. Savage Run Creek is an important elk calving area, and the sagebrush grasslands of the lower elevations provide winter range for elk and bighorn sheep. The northern goshawk and the pine marten are among the forest dwellers that can be found here.

RECREATIONAL USES: The trails along Savage Run Creek are suitable for both horsemen and backpackers. Trails in the Mullen Creek drainage have been abandoned, and this area offers a more primitive recreation experience. The Savage Run Wilderness is noted for producing trophy black bears and

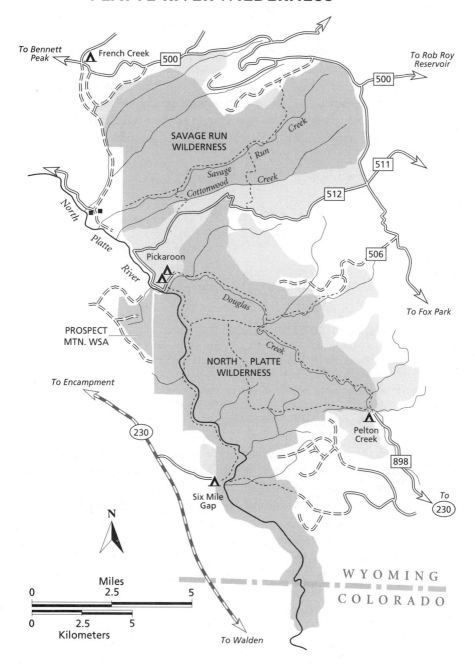

To Bennett Peak

French Creek

500

To Rob Roy Reservoir

500

SAVAGE RUN WILDERNESS

Creek

Run

Savage

Cottonwood   Creek

511

512

North

506

Platte

River

Pickaroon

To Fox Park

Douglas

PROSPECT MTN. WSA

Creek

NORTH   PLATTE WILDERNESS

To Encampment

Pelton Creek

230

898

To 230

Six Mile Gap

N

Miles
0   2.5   5

0   2.5   5
Kilometers

WYOMING

COLORADO

To Walden

mountain lions, although these animals are never abundant. Blue grouse nest within the wilderness, and provide some upland bird hunting in the autumn. Cottonwood Creek boasts a fishable population of rainbow and brown trout, mostly in the pan-sized class. Savage Run Creek is home to small brookies.

ACCESS: One must follow a maze of logging roads to reach the Savage Run Wilderness. The upper trailhead is accessed via FR 500 west of Rob Roy Reservoir, and low-clearance vehicles and trailers will have trouble making the last 1.5 miles to the trailhead. The two lower trailheads are reached via FR 512 and can be reached by any vehicle. The western end of the Savage Run Trail runs onto the privately owned A-Bar-A Ranch, and there is no public access to this entry point.

Day Hike, Backpack, or Horse Trip

Savage Run Trail

Distance: 7.0 miles one way.
Difficulty: Easy (E to W); Moderate (W to E).
Starting and minimum elevation: 9,750 feet, 8,300 feet.
Topo map: Keystone, Overlook Hill.
Getting there: The upper trailhead can be reached by following Wyoming 230 west from Laramie to the top of the Medicine Bow Mountains. Turn north on Forest Road 512, following this gravel trunk route past the railroad siding of Foxpark and then northwest through the clearcuts to meet Forest Road 511, some 15.5 miles from the highway. Continue straight ahead on 511 for 3 miles, then turn left (west) on FR 500. After 2 miles, turn left onto logging road B8, following signs for the Savage Run Trailhead. High clearance is required to drive the remaining 1.3 miles to the well-marked trailhead. The Cottonwood Extension Trailhead is reached by driving west on FR 512 from its junction with FR 511 for 8 miles.

This trail offers the primary route through the Savage Run Wilderness, following Savage Run Creek from the forested uplands down to the meadowy foothills. Horsemen will find it easiest to start from the Cottonwood Extension trailhead and ride up the trail and down again for a solid day's ride. From the clearcuts, the trail descends to the forest edge at the wilderness boundary. A pristine woodland of spruce and lodgepole pine shades the initial descent, and at the bottom the trail breaks out of the forest beside the wet meadows of upper Savage Run Creek. Watch for evidence of beaver activity amid the willows and dwarf birch of the watercourse.

After a short distance, the creek enters a narrow and timbered canyon where bedrock knobs rise from the steep slopes. Here, the stream gurgles through mossy rocks and woodland wildflowers, splashing down a succession of miniature waterfalls. Upon meeting a second stream branch, the valley widens and

Falls on Savage Run Creek.

the gradient decreases. The timbered bottomlands are broken occasionally by marshy glades. The trail runs through a young stand of lodgepole choked with blowdowns en route to the Cottonwood trail junction. Below the junction, open marshes again fill the bottoms, forming prime beaver habitat.

The trail passes extensive aspen stands and sagebrush meadows on its way to meet the Cottonwood Extension Trail. Turn left at this junction as the Extension trail fords Savage Run Creek, then climbs to the ridgetop beyond. Open slopes bear the trail down to Cottonwood Creek, where a footbridge leads to a gentle climb through the forest. The trail ends at the Extension trailhead, on the next ridgetop.

Platte River Wilderness 61

Location: 60 miles southwest of Laramie; 22 miles southeast of Encampment.
Size: 37,525 acres.
Administration: Medicine Bow National Forest (Laramie District), BLM (Rawlins Field Office).
Management status: Platte River Wilderness (22,749 acres), Prospect Mountain BLM Wilderness Study Area (1,145 acres), adjacent roadless lands (13,631 acres).
Elevation range: 7,380 feet to 9,350 feet.
System trails: 29.7 miles.
Maximum core to perimeter distance: 2.3 miles.
Activities: Hunting, fishing, camping, hiking, horseback riding, rockhounding, whitewater rafting.
Best season: Mid-May through October.
Maps: Platte River Wilderness map and brochure, Medicine Bow National Forest Map, Saratoga 1:100,000. See map on page 359.

Along the western margin of the Medicine Bow Mountains, the North Platte River has carved Northgate Canyon 1,000 feet deep into granite that is 1.4 billion years old. From here, the slopes mount up to rolling uplands robed in a verdant forest of lodgepole pine. Northgate Canyon has become the centerpiece of the Platte River Wilderness, a magnet for anglers, whitewater rafters, and wintering herds of game animals.

It would seem to be a geological anomaly that a river should abandon a perfectly good basin and turn instead into a rocky range to ply its course behind the first range of foothills. This strange occurrence has its origins in the Miocene period, some 20 million years ago. At that time, the Medicine Bow Range was buried to its rounded summit in sediment, and the Platte River held a course that reflected the lowest route through the plains. As the land rose in the intervening years, the sediments washed away at an accelerated rate, excavating this ancient range once more. But the river held to its original course, and its erosion was more than equal to the uplift. As a result, the river was able to gouge its canyon into the granite bedrock along the flanks of the Medicine Bows rather than sliding westward into the lower country of a syncline basin.

The sagebrush-bitterbrush grasslands that dominate the foothills form the primary winter range for approximately 500 head of elk from the Snowy Range herd, and about 200 head use the area year-round. These same slopes

Looking up Northgate Canyon from Six Mile Gap.

are a transitional range for mule deer that winter in the Encampment River basin and serve as year-round habitat for a reintroduced population of around 80 bighorn sheep. The peregrine falcon, bald eagle, and northern goshawk have been known to nest along Northgate Canyon.

Extensive stands of aspen can be found in the draws and north-facing slopes of the foothills, imparting a golden hue to the landscape in October. The upper reaches of the Platte River Wilderness are robed with a forest of lodgepole pine, broken only by riparian bottomlands choked with willows and south-facing slopes covered in sagebrush meadows. Black bears are common throughout the forested area, and wolverines have also been sighted. Beaver are abundant on the small tributaries of the highlands.

RECREATIONAL USES: The North Platte Wilderness is an angler's paradise and most of its recreational use is associated with fishing. The North Platte itself is a blue ribbon trout stream, and its tributaries can also offer fine fishing. The main river is home to trophy-sized brown and rainbow trout. Douglas Creek boasts a fine mixture of pools, runs, and pocket water, and many of the big sow browns from the river migrate into it to spawn. The smaller tributaries have been dammed by beaver in many places, and the resulting ponds can produce fast fishing for pan-sized brookies.

The North Platte River is also a popular waterway for whitewater rafting. During spring runoff, the section between Salt Creek and Six Mile Gap provides Class IV whitewater through the most visually spectacular parts of the canyon. As water levels drop, boulders emerge to make this section almost unfloatable (but some paddlers float it anyway). This float typically takes 3 hours. The lower section between Six Mile Gap and Pickaroon Campground has only a few rapids reaching no more than Class III, and it is a 2-hour scenic float suitable for canoes as well as rafts.

The trails of the Platte River Wilderness are well suited to day hikes, backpacks, and horse trips. The Platte Canyon trail is not recommended for horses because of steep talus and brush that must be traversed in places, and hikers are warned that you cannot hike from Six Mile Gap to Pickaroon Campground without fording the river. The BLM lands that border the Wilderness are a popular hunting destination for locals. Blue grouse can be found high on the ridgetops of the main wilderness during hunting season.

ACCESS: The improved gravel road to Six Mile Gap from Wyoming 230 is the most direct access to the North Platte River. It is a long journey by all-weather logging roads to reach the Pickaroon Campground at the downstream end of the wilderness. It is necessary to ford the river (possible only from mid-August through September) to reach the Platte Canyon trail from the campground. The upper end of the wilderness is accessed at Pelton Creek Campground, which is reached via a gravel spur road from Wyoming 230.

Floaters typically put in at the marked forest access 4 miles south of the state line on Colorado 125 and take out at Pickaroon Campground. The North Platte can also be accessed via the BLM lands adjoining the wilderness. Roads in this area are jeep trails that are so rough and steep that the BLM recommends that only expert four-wheelers attempt them. Unimproved cattle trails descend to the river via Stovepipe Gulch, Deerhorn Point, and Elkhorn Point.

Day Hike, Backpack, or Day Horse Loop

Platte Ridge Loop

Distance: 13.7 miles overall.
Difficulty: Moderately strenuous.
Starting and maximum elevation: 8,250 feet, 9,000 feet.
Topo map: Horatio Rock, Elkhorn Point.
Getting there: Drive Wyoming 230 south to the Colorado border, then head northwest on FR 898 to reach the Pelton Creek campground at its end. Parking at the trailhead in the campground requires a fee; the horse trailhead just outside the camp is free.

Upper Douglas Creek.

This route descends along Platte Ridge for aerial views of Northgate Canyon, then returns via Douglas Creek with fine fishing opportunities on the way back. From the Pelton Creek Campground, the trail follows an old roadbed up the beaver-dammed course of East Walbright Creek. Upon reaching the top, a journey through the pines leads to a similar descent into the West Walbright drainage. Follow the main creek downward at the first major stream forks. The trail turns northeast and starts climbing at a grassy cove lined with aspens. There is a good camp spot on the slopes above this meadow.

The trail now follows the draw upward into timbered country. Upon reaching the crest of Platte Ridge, a long up-and-down journey ensues through a lodgepole forest broken at long intervals by stands of aspen. At long last, a steep descent leads to a saddle beside an open hilltop; a side trip to the sagebrush slopes yields views of the distant Park Range in Colorado and the North Platte River far below. The trail rounds this summit and drops into the next saddle, where a buck-and-pole fence marks the intersection with trails descending east and west. Turn right (east) as our route follows an open draw to intersect Douglas Creek just above its confluence with Devils Gate Creek.

Ford Douglas Creek and turn right on the trail that follows it upstream. It leads past pools and runs beneath timbered slopes on the northeast exposures and sagebrush slopes that face southwest. The trail alternates between level meadows and steep detours onto the rocky slopes above the stream. Near Pelton Creek, the mountains dwindle into wooded hills, and soon the trail threads its way among placer mining spoils and willow thickets to make the final ford that leads back to the trailhead.

Encampment River Wilderness 62

Location: 2 miles south of Encampment.
Size: 19.027 acres.
Administration: Medicine Bow National Forest (Brush Creek–Hayden District), BLM (Rawlins Field Office).
Management status: Encampment River Wilderness (13,840 acres); Encampment River Canyon BLM Wilderness Study Area (4,547 acres), unprotected roadless state lands (640 acres).
Ecosystem: Rocky Mountain Province western spruce-fir forest.
Elevation range: 7,380 feet to 9,680 feet.
System trails: 19 miles.
Maximum core to perimeter distance: 1.5 miles.
Activities: Hiking, backpacking, horseback riding, hunting, fishing, wildlife viewing, kayaking, rockhounding, historical study, and recreational goldpanning.
Best season: May through October.
Maps: Medicine Bow National Forest Map, Saratoga 1:100,000.

The Encampment River flows north from Colorado, where it begins in the Mount Zirkel Wilderness. Upon entering Wyoming, its gradient increases as it descends through a tumultuous series of rapids and runs through the steep-walled canyon of the Encampment River Wilderness, lined with dense forests and occasional buttresses of granite 1.4 billion years old. The river then continues through the arid foothills, passing reminders of the prospecting era that lie within a BLM wilderness study area.

The Encampment River is the site of one of the storied mining booms in Western lore. Gold prospectors moved through the region in the 1860s, but found little and moved on. The real boom came in the late 1800s with the discovery of copper lodes in the Sierra Madre. In 1902, the North American Copper Company built a smelting plant outside the sprawling mining camp known as the Grand Encampment, which boasted a booming population that made it one of Wyoming's principal cities. A wooden pipeline 4 miles in length was then built from a check dam in the lower reaches of the Encampment Canyon. The pipeline brought water for the smelting process and to turn giant turbines to produce electricity for the plant. The pipeline's supports and the old diversion dam can still be seen within the Encampment Canyon WSA, along with the ruins of cabins, prospect pits, and abandoned mineshafts.

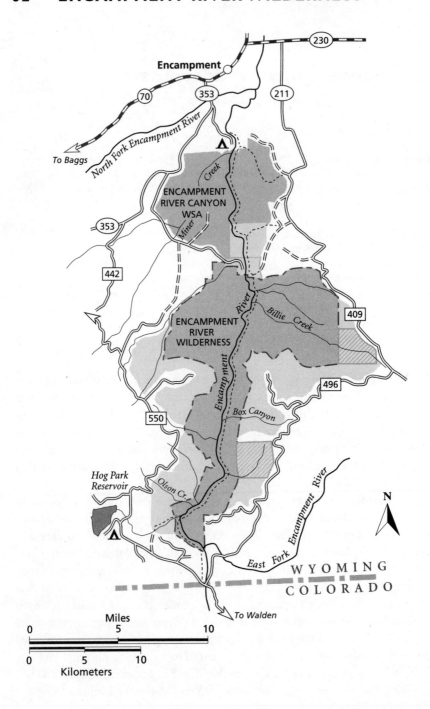

Ecologically, the mouth of the Encampment River Canyon is characterized by an arid landscape. Sagebrush, mountain mahogany, serviceberry, and bitterbrush are interspersed with bunchgrasses on the open slopes, and limber pine and juniper can be found on the flats. A lush growth of cottonwood and other hardwoods crowds the riverbanks, offering superb habitat to a wide array of bird life including ospreys, water ouzels, kingfishers, and songbirds. Groves of aspen are common in the middle recesses of the canyon, and the upper reaches of the river that fall within the Encampment River Wilderness are robed in a velvety forest of spruce, fir, and lodgepole pine.

The canyon of the Encampment River is noted for its variety of butterflies and hummingbirds, which peaks in early summer. Between 100 and 500 mule deer drop their fawns in the bottomlands and aspen groves of the lower reaches of Encampment Canyon. Elk winter in the lower canyon, and the forested upper reaches of the river are a critical yearlong habitat for the Baggs elk herd. The Encampment River is home to such rare species as the black-crowned night heron, boreal owl, boreal toad, and river otter. The canyon is also known for its concentration of raptors. Great gray owls, prairie falcons, bald eagles, and northern goshawks nest within the roadless area.

The Encampment River Canyon was originally a favorite haunt of bighorn sheep, but with the influx of miners into the region in the late 1800s, the sheep population was driven to extinction. Bighorns were reintroduced in 1976 and did well for a time, but now they are once more on the decline due to lack of suitable summer range. Open slopes on the western side of the area within the proposed Encampment Canyon Wilderness are used by the sheep as a lambing area. Watch for them here in early summer. The bighorns also winter in the lower reaches of the canyon.

The entire Encampment Canyon WSA has been recommended for wilderness designation by the BLM. The primary threat to the wilderness character of the Encampment Canyon comes from mining claims for copper, gold, and silver that were established following the passage of the Federal Lands Planning and Management Act. Upon wilderness designation, claims would be assessed and development of valid claims would be allowed, with some restrictions to minimize the impact on the wilderness. The wilderness experience along the Encampment River has already been badly damaged by a tasteless, neo-Californian summer home development on private and state lands between Forest Service and BLM wildernesses. It would certainly be in the public interest (though not very likely) for the federal government to acquire these inholdings outright and restore them to a pristine state.

RECREATIONAL USES: By far, the lion's share of recreational use centers around fishing in the Encampment River. Most of the hiking and backpacking use is also involved with fishing. During the peak of spring runoff (usually May and June), the Encampment River can be floated by expert kayakers. The river has a very steep rate of fall, with dangerous rapids that reach Class V. By midsummer, the water level drops, exposing boulders and shallows that make it unfloatable.

Conflicts between cattle and campers are frequent, because cattle concentrate on the same alluvial bottomlands that make the most attractive campsites. Both cattle and campers contribute to a level of fecal coliform bacteria in the waterways that is in violation of federal water quality standards. Acid drainage from abandoned mines leads to dangerously high levels of copper, lead, cadmium, silver, and manganese in the Encampment River during spring runoff.

Hunters will find that elk are common here, and the Encampment Canyon is rated as a potential trophy area for mule deer. Moose and antelope are also present in small numbers. Blue grouse can be found on the forested ridgetops, and may become abundant during peak years in their population cycle. The entire BLM Wilderness Study Area is closed to all entry during winter to safeguard wintering game animals. It is currently open to motorized use during some seasons.

ACCESS: The upper trailheads can be reached by driving west from Encampment for 8 miles to reach Forest Road 550 (marked "Bottle Creek Campground") and following this gravel trunk road to reach the trailheads just beyond Hog Park Reservoir. The lower trailhead is reached via County 353, a good gravel road that is accessible by all vehicles. The Palmer Gulch Road (Forest Road 409), which accesses a trailhead on the east side of the BLM wilderness study area, is so steep and rough that even four-wheel-drive vehicles are warned away.

Backpack

Encampment River

Distance: 13.3 to 15.5 miles one way.
Difficulty: Moderately strenuous.
Starting and maximum elevation: 7,230 feet, 8,370 feet.
Topo Maps: Encampment, Dudley Creek.
Getting there: Drive to the west edge of Encampment on Wyoming 70. Just 0.5 miles outside of town, turn left (south) on County 353. Follow this broad gravel road for 1 mile to a junction at the top of the hill, then go straight ahead to descend to the BLM trailhead next to the I.O.O.F. Camp. There is no fee for trailhead parking, and the primitive campsites on the far bank of the river are also free of charge.

Above the canyon, granite outcrops rise above Encampment River.

This good trail follows the river along the length of the Encampment River Canyon, passing mine ruins in the arid lower reaches and shady forests farther up. From the BLM trailhead, cross the footbridge and follow the east bank of the river past the I.O.O.F. camp and into the arid sagebrush hills. The verdant woodland of the river bottoms contrasts sharply with its arid surroundings. With upstream progress, Douglas fir and aspen appear amid the cottonwoods beside the river. As the canyon widens, there is easy progress across the riverside flats. An old burn reveals the tailings heaps and mine portals from the copper boom, and in the rivercourse are the ruins of an old check dam that once supplied a wooden pipeline to feed water to the old Encampment smelter.

A trail descends from the hills at Mason Gulch, and not far beyond it is a private inholding at the mouth of Miner Creek, now developed into some kind of Californicated country club. After passing this tasteless eyesore, the trail climbs high above a stony gooseneck and then descends to the Purgatory Gulch Trailhead. The main trail now enters the Encampment River Wilderness, managed by the Forest Service. The climax coniferous forest of spruce and Douglas fir now robes the canyon walls, and the trail crosses several small tributaries. Beyond Billie Creek, the river boils through a series of rapids guarded by massive gates of granite.

The trail now climbs and falls in breath-stealing grades as it labors to avoid the outcrops. At the mouth of Box Canyon, the river settles into quiet runs and riffles, but the path continues its up-and-down exertions. The hills begin to dwindle as the trail passes Dudley Creek, and lodgepole pine take over the forest. Striking outcrops of granite now rise from the hills, bracketing the mouth of Olson Creek. In short order, a bridge leads across the Encampment River to reach the Hog Park trail junction. The Hog Park trailhead is a mile to the southwest, but the main trail swings east, following the river for an easy jaunt through the trees. At the confluence with the East Fork, the trail follows the main river south into Commissary Park. Here, willows and grassy meadows lead to the trek's end at FR 550.

Huston Park Wilderness   63

Location: 55 miles southeast of Rawlins; 15 miles west of Encampment.
Size: 39,000 acres.
Administration: Medicine Bow National Forest (Brush Creek–Hayden District).
Management status: Huston Park Wilderness (31,300 acres); unprotected roadless lands (7,700 acres).
Ecosystem: Rocky Mountain forest province, Ponderosa pine–Douglas fir Ecosystem.
Elevation range: 7,740 feet to 10,443 feet.
System trails: 31 miles.
Maximum core to perimeter distance: 2.3 miles.
Activities: Hiking, backpacking, horseback riding, upland bird and big game hunting, fishing, recreational goldpanning.
Best season: August through September.
Maps: Medicine Bow National Forest Map; Saratoga and Baggs 1:100,000.

The core of the Sierra Madre is made up of rounded summits of Precambrian granite, dolomite, and amphibolite about 1.4 billion years old. This area was mantled in a thick ice cap during the Pleistocene, and the glaciers left behind extensive deposits of till. In modern times, these have become the flower-strewn meadows and forested slopes of the Huston Park Wilderness.

To the west of the Sierra Madre, the forelands are composed of a series of level, sedimentary ridges mantled in vast stands of aspen with spruce groves on some of the north-facing slopes. Meadows in this region tend to be dominated by tall grasses like timothy, with sagebrush becoming locally dominant in dry locales.

The granitic origins of the soil combine with cool soil temperatures to slow plant growth at high elevations. The heights of the range are also subject to extremely high wind speeds. Sustained winds of 60 miles per hour and gusts of over 100 m.p.h. rake the crest of the range, tearing at the vegetation. The upper slopes and stream bottoms are mantled in a spruce-fir woodland, while the crest harbors a network of wet meadows where a diverse array of wildflowers bloom beside springs and seeps. Extensive wildfires burned through the lower slopes of the Sierra Madres following a battle between fur trappers and Native Americans in 1841, stimulating the growth of extensive stands of lodgepole pine and aspen.

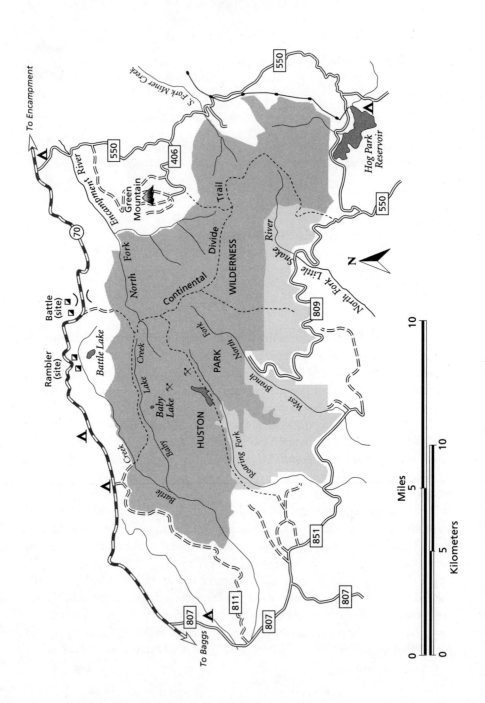

The Sierra Madre is a major summer range for elk, and it is not uncommon to see herds of several hundred head during the twilight hours. The high meadows are also an important calving area for these elk. Coyotes are abundant in the highlands. The streams that flow westward from the crest of the Sierra Madre support a pure strain of the rare Colorado River cutthroat trout.

The first prospectors filtered through the Sierra Madres during the late 1860s, searching for gold and silver, which they never found in great quantities. The real mining boom came in 1897 with the discovery of the Ferris-Haggerty copper lode, north of the wilderness. This mine was to produce over $1.4 million of copper ore over the span of its operation, and it ignited a copper boom that led to a proliferation of small communities of miners and prospectors in the Sierra Madre. With names like Rudefeha, Hog Park, Copperton, and Battle, some of these settlements boasted miniature downtown districts and even their own newspapers.

These were years of high copper demand, and in 1902 an aerial tramway was built from the crest of the Sierra Madres to the newly built smelter in Encampment to carry the ore. In its day, it was the largest aerial tram in the world. The copper market collapsed in 1907, and soon thereafter most of the mines had closed and the mining camps stood abandoned.

In modern times, the mining district is of little economic significance. The Verde Mine in the southwestern quadrant of the wilderness is still being worked on a sporadic basis. Miners are permitted to drive their ATVs to the Verde Mine, which exists on a private inholding within the wilderness. There has been some oil exploration in the sedimentary strata along the western edge of the wilderness, but test wells have come in dry.

The high parks of the Sierra Madre were used as a summer range for the great herds of domestic sheep that wintered in the Red Desert at the turn of the twentieth century. The numbers of domestic sheep in Wyoming have dropped markedly in recent decades, and now sheep no longer graze in the wilderness. Cattle are herded along the crest of the range between Highway 70 and Long Park, and visitors are likely to encounter them along the Continental Divide trail.

There is a long history of timber harvesting along the timbered slopes to the east of the Huston Park Wilderness. Although this area produces only spindly lodgepole of negligible commercial value, the Forest Service pursued an aggressive program of clearcutting from the 1940s through the 1970s. Many of the clearcuts extend right up to the wilderness boundary, leaving no buffer zone.

RECREATIONAL USES: Recreational use of the Huston Park Wilderness is quite low overall; only during the fall hunting season does the area attract many visitors. Since the wilderness is only 40 miles north of Steamboat Springs, many of its visitors come from Colorado. The Continental Divide

National Scenic Trail follows the crest of the Sierra Madre along the entire length of the wilderness, but as yet it receives only light use. Many of the trails along the crest of the Sierra Madre lack a defined tread and have been overtaken by meadow plants; it will be necessary to follow cairns and blazes in this area. From meadows at the southern end of the range, views stretch into Colorado to encompass the tall peaks of the Park Range and the granite crags of the Mount Zirkel Wilderness.

There are no notable lakes in the wilderness, and streams tend to be small. Hard-core fishermen will be able to find pan-sized trout in most of the waterways that drain westward from the wilderness. The boggy meadows at the crest of the range are a breeding ground for mosquitoes and biting flies, which become a major nuisance from mid-June to mid-August. The wilderness offers fine elk hunting, particularly during the bowhunting season. Blue grouse are prevalent in the upland forests, providing opportunities for small game hunting.

There is a considerable amount of off-road vehicle use on the trails that lead up to the western boundary of the Huston Park Wilderness. Thus far, the Forest Service has done a poor job of segregating motorized and non-motorized users in this area, and it could better serve the wilderness experience of visitors by closing all trails that lead into the wilderness to motorized vehicles.

ACCESS: Wyoming Highway 70 provides good paved access to the northern edge of the Huston Park Wilderness, and an all-weather trunk road (Forest Road 550) tracks along its eastern side. Many of the roads that approach the western side of the wilderness are little more than rutted jeep tracks that become mud pits when it rains.

Day Hike

Green Mountain Trail

Distance: 2.0 miles.
Difficulty: Easy.
Starting and maximum elevation: 10,040 feet, 10,270 feet.
Topo map: Solomon Creek.
Getting there: Drive west from Encampment on Wyoming 70. After 8 miles, turn left (south) on Forest Road 550, following signs for the Bottle Creek Campground. Follow this good trunk road for 5.2 miles, then turn right on FR 406. Stick to the uppermost road, which becomes a bit rocky as it climbs. At the 2.5 mile mark, turn left on the short spur road to the trailhead.

This trail makes a short and easy trip to the crest of the Sierra Madre, where open meadows yields vast southward views. The trip begins with a level and sometimes muddy stroll through a dense woodland of subalpine fir. After a

Aspen and bracken fern in the lowlands west of the Sierra Madre.

Looking across from alpine meadows at the south end of the Sierra Madre.

short distance, the path begins a moderate climb through a forest interrupted by boggy clearings and fields of broken granite. A gentle grade leads up to the crest of the range, where lush meadows are studded with boulders and clusters of fir. Hike over the low saddle to intersect the Continental Divide trail (which is really no more than a series of cairns in the trackless grasslands). Follow this route westward a short distance to reach a fire-scarred hill that offers superb views of the high peaks of the Park Range across the Colorado border.

Day Hike or Backpack

Roaring Fork

Distance: 7.0 miles one way.
Difficulty: Moderate.
Starting and maximum elevation: 8,020 feet, 10,100 feet.
Topo map: Fletcher Peak.
Getting there: Drive east from Baggs or west from the crest of the Sierra Madre on Wyoming 130. Turn south on FR 807, following signs for Battle Creek Campground. A good gravel road descends to the camp, but the road deteriorates (four-wheel drive recommended) as it crosses Battle Creek and climbs to Cottonwood Park. Bear left, following FR 807 to FR 851, and about 7.5 miles from the highway you will turn left (east) at a weather-beaten sign for the Roaring Fork trail. Park at the top of the hill and walk the road from there.

This trail follows a major drainage from the aspen lowlands to the west of the Sierra Madre to the alpine meadows at the crest of the range. It visits the ruins of old copper mines along the way. From the hilltop, hike the badly rutted jeep trail down through the aspens to reach the Roaring Fork trailhead.

From here a trail descends to ford the Roaring Fork (no more than a small brook) and follows posts upstream. The valley is narrow at first, but soon it widens into a broad basin as the route adopts an ATV trail. It passes through meadows of tall grass and groves of old aspens as it continues upstream. Watch for blazed trees as steep ridges rise on either side of the valley. Aspens continue to dominate the forest as the trail climbs modestly up the valley to reach a boggy meadow.

Beyond this point, the trail is quite faint as cairns and blazes lead through spruce bottoms and meadows choked with granite boulders. After passing some cabin ruins, the gradient increases as the path climbs along the north bank of the Roaring Fork to reach the Etna Mine. Here, tailings are piled below the sealed portal, and old Pelton wheels and boilers rust nearby. The trail continues up the north bank, passing more fallen cabins en route to the broad and rolling meadows at the top of the range. It is necessary to hike northeast for some distance to meet the crest trail.

APPENDIX A:

Trips at a Glance

GREATER YELLOWSTONE ECOSYSTEM

Trip Name	Area and (Page #)	Type	Round-trip Distance	Difficulty
Beartooth Butte	Absaroka-Beartooth(24)	Day hike	6.5–8.5 miles	Moderate
Beartooth Loop	Line Creek (30)	Day hike/ backpack	12.3 miles	Moderate
Bechler Canyon	Yellowstone N.P. (18)	Backpack	24 miles	Moderate
Bliss Pass	Yellowstone N.P. (16)	Backpack	20.6 miles	Moderately strenuous
Dead Horse Pass	Jedediah Smith (75)	Day hike	11–12.6 miles	Moderately strenuous
Death Canyon Loop	Grand Teton N.P. (69)	Backpack	25 miles	Moderately strenuous
Ditch Cr.–Horsetail	Mount Leidy Highlands (61)	Day hike/ Horse/Mountain Bike	12.2 miles	Moderate
Fish Lake	Winegar Hole (79)	Day hike	1.2 miles	Easy
Grinnell Creek	North Absaroka (39)	Day hike/ Horse trip	10 miles	Moderate
Holmes Cave	Teton Wilderness (53)	Day hike/ Horse trip	10 miles	Moderately strenuous
Lost Lake	Absaroka–Beartooth (23)	Day hike	4.8 miles	Moderate
Mount Hunt Divide	Grand Teton N.P. (68)	Day hike/ Backpack	15 miles	Moderately strenuous

GREATER YELLOWSTONE ECOSYSTEM (CONTINUED)

Trip Name	Area and (Page #)	Type	Round-trip Distance	Difficulty
Pacific Creek	Teton Wilderness (54)	XC-Ski trip	20.6–26.6 miles	Moderate
Pilot Creek	North Absaroka (37)	Day hike	14 miles	Moderate to Strenuous
Red Hills	Mount Leidy Highlands (59)	Day hike	3 miles	Moderately strenuous
Sheep Mesa	Washakie (45)	Day hike	10.6–12.6 miles	Strenuous
Spread Cr. Loop	Mount Leidy Highlands (58)	Day hike/ Horse trip	16.2 miles	Easy
Turbid Lake	Yellowstone N.P. (15)	Day hike/ Horse trip	6.6 miles	Moderate
Warhouse Loop	Washakie (47)	Backpack/ Horse trip	17.3 miles	Moderately strenuous
Wind Cave	Jedediah Smith (74)	Day hike	6.8 miles	Moderate
Winegar L. Loop	Winegar Hole (79)	Day hike	4.1 miles	Moderate

WESTERN RANGES

Trip Name	Area and (Page #)	Type	Round-trip Distance	Difficulty
Bear Creek Loop	Salt River Range (107)	Day hike/ Backpack	14.5 miles	Moderately strenuous
Blue Miner Lake	Gros Ventre (88)	Day hike/ Backpack	13 miles	Moderately strenuous
Granite Highline	Gros Ventre (86)	Backpack	24 miles	Moderate
Grayback Ridge	Hoback Peak (95)	Day hike/ Horse trip	6 miles	Strenuous
Hoback High Line	Hoback Peak (96)	Day hike	6.4 miles	Moderately strenuous
Indian Ridge	Commissary Ridge (113)	Day hike	9 miles	Moderately strenuous
North Crest Loop	Raymond Mountain (119)	Day hike	7.7 miles	Moderately strenuous
Red Park	Commissary Ridge (115)	Day hike/ Horse trip	3.4–8.6 miles	Moderate
Wagner Lake	Salt River Range (109)	Day hike	7 miles	Strenuous
West Miner Creek	Gros Ventre (87)	Day hike	7.6 miles	Moderate
Wolf Mountain	Palisades (91)	Day hike	7 miles	Moderately strenuous
Wyoming Range Tr.	Wyoming Range (100)	Backpack/ Horse trip	36.2 miles	Strenuous

WIND RIVER RANGE

Trip Name	Area and (Page #)	Type	Round-trip Distance	Difficulty
Bears Ears Trail	Popo Agie (137)	Backpack	22.6-28.8 miles	Strenuous
Dream L.– Boulder Can.	Bridger (128)	Backpack/ Horse trip	26 miles	Moderate
Mason Draw	Dubois Badlands (146)	Day hike	10 miles	Easy
New Fork– Doubletop	Bridger (130)	Backpack	29.5 miles	Moderately strenuous
Silas Canyon	Popo Agie (134)	Day hike	6.6-10 miles	Moderate
Whiskey Mountain	Fitzpatrick (141)	Day hike	11.1 miles	Strenuous

BIGHORN BASIN

Trip Name	Area and (Page #)	Type	Round-trip Distance	Difficulty
Alkali Cr. Canyon	Alkali Creek (179)	Day hike	3.4 miles	Moderate
Big Cottonwood	The Honeycombs (184)	Day hike	6 miles	Moderately strenuous
Birdseye Cr. Badlands	Birdseye Creek (192)	Day hike	1.2 miles	Easy
Bobcat Draw	Bobcat Draw (169)	Day hike/ Backpack	9.2 miles	Moderately strenuous
Deer Creek Overlook	McCullough Peaks (159)	Day hike	4 miles	Moderate
Devil Canyon	Bighorn Canyon (155)	Canoe trip	13.6 miles	Moderate
Dorsey Creek	Sheep Mountain (164)	Day hike	4.4 miles	Easy
Elk Creek	Sheep Mountain (166)	Day hike/ Horse trip	7 miles	Easy
Neiber Draw Divide	Cedar Mountain (187)	Day hike	1.8 miles	Moderate
Red Butte	Red Butte (174)	Day hike	4.4 miles	Moderate
Red Butte Badlands	Red Butte (174)	Day hike	4 miles	Easy
W. Birdseye Basin	Birdseye Creek (193)	Day hike	1.4 miles	Moderate
Whistle Cr. Breaks	McCullough Peaks (160)	Day hike	4.2 miles	Moderately strenuous

BIG HORN MOUNTAINS

Trip Name	Area and (Page #)	Type	Round-trip Distance	Difficulty
Bull Elk Park	Little Bighorn (200)	Day hike/ Backpack/ Horse trip	12 miles	Moderate
Firebox Park	Cloud Peak (216)	Day hike	5.6 miles	Moderately strenuous
Hazelton Peak	Hazelton Peaks (219)	Day hike	6.4 miles	Moderately strenuous
Highland Park	Cloud Peak (213)	Backpack/ Horse trip	45–51.8 miles	Moderately strenuous
Little Bighorn Can.	Little Bighorn (201)	Day hike/ Horse trip	4.8 miles	Moderate
Medicine Lodge Can.	Medicine Lodge (232)	Day hike	6.4 miles	Moderately strenuous
Paint Rock Canyon	Paint Rock Canyon (237)	Day hike/ Backpack/ Horse trip	25.6 miles	Moderate
The Arch	Medicine Lodge (231)	Day hike	2.6–8.6 miles	Moderate
Trapper Canyon	Trapper Canyon (224)	Backpack	9.1 miles	Strenuous
Walker Prairie	Walker Prairie (206)	Backpack/ Horse trip	18.2 miles	Moderately strenuous

POWDER RIVER BASIN AND HIGH PLAINS

Trip Name	Area and (Page #)	Type	Round-trip Distance	Difficulty
Cottonwood Notch	South Fork Powder (255)	Day hike	11.7 miles	Easy
Gardner Mountain	Gardner Mountain (249)	Day hike/ Horse trip	12.4 miles	Moderate
Miller Hills	Cow Creek Buttes (262)	Day hike/ Horse trip	12–16 miles	Moderate
Owl Creek Loop	Cow Creek Buttes (261)	Day hike/ Horse trip	6 miles	Moderate

OREGON TRAIL COUNTRY

Trip Name	Area and (Chapter #)	Type	Round-trip Distance	Difficulty
Heaths Peak	Pedro Mountains (273)	Day hike/ Climb	8 miles	Strenuous
Nolen Pocket	Sweetwater Rocks (286)	Day hike	8.4 miles	Moderate
Number 2 Gulch	Bennett Mountain (269)	Day hike/ Horse trip	6 miles	Moderately strenuous
Split Rock	Sweetwater Rocks (286)	Climb	2.6 miles	Moderately strenuous
Sweetwater Canyon	Sweetwater Canyon (292)	Day hike/ Backpack	8.2–18.6 miles	Moderate
Youngs Pass	Ferris Mountains (279)	Day hike	5 miles	Moderate

RED DESERT REGION

Trip Name	Area and (Page #)	Type	Round-trip Distance	Difficulty
Alkali Draw	The Pinnacles (310)	Day hike/ Horse trip	11.7 miles	Moderate
Beef Steer Creek	Red Creek Badlands (331)	Day hike/ Horse trip	7 miles	Easy
Black Mountain Overlook	Black Mountain (335)	Day hike	3 miles	Moderate
Continental Peak	Honeycomb Buttes (305)	Day hike	3 miles	Moderately strenuous
Devils Playground	Black Mountain (336)	Day hike	2 miles	Moderate
Dunes Trek	Killpecker Dunes (315)	Day hike	2–7 miles	Moderate
East Fork Point	Adobetown (327)	Day hike	3.4 miles	Moderate
Honeycombs Loop	Honeycomb Buttes (305)	Day hike/ Backpack	14.8 miles	Moderate
Luman Dunes	Red Lake Dunes (320)	Day hike	4 miles+	Moderate
Monument Valley	Adobetown (326)	Day hike	6.5 miles	Moderate
N. Oregon Butte	Oregon Buttes (301)	Day hike	4.6 miles	Moderately strenuous
Pinnacles Loop	The Pinnacles (309)	Day hike	6.1 miles	Moderate
Telephone Canyon	Red Creek Badlands (331)	Day hike	4.6 miles	Moderate

SOUTHERN RANGES

Trip Name	Area and (Page #)	Type	Round-trip Distance	Difficulty
Browns Peak	Snowy Range (356)	Day hike/ Backpack	10.5 miles	Easy
Encampment River	Encampment River (371)	Backpack	26.6–31 miles	Moderately strenuous
Green Mountain	Huston Park (376)	Day hike	2 miles	Easy
Laramie Peak	Laramie Peak (341)	Day hike/ Backpack/ Horse trip	10.4 miles	Moderately strenuous
Platte Ridge Loop	Platte River (365)	Day hike	13.7 miles	Moderately strenuous
Reynolds Hill	Vedauwoo (346)	Day hike	1.9 miles	Moderate
Roaring Fork	Huston Park (378)	Day hike/ Backpack	14 miles	Moderate
Savage Run Trail	Savage Run (360)	Day hike/ Backpack/ Horse trip	7–14 miles	Easy to Moderate
Sheep Mountain	Sheep Mountain Refuge (351)	Backpack/ Horse trip	21.2 miles	Moderate
Turtle Rock Trail	Vedauwoo (346)	Day hike	2.8 miles	Easy
Twin Mountain Meadows	Vedauwoo (347)	Horse Trip	3 miles	Easy

APPENDIX B:

Resources

Bureau of Land Management

Wyoming State Office
5353 Yellowstone Road
P.O. Box 1828
Cheyenne, WY 82003
(307) 775-6082

Casper Field Office
1701 East E Street
Casper, WY 82601
(307) 261-7600

Buffalo Field Office
1425 Fort Street
Buffalo, WY 82834
(307) 684-1100

Rawlins Field Office
1300 North Third Street
P.O. Box 2407
Rawlins, WY 82301
(307) 328-4200

Lander Field Office
1335 Main Street
P.O. Box 589
Lander, WY 82520
(307) 332-8400

Rock Springs Field Office
280 Hwy. 191 North
Rock Springs, WY 82901
(307) 352-0256

Kemmerer Field Office
312 Hwy. 191 North
Kemmerer, WY 83101
(307) 877-4500

Worland Field Office
101 South 23rd Street
P.O. Box 119
Worland, WY 82401
(307) 347-5100

Cody Field Office
1002 Blackburn
P.O. Box 518
Cody, WY 82414
(307) 587-2216

National Park Service

Yellowstone National Park
P.O. Box 168
Yellowstone, WY 82190
(307) 344-7381

Grand Teton National Park
P.O. Drawer 170
Moose, WY 83012-0170
(307) 739-3300

Bighorn Canyon National
Recreation Area
P.O. Box 7458
Fort Smith, MT 59035-7458
(406) 666-2412

USDA Forest Service

Intermountain Regional Office
Federal Building
324 25th Street
Ogden, UT 84401-2310
(801) 625-5352

Rocky Mountain Regional Office
740 Simms Street
P.O. Box 25127
Lakewood, CO 80225
(303) 275-5350

Medicine Bow–Routt National Forest
2468 Jackson Street
Laramie, WY 82070-6535
(307) 745-2300

Brush Creek–Hayden Ranger District
South Highway 130
Saratoga, WY 82331
(307) 326-5258

Encampment Ranger Station
204 West 9th Street
Encampment, WY 82325
(307) 327-5481

Laramie Ranger District
2468 Jackson Street
Laramie, WY 82070-6353
(307) 745-2300

Douglas Ranger District
2250 East Richards
Douglas, WY 82633
(307) 358-4690

Parks Ranger Disrtict
Walden Office
100 Main Street
P.O. Box 158
Walden, CO 80480
(970) 723-8204

Thunder Basin National Grassland
2250 East Richards
Douglas, WY 82633
(307) 358-4690

Bighorn National Forest
1969 South Sheridan Avenue
Sheridan, WY 82801
(307) 672-0751

Powder River Ranger District
1425 Fort Street
Buffalo, WY 82834
(307) 684-1100

Medicine Wheel Ranger District
604 East Main Street
Lovell, WY 82431
(307) 548-6541

Tongue Ranger District
1969 South Sheridan Avenue
Sheridan, WY 82801
(307) 672-0751

Shoshone National Forest
808 Meadow Lane
Cody, WY 82414
(307) 527-6241

Clarks Fork Ranger District
Greybull Ranger District
Wapiti Ranger District
203A Yellowstone
Cody, WY 82414
(307) 527-6921

Washakie Ranger District
333 East Main
Lander, WY 82520
(307) 332-5460

Wind River Ranger District
1403 West Ramshorn
Dubois, WY 82513
(307) 455-2466

Targhee National Forest
420 North Bridge Street
P.O. Box 208
St. Anthony, ID 83445
(208) 624-4049

Ashton Ranger District
P.O. Box 858
Ashton, ID 83420
(208) 652-7442

Palisades Ranger District
3659 East Ririe Highway
Idaho Falls, ID 83401
(208) 523-1412

Teton Basin Ranger District
P.O. Box 777
Driggs, ID 83422
(208) 354-2431

Bridger–Teton National Forest
340 North Cache Street
P.O. Box 1888
Jackson, WY 83001
(307) 739-5500

Big Piney Ranger District
315 South Front Street
P.O. Box 218
Big Piney, WY 83113
(307) 276-3375

Greys River Ranger District
125 Washington
P.O. Box 388
Afton, WY 83110
(307) 886-3166

Jackson Ranger District
25 Rosecrans Drive
Jackson, WY 83001
(307) 739-5400

Kemmerer Ranger District
Highway 189
P.O. Box 31
Kemmerer, WY 83101
(307) 877-4415

Pinedale Ranger District
210 West Pine Street
P.O. Box 220
Pinedale, WY 82941
(307) 367-4326

Custer National Forest
Beartooth Ranger District
Route 2, Box 3420
Red Lodge, Montana 59068
(406) 446-2103

Wyoming Game and Fish Department

Statewide Office
5400 Bishop Boulevard
Cheyenne, WY 82006
(800) 654-1178

APPENDIX C:

Conservation and Environmental Organizations

American Lands
726 7th Street SE
Washington, DC 20003
(202) 547-9105

American Wildlands
40 East Main, Suite 2
Bozeman, MT 59715
(406) 586-8175

Bighorn Audubon Council
994 West Loucks
Sheridan, WY 82801
(307) 672-2618

Bighorn Forest Users Coalition
P.O. Box 280
Story, WY 82842
(307) 683-2842

Biodiversity Associates
P.O. Box 6032
Laramie, WY 82073
(307) 742-7978

Greater Yellowstone Coalition
Box 1874
Bozeman, MT 59771
(406) 586-1593

Jackson Hole Conservation Alliance
P.O. Box 2728
Jackson, WY 83001
(307) 733-9417

National Bighorn Sheep Center
907 West Ramshorn
Dubois, WY 82513
(307) 455-3429

Rocky Mountain Elk Foundation
2291 West Broadway Street
Missoula, MT 59808
(406) 523-4545

The Nature Conservancy
258 Main, Suite 200
Lander, WY 82520
(307) 332-2971

The Wilderness Society
Northern Rockies Regional Office
105 West Main St., Suite E
Bozeman, MT 59715
(406) 586-1600

Wyoming Chapter of the Sierra Club
23 N. Scott, #27
Sheridan, WY 82801
(307) 672-0425

Wyoming Outdoor Council
262 Lincoln
Lander, WY 82520
(307) 332-7031

Wyoming Wildlife Federation
P.O. Box 106
Cheyenne, WY 82003
(307) 637-5433

Wyoming Wilderness Association
863½ Main Avenue
Durango, CO 81301
(970) 247-8788

INDEX

Note: page locators with * indicate maps for wilderness region.

SPECIAL INDEX

ABOUT THE AUTHOR

Erik Molvar has explored wildlands throughout the American West. He holds a Master's degree in wildlife management from the University of Alaska-Fairbanks, where he performed groundbreaking research on moose in Denali National Park. Erik has hiked over 10,000 miles of trails, in areas stretching from the Arctic Ocean to the Mexican border. This total includes over 1,500 miles in Wyoming's wild country, encompassing all of the roadless areas and trails in this book. He currently works for Biodiversity Associates, a non-profit conservation organization in Laramie, Wyoming.

Also by the Author:
Hiking Wyoming's Cloud Peak Wilderness
Hiking Glacier and Waterton Lakes National Parks
Hiking Montana's Bob Marshall Wilderness
Hiking Colorado's Maroon Bells–Snowmass Wilderness
Hiking Arizona's Cactus Country
Hiking Zion and Bryce Canyon National Parks
Hiking Olympic National Park
Hiking the North Cascades
Alaska on Foot: Wilderness Techniques for the Far North
Scenic Driving Alaska and the Yukon